AF669419

WARSAW INDOLOGICAL STUDIES

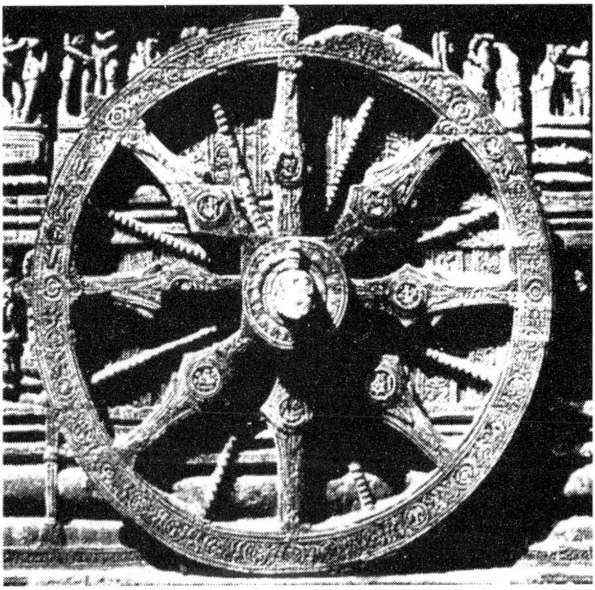

VOLUME 4

Editors:
Piotr Balcerowicz
in collaboration with
Jerzy Malinowski

WARSAW 2011

Art, Myths and Visual Culture of South Asia

Edited by

Piotr Balcerowicz

in collaboration with

Jerzy Malinowski

MANOHAR
2011

A PUBLICATION OF
THE FACULTY OF ORIENTAL STUDIES, UNIVERSITY OF WARSAW,
AND THE POLISH INSTITUTE OF WORLD ART STUDIES

WARSAW INDOLOGICAL STUDIES SERIES
VOLUME 4

EDITORS:
Piotr Balcerowicz
in collaboration with
Jerzy Malinowski

Cover design: Piotr Balcerowicz
Layout design and fonts, typeset by: Piotr Balcerowicz

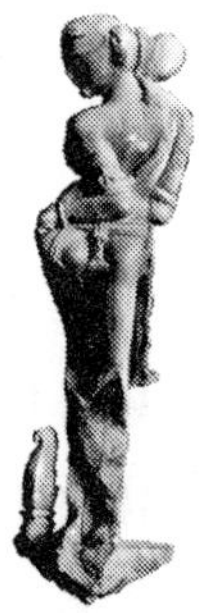

Publication supported by
the Embassy of the Republic of Poland in New Delhi
and the Faculty of Oriental Studies, University of Warsaw

First Edition: Delhi, 2011

Copyright © 2011 by *The Editors*

All rights reserved. No part of this publication may be reproduced or transmitted, in any form or by any means, without prior permission of the editors and the publisher.

ISBN 978-81-7304-951-4

Published by
Manohar Publishers & Distributors
4753/23 Ansari Road, Daryaganj
New Delhi – 110 002

Printed at
Salasar Imaging Systems
New Delhi 110 035

TABLE OF CONTENTS

Preface

The volume presents a collection of papers linked by a common theme which incorporates various aspects of art, religion, myths, symbols, literature and visual culture of the region of South Asia, but in certain aspects goes beyond the geographical boundaries and reaches out to South-East Asia.

The collection offers an entirely new material which explores a range of important motives and themes concerned with the art and visual culture of the region of South Asia, and partially with South-East Asia. They comprise various aspects of South Asian art, including sculpture, painting and decorative art, related to religious practice, mythology and cult, politics and power as well as the history and spread of artistic and mythological motives from South Asia to other parts of the world.

Monika Zin ('The Parable of 'The Man in the Well'. Its Travels and its Pictorial Traditions from Amaravati to Today') investigates a fascinating journey which an Indian Buddhist motif, primarily known from the sites of Nāgārjunakoṇḍā and Amarāvatī, made to various parts of Asia and Europe and analyses how the parable was represented in various pictorial traditions. Her meticulous examination unveils a fascinating nexus of narrative, mythological, artistic and historical layers and themes which lie behind the Parable of 'The Man in the Well' and its numerous versions in Europe and Asia.

In her study of the textual and archaeological evidence for temple consecration rituals in the Hindu tradition of South and South-East Asia, Anna Ślączka ('Temple Consecration Rituals in the Hindu Tradition of South and South-East Asia: A Study of the Textual and Archaeological Evidence') demonstrates how consecration ritual practice spread from South Asia to the regions of South East Asia, how it was reflected in artefacts, and how important it is to correlate archaeological findings with textual evidence of Sanskrit treatises. A research which closely combines and expertise in textual sources and sound knowledge of archaeology can certainly lead to a better understanding of culture and art, and yield important and revealing results.

Art, Myths and Visual Culture of South Asia
Warsaw Indological Studies 4 (2011) 7–11.

Two papers delve on the history of Buddhism in Sri Lanka and its reflection in Sri Lankan art, architecture and painting. Interestingly, the spread of Buddhism and its later development, especially in confrontation with external colonial forces, was closely linked to political power, attempts to win it or preserve it, and to the personage of the king. Both studies come up with ample evidence of how politics and royal power reshaped and determined further development of religious mythical 'history' of Buddhism on the island, the topography of the places of pilgrimage, historical myths, the interpretation of the history, the contents and style of paintings and murals. In the first study, Silke K. Yasmin Fischer ('The Spread of Buddhism from India to Sri Lanka: Its Visual Representation') examines how the Buddhist legend of the monk Mahinda arriving to Sri Lanka and bringing Buddhism to the island is revitalised and utilised in concrete political and historical circumstances which eventually introduce a new tradition and shape the way the beginnings of Buddhism in Sri Lanka are perceived, interpreted and disseminated by the Sri Lankan Buddhists themselves. And important instrument in the process and a reflection of it is, of course, pictorial tradition, which incorporates various media ranging from temple narrative paintings to modern state school textbooks. Asoka de Zoysa's detailed analysis of a selection of images from Buddhist temples of the Kandyan Era ('Reading images and interpreting the context: Differentiating Between Iconography and Iconology According to Erwin Panofsky's Three Phase Analysis') pursues the problem of the junction of religion, politics and art, and of how political programme influenced the topography of religious pilgrimages sides, architecture and temple paintings, resulting in rewriting history reflected both in text and painting. On the theoretical level, the author takes recourse to the methodology developed by Erwin Panofsky and the distinction of iconography and iconology. In short, his study unveils facts and events hidden behind the surface of painted murals.

Valdas Jaskūnas' paper ('Building Visual Order in Kashmir. Analysis of Architectural Structures as Described in the *Viṣṇu-dharmôttara-purāṇa*') shifts the focus from the southernmost part to the north of the Indian Peninsula. He analyses some passages devoted to architecture and temple models in the *Viṣṇu-dharmôttara-purāṇa* and compares them to the actual structures found in Kashmir. Of particular interest is the model of the *sarvato-bhadra* type of temple which is related to the iconographical program of Pāñcarātra Viṣṇuism. In his analysis, the material devoted to architecture found in the *Viṣṇu-dharmôttara-purāṇa* proves to be a conscious attempt to establish a new visual order, which echoes the ascendance of

Viṣṇuism and its domination over Buddhism in the region. As it usually happens, previous architectonic tradition or topography of sacred sites is not obliterated, but is rather creatively adopted by the new religious tradition and political elites in order to gain legitimacy and buttress their control and influence.

Barbara Grabowska ('Acts of Master Viśvakarman in Bengali Poems') takes up a theme of how art, artistic endeavour and artisanship were conceived in myth and literature. To illustrate the process, she analyses the motif of Viśvakarman, the mythical divine artisan, and his artistic undertakings the way they were depicted in Bengali religious tradition and poems.

An image of quite a homogenous material culture and art, especially with respect to terracotta art, in the Gangetic Valley of the golden ages of the Gupta period emerges from the paper of Samir Kumar Mukherjee ('Terracotta Art in the Gangetic Valley under the Guptas'), who inspects a range of terracotta figurines found at various archaeological sites in the Gangetic valley. The quality and workmanship of the terracotta objects, finer than in previous periods, reflects a general improvement in economic and social conditions during the reign of the Guptas. Mukherjee's findings reveal a close link between the themes displayed in the terracotta figurines and various aspects of social life and mythology.

In pursuing the imperative to study of art in itself, David Smith's paper ('Facial Expression in the Erotic Art of Khajurāho. A Preliminary Investigation') offers a new take on temple sculptures of Khajurāho, whereby he slightly diverges from traditional historians' approach to the erotic art of Khajurāho. He discusses the erotic sculpture of Khajurāho in terms that are somewhat parallel to the type of study which is the norm in Western art history. Smith analyses the expressive contents of the sculptures, with the emphasis on facial expression, and scrutinises the range of emotions expressed and images conjured up by the sculptor, searching for interpretative underpinnings of and artistic practice behind the sculptural forms, thereby disclosing the individualism and originality of the artists.

The team of M. Singh, R.S. Trambake, D.A. Gupta ('Chemical Conservation of Hīnayāna Paintings of the 2nd BCE, Cave No. 10, Ajanta') brings in a very practical dimension, vital to the survival of art and artefacts which art historians examine, namely the problems of restoration and conservation of ancient paintings and murals. They focus on chemical conservation of Hīnayāna paintings of the 2nd BCE of Cave No. 10, Ajantā, briefly presenting the history of the murals, their discovery and subsequent problems related to their preservation. Various conservation techniques of the past proved ultimately unsuccessful, but even latest methods of preservation of the paintings may prove futile when confronted with a large number of visitors, which in itself poses a serious threat to invaluable pieces of art in art collections and monuments all over the world.

Piotr Balcerowicz's study ('The Body and the Cosmos in Jaina Mythology and Art') investigates the roots, history and subsequent development of the image of 'the cosmic man' (*loka-puruṣa*) featuring in Jaina art and cosmology, the relation of the cosmic man to Mount Meru and to the concept of liberation.

The present volume has been inspired by and is, in a sense, a follow-up of an International Conference on Art and Visual Culture of India, which was held on 18–19 April, 2008, in Warsaw, Poland. It was the first conference devoted strictly to the Art of South Asia, and attracted scholars from Poland and abroad, including Great Britain, Holland, Austria and Lithuania. Some of these presentations are included here. The conference was organised by (1) the Polish Society of Oriental Art (now the Polish Institute of World Art Studies), represented by Jerzy Malinowski, Dorota Kamińska and Agnieszka Staszczyk of the Section of Oriental Art, Nicolaus Copernicus University in Toruń, and by (2) Piotr Balcerowicz (no affiliation), with active participations of the members of the Department of South Asia, Faculty of Oriental Studies, the University of Warsaw. The program of the conference comprised the history of architecture, sculpture, painting and decorative art from antiquity to modern times, as well as the iconography, mythology and symbolism of South Asia. The proceedings of the Conference were subsequently published in Polish as *Sztuka i kultura wizualna Indii* [*Art and Visual Culture of India*], edited by Piotr Balcerowicz and Jerzy Malinowski, Wydawnictwo DiG, Warszawa 2010 (171 pp., 127 photos, A4).

The tradition of the study of South Asia and South Asian art in Poland goes back to the beginnings of the nineteenth century and commences with the research and activities of such historians as, for instance, Joachim Lelewel (1786–1861), the author of *The History of Ancient India* (Cracow, 1820), and Orientalists such as Szymon Żukowski (1782–1834), Józef Kowalewski (1801–1878), Józef Sękowski (1800–1858), Leonard Chodźko (1800–1871), Haji Seraja Szapszał (Haji Seraya Shapshal, 1873–1961), a hakham and leader of the Karaim community of Eupatoria and Troki, or Indologists, primarily Stanisław Schayer (1899–1941), the founder of the Institute of Oriental Studies in Warsaw. First Polish explorers, it seems, ventured to various parts of South Asia during the Renaissance. We know just of a handful of names, including Poznań-born Kaspar (c. 1450–c. 1510), Paweł Palczewski (or Palczowski; died c. 1609), the author of (lost) *Topography*, and Erazm Kretkowski

(1508–1558), the envoy of Sigismund II Augustus to India. When Vasco da Gama reached India for the first time, Kaspar, referred to by the Portuguese as Gaspar da Gama or Gaspar da India, was already there for a number of years serving as a secret service agent at the court of the sultan of Bījāpur, Yusuf Ādil Shāh (1459–1511), whom the Portuguese knew as Adil Khan or Hidalcão. The first reliable account about India preserved in Polish language is a letter of Gdańsk-born Krzysztof Pawłowski (died 1603) written in Goa and posted on 20th November 1596 to his friends in Cracow (*Perygrynacja do Indyi ... w roku 1596 / Peregrinations to India ... in 1569*), first published in 1915 and later redacted by Stefan Stasiak ('Les Indes Portugaises à la fin du XVIe siècle d'aprés la Relation du voyage fait à Goa en 1596, par Christophe Pawlowski, gentilhomme polonais', *Rocznik Orientalistyczny* 3/4 (1925–27)). Pawłowski describes his journey to India from Gdańsk via Lisabon in rather unsophisticated language. There is still another travel account by Maksymilian Wikliński (*Les voyages de Joseph Maximilien Cajetan Baron de Wiklinski aux Iles de France, aux Indes en Perse et dans les pays de proche Orient 1768-1781*, Port-Louis 2004), who visited India twice. These and similar accounts were collected and described by Eugeniusz Słuszkiewicz ('India as seen by Polish travellers up to the 19th century', *Indo-Asian Culture* 9,4 (1961) 385–403, and 'India as seen by Polish travellers of the 19th century', *Indo-Asian Culture* 10,3 (1962) 336–339).

The study of South Asian art requires not only expert knowledge of an art historian, but also sound philological proficiency and cultural competence of an Indologist. This calls for a close cooperation of specialists in both fields, and the present volume is a good exemplification of this vital principle.

This publication would not be possible without the financial support of the Ministry of Foreign Affairs of the Republic of Poland and the Embassy of the Republic of Poland in New Delhi, for which the Editors extend their words of thanks. The Editors express their thanks also to the Faculty of Oriental Studies, University of Warsaw, which likewise contributed to the publication.

Piotr Balcerowicz
Warsaw, September 2011

Table of transcription of Sanskrit terms and some editorial rules

a) Vowels:

simple: अ/अ a आ/आ ā इ i ई ī उ u ऊ ū ऋ ṛ ॠ ṝ ऌ ḷ

diphthongs: ए e ऐ ai ओ o औ au

b) Consonants:

1. gutturals:	क ka	ख kha	ग ga	घ gha	ङ ṅa
2. palatals:	च ca	छ/छ cha	ज ja	झ jha	ञ ña
3. cerebrals:	ट ṭa	ठ ṭha	ड ḍa	ढ ḍha	ण/ण ṇa
4. dentals:	त ta	थ tha	द da	ध dha	न na
5. labials:	प pa	फ pha	ब ba	भ bha	म ma
6. semivowels:	य ya	र ra	ल la	व va	
7. sibilants:	श śa	ष ṣa	स sa		
8. aspirate:	ह ha				

Additional signs: ं ṁ (*anusvāra*), ँ ˜ (*anunāsika*), : ḥ (*visarga*), ळ ḷa (retroflex).

In quotations from Sanskrit, Pāli etc., words are separated (e.g.: *jñānam etad*, not: *jñānametad*); elements of compounds (including titles) are divided with a hyphen (e.g.: *mahā-phala*, *Ṛg-veda*; not: *mahāphala*, *Ṛgveda*). The latter rule does not concern proper names (e.g. Bhartṛhari; not: *Bhartṛ-hari) and geographical names (e.g. Rājagṛha; not: *Rāja-gṛha). All quotations from Indian languages (e.g. Sanskrit, Pāli, Hindi etc.) and single foreign terms (e.g. Sanskrit terms) are in italics. In addition, in compounded terms, wherever their conjunction results in the *sandhi* of vowels, that is also marked with the cicumflex sign ˆ (e.g. *yogânuśāsana*, not *yogānuśāsana*; *Chandogyôpaniṣad*, not *Chandogyopaniṣad*).

Note on Contributors

Piotr Balcerowicz (www.orient.uw.edu.pl/balcerowicz), Professor of Indian studies at the University of Warsaw (Department of South-Asian Studies) and Professor of international relations at the Warsaw School of Social Sciences and Humanities (Department of International Relations), specialises in Indian philosophical tradition, with emphasis on Indian epistemological thought and Jainism. He lectures on Indian philosophy and Indian religions as well as on intercultural relations and contemporary history of Asia, esp. South-Asia, Central Asia and the Middle East. He received his M.A. degree in Indology from the University of Warsaw in 1990 and his Ph.D. degree in Sanskrit and Indian Studies from Hamburg University in 1999. He studied Sanskrit, Prakrits and Pāṇini at Banaras Hindu University in 1987–1988 and Western philosophy at postgraduate level at Polish Academy of Sciences, Warsaw in 1990–1994. He earned his post-doctoral degree ('Habilitation') in Eastern philosophies in 2005 from Polish Academy of Sciences with his postdoctoral thesis (*History of Classical Indian Philosophy. Part One: Beginnings, Analytical Trends and Philosophy of Nature*. Warsaw 2003). He published extensively on Indian philosophy, but also on the Middle East and Central Asia, and authored a number of books on Indian philosophy, Jainism and history of Afghanistan.

Silke K. Yasmin Fischer (SilkeYasmin.Fischer@lrz.uni-muenchen.de), PhD, studied Fine Arts at the Academy of Fine Arts as well as Indology, Philosophy, Catholic Theology and Religious Studies at Ludwig-Maximilians-University in Munich, Germany. Since 2004 she has been assistant lecturer and research assistant at the Institute of Indology and Tibetology, as well as study affairs coordinator at the Department of Asian Studies at Ludwig-Maximilians-University in Munich, Germany. Her academic interests include Buddhism in Sri Lanka, South Asian schoolbooks, popularisation of Buddhism and Hinduism, intercultural constructions of meditation and enlightenment, and the *Ṛg-Veda*. She has published on Buddhism in Sri Lanka and South Asian schoolbooks. Her publications: 'Die Einheit der Religionen in einem indischen Schulbuch'. (2009), 'Wie lernt man Buddhismus?' (2009), *Erzähl-*

Art, Myths and Visual Culture of South Asia
Warsaw Indological Studies 4 (2011) 15–18.

tradierung als Interpretationsprozess. Eine diachrone Analyse zweier staatlicher Buddhismus-Religionsbücher aus Sri Lanka. (Wiesbaden, 2011).

Barbara Grabowska is a Professor of Bengali Language and Literature at the University of Warsaw. She has published several works (in Polish) on the medieval and modern literature of Bengal, such as: *Lyric Poetry of Bengal* (1995), *Bengali Theatre and Drama. A Survey* (co-authors: Elżbieta Walter, Bożena Śliwczyńska) (1999), *The World of the Snake Goddess Manasa* (2002), *Krishna and Bengali Literature* (2008). Her current projects include reserach on Caṇḍī, Satī, Parvatī.

Deepak A. Gupta is conservator whose main area of work is mural paintings. In 1996 he began his conservator career from Ajanta Caves, where he worked till 2003. From 2003 to 2009 he worked on many monuments in Maharashtra state. In 2009 he was again posted to Ajanta Caves for conservation of mural paintings. He has an experience of conservation on five world heritage site of India, viz. Ajanta Caves, Ellora Caves, Goa churches, Elephanta Caves and Hampi group of monuments. Further, he has also taken training at Air Pollution Lab, Taj Mahal.

Valdas Jaskūnas (valdas.jaskunas@oc.vu.lt), Associate Professor of Indian Studies at the Centre of Oriental Studies, Vilnius University. His research interests focus on the system of knowledge of traditional Indian art and architecture and Indian visual culture. He is an author of a book in Lithuanian: Visual Identities. Reception of Indian Art in the West (Vilnius, 2005). Center of Oriental Studies, Vilnius University, Universiteto St. 5, LT-01513 Vilnius, Lithuania.

Jerzy Malinowski (jmalin@poczta.onet.pl), President of the Polish Institute of World Art Studies (former Polish Society of Oriental Art); full (ordinary) professor of history of art and head of the Departments of History of Modern and Oriental Art at the Nicolaus Copernicus University in Toruń; Former deputy director of the Institute of Art of the Polish Academy of Sciences, deputy director of the National Museum in Warsaw, chairman of the Scientific Council of the Jewish Historical Institute in Warsaw. He studied and earned his Ph.D. and post-doctoral degree at the Jagiellonian University in Kraków. He was a lecturer at a number of universities in Asia and Europe and organizer of international conferences. His academic interests include modern and contemporary European art and art criticism (Symbolism, Expressionism, École de Paris, Avant-garde art), Jewish art and art of East Asia. He has published numerous books, articles and exhibition catalogues in English, Chinese, French, German, Hebrew, Japanese, Polish and Russian.

Samir Kumar Mukherjee—Former Professor and Head of the Departments of Archaeology and Museology, University of Calcutta, Kolkata, a specialist in Indian archaeology, museology and art history.

Manager Rajdeo Singh (m_singh_asi@yahoo.com), superintending archaeological chemist, Aurangabad has been in the service of the Archaeological Survey of India in various capacities since 1990. Prior to this, he served the defence R&D Laboratory and Geological Survey of India Laboratories in Bangalore for about twelve years. He was very closely associated with the scientific conservation and preservation of Ajanta Caves murals (WHS) from 1997 to 2008 and published about a dozen papers on various aspect of conservation of Ajanta murals. He has also published number of research articles on lime mortars, metals, coins etc. in Indian context. He has devised new methodology for the conservation of paintings and delivered many lectures in India and abroad in the field of conservation.

Anna Ślączka Anna A. Ślączka (a.slaczka@rijksmuseum.nl) is curator of South Asian art at the Rijksmuseum (the National Museum) in Amsterdam, the Netherlands, since 2009. She obtained her PhD in Indology from Leiden University in 2006 working on the South Indian *śaivâgama*s. Hereafter she conducted research at the International Institute for Asian Studies (Leiden, the Netherlands) and the Ecole française d'Extrême Orient in Pondicherry, and worked as a lecturer in Sanskrit at Leiden University. Her research interests comprise Śaiva Sanskrit texts, temple rituals, Indian and South-East Asian art and architecture. Her recent publications include: 'The brick structures of Go Thap: tombs or temples?', 'The iconography of the deities in the Devyâmata and the art of Bengal' (2011), 'The iconography of the Hindu deities in the Devyâmata, an early Śaiva *pratisthâtantra*' (2011) and *Temple Consecration Rituals in Ancient India* (Brill, Leiden 2007).

David Smith taught South Asian Religions and Sanskrit at Lancaster University from 1974 to 2011. His principal publications are *Ratnakara's Haravijaya: An Introduction to the Sanskrit Court Epic*, Oxford University Press, 1985; *The Dance of Siva: religion, art and poetry in South India*, Cambridge University Press, 1996; *Hinduism and Modernity*, Blackwell, 2003. He is currently writing *Hindu Eroticism*, to be published by I.B.Tauris; and preparing a study of Khajuraho.

R.S. Trambake (trambakers@yahoo.com), project modeller has been in the service of the Archaeological Survey of India for last 35 years. In his present assignment, he has been associated with the task of conservation of murals of Ajanta and consolidation, mending work of painted plasters and sculptures of Ajanta since 1993. He has to his credit about a dozen published papers in various journals. He is associated in the execution of some extraordinary work of mending of various Indian sculptures in the country.

Monika Zin, Professor, studied art history, Indology and dramatics in Krakow and Munich. She wrote her dissertation on the *Plays from Trivandrum in the History of Development of the Udayana Narrative* in 1991 and finished her habilitation in 2000 on the topic of Ajanta paintings. She teaches since 1994, at the Institute for Indology in Munich and since 2010 at the Freie Universitaet in Berlin. She has contributed monographs regarding Ajanta and the Buddhist tales and representations—*Ajanta Handbook of the Paintings, 2: Devotional and Ornamental Paintings*, 2003; *Pity and Miracles. Difficult Conversions and their iconography in Indian Buddhism*, 2006; *Samsaracakra, The Wheel of Rebirth in Indian Tradition* (together with Dieter Schlingloff), 2007—all written in German. She published articles dealing with the identification of narrative art in South, Southeast, and Central Asia and with Indian drama. Her current publication project deals with the *Narrative Reliefs from Amaravati and Nagarjunakonda.*

Asoka de Zoysa (asoka_de_zoysa@hotmail.com), Senior lecturer: German Studies, Department of Modern Languages, University of Kelaniya, Sli Lanka. He Studied Indian Philology and History of Art at the Freie Universität Berlin, Germany, where he obtained a PhD in Germanic studies. In his doctoral thesis he focused on the representation of the 'Other', examining unresearched documents of Germany, France and England which depict 'India' in popular genres (novels, operas, dramas and fictional autobiographies) of the first years of colonisation of the Subcontinent. Affiliated to the University of Kelaniya since 1997, he is the Head of German Studies at the Department of Modern Languages.

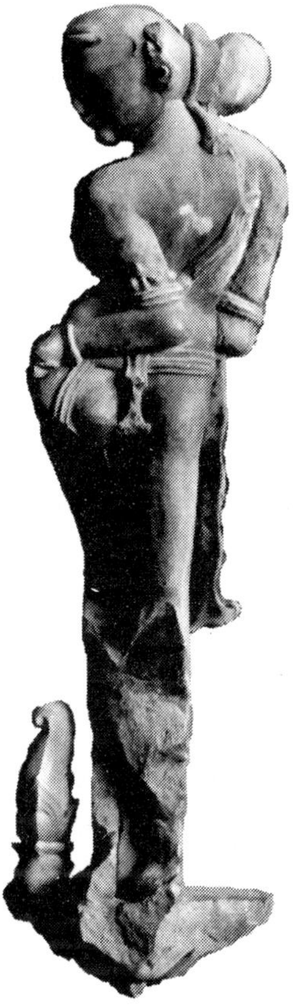

Myth, Parable and Art

Acts of Master Viśvakarman in Bengali Poems

BARBARA GRABOWSKA
(University of Warsaw)

Viśvakarman, the all-achieving, creator of all things, personification of creative power, in the *Ṛg-veda*, identified with god Prajāpati, was the creator of the skies and the earth. In the later period, in *Purāṇa*s and in the epic, he was reduced to the role of a versatile divine architect, gifted craftsman and protector of art and crafts, who equips gods with towns, chariots, weapons and ornaments. He made the disc for Viṣṇu, trident for Śiva, weapon for Kubera, lance for Kārttikeya, he built Laṅkā for the demons.

He was sometimes recognized as a son of Prabhāsa, the eighth Vasu, and Varastrī, the sister of Bṛhaspati, or sometimes as a son of Brahma. His wife was Yogasiddhā. He had five sons and four daughters (MANI (1996: 869–872)).

In Sanskrit texts Viśvakarman is described with such epithets as Kāru ('doer; workman; artisan'), Takṣaka ('carpenter'), Devavārdhika ('builder of the gods'), in Bengali texts his name is usually changed to Viśāi.

The most interesting and most detailed account of Viśvakarman's work is given in a poem by a renowned poet and dramatist Madhusudan Datta, entitled *The Birth of Tilottamā* (*Tilottamā-saṁbhav*) published in 1860. The text narrates the creation of the enchanting Tilottamā, 'Perfect in Minutest Detail', the most beautiful work of art ever accomplished by Viśvakarman.

The circumstances of Tilottamā's birth are described by the poet in blank verse; in fact, *The Birth of Tilottamā* is the first Bengali poem of such kind (MR 494–497).

After practicing exceptionally austere asceticism, two demon brothers Sunda and Upasunda gained, thanks to Brahma's grace, the boon of near-immortality: no one could ever kill them, except for themselves, however they were extremely devoted and loyal to each other. They ruled the world on their own, driving the gods from the skies. The gods, after a debate, decided that the only solution was to instigate a conflict between the two brothers, using for that purpose a beautiful woman. Viśvakarman was supposed to create the woman. Pavana, the god of wind, was sent

Art, Myths and Visual Culture of South Asia
Warsaw Indological Studies 4 (2011) 21–31.

to bring him to the gathering of the gods. The abode of the divine artisan (*deva-śilpin*) was at the end of the world, far beyond the Earth, beyond the world of Yama, the Moon and the Sun. Thick smoke covered the mountains of metals and minerals. God Viśvakarman sat on a golden throne in his palace.

Viśvakarman's reaction to the Wind is quite revealing in showing which tasks were traditionally assigned to him. Viśvakarman thought that the Wind had come to him to get a jewel for his new beloved. He offered him ornaments he had made: foot bracelets sounding like Sarasvatī's lute, an ornamented hip band, a pearl necklace that would rest between woman's breasts, bracelet laden with jewels, coral earrings, head ornament that would decorate hair resembling night sky.

Pavana took Viśvakarman to the gold city of Brahma (*svarṇamay brahmapurī*), built of gold and diamonds, also a creation of the divine architect. There Viśvakarman listened to gods' request: he was expected to create a charming woman taking bits (*tila tila*) of everything what was there in the world, things moving and unmoving. Now, the poet presents how the master worked. The master of all artists sunk into deep meditation and performed strict austerities: with the power of a potent mantra he brought to the city of Brahma all that he needed. It is worth noting that the ingredients used to create Tilottamā's body are elements of nature generally used in metaphors of woman beauty.

Viśvakarman made the maid's two feet of lotus, which he painted with lighting as if he would do it with the *lākṣa-rasa* lac dye. Her thighs were made of banana trees, a lion gave her the slim waist, the skies made up her buttocks with full circles, and the Milky Way girded them like a belt. Her shoulders were made of lotus branches. Pomegranate competed with *kadamba*[1] for the place on her chest; the artist, however, opted for Mount Meru. The Moon became her face thanks to the power of asceticism; it was impeccable and spotless. Then, a cloud took shape of her hair. Although a gazelle offered her eyes humbly at his feet, Viśvakarman made the eyes of the *tejaḥ-puñja* glow, divided into two separate circumferences. Her lips he made of the red *bimba* fruit and he smeared them with nectar; elephant pearls shone as her teeth. The god of love himself placed his bow as the maid's eyebrows; the artist grasped Kāma's quiver, took sharp flower-arrows from it and offered them to Tilottamā's eyes. The Earth presented gems to adorn the maid's body. Golden magnolia and water lily flowers as well as gold contested to give her their colour, but Viśvakarman painted her body with yellow orpiment. Kokila, the friend of spring, wanted to give the maid her own voice, but Sarasvatī conferred all *rāga*s and *rāgiṇī*s, incarnated melodic models, on her as her voice. Goddess of speech Vāgīśvarī fixed

[1] *Kadamba* (*Nauclea kadamba*), a tree with yellow scented flowers, in bloom during the rainy season.

her tongue. The divine master of all artists brought her to life with the help of nectar and Tilottamā stood like incarnated glow.

When they saw Tilottamā of divine beauty, the demon brothers Sunda and Upasunda quarrelled over her and, as a result, killed each other.

The Creation of Goddess Padmāvatī

The snake goddess was created in similar way, according to the *Story of Padma* (*Padma-purāṇa*) by Vijay Gupta, published in 1906. When the potent seed of Śiva fell to the underworld, snake Vāsuki summoned the *nirmmāṅkārī* ('creator', 'maker', 'craftsman') and ordered him to create a daughter for a god of it. He remembered that Śiva already had two sons. The poet does not actually mention the name of Viśvakarman; he only uses the term *nirmmāṅkārī*, but there can hardly be any doubt that whom he means is the divine artist: it would be very unlikely that a regular craftsman could create a goddess.

When he was brought to the underworld, the accomplished creator wondered how to fulfil his task as he did not have any standard or model (*rūpa*). In the end he created an exceptionally beautiful goddess, mostly with lotuses, and gave her the name of Lotus Lady—Padmāvatī. She was brought to life with water mixed with nectar from the pond (*amṛta-kuṇḍa-jala*) of Sarasvatī (PP 6).

Not only had Viśvakarman his part in creation of Padmavatī but he also prepared for her an appropriate room called *karaṇḍī*. When the goddess wanted to go to the house of her father Śiva on the mountain of Kailāsa, Śiva called for Viśvakarman and told him to build the *karaṇḍī*. The four walls of the *karaṇḍī* were decorated with thousand of lotuses, four roofs were made of gold, four doors were protected by snakes, and additionally there was a snake *maṇḍala* situated on an elevation. Śiva put the goddess in the *karaṇḍī,* covered her with various flowers and set off with her on a bull.

Asutosh BHATTACHARYYA (1977: 253–254), a renowned Bengali anthropologist, emphasizes that even today *karaṇḍī* plays a big part in the offering ritual for the snake goddess. The author explains that it is a small object in the shape of a little house, around half a meter high, made of Indian cork (*śola*). Roof and walls are decorated with colourful drawings of snakes, their mistress and images of heroes of the snake goddess story. *Karaṇḍī* is only found in eastern and north-eastern Bengal.

Of the remaining exploits of Viśvakarman, described in Bengali texts, one could mention the making of Indra's weapon, the construction of a city, temple, house and the making of parts of female robe, i.e. goddess' bra decorated with jewels. The source texts used here are texts by Dvija Mādhav (MG), Mukundarām (CM) and Rāmdev (AM) as well as the Bengali version of *Mahā-bhārata* (MBh).

The Making of Indra's Weapon

Viśvakarman's great feat was the making of a powerful weapon, known as *vajra*, meant for the god of war Indra, so that the god could defeat the demon Vṛtra. The Bengali version of the *Mahā-bhārata* relates the story twice: in the *Vana-parvan* (MBh 405–406) and in the *Gadā-parvan* (MBh 854–860).

Indra's fight with Vṛtra, who held the waters hostage, is known already from the *Ṛg-veda* hymns. The oldest version of this myth is not particularly detailed and we do not know any details concerning either the fight itself or the creation of the weapon; these are however, provided by a later epic version.

As narrated in the *Vana-parvan*, Vṛtra drove away the gods from the skies and sat on Indra's throne. The gods asked Brahma for help, who replied that the demon could not be defeated with any regular weapon made of iron, wood or stone. The gods should go to the sage Dadhīci to ask him for his bones and from them make the weapon called *vajra*, with which Indra would be able to kill Vṛtra. In *Gadā-parvan* Brahma sends the gods to Viṣṇu, who gives them the same advice.

The gods went to the sage's hermitage on the Sarasvatī river, where they saw Dadhīci with body his glowing more intensely than fire, the sun or the moon. When implored, the sage, to the admiration of all present, decided without any hesitation to abandon his own body for the benefit of others. With his bones the gods returned to the divine artist, Viśvakarman.

However, in the *Gadā-parvan* the sage expressed his doubt and had some difficult moments of hesitation. Thanks to his many merits acquired after a long journey through 84,000 incarnations, he assumed a birth in human body, which is difficult to obtain in itself; moreover, it was the best possible of human births: that of a Brahmin. Thanks to asceticism he developed powers that equalled those of gods. And now why should he give it all up? However, seeing the gods sitting in desperation, dispirited with lowered heads, he felt sympathy and made up his mind. In the state of *yoga*, he breathed his last breath.

Indra took his bones and summoned the god Viśvakarman to tell him to prepare a *vajra*. Viśvakarman invested in it the accumulated power of all weapons and handed the infallible weapon over to Indra. Indra proceeded to Brahma, who performed the *abhiṣeka* rite over the weapon, charmed it with a special divine mantra (*brahma-mantra*), brought it to life (*jīva-nyāsa*) and said: 'With this weapon, you will defeat the demon!'

According to the *Mahā-bhārata*[2], Vṛtra opened his mouth and swallowed Indra. Gods felt really worried and created the yawn. When Vṛtra yawned, Indra got out of his body. The theme recurs in the *Bhāgavata-purāṇa* (BhP 609). The gigantic Vṛtra swallows Indra together with Airāvata, like a python swallows an elephant. Indra descends to the demon's stomach, slits it open with the *vajra* and manages to get out.

This theme is also mentioned by Hemchandra Banerji in his best known text, an epic poem entitled *Killing of Vṛtra* (*Vṛtra-samhār*, 1875–1877) (SEN (1962: 370–380). The poet filled the framework of the old myth with loose episodes of his own creation. While the Bengali version of the *Mahā-bhārata* focuses on the heroic decision of the sage Dadhīci, in Hemchandra's text the focal point is the conflict between two women: the proud and envious Aindrilā, Vṛtra's wife, and Śacī, Indra's wife. The wife of the victorious demon Vṛtra relishing the pleasures of the paradise wants to humiliate the goddess Śacī and reduce her to the status of her own slave. Rape and abuse of the goddess leads to the demon's defeat. Infuriated Śiva informs Indra how to defeat Vṛtra: with the weapon made from the sage Dadhīci's bone. Although the focus of the story is on Dadhīci's sacrifice, the poet does not devote much attention to it and it the main character of the poem is not Dadhīci but Aindrilā.

This is how the poet describes Viśvakarnan's workshop:

> 'Deep in the womb of the earth, in thick darkness,
> In a deserted and hardly reachable place,
> Wide and spacious was Viśvakarman's workshop.
> Terrifying sounds were to be heard there constantly,
> Searing the ears—terrible hits of the hammer,
> As though a club sent a million blows,
> With powerful hiss—as though a million Vāsuki snakes were hissing—
> —A stream of melted metals ran quickly to the water.
> Clouds of thick smoke and steam covered the area,
> Heaps of ashes were floating, smell of burning lingered.'[3]

The Construction of Cities

It transpires from the text by Madhusudan Datta, mentioned above, that Viśvakarman is city builder. The golden Brahmapurī, Brahma's City, is one of his creations. From poems dedicated to the snake goddess we learn that also her city

---

[2] BHATTACHARJI (1970: 258).

[3] BANDYOPADHYAY (1999: 387).

was built by the divine artist. The goddess Maṅgalacaṇḍī ordered the creation of the city of Gujarāṭ, the capital of her dedicated servant Kālketu. Its inhabitants made sacrifices to the divine wife of Śiva. The poets emphasize that the construction was started in an auspicious moment with a favourable position of the stars.

The description of the construction by Rāmdev (AM 73) is exceptionally short. The poet only informs that the goddess called for Viśvakarman and told him to go to Gujarāṭ and build a city there. As a result, the city was created overnight. The buildings were said to be glorious, but the poet only mentions rooms for elephants, stables and a theatre.

More details are given by Mukundarām (CM 311–313).

The divine artist built for Kālketu a city similar to Ayodhyā. He built it on the 13th day of the light half of the month of Kārtik (October–November), when the moon coincided with the planet Jupiter. Viśvakarman, together with Hanumant and his son Dāruvarman, raised buildings with stone walls as high as mountains. They also built houses of clay with four rooms and four roofs with verandas. Every house was equipped with a well. The team made gates of stone. In the east they built a temple of Viṣṇu (*deul*). The god's statue was decorated with diamonds and sapphires and, as a result, it glared like fire. On the left there was a temple of Durgā, next to it was a dance room. To the east of the main gate they dug a pond. In the north there was a second gate. In the meeting point of four roads in the city they built a temple of Śiva, shelter for orphans (*anātha-maṇḍapa*) and a charity house where alms were distributed (*bhāt-śālā*). They built bazaars and large (*dīghala*, lit. 'long') houses for travellers. For Kr̥ṣṇa they made a swing of diamonds and sapphires and hung it in the Kadam forest (*kadamba-kānana*). In the western part of the city they built a mosque.

The Construction of the Temple of the Goddess Maṅgalacaṇḍī

The construction of a temple (*maṭh*) was probably a theme which easily captivated the attention of listeners, which explains why it is present in texts by Mādhav, Mukundarām and Rāmdev.

Descriptions by Mādhav (MC 24–26) and Rāmdev (AM 27–29) are complementary; the former is interested mainly in the construction, whereas the latter in the pond adjacent to and the garden surrounding the temple. The most detailed description is provided by Mukundarām (CM 122–125).

The goddess Maṅgalacaṇḍī requested the divine architect, whom she called her son, to build a temple in the city of Kaliṅga on the riverside of Kaṁsa. Viśvakarman went there with Hanumant. In an auspicious moment he started the construction at the foot of the *tamāla* tree. With a thread, he measured 57 *banda*s and he built the temple overnight. Hanumant transported rocks on his head. Also the servants brought everything that was needed: stones, corals, pearls, rubies, silver and gold. The artist laid down the cornerstone and installed the columns, whereupon he placed a thatch roof with four quarters (*cau-cāl*). The four stone walls were incrusted with mirrors, a pinnacle was decorated with diamonds, sapphires and emeralds, on the top (*śiras*) of the temple white fans and flags flapped. Inside there were numerous chambers—dance rooms, ablution rooms, treasury, laboratory full of metals and minerals, guestrooms, treasury full of diamonds, corals and other jewels.

Viśvakarman made various paintings representing the three worlds, Indra and all gods, the guru of the immortals, the *asura*s and sages and the wish-granting *kalpa-taru* tree. Sacrifice place was also prepared. A golden figure of the ten-handed goddess Maṅgalacaṇḍī was placed on the silver altar: with a diadem on her head, she stood on a lion's back, next to her there were two golden jugs and figures of Maheśa sitting on a bull, Kārtttikeya on a peacock and Ganeśa on a rat, all laden with jewels. Implored by the goddess, Hanumant engraved a description of a sacrifice ritual in the stone (*pūjār paddhati*).

Hanumant dug a pond with his claws, incrusted four ways into the water with stones, and filled it with water from the underground river of Bhogavatī. The pond was covered with alluring white, blue and red lotuses, which bloomed all night and day, and with water lilies. Viśvakarman surrounded the pond with a garden and planted *tamala* trees, various flower trees and blooming bushes on the banks. He replanted the sandal trees from the Malaya Mountains. Kokilas were singing in branches of mango trees. The trees had flowers and fruits at the same time, animals hostile to each other by nature lived there together in peace: a lion next to an elephant, a frog next to a snake, a mouse played with a cat.

Rāmdev (AM 27–29) particularly praises the charm of the pond adjacent to the temple. The only information about the actual structure of the building is that it was made of various jewels (*maṇi-maya maṭha-gṛha*), pearls, coral, emeralds and gold.

One could get the impression that preparation of the garden was as extraordinary as the building of the temple.

The Construction of a Swing

While describing the construction of the city, Mukundarām mentions a swing for Kṛṣṇa. We can imagine what the swing looked like or what was its purpose thanks to a poem by Paraśurām, a poet flourishing in the seventeenth century. His popular poem *Kṛṣṇa-maṅgala* is a free translation into Bengali of the tenth book of *Bhāga-vata-purāṇa*, which in itself serves as an object of worship, especially for

Vaiṣṇavas. The poet added some folklore themes about Kṛṣṇa's love for Radhā to the classical story.

Dola-līlā ('swing-play') is a new and so far unknown theme introduced into the Kṛṣṇa's adventures by Paraśurām (PK 259–266). Kṛṣṇa's swing-play in the light half of the month of Phālgun (February—March) is mentioned in the *Padma-purāṇa* and *Skanda-purāṇa*, whereas according to *Garuḍa-purāṇa* it takes place in the month of Caitra (March–April).

During spring in the month of Phālgun Kṛṣṇa decided to play with the red powder known as *phāgu*. On his request, Indra called for Viśvakarman and asked him to build a pavilion with a swing for Kṛṣṇa. The divine craftsman came various tools. From Kubera's treasury, he took diamonds, rubies, pearls, corals, gold and silver and went to Gokula in search of a beautiful place. He liked Vṛndāvana on the shore of Yamunā. He created the pavilion within one night. Two columns were of emeralds, the walls of gold, the floors of crystal. He decorated the pavilion with strings of pearls, flags, golden jugs, and installed there four sculptures of Garuḍa made of gold. The pavilion was so beautiful that there was none that could equal it even in the Viṣṇu paradise. It was admired by Indra himself, who informed all other gods about it. The gods, with a magnificent retinue of musicians and dancers, arrived to pay obeisance to Kṛṣṇa, swing him and to smear his body with the *phāgu* powder. In the morning, shepherds arrived for the same reason. Rādhā sat on the swing next to Kṛṣṇa.

The Construction of a House (CM 309–311)

Solicited by the goddess Caṇḍī, Viśvakarman together Hanumant built a house for her dedicated worshiper Kālketu. Starting their work at an auspicious conjunction of stars, first they built four walls which they decorated with precious stones and incrusted their copings with wood; the roof was divided into four quarters. The interior of the building consisted of four exquisite rooms. The house was surrounded with a stone (*śilā*) terrace. On the women's side of the house, Hanumant dug a pond and inlaid four paths leading to the water with stones and gravel (*pāṣāṇa*). On the northern side, there was a back gate, whereas the main entrance was from the east. Next to the house they built a dance room and a temple for Caṇḍī. They decorated it with paintings, and installed an altar full of jewels. They put jugs and a figure of Caṇḍī on the altar.

Women's Ornaments

Interestingly, the production of women's ornaments was a field traditionally associated with Viśvakarman. Several poems describe the jewel-incrusted brassiere of the goddess Maṅgalacaṇḍī. According to Rāmdev, the divine artist manufactured it in a blink of an eye, even though the work was complicated. We learn of how he cut, stitched and sewn the fabric and then decorated it with paintings of three worlds and plants (AM 64–65).

The decoration of the brassiere was described in detail by Dvija Mādhav (MG 54–56). Viśvakarman represented there the paradise, the world of the mortals and the underworld. First, he portrayed the god Dharma, Indra on the elephant Airāvata, Agni on a ram (*aja-vāhane*), the sage Nārada on a pedal tool for husking rice (*ḍheniki*), spirits (*pramather gaṇa*) of Śiva with tridents in their hands, the lord of death Yama, riding on a buffalo, and the goddesses: Lakṣmī, Sarasvatī, Caṇḍī and Camuṇḍā. Then he depicted all mountains and rivers, the sun and the bird Garuḍa behind it. He further pictured ponds and lakes and, finally, a flower garden with various species of lotuses and other flowers (the poet mentions, in fact, over 20 names here).

The goddess's fanciful brassiere decoration is even richer the way it is depicted in the text by Mukundarām (CM 233–240). The author maintains that the master used stories of *Purāṇa*s and the *Mahā-bhārata.* Viśvakaraman took a brush into his hand and, first, he painted ten incarnations of Viṣṇu: the fish, turtle, boar, the man-lion Narasiṁha, the dwarf, Paraśurāma, Rāma, Balarāma, the Buddha and Kalkin. The poet describes each of the incarnations the way Viśvakarman painted them, e.g. how Viṣṇu's incarnated into a boar, which saved the Earth, went into the underworld kingdom, killed the first among the demons, spared the earth with tusks and took it out of water.

The poet treats the Kalkin incarnation as belonging to the past. The protagonist in next paintings is Kr̥ṣṇa, the son of Yaśodā (sic!) and his youthful frolics, a theme especially endearing to the Bengali heart. The poet mentions all important episodes of Kr̥ṣṇa's life in Vr̥ndāvana Vr̥ndāvana, such as the killing of Pūtanā, defeating of the snake Kāliya, raising of the mountain of Govardhana, dalliance with shepherd girls, or the killing of Kaṁsa.

On the right side of the brassiere, according to Mukundarām, Viśvakarman painted sages and divine fortune-tellers (the poet lists a large number of names), various birds surrounding Garuḍa (around 30 bird species), 20 species of animals, numerous apes, know from *Rāmāyaṇa*, and snakes. In the middle of the brassiere he painted the Vr̥ndāvana Vr̥ndāvana forest, the *kadamba* forest, the banks of Yamunā, Kr̥ṣṇa's swing and plentiful plants (here follows a catalogue of over 30 plants).

In the description of Viśvakarman's acts found in Bengali poems, one can find, beside the numerous imaginative elements, also the reality of the medieval Bengal. The temple of the goddess Maṅgalacaṇḍī can serve as an example here.

In Bengal's history written by MAJUMDAR (1974: 330–332) we find the information that in the medieval Bengal the Hindu temples were built in two styles, known as *rekha deul* and *kuṭir deul.* Characteristic features of *kuṭir deul* were the roofs divided into two or four quarters typical of Bengali thatched huts, as MAJUMDAR (1974: 331) explains: 'In this structure four triangular roofs places on the four walls move up to converge on a curved line of a pint, just like a four-roofed thatched hut'. The walls of temples were decorated with paintings of plants, animals, birds and people. Such temples, typical of local culture, dominated in Bengal since the sixteenth century. The temple of the goddess Maṅgalacaṇḍī described by poets as a creation of the divine craftsman, is in fact temple in the *kuṭir deul* style.

It may at first be a little puzzling why the narrative poems introduced Viśvakarman into their plots at all. In fact, their main characters were folk deities worshiped initially by the low castes. Both the deities revered by the lower classes and the myths narrated by them had to be modelled after renowned and established examples in order to find the approval of the higher castes. Folk stories were Sanskritised through the poems and the tribal gods gradually found their way into the Hindu pantheon. In order to bestow more prestige on the folklore themes, they were composed in genres resembling Sanskrit *Purāṇa*s and populated with folklore protagonists. Since one goddess of another, either Maṅgalacaṇḍī or Padmavatī, were attended by the divine craftsman, and to her orders Viśvakarman constructed a temple or manufactured even an ordinary brassiere, thereby additional prestige accrued to her.

BIBLIOGRAPHY

AM = Dvija, Rāmdev: *Abhayā-maṅgal.* Āsutoṣ Dās sampādita, Kalikātā Visvavidyālay, Kalikātā 1957.

BANDYOPADHYAY 1999 = Bandyopādhyāy, Asitkumār: *Bāṁlā sāhityer sampūrṇa iti-vṛtta.* Maḍārṇ Buk Ejensī Prāibheṭ Limiṭeḍ, Kalikātā 1999.

BHATTACHARYYA 1977 = Bhattacharyya, Asutosh: *The Sun and the Serpent Lore of Bengal.* Firma KLM Private Limited, Calcutta 1977.

BHATTACHARJI 1970 = Bhattacharji, Sukumari: *The Indian Theogony. A Comparative Study of Indian Mythology from the Vedas to the Purāṇas.* Cambridge At the University Press, Cambridge 1970.

BhP	= *Bhāgavata-purāṇa*. Goswami, C.L.: *Śrimad Bhāgavata Mahāpurāṇa*. with Sanskrit Text and English Translation, Part I and II, Gita Press, Gorakhpur 2001.
BK	= *Bāiśkavi Śrī-śrī-padma-purāṇa bā Manasā puṁthi*. Madangopāl Gupta sampādita, Rājendra Lāibrerī, Kalikātā, no publication date.
CM	= Mukundarām Cakravartī: *Caṇḍī-maṅgala*. Śrīkumār Bandyopādhyāy & Viśvapati Caudhurī sampādita, Kavikaṅkaṇ-Caṇḍī, Kalikātā Viśvavidyālay, Kalikātā 2002.
KK	= Kṣemānanda, Ketakādās: *Manasā-maṅgala*. Akṣaykumār Kayāl o Citrā Dev sampādita, Lekhāparā, Kalikātā 1977.
MANI 1996	= Mani, Vettam: *Purāṇic Encyclopaedia*. DC Books / Motilal Banarsidass, Delhi 1996.
MBh	= Kāśīrām Dās: *Mahā-bhārata*. De'j Pābliśiṁ, Kalikātā 1991,
MG	= Mādhav, Dvija: *Maṅgalacaṇḍīr gīt*. Sudhībhūṣaṇ Bhaṭṭācārya sampādita, Kalikātā Viśvadyālay, Kalikātā 1965.
MAJUMDAR 1974	= Majumdar, R.C.: *History of Mediaeval Bengal*. G. Bharadvaj & Co., Calcutta 1974.
MR	= Datta, Māikel Madhusūdan: *Māikel-racanā-saṁbhār*. Pramathnāth Biśī sampādita, Mitra o Ghoṣ, Kalikātā 1966.
PK	= *Paraśurāmer Kṛṣṇa-maṅgala*. Dāś Gupta Nalinīnāth sāmpadita, Kalikātā Viśvavidyālay, Kalikātā 1957.
PP	= Vijay Gupta: *Śrīśrīpadmapurāṇa bā Manasā-maṅgala gīta*. Kalimohan Vidyaratna sāmpadita, Kalikata 1906.
SEN 1962	= Sen, Sukumar: *Bāṅglā sāhityer itihās*. Vol. 2, Iṣṭārṇ Pābliśārs, Kalikata 1962.

The Parable of 'The Man in the Well'
Its Travels and its Pictorial Traditions from Amaravati to Today

MONIKA ZIN
(Ludwig Maximilian University of Munich)

Dedicated
to HRH Maha Chakri Sirindhorn
Princess of Thailand,
in memento of Her visit to Munich
in July 2008

Among the Buddhist reliefs found in Nagarjunakonda (Nāgārjunakoṇḍā—Eds.), the ancient Vijayapurī of the Ikṣvāku in the 3rd century CE, there are still many whose meaning has not been satisfactorily explained. Nagarjunakonda was discovered in the 1920s and excavated some years later.[1] The most extensive excavations were made in the 1950s, before the dam was built and the water of the river Krishna submerged the entire valley which became the Nagarjunasagar, covering the archaeological site for ever (SOUNDARARAJAN (2006)).

The Ikṣvāku were a local dynasty who tried to imitate the great Sātavāhanas from Dharaṇikoṭa, the place ca. 125 km downstream which is known today as Amaravati (Amarāvatī—Eds.). Like the Sātavāhanas, the Ikṣvāku were not Buddhist, but their wives, sisters and many of their subjects were (ROSEN STONE (1980)). Buddhism must have been very important and must have had the support of the rulers, since there were many Buddhist sites with *stūpa*s, temples and monasteries in the close vicinity of the capital Vijayapurī. The reliefs from those sites are today held in the museum on Nagarjuna Island as well as in museums in India and all over the world. Explanations of the subjects of the reliefs are principally found in VOGEL (1929, 1932, 1933), LONGHURST (1938) and RAO (1956).

---

[1] For discovery of the site and excavations cf. ROSEN STONE (1994: 1–3).

Art, Myths and Visual Culture of South Asia
Warsaw Indological Studies 4 (2011) 33–93.

The reliefs from Nagarjunakonda and Amaravati include many subjects which have no parallels in any other Buddhist schools; however, because their motifs are repeatedly depicted, we are lead to believe that their themes must have been popular, whether or not their meanings have been explained.

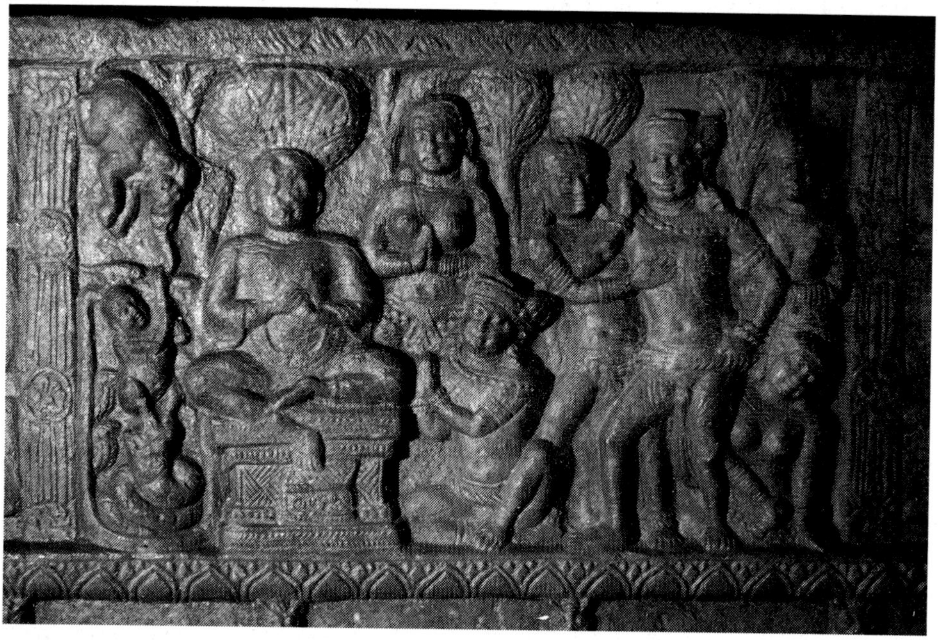

Fig. 1. Nagarjunakonda, Site 9, Nagarjunakonda Museum, No. 24, frieze, ill.: VOGEL (1937: pl. 34a); LONGHURST (1938: pl. 31b); RAO (1956); ROSEN STONE (1994: fig. 64, pl. 81); ZIN (2004: fig. 15 / drawing). ©Monika Zin. [For a colour print, see the Appendix]

One such theme was a story which is represented in a relief kept on Nagarjuna Island [fig. 1]. The scene is a part of a long frieze and shows two consecutive scenes of the narrative in one register. The story is clearly set outdoors because there are some trees in the background. On the right-hand side there is a man who is characterised by a princely head-dress and an ornament above his left ear. The man is holding a spear in his left hand and his right hand is lifted so that the tip is pointing upwards. The man seems to be stepping forwards while three women try to stop him. The next scene, further to the left, depicts the same man sitting by the throne of a preaching monk (it is a monk, not the Buddha, since the *uṣṇīṣa*, the *ūrṇā* and the long earlobes are lacking). The man clasps his hands together in a gesture of worshipping with respect to the monk, as does a woman who is at the side of the throne;

the man is no longer in an aggressive position as if due to the sermon he is listening to. On the other side of the monk, on the left-hand edge of the register, something very peculiar is represented [fig. 2 a–b]. The tiny figure of a man can easily be recognised: he seems to be naked, his arms are held high and his legs are bent at the knees, which implies that he is hanging. Below his feet there is a huge, coiled snake with open jaws, ready to catch him. On the sides there is a sort of a frame, out of which four cobras emerge. In the upper part there is a tree and to the left the most prominent feature: an elephant which is shown as if falling down. It is possible to recognise a little animal to the left of the man's hands and there may be another one to the right.

The same narrative can be recognised on another relief in the Nagarjunakonda Museum [fig. 3]. Here as well there is an aggressive, princely looking man with a spear in his left hand and a lifted right index finger; in this relief he is coming out of a building where some women try to stop him. To the left there is the scene with the preaching monk and to the side of the monk there is again an additional scene, here depicted diminutively, which contains the same elements [fig. 4 a–b]: the hanging man with drawn up legs, the giant snake with opened jaws below and four cobras to the sides. Above the upper part of the frame there is the tree, the elephant and a small animal (or again perhaps two animals). The frame in this relief is more easily decipherable since there are regular blocks of stones on its outer wall: the frame must be a well.

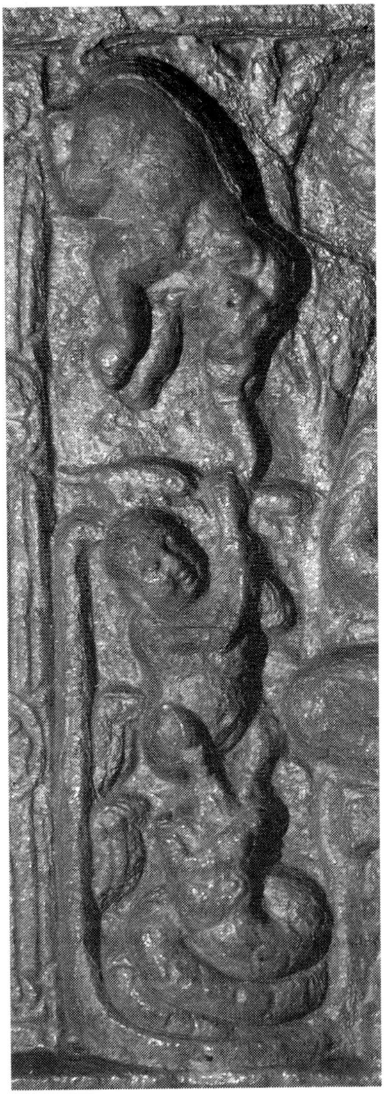

Fig. 2

There is another example of the same narrative which is now kept in Paris [fig. 5]. The relief is more elaborate—the woman's attempt to stop the man is depicted in dramatic scenes—but it also more mutilated; however, the same elements are recognisable. The diminutive scene on the side of the preaching monk [fig. 6] is certainly the same; an umbrella lying on the side can be explained as having been dropped by the man.

In addition to the depictions discussed above, there are three more examples of the same narrative but these are not from Nagarjunakonda but from Amaravati. The representations are very small; they are shown in the decoration of the *stūpa*s depicted on slabs, so they are only a few centimetres high. It is only our knowledge of the bigger examples which allow us to recognise the contents of these tiny versions. One of these miniature scenes is to be found in the Archaeological Site Museum at Amaravati [figs. 7 a–b], another one in the British Museum [fig. 8], recognised by ROSEN STONE (1994: 38), and perhaps also one more on a slab in the Amaravati Museum [fig. 9]; on this last however, the part with the seated monk has not survived. The importance of these diminutive depictions is that they provide us with evidence that the story must have been known before they were created, since there must have been bigger, more elaborate depictions to enable the viewer to understand the miniature ones.

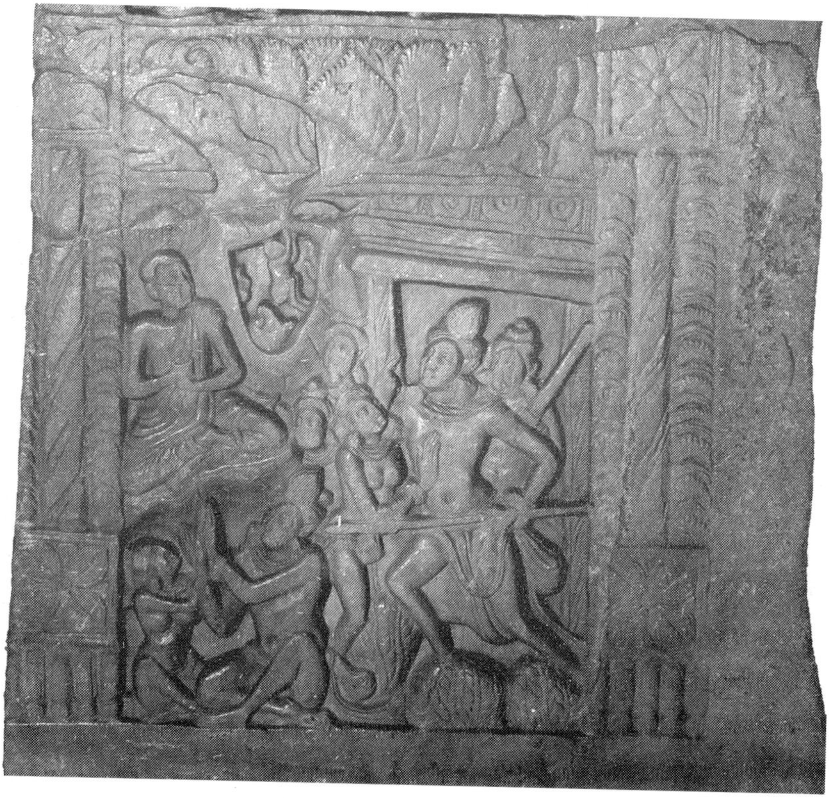

Fig. 3. Nagarjunakonda, Site 2, Nagarjunakonda Museum, No. 18, *stûpa* slab, ill.: LONGHURST (1938: pl. 49b); EINHORN (1972: fig. 117); ROSEN STONE (1994: fig. 222, 223); ZIN (2004: fig. 17 / drawing); SUGITA (2007: fig. 4). © Monika Zin [For a colour print, see the Appendix]

The representations from Amaravati shift the dating of the motif back, since the slabs can be dated to the beginning of the 3rd or even the end of the 2nd century CE.

The reliefs in Nagarjunakonda Museum [figs. 1, 3] are labelled as the 'Subjugation of Āṭavika'[2], however, this identification can be refuted because the Yakṣa Āṭavika was converted by the Buddha himself, not by a monk; moreover, Hastaka, a boy who played a crucial role in this conversion is not represented in any of our reliefs.[3]

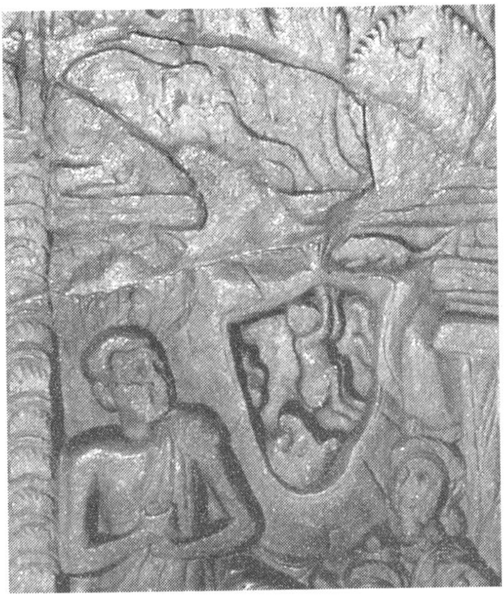

Fig. 4a

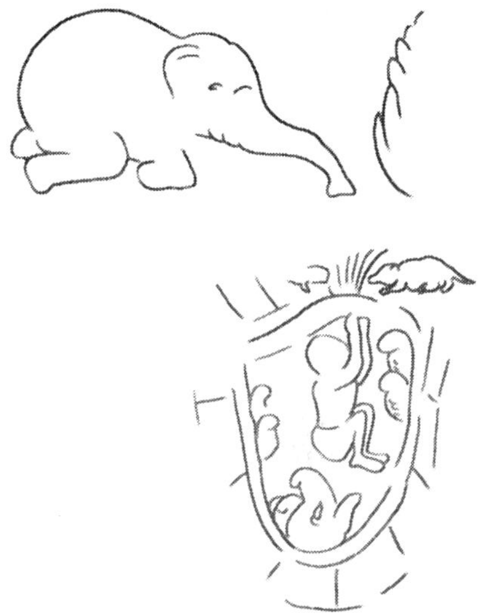

Fig. 4b

This identification of the scene as a depiction of the Āṭavika narrative has become established in spite of the fact that VOGEL had already recognised the crucial element of the relief in 1937, when he identified the diminutive scene of the preaching monk as the parable of 'The Man in the Well'. VOGEL (1937: 113–15) explained the rest of the relief with reference to an unknown version of a narrative about King Udayana, which still remains unknown (cf. *infra*, p. 78). Even so it is certain that this is the parable of 'The Man in the Well', and it is to the great credit of Jean Philippe VOGEL that he recognised it.

VOGEL renders the story of the parable as follows (1937: 112–13):

[2] The identification was first made by LONGHURST (1938: 45–46), repeated by RAO (1956) and (1984), and in the popular guide by SARKAR–MISRA (1966).

[3] For the literary and pictorial tradition of the narrative cf. ZIN (2006: Ch. 1).

'Once on a time a man, while traversing a desert, saw himself pursued by a furious elephant. He was seized with fright and knew not where to find a refuge when he perceived a dry well near which grew the long roots of a tree. He seized those roots and let himself glide down into the well. But two rats, one black and the other white, gnawed together the roots of that tree. At the four sides of the tree there were four venomous snakes which endeavoured to bite him, and beneath there was a dragon gorged with poison. In the depth of his hearth he equally feared the dragon's poison, the serpents and the breaking of the roots. There dwelled on that tree a swarm of bees which made five drops of honey trickle down into his mouth.'

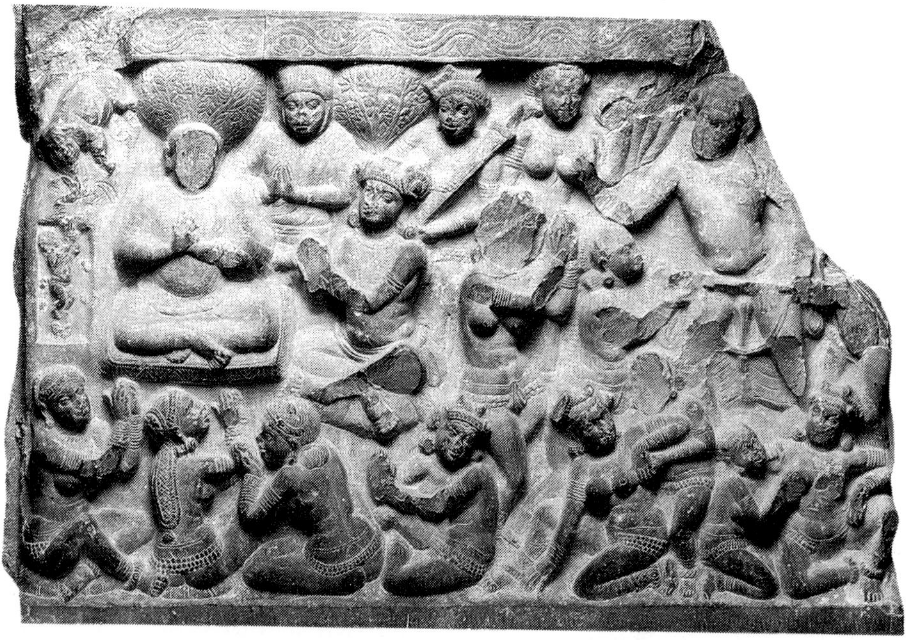

Fig. 5. Nagarjunakonda, Site 6 ?, Musée Guimet, No. 17067, *stūpa* slab, ill.: VOGEL (1937, pl. 33b); HACKIN (1931, pl. 5–7); DENECK (1970, pl. 82–85); ROSEN STONE (1994, fig. 113); ZIN (2004, fig. 16, drawing); SUGITA (2007, fig. 5, detail). Here after HACKIN.

The parable of 'The Man in the Well' was the object of Indological research long before VOGEL, as part of the 19th century vogue for comparative studies of literary motifs, and the story was therefore known in Europe. Friedrich Rückert, the pioneer of Oriental Studies and also a popular German poet, published the translation of the

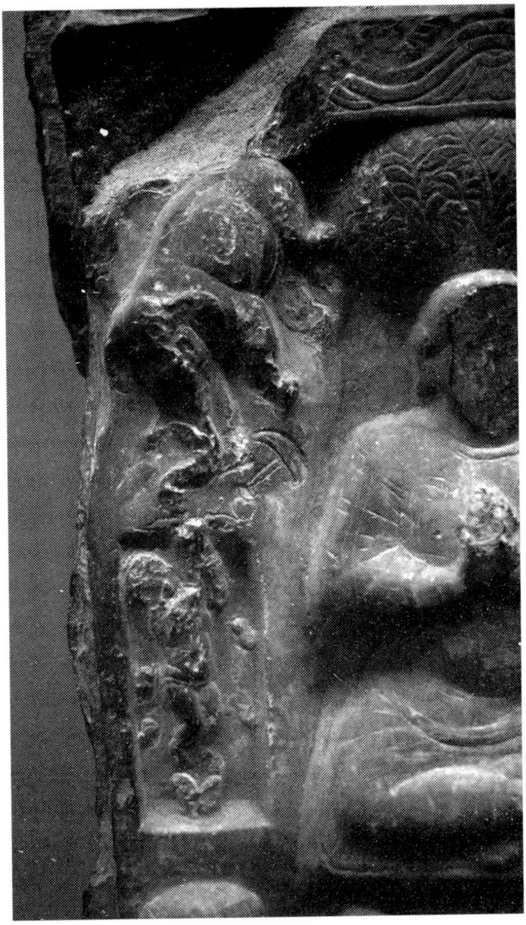

Fig. 6

parable in 1823[4] based on the poem of the 13th century Persian Sufi mystic, Rūmī (cf. *infra*, p. 54). Rückert's poem made the parable commonly known in Germany and shortly afterwards other versions began to circulate, including versions from India. In 1859 Theodor BENFEY, followed in 1860 by Felix LIEBRECHT and in 1888 by Ernst KUHN, was able to deliver the first summing up about the spreading of the parable.[5] KUHN (1888: 70) demonstrated beyond any doubt that the parable originally came from India since its elements were known from earlier Indian sources: the chase by an elephant and the fall into a pit were already referred to as similes in the *Br̥had-āraṇya-kôpaniṣad*.[6]

Today, our knowledge about the parable is more extensive: we know that it is rendered in the *Mahā-bhārata*[7], in four Jaina sources, namely in the *Vasudeva-hiṇḍi* of Saṅghadāsa[8], in the

[4] Cf. ALALI-HUSEINAT (1993: 154, n. 1); Friedrich Rückert, published it first in: *Frauentaschenbuch für das Jahr 1823*, Nürnberg: 352–54.

[5] The comparative research of the 19th century connected the parable with far-flung stories from European storytelling, in which the similarities of the story are not recognisable at first glance (German mythology of Iggdrasil, 'May-tree'), by seeing in it an archetypal understanding of human life; cf. VASIL'KOV (1995), references to the earlier research.

[6] For newer research about the subject cf. e.g. HARA (1985); von SIMSON (2010).

[7] MBh_1 11.5–6, pp. 19–24; MBh_2 37–38.

[8] VH_1 8.4–23, p. 8; VH_2 560–561; German translation in: METTE (1991: 55–56) and METTE (2010: 68–69).

Samarāicca-kahā of Haribhadra[9], in the *Pariśiṣṭa-parvan* of Hemacandra[10] and in the *Dharma-parīkṣā* of Amitagati[11]. The Buddhist sources did not survive in Indian languages but we have six Chinese translations, namely T 208 (Nj. 1366: 'The Saṁyuktāvadāna-sūtra, selected from various sūtras, of Kumārajiva', 405 CE)[12], T 217 (Nj. 735: 'Sūtra spoken by Buddha on [eight] comparisons')[13], T 1690 (Nj. 1347: 'Sūtra on the cause [Nidāna] of the preaching of the law [delivered] by Piṇḍola Bharadvāja to King Udayana' of Guṇabhadra, 435–443 CE)[14], T 2121 (Nj. 1473: '[A collection of extracts] on different subjects from Sūtras and Vinaya works',

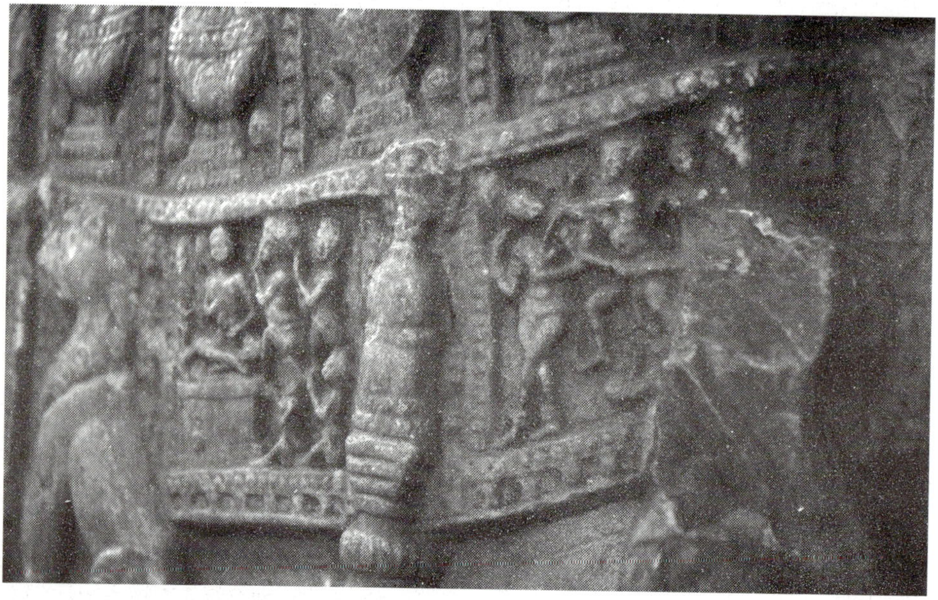

Fig. 7. Archaeological Site Museum of ASI, No. 22. © Monika Zin

[9] SK_1 110–14; SK_2 225–28.

[10] PP_1 68–69; PP_2 64–68.

[11] DhPar 2.5–21, analys. (1903: 39–40).

[12] T 208, *Tchong king siuan tsa p'i yu*, ed. Vol. 4, ch. 1, p. 533; French translation: JULIEN (1859–60: 190–93, no. 53), German translation: JULIEN (1903: 97–99); French translation: CHAVANNES (1910–1934 Vol. 2: 83–84, No. 205).

[13] T 217, *P'i yu king*, ed. Vol. 4: 801; French translation: JULIEN (1859–60: 131–34, no. 32); German translation: JULIEN (1903: 69–70; French translation: CHAVANNES (1910–1934 IV: 236–37, in commentary on No. 469).

[14] T 1690, *P'in t'eou lou t'ou lo chö wei yeou t'o yen wang chouo fa king*, ed. Vol. 32, p. 787.

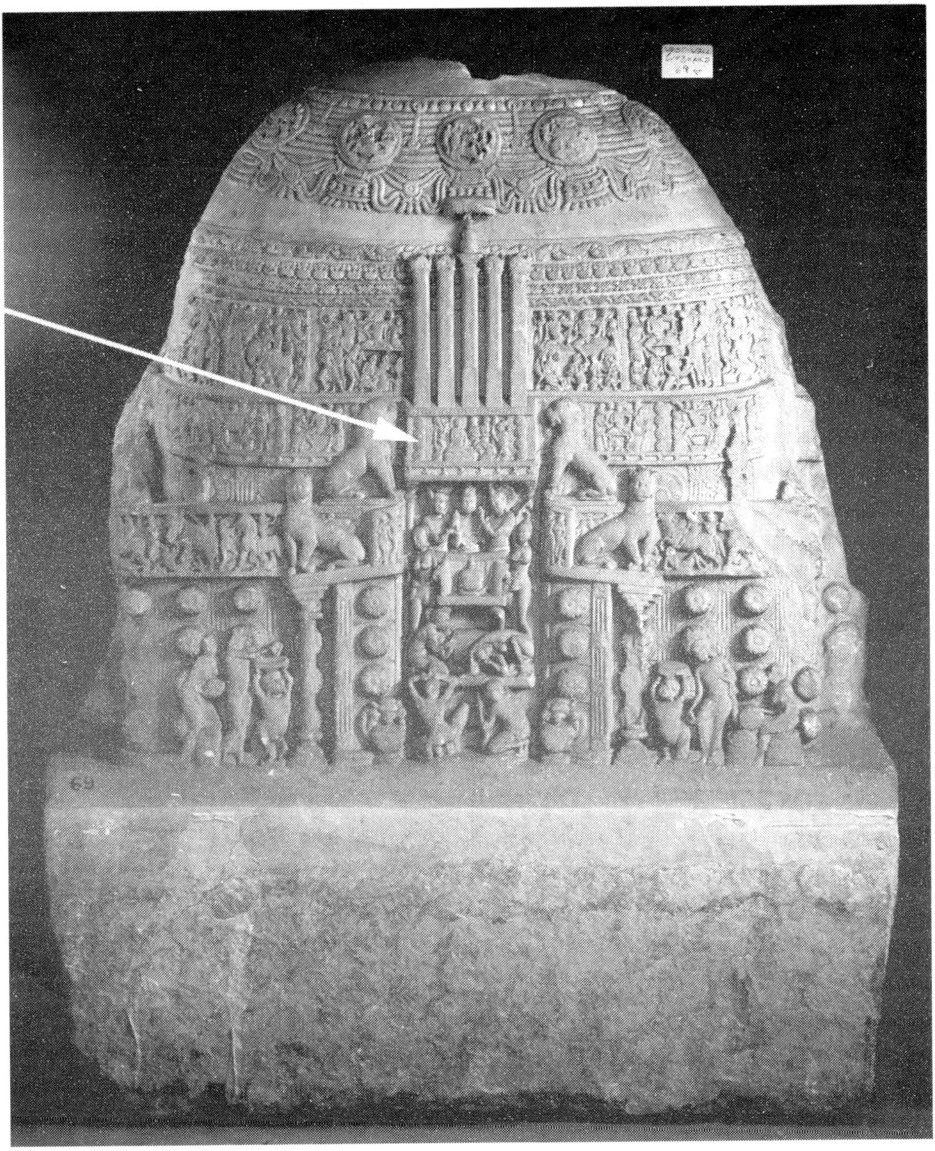

Fig. 8. British Museum, No. 69, ill.: FERGUSSON (1868: pl. 81.1); STERN–BÉNISTI (1952: pl. 43); KNOX (1992: no. 68, p. 130); ROSEN STONE (1994: figs. 67–68); ZIN (2004: fig. 18/drawing). © Trustees of the British Museum

compiled by Saṅ-min, 516 CE)[15], T 2122 (Nj. 1482: 'Pearl-grove of the garden of the law', compiled by Tao shi, 668 CE)[16] and T 2131 (Nj. 1640: 'A collection of the meanings of the [Sanskrit] names translated [into Chinese]' of Fa-yun, 1151 CE)[17]. There is also one Tibetan version, but it is very different from the Indian one.[18]

The sources differ from one another in the presence or absence of particular elements of the parable and through the explanation of the allegory. The Buddhist version quoted above (it is the Chinese text, T 217) continues (after VOGEL (1937: 113)):

> 'The tree and the desert figure the long night of ignorance; that man figures the heretics; the elephant figures the impermanence of things; the well figures the brink of life and death; the roots of the tree figure human existence; the two rats, white and black, figure day and night; the roots of the tree gnawed by those two animals figure the obliviousness of ourselves and the extinction of all thought; the four venomous serpents figure the four great things [, i.e. the four elements (Skt. *mahā-bhūtāni*)]; the bees figure the vicious thoughts: the honey figures old age and illness; the venomous dragon figures death.'

One can see at first glance that the explanations of the allegory are far from logical: if the roots of the tree from which the man is hanging stand for human existence, why should the man himself stand for heretics and not for everyone? Why is honey, whose main characteristic is its sweetness, explained as the ills of life, old age and illness? It looks as if, when the Chinese translation was made, the explanation of the parable was not true to its original meaning.

Another Chinese text (T 208) appears more logical. Let us quote it here in the German translation from JULIEN (cf. *supra*, n. 12):

> 'Es war einmal ein Mann, den das Unglück betroffen hatte, zum Tode verurteilt zu sein: Man hatte ihn in Ketten gelegt und ihn in's Gefängnis geworfen. Aufgeregt durch die Furcht vor dem Tode, zerbrach er seine Fesseln und entfloh. Wenn ein zum Tode Verurtheilter entflog, so sandte man nach des Gesetzen des Königreichs ihm einen wüthenden Elephanten zur Verfolgung des Verurtheilten los. Als dieser den Elephanten näher kommen sah, lief er schnell, um in einem ausgetrockneten Brunnen

---

[15] T 2121, *King liu yi siang*, ed. Vol. 53, ch. 45, pp. 223c–224a; cf. CHAVANNES (1910–1934 Vol. 4: 235–238, No. 469).

[16] T 2122, *Fa yuan tchou lin*, ed. Vol. 53, ch. 44, ed. p. 626a–b.

[17] T 2131, *Fan yi ming yi tsi*, ed. Vol. 54, p. 1141c.

[18] *Dpe-chos rin-chen spungs-pa* by Po-to-ba Rin-chen-gsal (1027/31–1105), Ch. 3, example 6, cf. ROESLER (2011: Teil I, Kap. 3.2 und Teil II, Beispiel 3.5+).

> zu gelangen. Aber auf dem Grunde desselben war ein giftiger Drache, dessen gähnender Schlund der Oeffnung des Brunnens zugekehrt war. Ausserdem sassen in den vier Ecken des Brunnens vier giftige Schlangen. Daneben war die Wurzel einer Pflanze. Der Verurtheilte, dessen Herz vor Angst verwirrt war, ergriff schnell diese Wurzel, aber an dieser nagten zwei weisse Ratten. In diesem verhängnisvollen Augenblick bemerkte er oberhalb des Brunnens einen grossen Baum, in dessen Mitte sich eine Scheibe Honig befand. Täglich fiel ein Tropfen Honig in den Mund des Unglücklichen. Nachdem er diesen köstlichen Tropfen bekommen hatte, dachte er nur noch an den Honig, vergass die schrecklichen Gefahren, die ihn von allen Seiten bedrohten und verlangte gar nicht mehr, aus dem Brunnen herauszukommen.
>
> Der heilige Mann (Buddha) schöpfte aus dieser Begebenheit verschiedene Gleichnisse. Das Gefängnis bedeutet die drei Welten, der Gefangene die gesamte Menschheit, der wüthende Elephant den Tod, der Brunnen den Wohnsitz der Sterblichen; der giftige Drache auf dem Grunde des Brunnens bedeutet die Hölle; die vier giftigen Schlangen bedeuten die vier grossen Dinge (Erde, Wasser, Feuer und Wind); die Wurzel der Pflanze die Wurzel des menschlichen Lebens; die weissen Ratten Sonne und Mond, die nach und nach das Leben des Menschen aufzehren, die es untergraben und jeden Tag vermindern, ohne einen einzigen Augenblick inne zu halten …'

In this version the man stands for mankind, the well for the abode of mortals, the root on which the man is hanging for life, the elephant for death and the dragon for hell. However, it is not clear why the venomous snakes should symbolise Earth, Water, Fire and Wind, moreover, both rats are here white, whereas as we will see, it is important that one rat (mouse) is white and the other black.

There is no surviving Buddhist version which would correspond with our depictions; T 2121 (cf. *supra*, n. 15) speaks about three snakes and does not mentioned the dragon, T 1690 talks in addition about the bush-fire that razes the tree to the ground (the same thing is also found in T 217) and the explanation of the allegory in those texts is incomprehensible in many points.

It seems that of all the sources known today it is the Jaina texts which have preserved the version which corresponds best with our reliefs. At the same time it is a very logical retelling. Let us quote here the parable from the oldest preserved version, the *Vasudeva-hiṇḍi*, in the new translation by METTE (2010: 68–69):

> 'Ein Mann, der sich auf einer weiten Reise befand, hatte sich einer Karawane angeschlossen und war mit ihr in eine wilde Gegend gezogen. Räuber zerschlugen jedoch die Karawane, der Mann wurde abge-

> sprengt und irrte umher, ohne die Richtungen zu kennen. Von einem wilden Elefanten überfallen, dessen Haupt von Brunftsaft feucht war wie ein Regentag, flüchtete er und erblickte einen alten, von Gras und Binsen ringsum bedeckten Brunnen. An dessen Rand stand ein gewaltiger Nyagrodha-Baum, von dem ein Ast in den Brunnen hineinragte. Von Furcht überwältigt, hängte sich der Mann an den Ast, hielt sich mitten im Brunnen schwebend und schaute um sich: Oh weh! Da war eine riesige Boa mit aufgerissenem Maul, bereit, ihn zu fressen! Die erblickte der Mann unten. Seitlich aber, in jeder der vier Himmelsrichtungen, waren grausige Schlangen, die ihn beißen wollten. An dem Ast über ihm nagten zwei Mäuse, eine schwarze und eine weiße. Der Elefant berührte mit dem Rüssel seine Haarspitzen. Auf dem Baum aber befand sich ein sehr bevölkertes Bienennest. Als nun der Baum von dem Elefanten geschüttelt wurde, sprühte der Wind einige Honigtropfen in den Mund des Mannes, und die kostete er. Die Bienen aber flogen von allen Seiten her um ihn herum und wollten stechen. Sag, was war wohl das Glück des Mannes in dieser Lage? Die Honigtropfen, die er begehrte, waren sein Glück, denke ich, alles übrige war Unglück.—So war es. Nun aber die Bedeutung des Gleichnisses: Wie im Gleichnis jener Mann, so ist die Seele, die im Strom der Wiedergeburten, im *Saṁsāra*, kreist; wie jene wilde Gegend, so—vielfältig durch Geburt, Alter, Krankheit und Tod—ist die Wildnis des *Saṁsāra*; wie der wilde Elefant, so der Tod; wie der Brunnen, so eine Wiedergeburt als Gott oder Mensch; wie die Riesenschlange, so eine Wiedergeburt in der Hölle oder Tierwelt; wie die anderen Schlangen, so Zorn, Stolz, Trug, Gier, die vier bösen Leidenschaften, die zu schlechten Wiedergeburten führen; wie der Ast, so die Lebenszeit; wie die beiden Mäuse, so die hellen und dunklen Monatshälften, die mit dem Zubiß von Nächten und Tagen das Leben kürzen; wie der Baum, so die Gründe für die Bindung von *Karman*, nämlich Unwissenheit (*ajñānam*), Haften an den Sinnesfreuden (*avirati*) und Irrglaube (*micchattaṁ / mithyātvam*); wie der Honig, so die Sinnesobjekte: der Ton, der Gegenstand der Berührung, der Geschmack, die Form und der Duft; wie die Bienen, so die Krankheiten, die den Körper anfallen und in ihm ausbrechen. Woher bezieht einer, der sich so in Angst und Not befindet, sein Glück?—Einzig aus der Süße des Geschmacks der Honigtropfen entsteht seine Vorstellung von Glück!'

The Jaina version must have preserved the oldest source which is no longer available in any of the Buddhist versions but which is shown in the Nagarjunakonda reliefs. All the depicted elements are there (and also the honey and the bees, which are not depicted probably because of the difficulties of representation). The explanations of the elements of the simile are also not only logical but also affect the reader deeply: in this version the elephant symbolises death, the giant snake hell, honey the delusion of the senses, the branch of the tree life, and the white and black mice stand for the days and nights which make life shorter.

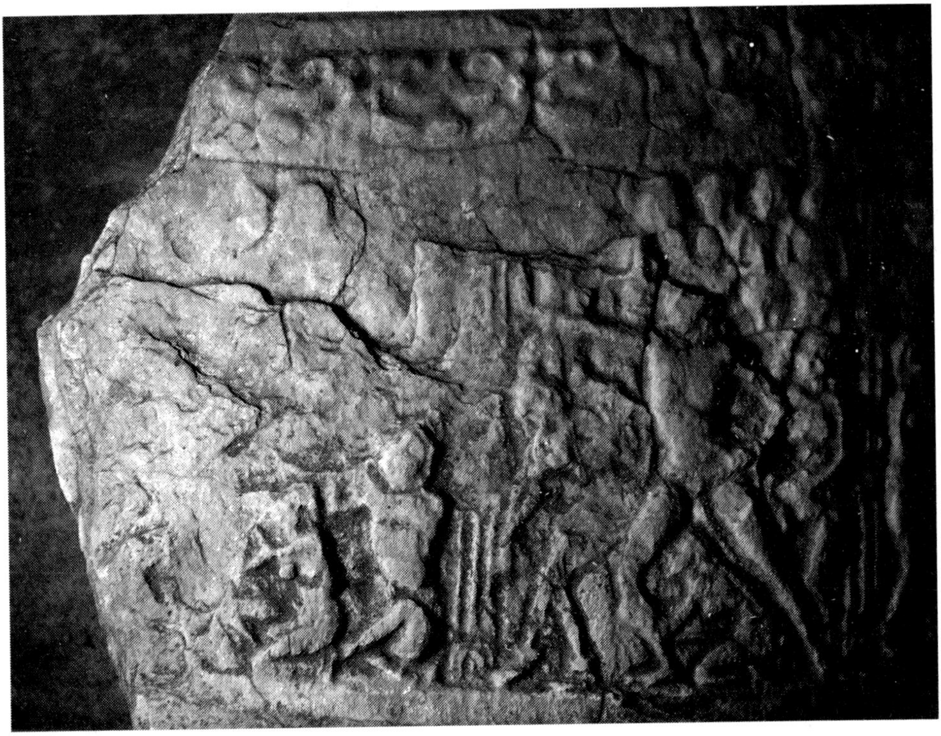

Fig. 9. Gummadidurru, Amaravati. Archaeological Site Museum of ASI, depot, No. 97. © Monika Zin

Compared with this, the version in the *Mahā-bhārata* (cf. *supra*, n. 7) is quite different and does not fit the Nagarjunakonda depictions at all. In this version, the man is hanging with his head down and there is no mention of the four venomous snakes. The elephant is not a normal one but is six-faced and twelve-legged, which according to the text represents the six seasons and twelve months—evidently an extension of the earlier 'days and nights'. The version in the *Mahā-bhārata* can by no means be treated as the oldest and original one, on the contrary, its details prove that it was taken from Buddhist sources; it even looks as if the Buddhist pictorial representations of the *Saṁsāra-cakra* ('the Wheel of Rebirth') could play a role in its imagery (cf. ZIN–SCHLINGLOFF (2007: 99, 144–45)). As von SIMSON (2010) observes, the description includes a terrible woman embracing wildness (*saṁsāra*) which brings to mind the (female) monster *anityatā* embracing the Wheel of Rebirths.

Excluding the Tibetan version (cf. *supra*, n. 18), which includes only the white and black mice, there are 11 versions from India (five in Indian languages and six in Chinese translations). Although this would seem to be a lot, in fact, the Jaina versions are actually quotations renderings of one and the same content and the Chinese sources are collections of parables or compilations. From the Brahmanical sources we have only the *Mahā-bhārata* (cf. *supra*, n.7), where Vidura tells the parable to Dhṛtarāṣṭra as a simile of the impermanence of the world using a metaphor related to Buddhism. The parable has not found its way into popular literature: it was not incorporated into any story-collections such as the *Pañca-tantra* or the *Bṛhat-kathā* (the parable does not appear in the *Bṛhat-kathā-śloka-saṁgraha*, the *Kathā-sarit-sāgara* or the *Bṛhat-kathā-mañjari*, and in the *Vasudeva-hiṇḍi* it is a part of the introduction, not the main story), thus it seems that in India the parable was not very popular. As for pictorial representations, these are only found in Amaravati and Nagarjunakonda. The representations from Amaravati, which can be dated to the 2nd c. CE, are the earliest of all known, pictorial or literary, sources.

Even if it was not very popular in India, the parable managed to leave India and become part of the imagery of mankind. It did not travel by itself, rather it was carried on the back of two very popular narratives: one was a collection of animal fables of Brahmanical origin and the other one was a Buddhist romance.

The collection of fables was the *Pañca-tantra*, one of the most widespread and oft-translated narratives in the world.[19] As its translations relate, the Persian king Khostrou Anoširvān (531–579) sent his physician Borzōē to India to bring him the famous book. Borzōē brought the book and translated it into middle Persian (Pahlavi), and so the *Karīrak ud Damanak* came into existence (the name comes from Karaṭaka and Damanaka, the Sanskrit names of two jackals from the frame story of the *Pañca-tantra*). Now, Borzōē included the parable of 'The Man in the Well' in his text, placing it into his own biography, not into the collection of fables itself. Since the Indian *Pañca-tantra* does not incorporate the parable, Borzōē's source is unknown (DE BLOIS (1991a, esp. 34–37)); but according to the examination of the paper in hand, the version must have been close to the version as it is preserved in the *Vasudeva-hiṇḍi* (cf. *supra*, p. 43 f.).

Borzōē's translation of the *Pañca-tantra* has not survived the times, but there are two further translations which are based directly on his. One of them, the *Kalīlaw-Damnağ*, a translation into Syrian written about 570 by the Persian Christian named

[19] Cf. EM Vol. 7: cols. 888–95 (GROTZFELD–MARZLOPH) and DE BLOIS (1991: 35).

Būdh (it is preserved in only one manuscript from the 16th century, cf. WRIGHT (1884)), did not play an important role in spreading of the narrative. The second one, the *Kalīla wa-Dimna* (known mostly as *The Fables of Bidpai*) was the translation into Arabic by Abdallāh ibn al-Muqaffa[20]; this translation was not only of importance in itself but it also because it became the basis for translations into further languages, including nearly all the European ones.[21]

Al-Muqaffa was Manichaean and he was executed in 757, so the Arabic translation must have been written around the middle of the 8th century.

The version by al-Muqaffa is as follows (after (WOLFF 1839: XXXVI–XXXVIII)):

> 'Man kann dasselbe (…) mit nichts besser vergleichen, als mit einem Menschen, welcher, vor einem wüthenden Elephanten fliehend, in einen Brunnen hinabsteigt; er hält sich fest an zwei Aesten, die über den Brunnen herhängen, er steht auf einem hervorstehenden Stein des Gemäuers. Vier Schlangen strecken ihre Köpfe heraus aus ihren Löchern in der Mauer; auf dem Boden des Brunnens gewahrt er einen Drachen, welcher, mit offenem Rachen, nur den Augenblick seines Falls erwartet, um ihn zu verschlingen. Seine Blicke richten sich auf die zwei Aeste, an denen er sich festhält, aber er sieht da zwei Ratten entstehen, eine schwarze und eine weiße, die ohne Aufhören an den Aesten nagen. Indeß bietet sich seinem Blick ein anderer Gegenstand dar, ein Bienenstock. Er macht sich an den Honig desselben und vergißt, ob solchem Genuß, der Schlangen, auf welchen seine Füße ruhen, der Ratten, welche die Aeste abnagen, an denen er sich festhält, und der drohenden Gefahr, eine Beute des Drachens zu werden, der auf den Augenblick seines Falles paßt. Seine Unbesonnenheit und seine Selbsttäuschung hören erst mit seinem Leben auf.
>
> Der Brunnen aber, das ist die Welt, voll von Gefahren und Elend. Die vier Schlangen, das sind die vier Säfte, deren Mischung unsern Körper bildet, die aber, wenn ihr Gleichgewicht gestört wird, eben so viel tödtendes Gift werden. Die zwei Ratten, die schwarze und die weiße, das sind der Tag und die Nacht, deren stete Folge die Dauer unseres Lebens verzehrt. Der Drache, das ist das unausweichbare Ziel, das uns alle erwartet. Der Honig endlich, das sind die sinnlichen Vergnügun-

[20] EI Vol. 3: 883–85 (GABRIELLI).

[21] SILVESTRE DE SACY (1816: 1–556); EI Vol. 4: 503–06 (C. BROCKELMANN); the genealogical tables of the spreading of the translations are very impressive, as found in the frontispieces of TAWNEY's translation of the *Kathā-sarit-sāgara* (see TAWNEY–PENZER (1924 V: 232 ff.) or GRUBE (1991a).

gen, deren falsche Süßigkeit uns verführt und uns von dem Wege ableitet, den wir gehen sollten.'

The tree from the Indian version, with branches which hang down inside the well (one immediately thinks of the Indian Banyan tree with its aerial-roots), has disappeared from the story; here the man is holding two branches which are hanging above the well. The text states at first that he is standing on a protruding stone, but then that he is standing on the snakes. The dangerous elephant is mentioned at the beginning as the reason for the man's flight but it is not explained at the end as one of the elements of the simile. For the symbol of death there is the dragon at the bottom of the well, while the snakes stand for troubles and illnesses (literary the four humours which, when their balance is destroyed, change into deadly poison), the well stands for the world and the branches for life: these are being shortened by the white and black rats which are again the days and nights which make life shorter (the branches are not explained). The honey is the false sweetness of the senses.

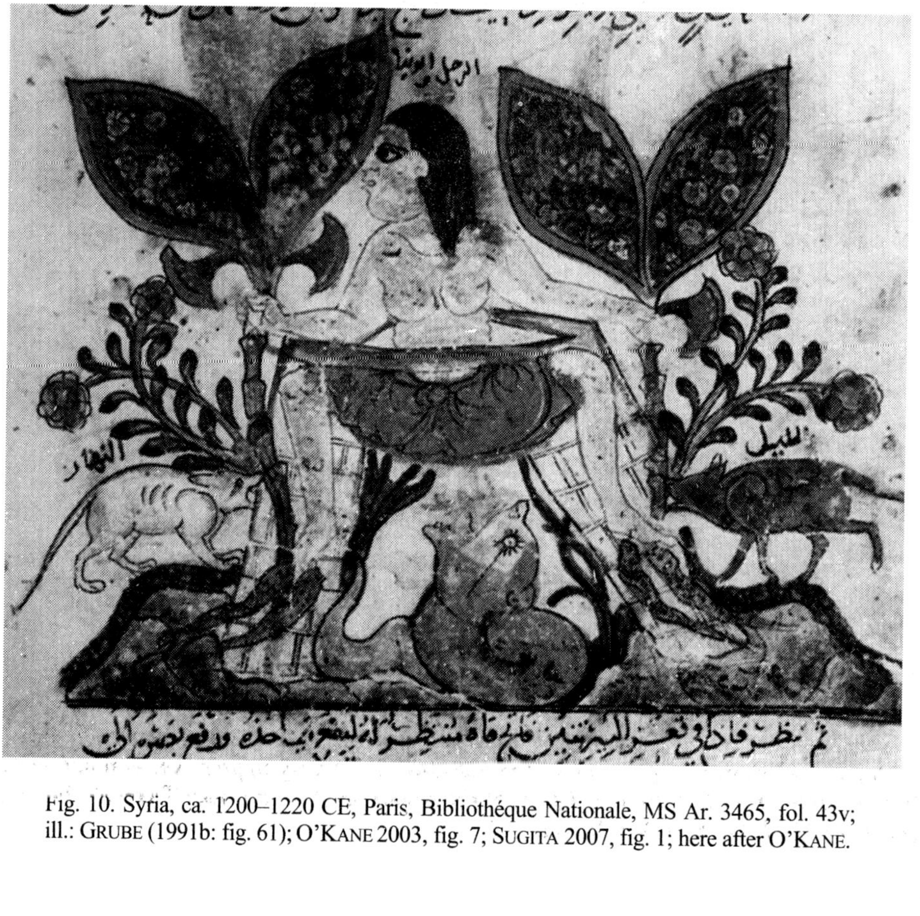

Fig. 10. Syria, ca. 1200–1220 CE, Paris, Bibliothéque Nationale, MS Ar. 3465, fol. 43v; ill.: GRUBE (1991b: fig. 61); O'KANE 2003, fig. 7; SUGITA 2007, fig. 1; here after O'KANE.

The *Kalīla wa-Dimna* was one of the first books of the Islamic world to have been illustrated[22] and there is an unbroken tradition of illustrating the manuscripts.[23]

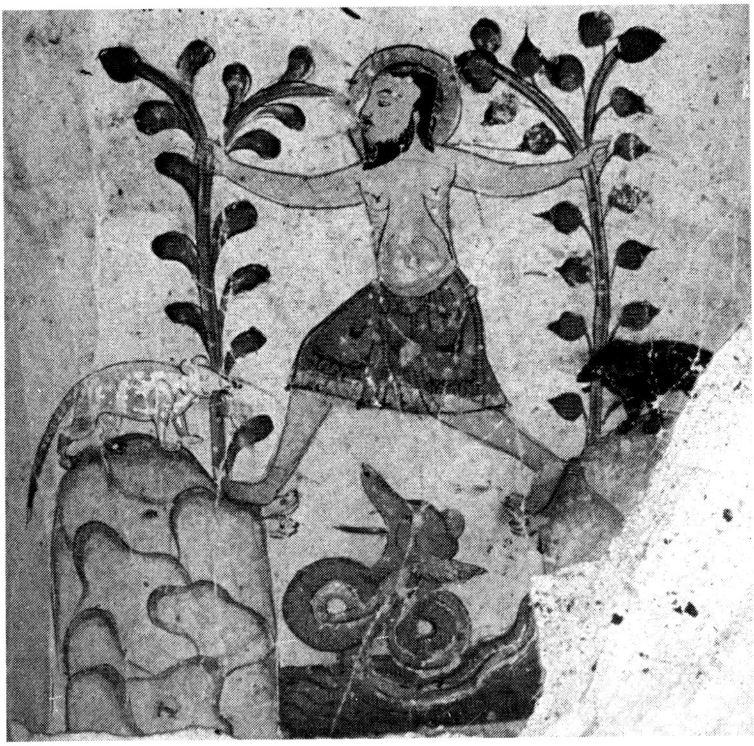

Fig. 11. Egypt or Syria, ca. 1340–1350, Munich, Bayerische Staatsbibliothek, Arab 616, fol. 40v, ill.: O'KANE (2003: fig. 9). © Bayerische Staatsbibliothek. [For a colour print, see the Appendix]

The oldest preserved manuscripts come from the Arabic 'classical tradition' (GRUBE (1990–91: 36)). The books from the 13th [fig. 10] and 14th centuries [fig. 11] include the illustrations of our parable. What the pictures show corresponds quite well with the text by al-Muqaffa when we bear in mind that 500 years of the

[22] GRUBE (1991a: 4) proceeds from the assumption that the *Kalīla wa-Dimna* of al-Muqaffa was already illustrated. RABY (1991: 22 ff. with notes) is more tentative and he debates if the earliest Pahlavi, Arabic and Persian translations were illustrated.

[23] Cf. RABY (1991: 17 ff.), a study about earlier depictions of the stories from the *Pañca-tantra* from India and Panjikent.

pictorial tradition (and a millennium since the creation of the depiction in Amaravati) are lost to us.[24] The man is represented inside the well, he is holding himself up by two plants (or trees) growing by the edge of it, the two mice gnawing on the plants are white and black, but they are as big as dogs. The dripping honey is alluded to through the man's open mouth, and in one case (O'KANE 2003: fig. 10) the artist painted an object in the branches of the tree which probably represents a nest of bees or a bee-hive. The biggest problem for the painters was the representation of the inside of the well: they made it transparent so as to be able to show the dragon at the bottom and the snakes, the man is standing on. The well is therefore depicted either as a circle around the man or it is not represented at all [fig. 11] in which case the man looks as if he is standing above a hollow. The elephant is not depicted in any of the illustrations.

The *Kalīla wa-Dimna* of al-Muqaffa was translated into Neo-Persian. There were several translations, the one from the 10th century by Rōdakī is lost (GRUBE (1990–91: 320)), another one *Dastānhā-ye Bidpai* by Moḥammad ibn Abdallāh al-Bokhari was not very popular, while the translation from the 12th century, the *Kalīle va Demne* by Abū'l-Ma'ālī Našrallāh Monši, known as Našrollāh, is popular in Iran even today.[25]

The version by Našrollāh kept some of the details from the *Kalīla wa-Dimna* but changed them partly: the cause of the man's flight is not an elephant but a camel. The man escapes not into the well but into a hollow. That can perhaps be explained not as a change made by al-Muqaffa but as the adaptation into the written text of the imagery from pictorial representations [fig. 11].

The Persian translations were also illustrated from the beginning. The *Šāhnāmeh*, from the middle of 10th century, relates how the Samanid ruler Našr ibn Aḥmad (913–42 CE) ordered Chinese artists to make pictures to accompany the translation by Rōdakī. 'The Chinese' should be understood here as the Manichaean Uyghurs (DE BLOIS (1991b: 14) and (1991a: 28, n. 2)).

The version by Našrollāh provides the basis for various illustrations of the parable in the Persian paintings; the *Kalīle va Demne* have been extremely popular through the centuries and were illustrated,[26] many manuscripts include depictions of our parable.[27]

---

[24] The illustrations are often referred to as 'the Perils of Life'; cf. also O'KANE (2003: 58–60); SUGITA (2007: figs. 1–3).

[25] Cf. EI Vol. 7: 1016–17 (E. BERTHOLD).

[26] For the 'Check-List' of the manuscripts cf. GRUBE (1990–91: 360–68) and the App. II in GRUBE (1991a: 168–70)

[27] GRUBE (1991a: App. I: Text Synopsis, B.13); O'KANE (2003: 61–68, 102–03); SUGITA (2007: figs. 8–12).

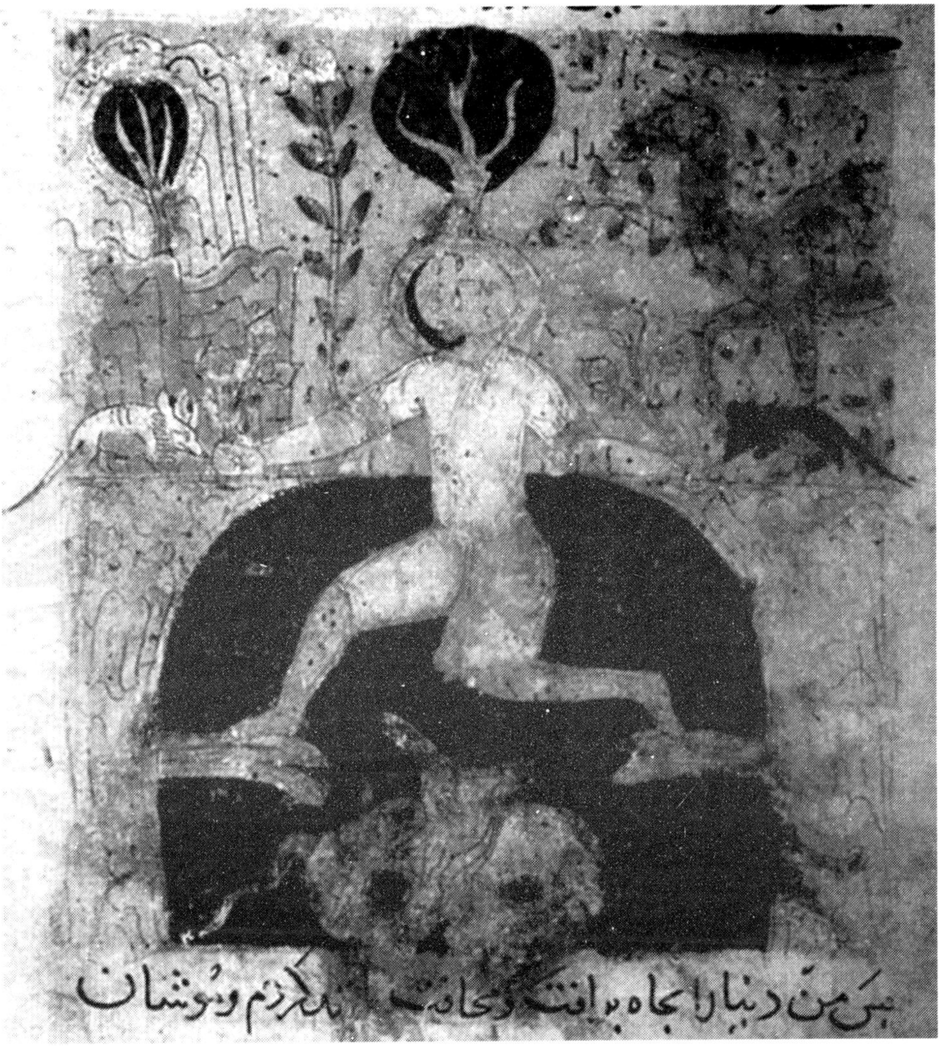

Fig. 12. Baghdad (?) ca. 1260–85, Istanbul Topkapı Saray Library, H 363, fol. 35b, ill.: ROGERS (1986: fig. 28); SMINÉ (1993: fig. 19); CAGMAN–TANINDI (1986: fig. 28); O'KANE (2003: fig. 12); SUGITA (2007: fig. 8); here after O'KANE.

In the beginning the pictorial pattern of the Persian illustrations does not differ much from their forerunners except that the camel appears to one side [fig. 12]. In later paintings the camel gets bigger so that the entire composition is changed sometimes into an asymmetrical one [fig. 13]. The painters face the same difficulties about depicting the inside of the hollow as their predecessors. They show the man inside the opening in the ground but an additional hole can be seen below this—as if the earth were transparent here. Through this hole, the inside of the ditch is visible with the dragon on the bottom and the snakes on which the man is standing. Further details remain unchanged, the man holds on to two plants which are being gnawed by the white and the black mouse and his mouth is open, allowing the dripping honey to fall into it from the round bees' nest on the tree.

The parable of 'The Man in the Pit' was popular in Persia as part of the collection of stories, but it was also known independently of it. Such independent literary work

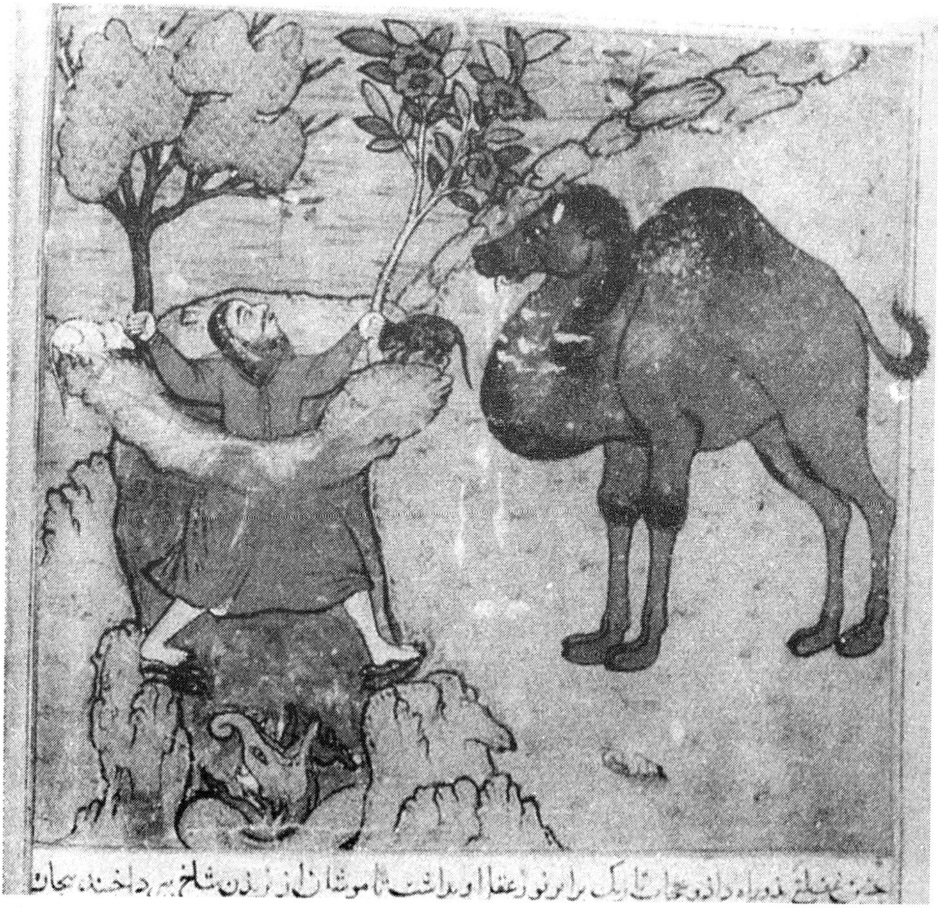

Fig. 13. Bagdad or Tabriz, AH 744 / 1343–44 CE, Cairo, National Library, MS Adab Farsi 61, fol. 16v, ill.: GRUBE (1991b: fig. 62); O'KANE 2003, fig. 16; SUGITA 2007, fig. 9; here after O'KANE.

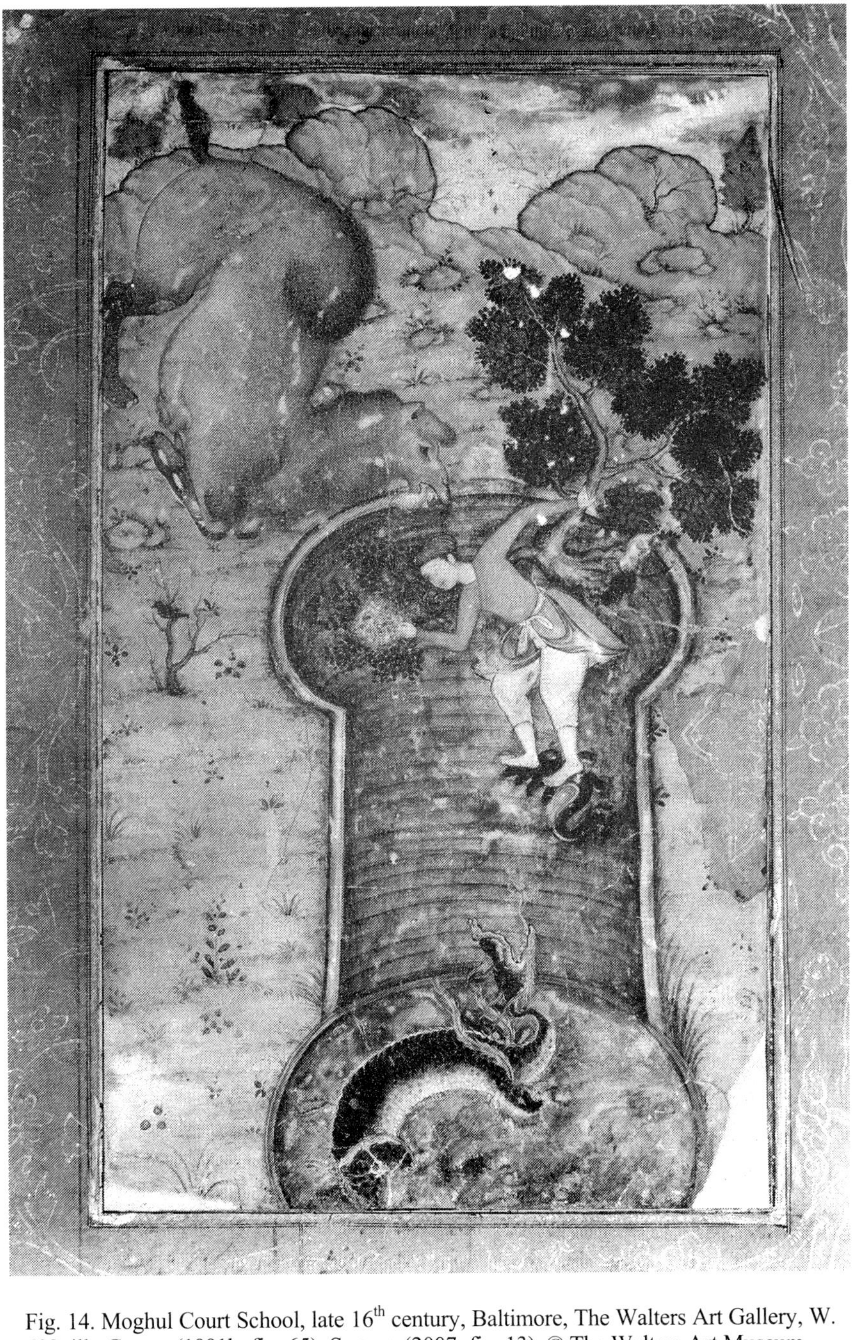

Fig. 14. Moghul Court School, late 16th century, Baltimore, The Walters Art Gallery, W. 692, ill.: GRUBE (1991b: fig. 65); SUGITA (2007: fig. 13). © The Walters Art Museum

must have been the prototype of the poem by Friedrich Rückert, *Es ging ein Mann im Syrerland, Führt' ein Kamel am Halfterband...* (cf. *supra*, n. 4); it is said that Rückert translated the poem of a Sufi mystic Ğelāllodin Rūmī (1207–1273)[28]. This version[29] is peculiar: the man is able to escape from the well and it is not honey which he desires but *manna* (Rückert changes it into blackberries). Interestingly the well and the *manna*, depicted as small white balls on a bush the man is trying to grasp, is represented in one very beautiful painting from Moghul India [fig. 14].

The old collection of animal fables finds its way back to India (DE BLOIS (1991b: 14), KHANDALAVALA–DESAI (1991)) in the book *Eyār-e dāneš* written 1587 for Akbar by Abū'l-Fazl Ibn Mobārak[30]. Perhaps the *manna*, as an alternative to honey, appears in translations known in India, it is possible, however, that the painter took the imagery from Rūmī's version. The miniature has been preserved on its own, not in a collection of the fables.[31]

Apart from this one exception from India the pictorial depictions of the parable in the Persian-speaking world remained without change till modern times (von SIMSON (2010)) and show the man inside the hollow reaching for the honey-comb.[32]

As stated above, the Arabic *Kalīla wa-Dimna* by Ibn al-Muqaffa was of importance not only for the Islamic world but also for Europe. In the 11th century came the Greek translation by Symeon Seth, *Stephanitēs kai Ichnēlatēs*[33] (SJÖBERG (1962)), in which the elephant which chases the man is replaced by a unicorn (cf. *infra*, p. 64), and in the 12th century there was a Hebrew translation probably by Rabbi Joel, who, however, is mentioned only by Doni in 16th century, so that his authorship is not entirely certain.[34] In this version the man flees from a lion. The 13th century saw the translation into Latin by the converted Jew, John of Capua (Johannes da Capua), the *Directorium humanae vitae alias Parabole antiquorum sapientum* (34,1–35, also with the lion)[35],

---

[28] Rūmī's poem is given by Joseph von HAMMER-PURGSTALL (1818: 183) as beginning with a verse prelude: *Messalëi chob u nik bad amed.*

[29] Rückert's direct source was the German translation by von HAMMER-PURGSTALL (cf. n. 28) ‚… hast du gehört, daß man im Syrerland Einst führte ein Kameel am Halfterband…'

[30] Cf. EI Vol. I: 117–18 (NURUL HASAN); according to GRUBE (1991a: 6, n. 19) the book of Abū'l-Fazl was translated in 1818 by A. I. Silvestre de Sacy as *The Fables of Pilpay*; I, however, have not seen a copy.

[31] GRUBE (1991a: 169) states: '56. *The Perils of life* (B.13). Painting from a lost manuscript of the *Anvar-i Suhayli* or the *Iyar-i Danish*…'

[32] Cf. illustration to the Našrollāh version from 1865, in MARZOLPH (2001: fig. 49); information about the picture is taken from von SIMSON (2010) where the picture is also reproduced.

[33] Cf. EM Vol. 12, col. 1240–43 (M. ANTON).

[34] For other Hebrew versions cf. SCHWARZBAUM (1979); DE BLOIS (1991: 13).

[35] EM Vol. VII: cols. 580–83 (U. KÜHNE).

which was to become the source for translations into national languages in the whole of Europe. The popularity of the book was enormous (cf. *supra*, n. 21) and the extent of the various pathways it took as it spread can hardly be revealed. It is worth mentioning one very popular version, *The Moral Philosophy of Doni*, a 16th century English translation by NORTH (2003), in which the jackals from the original were changed into a mule and an ass while the man escapes into the well from four lions [fig. 15]. The small animals do not look like mice; the text calls them 'two beasts, of colour white and black'. The text also talks about a terrible dragon inside the well and about 'a little hole behind him [the man] wherein there was a pot full of honey, laid there by chance by some shepherd passing by the way' (NORTH (2003: 241–43)) though these are not depicted. According to this version the man reaches for the honey, falls into the well and dies.

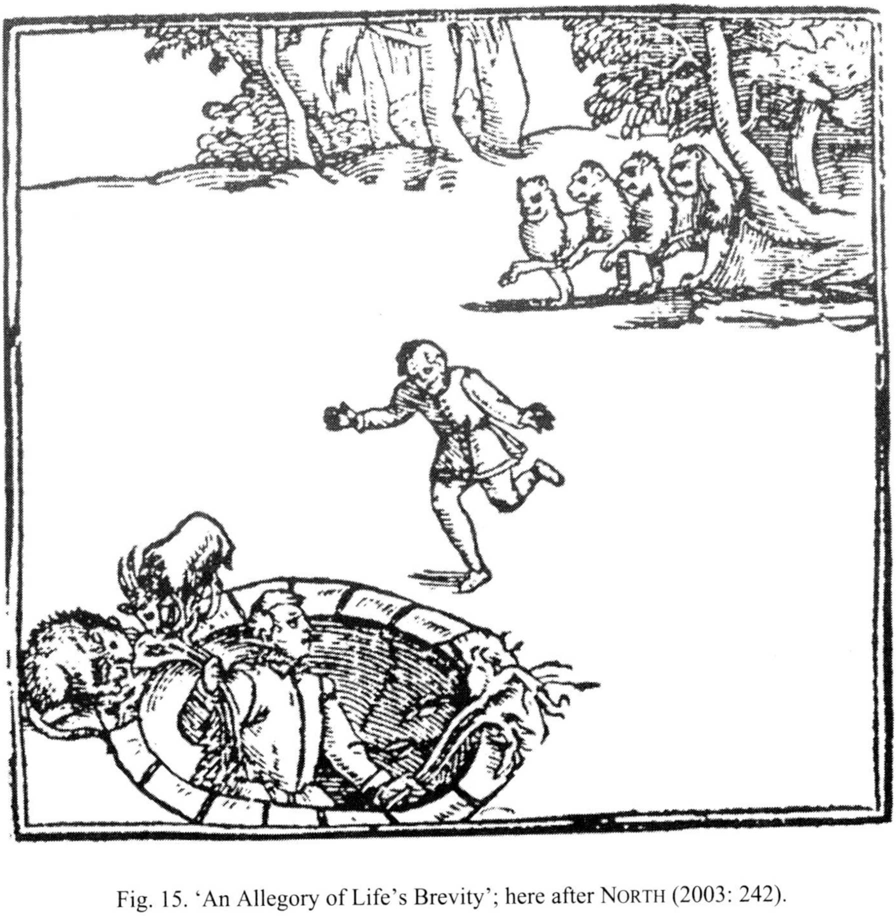

Fig. 15. 'An Allegory of Life's Brevity'; here after NORTH (2003: 242).

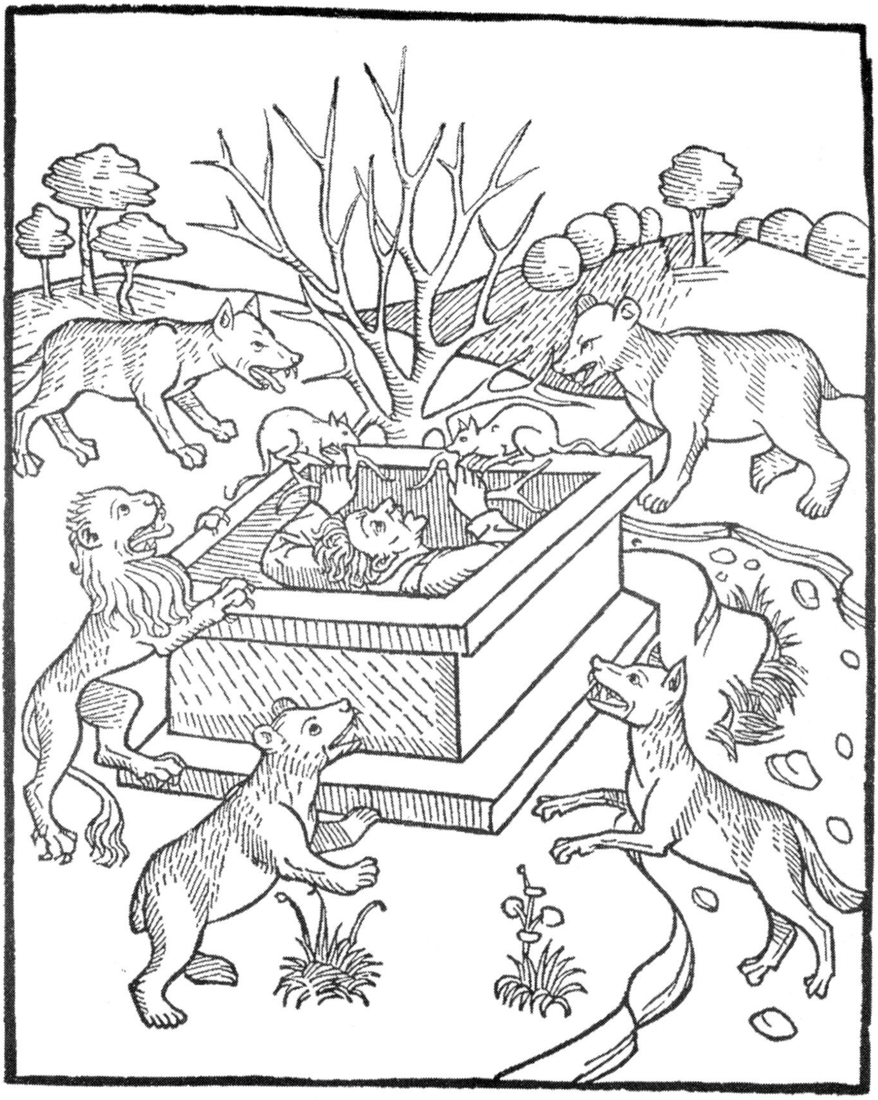

Fig. 16. *Die Inkunabeln des Directorium vitae humanae*, Ulm 1483; the same woodcut is repeated in several old German prints from the fifteenth and sixteenth centuries of the *Buch der Beispiele der alten Weisen* by Anton Pforr; here after SCHRAMM (1923 Vol. VII: No. 47).

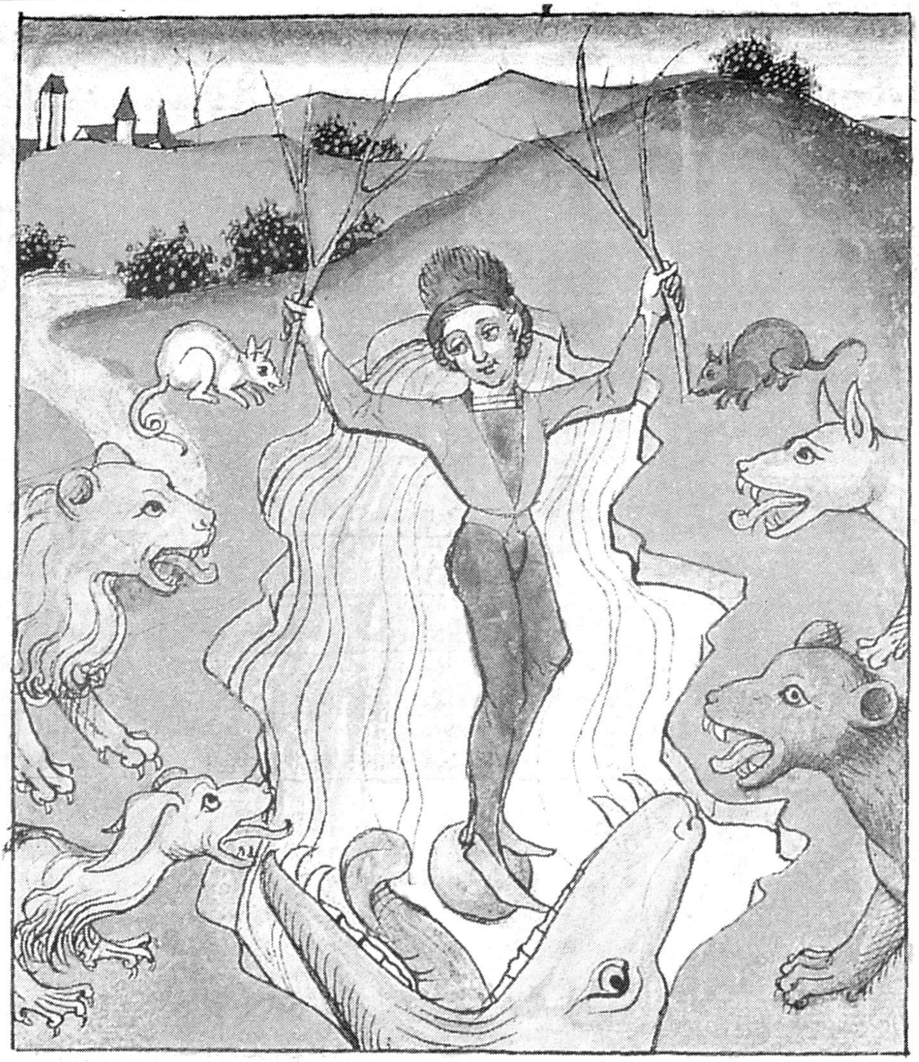

Fig. 17. Heidelberg, University Library, Cod. Pal. germ. 466, Buch der Beispiele, p. 25. © Universitätsbibliothek Heidelberg. [For a colour print, see the Appendix]

Illustrations based on the German rendering by Anton von Pforr[36] show the man inside the well around which different terrible animals are standing [fig. 16] (the

---

[36] Cf. ed. GEISSLER (1964: 14–15).

texts talk about *quattour animalia*); he holds on to two boughs of a tree which are being gnawed by two mice. The well can be replaced by the hollow [fig. 17] at the bottom of which the open mouth of the terrible dragon is depicted.

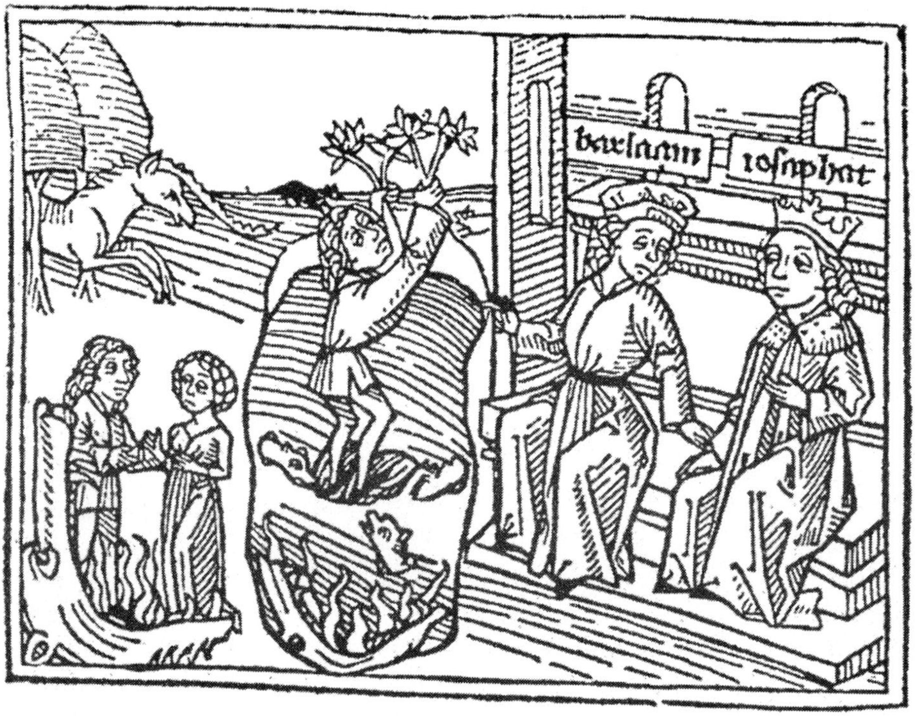

Fig. 18. Woodcut from the *Barlaam und Josaphat* by Günther Zainer, Augsburg ca. 1476; ill.: SCHRAMM (1923 Vol. 2: No. 559); EINHORN (1978: fig. 13). According to EINHORN (1972: 415, No. B, 14 A, fig. 1): 'Holzschnitt zum 15. Kap.: Barlaam und Josaphat, auf einer Bank mit hohen Lehnen sitzend; die deutende Rechte Barlaams weist auf die in der l. Bildhälfte dargestellte Parabel hin: Mann in einer Grube mit feuerspeiendem Drachenmaul und drei Schlangen versinkend, sich mit den Füßen auf einem Vorsprung abstützend und mit den Händen Zweige an der Abbruchkante ergreifend; Einhorn l. o. aus einem Wald hervorbrechend; l. u. Mann und Frau in den Flammen eines Drachenmauls'; here after SCHRAMM.

The collection of animal fables from the old Indian *Pañca-tantra* was not the only bearer of the parable of 'The Man in the Well' to the West. Another, perhaps even more important one, was the *Balavaar and Josaphat*, the best-selling romance of mediaeval Europe.[37]

[37] Cf. EM Vol. 1: cols. 1243–52 (I. LACKNER).

The Indian original is unknown; it probably never existed and the narrative was just a rendering of a commonly known tale about the life of the Buddha. The story finds its way to the Manichaean region in Central Asia. The whole of the Manichaean version has not survived, but there are still manuscript fragments from the 8th century found in Khocho (Xočo, pinyin: Gāochāng), written in the Uyghur language[38]. The version was translated into Arabic and from *bodhisatva*[*], via Manichaean *bwdysdf*, the Arabic *būḏāsf* was created. The Arabic translation has survived, it is the *Kitāb Bilawhar wa-Būḏāsf*, 'The book of Bilawhar and Būḏāsf'. In process of time the initial *b* was misread as *y* and so *Būḏāsf* was changed into Yosaph.[39]

The Arabic version can not have been very popular because it belonged to the Ismaili (Shī'a) tradition (GIMARET (1971))[40], however, its further translations were important because it was translated into Old-Georgian, and from there found a passage into the Christian world. There are two Old-Georgian translations in existence: the *Sibrdzne Balahvarisi*[41], which was known much earlier to western scholars, but which is only the condensed version of the longer account, and the *Balavariani*, preserved in only one manuscript, which is of much greater importance[42]. It was this version which was translated into Greek[43] (early research regarded this translation as the work of St. John of Damascus (8th century) and the source of the Georgian version (cf. DÖLGER (1953); PERI (1957) or John of St. Saba (cf. ZOTENBERG (1886)). From the Greek version, the *Barlaam cai Iosaph*, it was only a short step to Latin and from then the narrative starts its march through the literature of mediaeval Europe. It comes into the *Legenda aurea* of Jacobus de Voragine (chap. 180, *De sanctis Barlaam et Josaphat*); its numerous renderings and translations into national

---

[38] LE COQ (1909: 1202–05); LE COQ (1912: 5–7); LE COQ (1923: 25 ff.).

[*] In the paper, the spelling '*bodhisatva*' is consistently used instead of '*bodhisattva*' at the explicit wish of the Author—Eds.

[39] LIEBRECHT (1860); KUHN (1894); CHAUVIN (1887: 83–112); EIr Vol. 3.1: 801 (J.P. ASMUSSEN) (with further references); about other Arabic versions cf. GIMARET (1971: 25–61).

[40] Cf. also VOLK (2006: 191, and n. 196), with references, and also a note that in Spain the Hebrew translation of the *Barlaam* was made from the Arabic original, which proves that the text was nonetheless known in the territories of Sunni Islam.

[41] Translated by LANG (1957).

[42] Translated by LANG (1966); cf. the preface by I.V. Abuladze: 'The origin and history of "Balavariani" and its place among the treasures of world literature' (pp. 19–41).

[43] For the new edition of the Greek translation cf. VOLK (2009); also after the discovery of the *Balavariani*, the Greek version was regarded as the opus of John from Damascus, cf. e.g. introduction to the English translation from Neo-Greek by KANTIOTES (1997).

languages can hardly be followed today.[44] The story was also repeated in innumerable versions in the theatre, from the *Sacra representationi* and stage production of the Jesuits to the pieces of high literary value, such as the *Barlaán y Josafat* by Lope de Vega[45]. The attractiveness of the story for literature and the theatre is mirrored by the importance of its religious aspect: the Catholic and the Orthodox churches (the Old-Russian *Poviest' o Varlaame i Ioasafe* (see LEBEDEVA (1985)) was no less popular than its western counterpart) both incorporated the saints, Barlaam and Josaphat, into their calendars; there was—and still is today—a San Giosafato church in Palermo, and there are even relics of the Saint kept in St. Andreas church in Antwerp. Nevertheless Josaphat is nobody else than the Bodhisatva.

It is perhaps worth while at this point briefly recapping what the story in the *Barlaam and Josaphat* is about. The narrative is about King Abenner (Avenir) from India, who is a cruel persecutor of Christian monks. When a son, Josaphat (Ioasaph), is born to him and the fortune-tellers prophecy that he will become a Christian monk, the king builds a palace for the prince, where he lives shielded from real life. When he grows up the prince wishes to see the world outside and makes excursions during which he meets an old man, a sick man and a disabled man. It is not difficult to recognise that the story repeats the life-story of the Buddha.[46] In Buddhism, however, after the sight of the three suffering men comes the vision of a Buddhist monk, and this becomes the direct cause of the Bodhisatva leaving the palace and searching for enlightenment. The Christian version, however (and perhaps its Manichaean predecessor) changes the original so that the monk comes not in a vision but in person and it is he who brings the prince to the enlightenment. Enlightenment can come not from within a person but can only be given by a teacher: after seeing the three suffering men prince Josaphat enters a state of mental crisis; by divine revelation Barlaam (Balahvar), a banished Christian minister of King Abenner, gets to know about it, he comes to the palace and by means of parables prepares Josaphat for baptism. The king tries to discredit Barlaam and organises a philosophical dispute

[44] Out of the extensive secondary literature about the spreading of the romance only a few books can be named here: JACOBS (1896), SONET (1949–52); PERI (1959); VOLK (2009).

[45] The drama by Calderon dela Barca, *A vida a sueño* (1635), where the prince Sigismund is being kept in the palace shielded from the real world, must have its roots in the *Balavaar* narrative.

[46] In the old Arabic *Kitāb Bilawhar wa-Būḏāsf* there are still more reminders of the Buddha legend, such as that the future mother of the prince sees a white elephant in a dream (cf. GIMARET (1971. 66)) or in the name of the city 'Šawilâbaṭṭ', which still sounds like 'Kapilavastu'.

between him and a magician named Theodas (apparently a surrogate of the name of the Buddha's adversary Devadatta) who changes himself into the form of Barlaam to make him ludicrous in the eyes of the prince, but the Christian minister wins the debate despite all difficulties. In the end not only does Josaphat become a Christian monk, but Abenner is converted and stops his cruel persecution of Christianity.

Among the parables which Barlaam tells to Josaphat appears our story of 'The Man in the well'. The earliest preserved version, in the Arabic *Kitāb Bilawhar wa-Būḏāsf*, differs very little from the version in the *Kalīla wa-Dimna* by Ibn al-Muqaffa (cf. *supra*, p. 47), from the Indian original (GIMARET (1971: 88))[47]:

> 'Bilawhar—On raconte qu'un homme était parti dans un désert. Et comme il allait, voilà qu'un éléphant en rut se précipita sur lui. Alors, l'home prit la fruite, tournant le dos à l'éléphant qui le poursuivait. La nuit le surprit, et le contraignit à se jeter dans un puits, où il demeura suspendu, accroché à deux rameaux qui poussaient sur son bord, et les pieds posés pour les appuyer sur quelque chose qui était sur la paroi du puits.
>
> Le matin venu, il regarda les deux rameaux, et il vit à leur pied deux rats, l'un blanc, l'autre noir, qui rongeaient les deux rameaux sans cesse. Puis il regarda ce qui était sous ses pieds: c'étaient quatre vipères qui sortaient la tête de leurs trous. Puis il regarda au fond du puits: il y vit un dragon, la gueule béante, qui attendait de le dévorer. Puis il leva la tête vers la base des rameaux: ils portaient au haut en peu de miel. Alors, il approcha les rameaux de sa bouche, et goûta quelque peu de la douceur de ce miel. Et la douceur qu'il trouva à ce qu'il en avait goûté le retint dans ses jouissances immédiates, et le détourna de songer et de penser aux deux rameaux auxquels il était accroché, alors qu'il voyait bien la hâte des deux rats à les dévorer, aux quatre serpents sur lesquels il s'appuyait, sans savoir quand l'un d'entre eux s'élancerait sur lui, au dragon à la gueule béante, sans savoir ce qu'il deviendrait quand il tomberait au fond de son gosier.
>
> En bien, le puits, c'est ce monde, plain de malheurs et d'épreuves. Les deux rameaux, c'est cette vie blâmable. Les deux rats, blanc et noir, c'est le jour et la nuit. Leur hâte à dévorer les rameaux, c'est la hâte

[47] The translations of the parable into German (BLAU (1853: 401–02)) and English (REHATSEK (1890: 135–36)) do not follow the *Kitāb Bilawhar wa-Būḏāsf* directly but rather the Arabic text known as *Book of the King's Son and the Ascetic*, cf. ZOTENBERG (1886: 79–81).

> des jours et des nuits à dévorer la durée des existences. Les quatre vipères, ce sont les humeurs du corps, qui sont des poisons mortels. Le dragon à la gueule béante, prêt à dévorer, c'est la mort qui guette. L'éléphant, c'est la durée de l'existence qui tend vers elle. Et le miel, c'est l'aveuglement des hommes égarés par le peu de plaisir de la vie qu'ils obtiennent dans ce monde.'

The version is a little bit more logical than the one in the *Kalīla wa-Dimna*; there the man just did not see at first that he was standing on snakes, here we receive the information that he could not see them because it was dark and he noticed them in the morning.

Notwithstanding such minute changes, the versions in the *Kalīla wa-Dimna* and in the *Kitāb Bilawhar wa-Būḏāsf* are so similar that it looks as if one of them is taken from the other: they must have been written at exactly the same time, so which of the versions is the original is a point of controversy.[48]

The earliest Christian version, the Old-Georgian *Balavariani* (LANG 1966: 77–78), repeats the situation with all the details:

> 'Balahvar said to him: "This transitory life and all that cherish it resemble a man pursued by a raging elephant, which cornered him inside a fearsome abyss. As he fell down inside it he found two branches growing out over the precipice, so he hung on to them, and then managed to establish some sort of foothold. When he looked around him, he descried two mice, one white and the other black, which never ceased to gnaw at the roots of those trees on which he hung. Then he looked down into the chasm and noticed a dragon, which had parted its jaws and was intent on swallowing him up. And on the ledge on which his feet rested he discerned four heads of asps projecting from the cliff. Then he lifted up his eyes and saw that a little honey was dripping from the branches of the tree, and he began to eat it. And its flavour and sweetness so entranced him that he no longer worried about the perils which beset him and the fact that he might be bitten to death at any moment. As for the branches on which he was suspended, he saw

[48] DE BLOIS (1991a: 34–35) puts together different theories about the dependence of one text on another, he means that it was Burzōē, the translator of the *Pañca-tantra*, who took the Indian parable abroad, from his popular book it was taken into the *Kitāb Bilawhar wa-Būḏāsf*. Some scholars e.g. ALMOND (1987: 403), VOLK (2009: 109) assume that the Arabic *Kitāb Bilawhar wa-Būḏāsf* and the *Kalīla wa-Dimna* are the work of one and the same author, al-Muqaffa. French translations of parables from both texts are put in synoptic columns in VOLK (2006: 173–74).

> the tree's roots being gnawed away by the mice and—most dangerous of all—the dragon lying in wait to swallow him up, but all this failed to trouble him in the slightest.
>
> Now that elephant is the harbinger of death, which pursues the sons of Adam, and the abyss is the world, full of all manner of evil and pernicious snares. The two branches are a man's life span and the two mice—one white and the other black—are the days and nights that fret at it incessantly, and suddenly sever the thread of a man's life. The four asps signify the four elements from which a man's body is constructed, and when a single one of them is destroyed, life comes to an end. The dragon which opened its jaws and longed to swallow him up, is the image of hell, into which the lovers of this world enter after their death. And those few drops of honey are the brief delights of this world, by which it deceives those who are astray by the sweetness of corruption."'

A big modification comes with the Greek translation, even though many details remain unchanged. The version changes the elephant into the unicorn (μονόκερως), here in translation from Neo-Greek by KANTIOTES (1997: 156–59):

> '... these I consider to be like a man flying before the face of a rampant unicorn, who, unable to endure the sound of the beast's cry, and its terrible bellowing, to avoid being devoured, ran away at full speed. But while he ran hastily, he fell into a great pit; and as he fell, he stretched forth his hands and laid hold on a tree to which he held tightly. There he established some sort of foothold and thought himself from that moment in piece and safety. But he looked and discovered two mice, the one white, the other black that never ceased to gnaw the root of the tree whereon he hung and were all but on the point of severing it. Then he looked down to the bottom of the pit and espied below a dragon, breathing fire fearful for eye to see, exceedingly fierce and grim with terrible wide jaws, all agape to swallow him. Again looking closely at the ledge whereon his feet rested, he discerned four heads of asps projecting from the wall whereon he was perched. Then he lifted up his eyes and saw that from the branches of the tree there dropped a little honey. And at that he ceased to think of the troubles whereby he was surrounded; how outside the unicorn was madly raging to devour him: how below the fierce dragon was yawning to swallow him: how the tree which he had clutched was all but severed; and how his feet rested on slippery, treacherous ground. Yes, he forgot

> without care all those sights of awe and terror and his whole mind hung on the sweetness of the tiny drop of honey.
> This is the likeness of those who cleave to the deceitfulness of this present life,—the interpretation whereof I will declare to you immediately. The unicorn is the type of death ever in eager pursuit to overtake the race of Adam. The pit is the world, full of all manner of ills and deadly snares. The tree, which was being continually frayed by the two mice, to which the man clung, is the course of every man's life that is spent and consumes itself hour by hour, day and night, and gradually draws near its severance. The fourfold asps signify the structure of man's body upon four treacherous and unstable elements which, being disordered and disturbed, bring that body to destruction. Further more, the fiery cruel dragon presages the jaws of hell that is hungry to receive those who choose present pleasures rather than future blessings. The dropping of honey denotes the sweetness of the delights of the world, whereby it deceives its own friends nor suffers them to take timely thought for their salvation.'

The unicorn settles in the story and all successive Latin versions and their translations into European languages feature it. It will also be represented in art.[49]

The sudden emergence of the unicorn in the story is not explained, despite the exemplary study of this theme by EINHORN (1972). Further investigations by the same author (EINHORN (1978)), despite exhaustive research which produced the best ever collection of textual and pictorial references of the motif, did not provide answers as to why the unicorn which is normally a good beast in Christian iconography (symbolising Jesus, the resurrection and the overcoming of disease)[50] in our parable started to symbolise death, μονόκερως θάνατος, *unicornis id est mors*[51]. The unicorn as a symbol of death started to be so appropriate that it even passed into the Greek translation of the animal fables, the *Kalīla wa-Dimna*, by Symeon Seth (cf. *supra*, p. 54).

[49] Cf. e.g. W. STAMMLER, in: RDK Vol. 1: cols. 1452–57; DER NERSESSIAN (1936); RÉAU (1958: 177 ff.); STAMMLER (1962); LChI (1969: 244–45); EINHORN (1972).

[50] For meanings of the unicorn and the wandering of the motif since their Indian sources cf. RDK Vol. 4: cols. 1504–44 (L. WEHRHAHN-STAUCH); EINHORN (1978: esp. 32 ff.), HATHAWAY (1980); for the newest research cf. TAGLIATESTA (2007).

[51] Cf. EINHORN (1972: 387, 390); the unicorn starts to symbolise death in other contexts as well, cf. EINHORN (1972: 407–09); meaningful is a saying quoted there after EISELEIN (1840: 141): 'Daß dich der Einhurn in diesem Jar nit stoß' und in vilen Jaren nit!'

A comparison of the pictorial depictions accompanying this article leads to the conclusion that the unicorn could have been introduced into the parable through the simple misunderstanding of an illustration. For a European artist, who had never seen

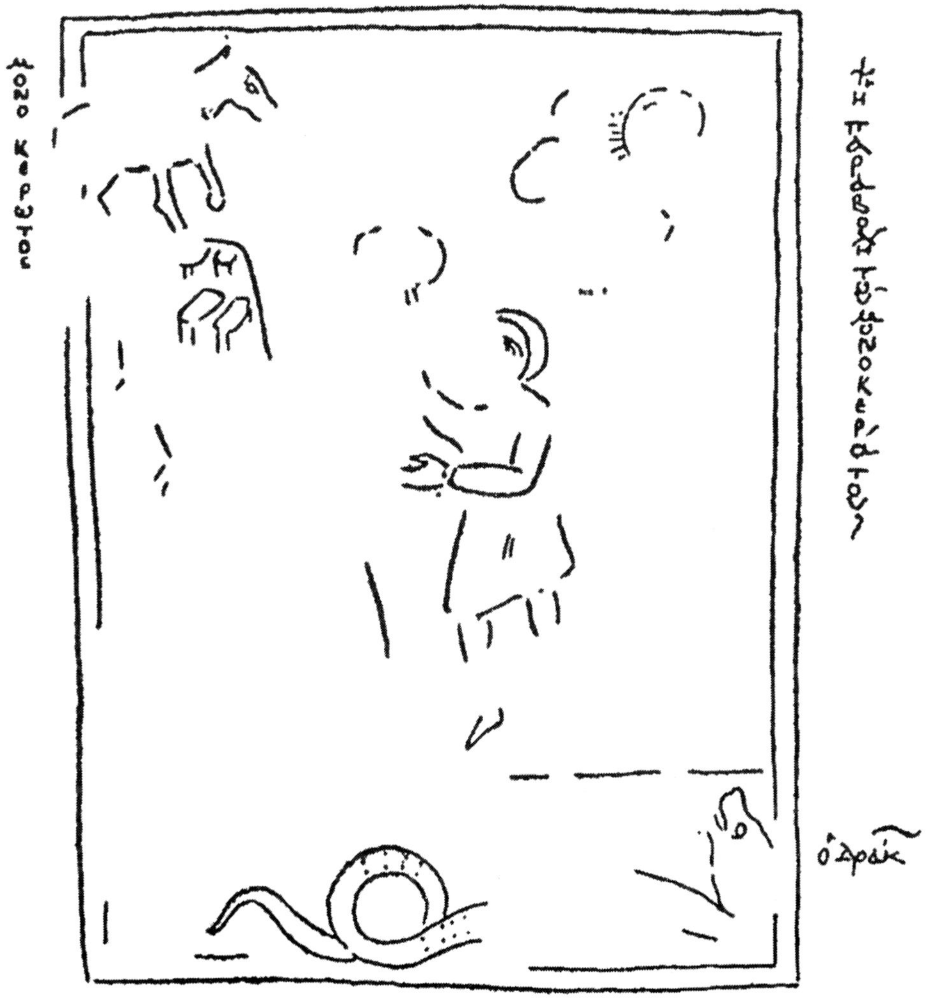

Fig. 19. According to EINHORN (1972: 410, No. A. II): 'Jannina, Epirus, Bibliothek der Schola Zosimala, fol. 54. 11./12. Jh. Ein Teil der Hs. in Cambridge, Univ.-Bibl. Add. MS. 4491. Stark beschädigt: Mann r. neben einer felswand; Einhorn, Laubwerk und Mäuse l.o.; Schlangen unkenntlich; Beischriften'; here after DER NERSESSIAN (1936: 63, fig. 24). VOLK (2003: 130, n. 4) refers to an article by E. D. Sampaniku (1990) in Greek as a source for further depictions, in the post-Byzantine wall-paintings in Greece.

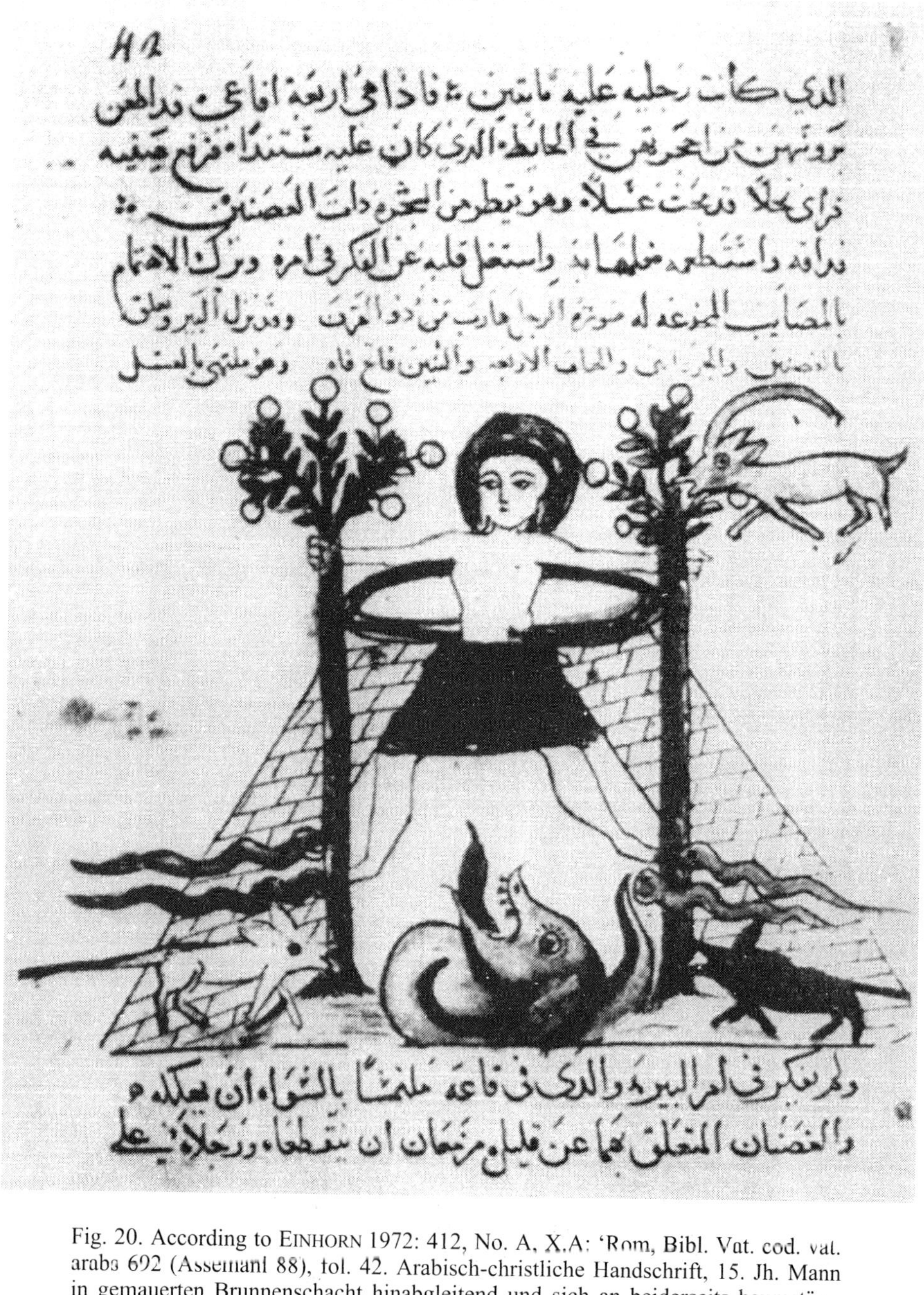

Fig. 20. According to Einhorn 1972: 412, No. A, X.A: 'Rom, Bibl. Vat. cod. vat. arabs 692 (Assemani 88), fol. 42. Arabisch-christliche Handschrift, 15. Jh. Mann in gemauerten Brunnenschacht hinabgleitend und sich an beiderseits baumstämmen festhaltend; Einhorn r.o.', fig. 100; Leroy (1955); here after Einhorn.

an elephant, such confusion seems highly probable.[52] Let us take as example an illustration of the parable from a German woodcut of the fifteenth century[53] [fig. 18]. Barlaam is shown here explaining the parable to Josaphat; he sits on the side and points at a representation of it with a finger: the man is hanging inside a hollow, holding himself up on two plants, by which the white and the black mouse are standing. Inside the hollow there is the open jaw of the monster and three snakes which are emerging from holes. But the snakes have ears and they are not under the feet of the man (as the text narrates) but on the sides of the hollow, like in Indian depictions. It looks as if the artist (or most probably his predecessor, generations earlier) did not understand that he was supposed to be representing snakes. The woodcut is thus following the pictorial rather than the literary tradition. The unicorn is coming from the woods, to the side of the hollow: this one-horned animal might also be traced back to an animal with a trunk which a European artist did not understand. The *quattour animalia* in the European renderings of the *Kalīla wa-Dimna* (cf. *supra*, p. 58 and figs. 16, 17) may have come from a misunderstanding of the snakes and of one pictorial version which gave them ears.

In fig. 18, on the side, there is the entrance to hell represented as the open jaw of a monster, very similar to the monster at the bottom of the hollow. Inside the jaw is an amorous couple. This additional depiction which should certainly demonstrate the abjection of sensualism which is being criticised in the parable; the artist has found no way to depict the dripping honey.

The Christian illustrations of the parable follow several patterns[54] that clearly demonstrate different pictorial traditions and do not allow a conclusion to be drawn about the chronological development of the depictions.

The early pictures, from 11th–12th century show [fig. 19] the unicorn standing above the pit with the man, inside the pit is a huge snake. By the legs of the unicorn two tiny animals are visible—these must be the mice whose presence signifies that

---

[52] VOLK (2006: 175–76) gives convincing evidence that the confusion of the elephant with the unicorn in the texts was improbable because descriptions of both animals were quite frequent and their characteristics well known; it seems all the more probable that the confusion took place not because of a misunderstanding of texual descriptions but because of a misapprehension of visual depictions.

[53] The textual tradition of the depiction is known, it is a Middle High German translation from the Latin so called 'Vulgat' translation from the 12th century, which is based on the Greek version—cf. EINHORN (1972: 384) with references to PERI (1959); in EINHORN (1972: 384–85) quotation of the text.

[54] EINHORN (1972: 386 ff.), references in the catalogue on pp. 41–17; many illustrations depicted, figs. 1–3, Pls. 97–122, and further bibliographical references.

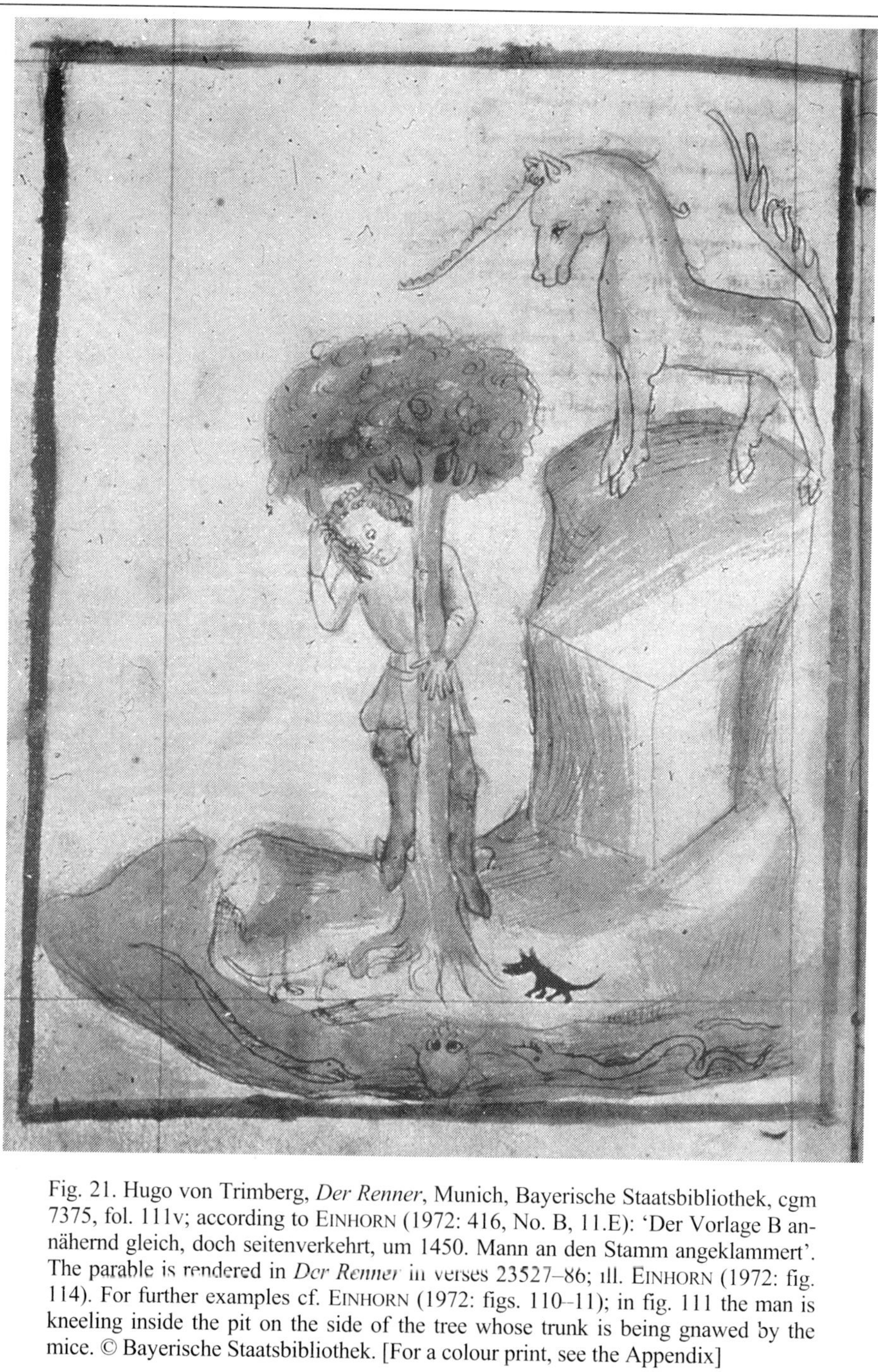

Fig. 21. Hugo von Trimberg, *Der Renner*, Munich, Bayerische Staatsbibliothek, cgm 7375, fol. 111v; according to EINHORN (1972: 416, No. B, 11.E): 'Der Vorlage B annähernd gleich, doch seitenverkehrt, um 1450. Mann an den Stamm angeklammert'. The parable is rendered in *Der Renner* in verses 23527–86; ill. EINHORN (1972: fig. 114). For further examples cf. EINHORN (1972: figs. 110–11); in fig. 111 the man is kneeling inside the pit on the side of the tree whose trunk is being gnawed by the mice. © Bayerische Staatsbibliothek. [For a colour print, see the Appendix]

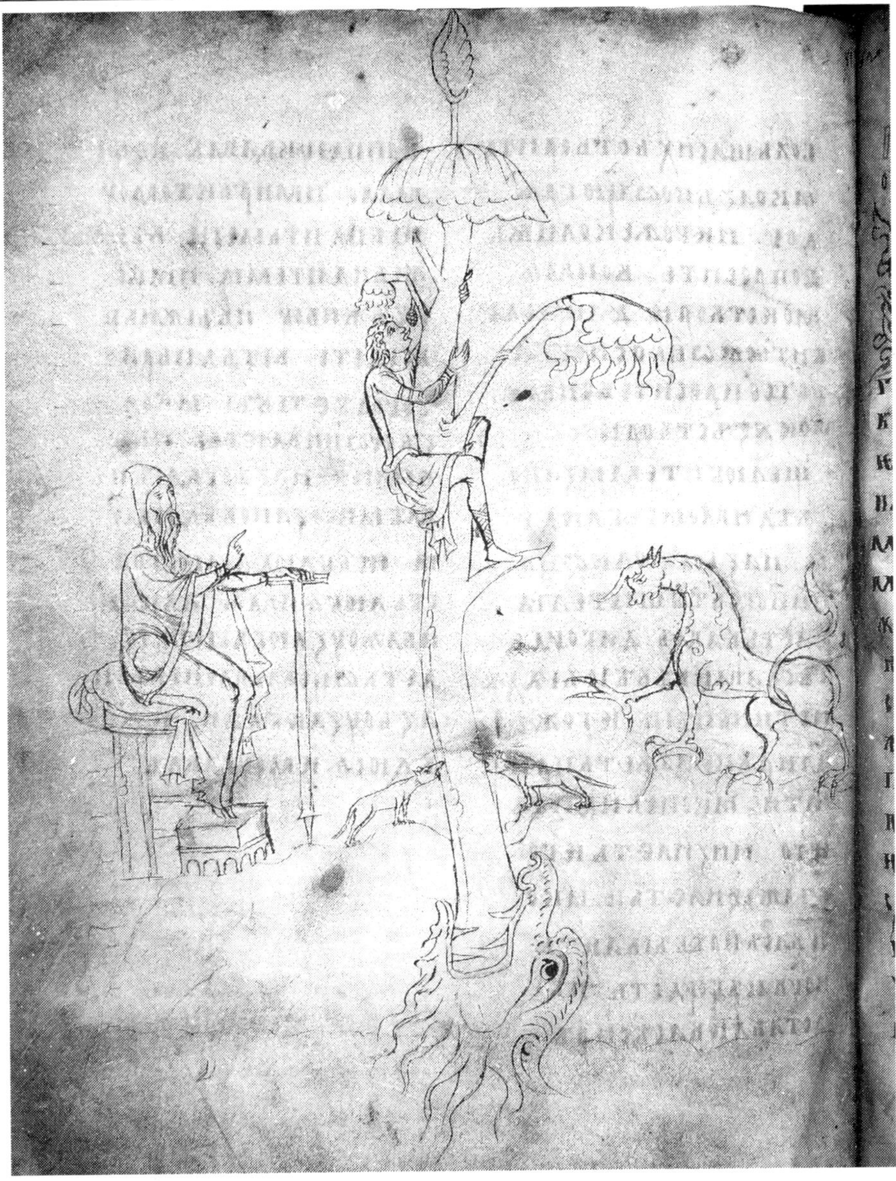

Fig. 22. Kraków, Czartoryskis' Library Sygn. 2097 IV, p. 78, (NOWAK (1999: 157–58)); according to EINHORN (1972: 412, No. A, VIII): 'Mann am Baumstamm angeklammert; l. Barlaam sitzend mit Kaputze und T-förmigem Stab, r. Einhorn mit Krallenfüßen; keine Schlangen' (Slavonic Evangeliary from Ławryszew; end of 14th century. Former Ortodox monastery in Ławryszew (now Laurishava) near Nowogródek (now Novahrudok), former Grand Duchy of Lithuania (now Belarus)); NAUMOW–KASZLEJ (2004): 13th century. © Fundacja Czartoryskich. [For a colour print, see the Appendix]

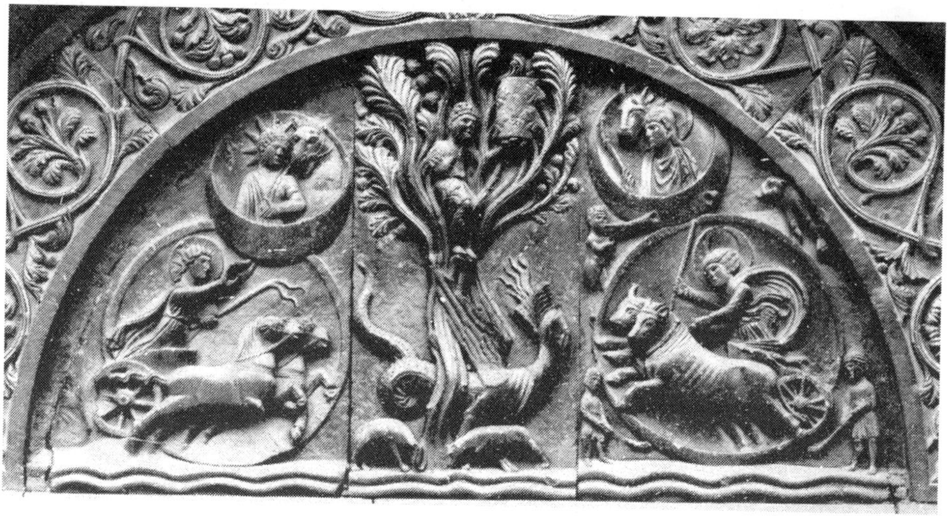

Fig. 23. Parma, portal on the Soutehern Facade of the baptistery, 1196–1220. Ill.: DE FRANCOVICH (1952 Vol. 2: pl. 149–52); POESCHKE (1998: pl. 116); here after DE FRANCOVICH (1952 Vol. 2: pl. 150).

the man was holding a branch; unfortunately the picture in fig. 19 is too badly damaged to ascertain if the four snakes were also depicted. Another pattern, from the Christian Arabic illustrations, follows precisely the Islamic tradition of the *Kalīla wa-Dimna* (like our fig. 10) but adds a unicorn on the side [fig. 20], also another pattern of illustrations (like our fig. 11) with the man standing above the hollow, is represented in illustrations of *Barlaam and Josaphat*[55].

The most widespread pattern shows the man sitting on a tree, which in these versions is the pan-European Tree of Life[56], the dripping honey is also sometimes replaced by the fruits of the tree. Sometimes the unicorn is on a high cliff (like in fig. 19), the man is holding himself on the bough, as if he would hang, and there is a pit

[55] Cf. SMINÉ (1993: fig. 5), the manuscript from 13th c. Syria, kept in Dayr al-Balmand Monastery (No. 147) in Lebanon. The unicorn is named in the description but not depicted in the illustration. In the Arabic Christian tradition our parable is depicted in later times as well, LEROY (1955, pl. 7.2) brings a miniature from a manuscript from 17th century. The picture shows the man above the well, which is opened from one side so that the bottom with the huge head of the monster can be seen. There are four snakes on the outside of the well and mice (white and black) gnawing branches of two trees the man is hanging on. The man is clad in the typical dress of Turkey of the 17th century, slippers and a very big turban.

[56] KÜNSTLE (1928: 200 ff.); OLSCHI (1928: 180 ff.); VETTER (1960: 216 ff.); EINHORN (1972: 392); ODENIUS (1972–73).

with snakes or dragon below [fig. 21], but in most of the cases the depictions show the man inside the crown of the tree and the unicorn, dragon and mice on the sides and below.[57] Only rarely is Barlaam depicted on the side [fig. 22]. As a rule the parable is depicted without an overt connection to *Barlaam and Josaphat*. The most famous of these depictions are the sculptures above the portal on the southern facade of the baptistery in Parma, built between 1196 and 1220 [fig. 23] and the relief in the pulpit in Ferrara from the 14th century [fig. 24]. In Parma the man sits on the tree and stretches to grasp a bee-hive, below, by the tree trunk, there is a fire-spitting, winged dragon and two animals (not resembling mice at all). The unicorn is not represented. The highly symbolical representation of Everyman is enhanced by means of the double depiction of the personifications of the Sun and the Moon. Also in Parma the animals biting the trunks of two trees, on which the man is standing, are not mice, but look rather like wolves. The head of the fire-spitting dragon shown in profile allows recognition of the earlier tradition. Also the bow-shaped band, on which the unicorn is standing, and which carries the inscription *unicornis iste insequitur animas hominum*, seems to repeat the rim of the well—the meaning of which was probably no longer understandable for the artist.

Such depictions of the parable in art, independent from the *Barlaam and Josaphat* narrative, correspond with the development in literature: the parable parts company from the story and starts to live an autonomous life[58]; it will become the epitome of the *conditio humana*. Only a few examples can be named here, such as the *Gesta Romanorum* (chap. 168: *De eterna dampnatione*) or two popular versions in Middle High German, *Ein paispel von ainem mensch, der gejagt wart* by Michael Beheim[59] or *Ein Bild des menschen elenden, gefährlichen Lebens* by Hans Sachs[60].

The reliance on the *Barlaam and Josaphat* narrative can be recognised, in literature and in art, by the presence of the unicorn. After *Barlaam* the unicorn stays and represents the danger from which the man escapes, as it does in the copper engraving by Boetius Bolsvert (1580–1633) [fig. 25]. The depiction confirms a continuation of the old pictorial tradition which has not been forgotten: apart from the unicorn, which might be a misconceived elephant (cf. *supra* p. 67), all the other elements which

[57] Cf. EINHORN (1972: figs. 101–02, 104–07, 109, 112, 113, 115); VOLK (2003: n. 4) connects early depictions of the Coptic textiles (earliest from the 6th century), showing the man inside a tree, with our parable, this, however, does not seems to be proven.

[58] For the overview of the versions cf. EINHORN (1972: 395–404).

[59] GILLE–SPRIEWALD (1970 Vol. II: 441–42).

[60] Hans Sachs (1557), ed. Nürnberg 1816: 336–39; for further versions from the mediaeval German literature cf. WEIZSÄCKER (1899).

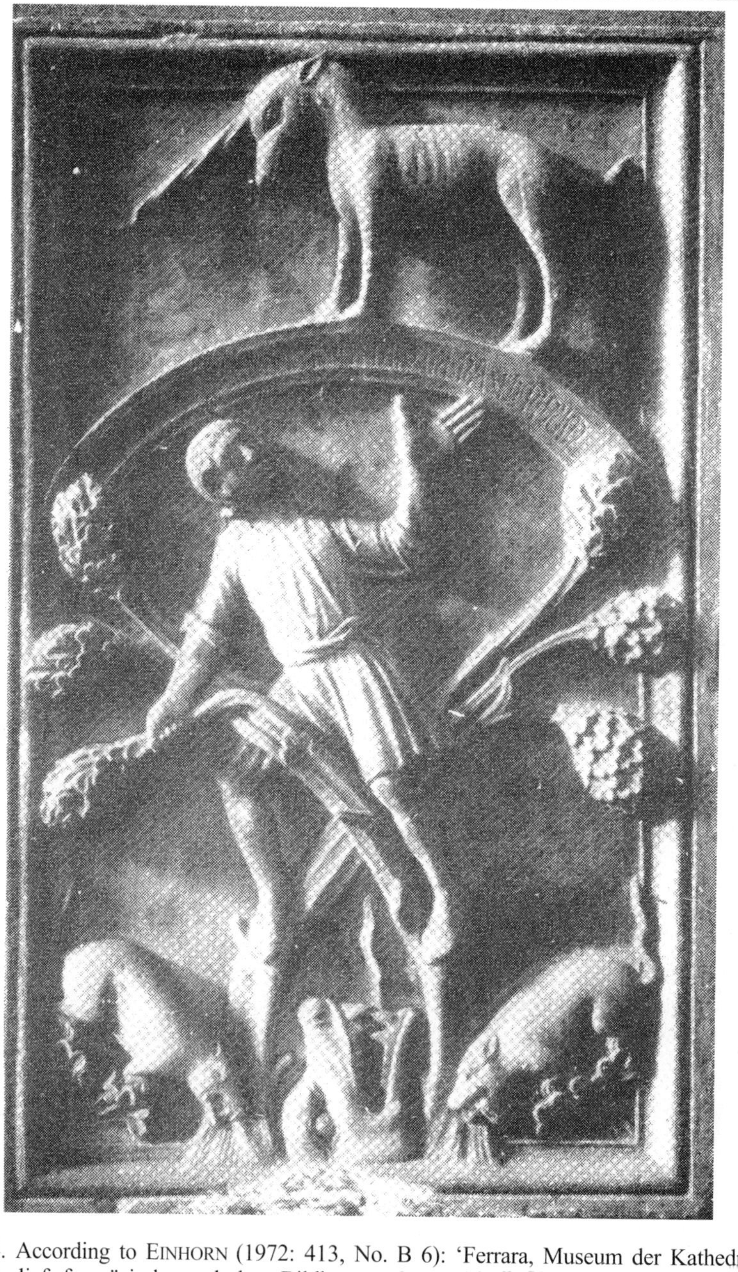

Fig. 24. According to EINHORN (1972: 413, No. B 6): 'Ferrara, Museum der Kathedrale, Kanzelrelief, französisch geschulten Bildhauers, frühes 14. Jh Unterhalb eines halbkreisförmigen Schriftbands VNICORNIS ISTE INSEQUITUR ANIMAS HOMINUM, auf dem ein Einhorn steht, ein Mann im Kreuzungspunkt zweier Baumstämme; feuerspeiender Drachenkopf; keine Schlangen'; ill. DE FRANCOVICH (1952, Vol. 1: 428); here after DE FRANCOVICH.

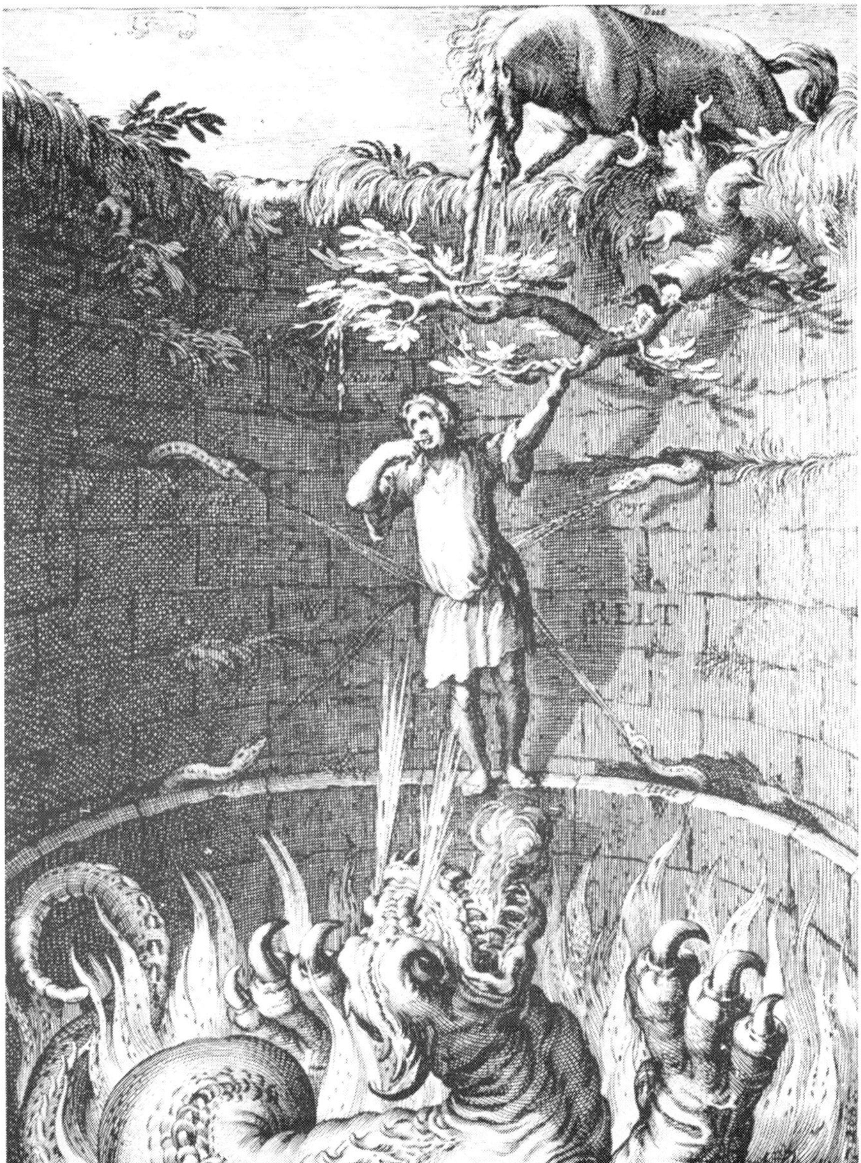

Fig. 25. According to EINHORN (1972: 417, No. B 16): 'Boetius Bolsvert (1580–1633). Kupferstich: in gemauerten Brunnenschacht auf einem Absatz stehend ein Mann, mit der Linken sich an einen Zweig anklammernd, die Rechte zum Munde führend; seitlich je zwei Schlangen, unterhalb feuerspeiender Drache; Einhorn o. am Brunnenrand', ill.: KNIPPING (1939 Vol. 1: fig. 5); WEHRHAHN-STAUCH / RDK, Vol. 4: col. 1527, fig. 16; HATHAWAY (1980: 73); SUGITA (2007: fig. 14); here after KNIPPING.

have been known since the earliest, Indian versions are still represented here: the man is again inside the well and holds onto a branch which is being gnawed by two mice—a black and a white one, four snakes are coming from the sides of the well and there is a terrible monster at the bottom, while honey is dripping from the tree.

One might assume that as the parable was so popular in the West it must have been frequently represented in the East, and yet this is not the case. In India, the parable is unknown apart from the reliefs in Amaravati and Nagarjunakonda [figs. 1–9] and the Moghul tradition [fig. 14].[61] The same can be said, to the best of my knowledge, about representations in regions such as Central and South-East Asia which copy the Indian pictorial tradition.

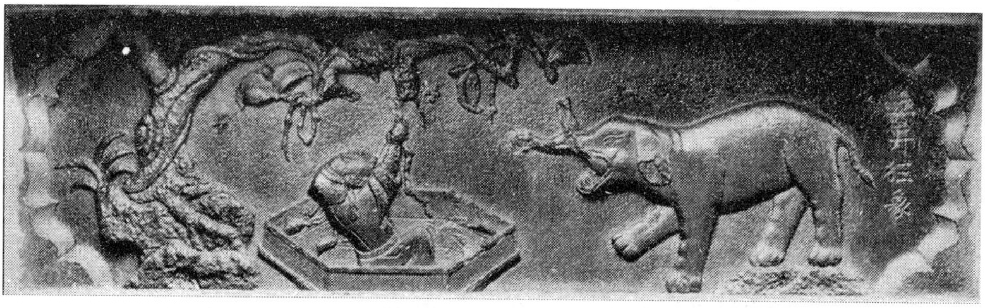

Fig. 26. Quanzhou, Twin Pagodas, Kaiyun Temple, 1238. Ill.: ECKE–DEMIÉVILLE (1935: fig. E base 18); EINHORN (1972: fig. 116); here after ECKE–DEMIÉVILLE.

An illustration of the parable from Song dynasty China can be found in the city of Quanzhou (泉州, known in the European sources as Zaitan) on one of the reliefs in the Kaiyuan Temple. It is among the reliefs on the base of the eastern of the so called Twin Pagodas, and dates from the year 1238 [fig. 26]. The relief shows the man hanging inside the well, holding on to the tree standing on its side. He is not, however, holding on to a branch of the tree but is apparently grasping a liana that is observable on the trunk. There are two mice above the man, one on the liana and another one on the branch, and two bees can be seen in the air. The mouth of the man seems to be open so that the viewer would imagine the honey dripping in. The sculptor did not manage to show the bottom of the well, but there are four snakes

[61] Similar in the literary tradition: the renderings of the parable from the Indian folk-storytelling (cf. DUBOIS (1906: 433–34); TAUSCHNER (1959, No. 58, 'Der törichte Jäger') are reminiscent of western versions, cf. *Speculum Morale* des Vincent de BEAUVAIS (analys. in SCHWARZBAUM (1979: 348)); to my mind they can not be taken as the development of the old Indian tradition but should be treated as due to the influence of the Christian mission, cf. below p. 79 f.

(one has broken off) coming from the lining of the well. An elephant is coming from the right-hand side of the relief and an inscription on its side pronounces 'the elephant and the empty well'.

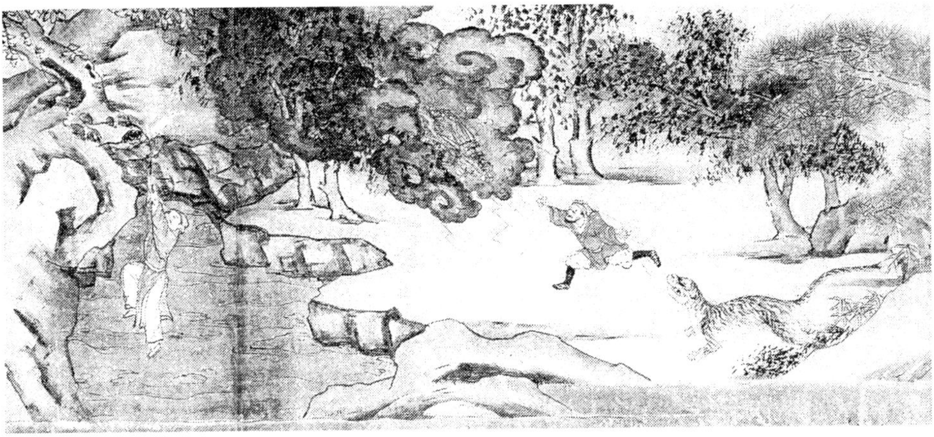

Fig. 27. Painting roll, Kamakura Period, 14th c. ill.: *Kamakura no Emaki* (1987: 34); SUGITA (2007: fig. 6); here after *Kamakura no Emaki.*

The elephant brings us back to the earliest texts and depictions, nevertheless it is impossible to state that this relief is a continuation of the old tradition because there is no proof that the imagery was transferred. Moreover, the seaport Quanzhou contained such a fusion of Buddhist, Hindu, Islamic, Christian and Manichaean traditions (SCHOTTENHAMMER (1998)) that even if the artist has depicted the parable in the way in which it is rendered in the Buddhist scripture, he could have take his inspiration from another faith.

One very interesting illustration of our parable comes from the Kamakura period in Japan (14th c.).[62] The picture is a part of a scroll several meters long which depicts the life stories of the legendary monks. The part with the parable illustrates the life of the famous monk Shendao Dashi (Zendō). The illustration shows the parable in two successive scenes[63], on the right-hand side the man is running away, on the

[62] I would like to state my gratitude to Prof. Seishi Karashima (Hochioji) and Mrs. Satomi Hiyama (Tokyo) for bringing my attention to this painting and providing me with references and copies.

[63] The parable is in two successive scenes, first the man running for his life and then the man hanging above the pit, this is also depicted in the early illustrations from the *Barlaam and Josaphat*, cf. EINHORN (1972: 410–11, Nos. A III, A IV, V A; Pls. 97–99); cf. also fig. 15.

left-hand side he is hanging above the pit [fig. 27]. He is running from a tiger, but on the other side of the man there is also a dark cloud with thunderbolts from which the head of a dragon is emerging. Clearly, this must symbolise a storm, but, as we

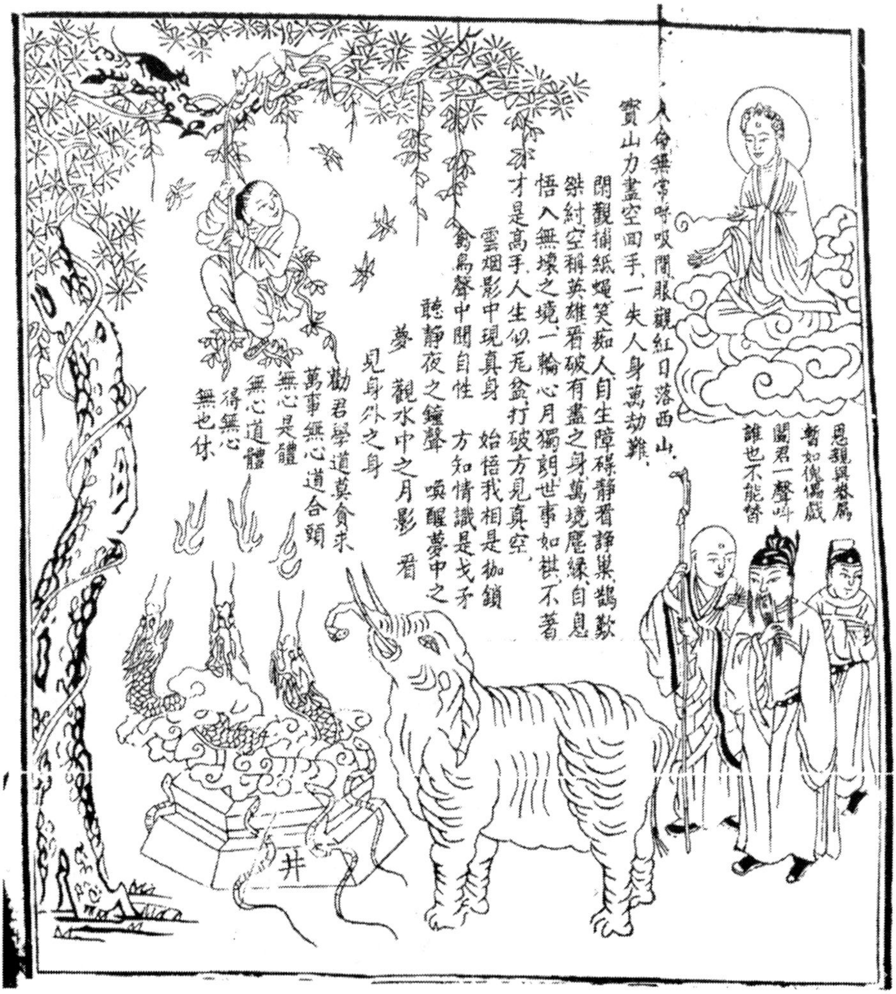

Fig. 28. Sheet print, China, 19th c.. Ill.: MOULE (1894); SUGITA (2007: fig. 7); here after MOULE.

will see, in later depictions the storm clouds will be placed underneath the hanging man—where the monster/dragon is normally represented. Perhaps the cloud with the dragon emerging from it was adopted from an older tradition which has not survived in which a cloud was represented above the well. The man is running with stretched out arms between those two dangers in the direction of a river which flows between high banks. In the next scene we see him hanging above the river, holding on to a liana which is growing along a very steep river-bank. Two mice, one black and one white, are shown next to the liana. Bees are flying around the body of the man.

Given that the scroll represents the life of Shendao Dashi, the only possible connection between the parable and the famous monk would seem to be the belief that he taught the parable to somebody and probably converted him by means of it. The parable was known in Japan, not only through knowledge of the Chinese *sūtra*s, but also in through commonly used imagery. In the famous collections of poems *Man'yo-shu* (*Collection of Ten Thousand Leaves*, Nara time) the passage about two mice and four snakes is taken to illustrate poem No. 793, (the passage is however in prose, so not as early as the main part of the collection).

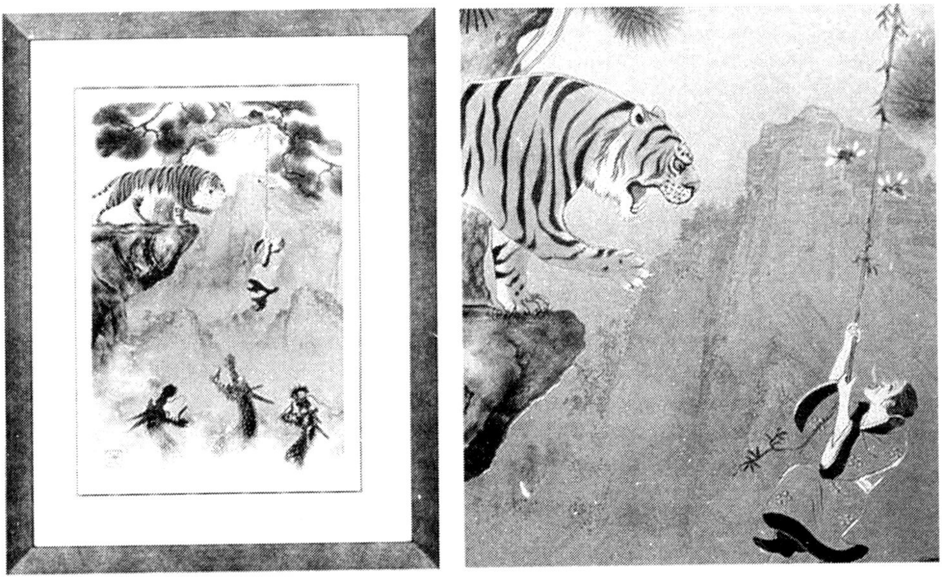

Fig. 29. Sakaki-Eiju from Nara, Mujo-no-Tora from 20th c.: www.family-art.co.jp/regular02.html [accessed: Spring, 2008]

The imagery of the parable seems to have been passed down through the ages in the Far East, even though the surviving depictions are few. A cheap print from 19th century China contains an illustration of the parable [fig. 28]. Its features—a hexagonal well with snakes on its lining, a tree covered with a liana, bees and (three) dragons emerging from the cloud which is above the well in this picture—together show a fusion of earlier pictorial traditions. On the right-hand side of the sheet the Buddha is represented and below him are three people, two laymen and a monk. The text identifies them as King Udayana (depicted with an attendant) and the monk Piṇḍola Bharadvāja. The depiction corresponds with the *Sūtra on the cause (Nidāna) of the preaching of the law by Piṇḍola Bharadvāja to King Udayana*, i.e. T 1690 (cf. *supra*, n. 14). The fact that out of all the parables cited in T 1690, it is the 'Man in the Well' that is depicted shows that there was knowledge of the parable in 19th century China.

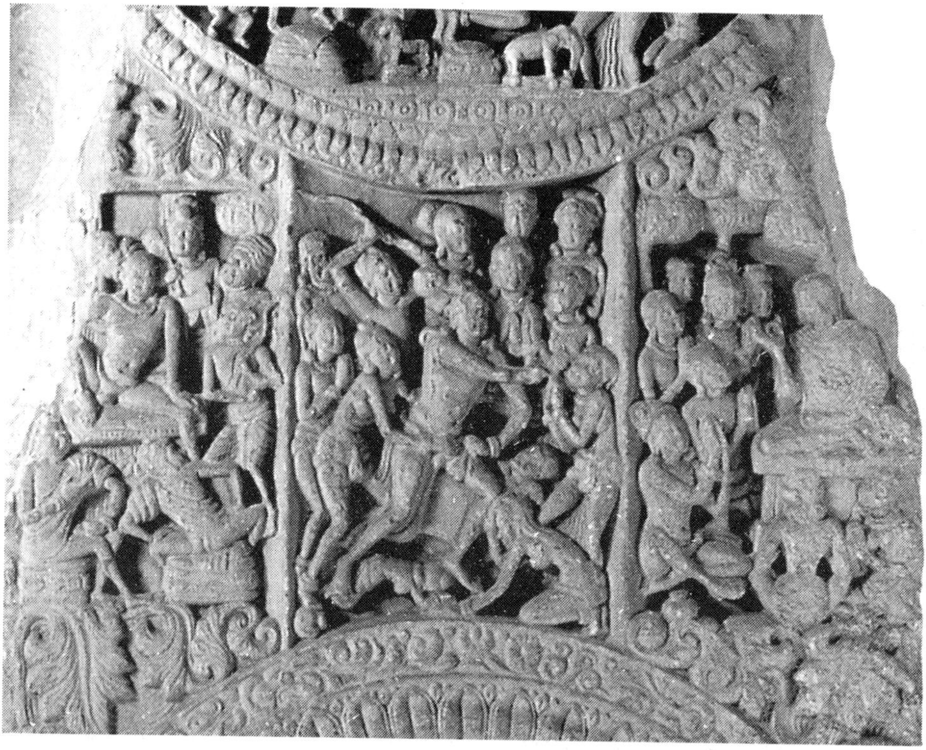

Fig. 30. Amaravati, British Museum, 11, FERGUSSON (1868: pl. 59.2); BARRETT (1954: pl. 29); STERN–BÉNISTI (1961: pl. 57a); SIVARAMAMURTI (1975: fig. 366); KNOX (1992: no. 12, p. 61); RAO (1984: pl. 174); ROSEN STONE (1994: figs. 67–68); ZIN (2004: fig. 19 / drawing); here after KNOX.

The same can be said about modern Japan, even though the continuation of the pictorial tradition can not be proved. Products of contemporary art (of doubtful artistic value), published on the Internet depict [fig. 29] the man hanging above the pit out of which three dragons emerge from fog. The man is holding on to a liana (even though the tree is a coniferous one) and his mouth is open to catch the drops of honey from the honey-comb. Two oversized bees are flying along half of the liana. On the branch of the tree there are two mice and on the overhang of the rock stands a huge tiger trying to grasp the man in its paw.[64] Not only do such pictures appear on the Internet but there are also texts of unknown derivation[65] about a man hanging on a vine from a cliff between two tigers, one on its top and one at its foot. The man in these texts is eating strawberries and this seems to associate the texts with the West.

The question of whether the parable was continuous known in Asia has important significance for how indigenous the Asiatic depictions are. The parable, and also the Buddha's life story, as told in *Barlaam and Josaphat*, came to Asia a long time ago from the West. Towards the end of the 16th century in Portuguese Goa, a Dominican friar Diogo do Couto (1542–1616) found out that the story of St. Josaphat and the life story of the Buddha were one and the same narrative. Diogo interpreted his finding in the only way which was thinkable for him (or perhaps in the only way which made him safe from the Great Inquisition), and that was, that the Indian pagans took the story about the Christian saint and transformed it into the Buddhist legend.[66] The scholarly, and ingenious, Society of Jesus applied the discovery of the pious Dominican for their own ends: In 1591 *Barlaam and Josaphat* was translated into Japanese and used for missionary work in Japan.[67] So the Jesuits evangelised in Japan and also China[68] and the Philippines[69] by explaining to people that the Buddha was in reality St. Josaphat.

---

[64] Mutsuo YANASE (1987) and Hideki SUGITA (2007) give the name of the painter as Sakaki-Eiju from Nara. YANASE writes also that the subject is known especially in the Jodoshund sect in Kansai district.

[65] Cf. www.story-lovers.com/liststigerstrawberrystory; www-usr.rider.edu/~suler/ zenstory/cliffhanger; www.zenstrawberry.com

[66] Cf. VOLK (2006: 159) for bibliographical references on the original text of Diogo de Counto and the secondary literature.

[67] Cf. IKEGAMI (1999).

[68] VOLK (2006: 160, n. 69) mentions two Chinese translations, one which existed before the year 1610 and another one *Shēng Jo-sa-fa shih-mo* (the life of St. Josaphat) by Niccolò Longobardi (1557–1654).

[69] Cf. VOLK (2006) for the translation into the Tagalog-language by Antonio de Borja, Manila 1712.

Let us return to the earliest version of our parable, the reliefs from Amaravati and Nagarjunakonda [figs. 1–9] and the narrative that is depicted there, the story of the man who goes armed to attack a monk and then worships this monk; his aggression doubtless changed by the parable the monk tells him. It might be that the echo of this story still sounds in the Christian narrative about the cruel king Abenner who killed monks before he was converted by Barlaam, or perhaps in the Japanese narrative about Shendao Dashi who used the narrative to convert somebody. The narrative

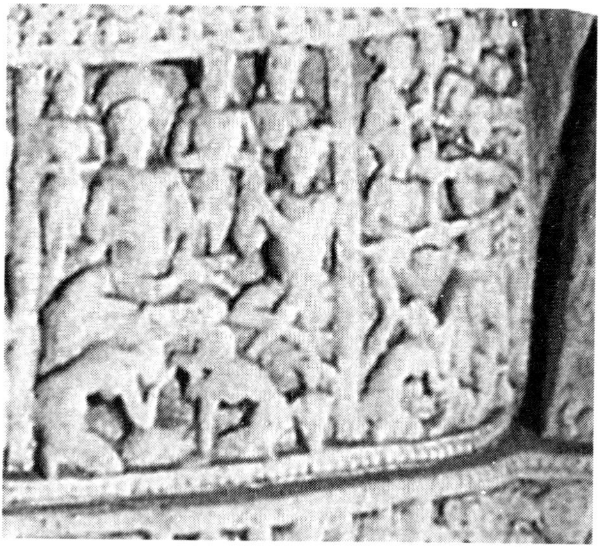

Fig. 31. Amaravati, British Museum, 87, FERGUSSON (1868: pl. 79.1); STERN–BÉNISTI (1961: pl. 51a); KNOX (1992: 151, no. 77); here after KNOX.

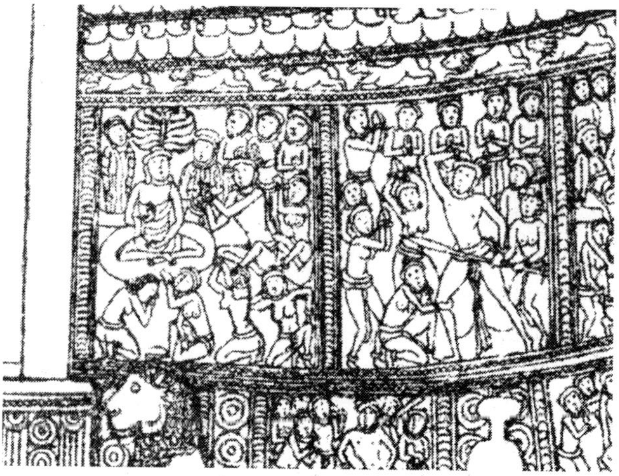

Fig. 32. Amaravati. Drawing by an assistant of Colonel Mackenzie, Signed: 'T.A. May 1817'. The British Library, WD1061, folio 68, according to the *Online Gallery of the Amaravati Album* (www.bl.uk/onlinegallery/features/amaravati/miscsubjects.html), ill.: BURGESS (1887: pl. 34b); here after BURGESS.

as such has not survived. VOGEL (1937: 113–15) tried to explain the depiction in the reliefs from Nagarjunakonda with narratives of King Udayana. He did this because in Pāli there is a story (Jātaka No. 497) about the aggressive Udayana (Udena) who martyrs the monk Piṇḍola Bharadvāja, while his wives try to protect him. The explanation sounds plausible (especially since there are also narratives in 'northern' Buddhism, and in the Chinese translation about the conflict between the two[70]) and matches the depictions well. The Pāli tradition, however, does not include even a small allusion to the parable, and the Chinese version of the parable, T 1690 (cf. *supra*, n. 14, fig. 28), which VOGEL (1937) supposed to be the literary basis for the Nagarjunakonda reliefs, knows nothing about the aggressive mood of Udayana.

The parable about a man who forgets to struggle for liberation from the ills of existence because of sensual pleasures would in fact be very appropriate to the character of Udayana. Udayana is famous for being keen on music and hunting and most of all for being a handsome philanderer. The sermon condemning sensual pleasures would therefore sit very well in his narrative. However, such narrative is unknown and the textual tradition of our reliefs remains unidentified. It might have been a story about Udayana and Piṇḍola but equally might have been about any aggressive king.

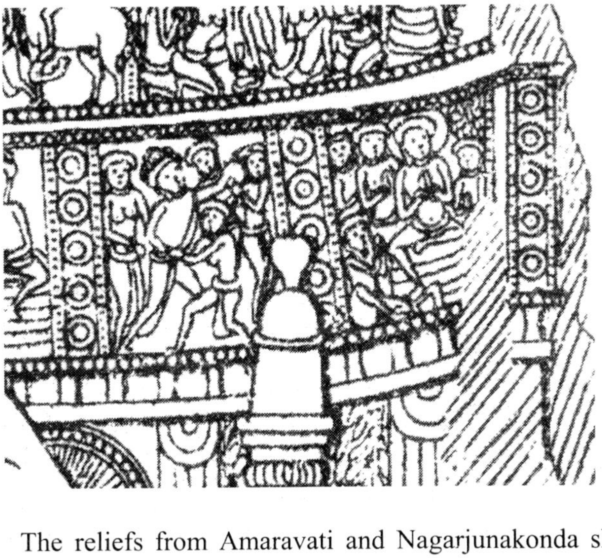

Fig. 33. Amaravati. Drawing by an assistant of Colonel Mackenzie, The British Library, WD1061, folio 79, signed 'T.A.', ill.: BURGESS (1887: pl. 39.1); here after BURGESS.

The reliefs from Amaravati and Nagarjunakonda should be connected with the textual sources preserved today in 'northern' Buddhism, not in the Pāli tradition (ZIN (2004)). As mentioned in the beginning, many of these reliefs remain unexplained and their textual basis seems to be lost.

[70] KŚ 6.1.6, pp. 22–24.

What is very peculiar about the reliefs of 'The Man in the well' is that the representation of the parable, that is the content of the sermon, and the person who is telling the sermon appear in one and the same picture. This type of 'story within a story' or rather 'depiction within a depiction', the *mise en abyme*, is unknown in older Indian art. Interestingly this pattern was adopted by the European depictions [figs. 18, 22].

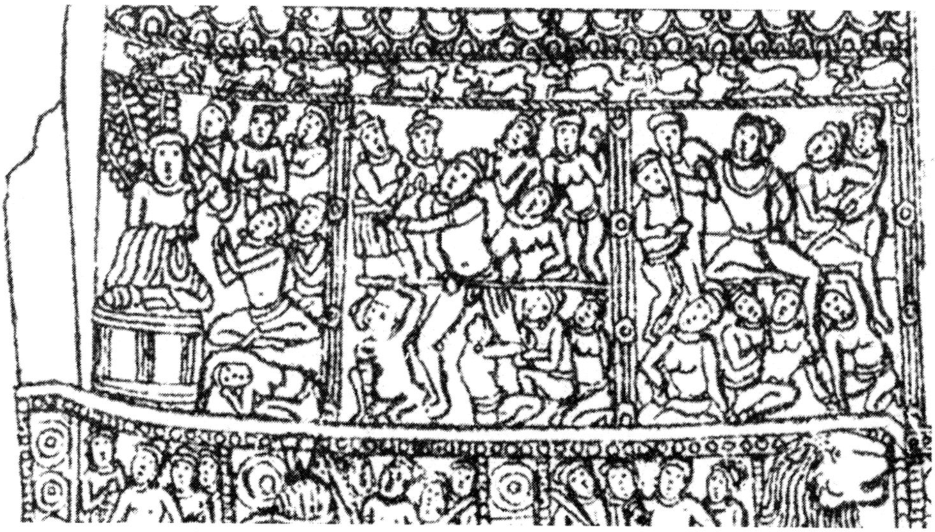

Fig. 34. Amaravati. Drawing by an assistant of Colonel Mackenzie, The British Library, WD1061, folio 33, signed 'T.A. 12th Nov'r 1816', ill.: BURGESS 1887, pl. 39.2; here after BURGESS.

In the reliefs from Amaravati we can find examples of apparently the same narrative but without the parable. Two such depictions are preserved in the British Museum [figs. 30, 31], three further are lost today but known from old drawings: [figs. 32, 33, 34]. The reliefs can contribute to the explanation of the depicted story: it seems that in the depiction on the pillar in British Museum [fig. 30] the beginning of the story is represented: in the left register the king is shown on the throne, accompanied by his ministers sitting below. He talks to two Brahmins, one of them characterised by the typically thrice bent stick (*kuṭila*). The same Brahmins are then depicted in the middle register, as if fighting the women who are trying to stop the king. The meaning of this first scene seems to be that the Brahmins inform the king about the monk and cause the king's aggressive mood. The reliefs remain, however, also with this detail not explained, i.e. the frame-story of the earliest representations of the parable 'Man in the Well' is unidentified. What we can say is that the narrative—with or without the parable—was depicted in Amaravati and Nagarjunakonda eleven times, and as such it belongs to the most common themes there.

It is impossible to say, however, why the parable was depicted in some reliefs and not in others. There is no appreciable difference in the date of the reliefs so it is not the case, for instance, that the reliefs without the parable are earlier and those with later. It must be mentioned, however, that there is not a single example without the parable from the later Nagarjunakonda. It is possible that not all artists represented the content of the sermon, even though 'The Man in the Well' belonged to the narrative from the very beginning, because the 'depiction inside the depiction' was not for everybody.

* * *

This paper is an attempt to deal in only a few pages with such an exceedingly widespread motif that one could devote one's life to investigate the questions raised here.

Let us sum up its findings.

The parable about 'The Man in the Well' originated in India, in all probability in Buddhist bearing. The oldest references are the frequent depictions in Buddhist reliefs from the Amaravati School, which connect the parable with the frame-story (probably the story about King Udayana and the monk Piṇḍola Bharadvāja) which is lost. Judging from their coherence, the surviving Buddhist texts of the parable, preserved in Chinese, do not include the original version. The only version from orthodox India, in the *Mahā-bhārata*, is late and does not correspond with the depiction and other literary versions at all. The coherent version survived in the later Jaina texts, even when those texts themselves must be dated much later.

It was the coherent Indian version, like those which survived in the Jaina texts, which left India and was carried to the West with the romance of *Barlaạm and Josaphat* and the animal fables *Kalīla and Dimna*.

Apart from the transition of the parable in literary, and presumably also oral sources, it must have been transmitted through pictorial models. In some cases, and in these can be counted the changing of the elephant into a unicorn, the deviation in the visual tradition can be explained as a misunderstanding of the visual patterns.

Also, the 'depiction within a depiction', the way in which the parable is represented together with the person who is explaining it, in what for India is a very uncharacteristic fashion, also appears in the non-Indian representations [figs. 18, 22, 28]. Was it a method of depiction which just presented itself as natural for the iconography of parables or is it the luminous creation of the Amaravati artists who produced a mode of representation which, however, disappeared from India?

The parable forges its real career outside India.

It is saying much that in the 19th century the parable was worked on by scholars who knew the Islamic and Christian versions; their research on the Indian sources was only carried out in order to ascertain the beginning of the motif, their real interest was in the later texts. This is the case, for example, with a researcher like BENFEY (1859: 80)—in the book about the Indian *Pañca-tantra* where the parable does not appear—or Bishop MOULE of Hanchow (1884) who brings together the Chinese version with the Greek text of the parable by John of Damascus. WINTERNITZ (1909: 351, Engl.: 1927: 48) starts the passage about the parable with a reference to Rückert.

Thus the Indian original was always understood merely as the beginning of a tradition which only subsequently started to be of immense importance. It might be that this perspective is proper. The parable obtains greatest significance in Islam and in Christianity—as if these religions, in which death is understood as a final exit from this world, could obtain most significance from the imagery of the person hanging in the well and forgetting about all dangers for a drop of honey—as the embodiment of the *conditio humana*.

BIBLIOGRAPHY

ALALI-HUSEINAT 1993 = Alali-Huseinat, Mahmoud: *Rückert und Orient. Untersuchungen zu Friedrich Rückerts Beschäftigung mit arabischen und persischer Literatur*. Frankfurt am Main 1993.

ALMOND 1987 = Almond, Philip: 'The Buddha of Christendom', *Religious Studies* 23 (1987) 391–406.

ANTON / EM = Anton, Manuela: 'Stephanites und Ichnelates', EM Vol. 12, col. 1240–43.

ASMUSSEN / EIr = Asmussen, J.P.: 'Barlaam and Iosaph', EIr Vol. 3.1: 801.

BARRETT 1954 = Barrett, Douglas: *Sculptures from Amaravati in the British Museum*. Trustees of the British Museum, London 1954.

BENFEY 1859 = Benfey, Theodor: *Pantschatantra: Fünf Bücher indischer Fabeln, Märchen und Erzählungen, aus dem Sanskrit übersetzt mit Einleitung und Anmerkungen*. 2 Vols. Brockhaus, Leipzig 1859 [reprinted: Hildesheim 1966].

BERTHOLD / EI = Berthold, E.: 'Naṣr Allāh Muḥammad', in: EI Vol. 7: 1016–17.

BLAU 1853 = Blau: 'Aus einem Briefe des Gesandschafts-Attaché Blau an Prof. Fleischer', *Zeitschrift der Deutschen Morgenländischen Gesellschaft* 7 (1853) 400–03.

BROCKELMANN / EI = Brockelmann, C.: 'Kalīla wa-Dimna', in: EI Vol. 4: 503–06.

BURGESS 1887 = Burgess, James: *The Buddhist Stupas of Amaravati and Jaggayyapeta in the Krishna District, Madras Presidency, Surveyed in 1882*. Archaeological Survey of Southern India 1, London 1887 [reprinted: Varanasi 1970].

CAGMAN–TANINDI 1986 = Çağman, Filiz; Tanındı, Filiz ve Zeren: *The Topkapı Saray Museum. The Albums and Illuminating Manuscripts*. London 1986.

CHAUVIN 1887 = Chauvin, Victor Charles: *Bibliographie des ouvrages arabes ou relatifs aux Arabes publiés dans L'Europe chrétienne de 1810 à 1885*. Vol. 3, Liège 1887.

CHAVANNES 1910–1934 = Chavannes, Édouard: *Cinq cents contes et apologues, extraits du Tripitaka chinois et traduits en français*. Vols. 1–4, Paris 1910–34 [reprinted: 1962].

DE BLOIS 1991a = De Blois, François: *Burzōy's Voyage to India and the Origin of the Book of Kalīlah wa Dimnah*. London 1991.

DE BLOIS 1991b = De Blois, François: 'The *Pancatantra*: From India to the West—and Back', in: GRUBE (1991A: 10–15).

DE FRANCOVICH = De Francovich, G.: *Benedetto Antelami, architetto e scultore e l'arte del suo tempo*. 2 Vols. Milano–Firenze 1952.

DENECK 1970 = Deneck, Marguerite-Marie: *La Sculpture Indienne*. Paris 1970.

DER NERSESSIAN 1936 = Der Nersessian, Sirarpie: *L. illustration du Roman de Barlaam et Joasaph*. Paris 1936.

DhPar = Amitagati: *Dharma-parīkṣā*. [Analysis in:] Nikolai Vladimirovich Mironov: *Die Dharmaparīkṣā des Amitagati, Ein Beitrag zur Literatur und Religionsgeschichte des indischen Mittelalters*. Dissertation Strassburg, G. Kreysing Leipzig 1903.

DÖLGER 1953 = Dölger, Franz: *Der griechische Barlaam-Roman, ein Werk des hl. Johannes von Damaskos*. Studia Patristica et Byzantica 1, Ettal 1953.

DUBOIS 1906 = Dubois, Jean Antoine: *Hindu Manners, Customs and Ceremonies*. Translated and edited by H.K. Beauchamp. Oxford 1906.

ECKE–DEMIÉVILLE 1935 = Ecke, Gustav; Demiéville, Paul: *The Twin Pagodas of Zayton, A Study of Later Buddhist Sculpture in China*. Cambridge (Massachusetts) 1935.

EI = Gribb, H.A.R. et al. (eds.): *Encyclopaedia of Islam*. 2nd edition, E. J. Brill, Leiden 1960–2005.

EINHORN 1972 = Einhorn, Jürgen W.: 'Das Einhorn als Sinnzeichen des Todes: Die Parabel vom Mann im Abgrund', *Jahrbuch des Instituts für Frühmittelalterforschung der Universität Münster* 6 (1972) 381–415.

EINHORN 1978 = Einhorn, Jürgen W.: *Spiritalis unicornis, das Einhorn als Bedeutungsträger in Literatur und Kunst des Mittelalters*. 2n edition, München 1978.

EIr = Yarshater, Ehsan et al. (ed.): *Encyclopaedia Iranica*. Center for Iranian Studies, Columbia University, London–New York 1985–2009.

EISELEIN 1840 = Eiselein, Joseph: *Die Sprichwörter und Sinnreden des deutschen Volkes in alter und neuer Zeit*. Freiburg i. Br 1840.

EM = Brednih, R.W. et al. (eds.): *Enzyklopädie des Märchens. Handwörterbuch zur historischen und vergleichenden Erzählforschung. Begründet von Kurt Ranke*. Vols. 1–10, Berlin–New York 1999–.

FERGUSSON 1868 = Fergusson, James: *Tree and Serpent Worship: or Illustrations of Mythology and Art in India in the First and Forth Centuries after Christ from the Sculptures of the Buddhist Topes at Sanchi and Amaravati*. London 1868 [reprinted: Delhi 1971].

GABRIELLI / EI = Gabrielli, F.: 'Ibn al-Muḳaffa<', in: EI Vol. 3: 883–85.

GEISSLER 1964 = Geißler, Friedmar: *Anton von Pforr: Das Buch der Beispiele der alten Weisen kritisch herausgegeben nach der Straßburger Handschrift, mit den Lesarten aller bekannten Handschriften und Drucke des 15. und des 16. Jahrhunderts*. Berlin 1964.

GILLE–SPRIEWALD 1970 = Gille, Hans; Spriewald, Ingeborg: *Die Gedichte des Michael Beheim*. Berlin 1970.

GIMARET 1971 = Gimaret, Daniel: *Le livre de Bilawhar et Būḏāsf selon la version arabe ismaélienne*. Genf–Paris 1971.

GROTZFELD–MARZLOPH / EM = Grotzfeld, H. S.; Marzloph, U.: 'Kalila wa_Dimna', in: EM Vol. 7: cols. 888–95.

GRUBE 1990–91 = Grube, Ernst J.: 'Prolegomena for a corpus Publication of Illustrated Kalīla wa Dimnah Manuscripts', *Islamic Art* 4 (1990–91) 301–481.

GRUBE 1991a = Grube, Ernst J. (ed.): *A Mirror for Princes from India. Illustrated Versions of the* Kalilah wa Dimnah, Anvar-i Suhayli, Iyar-i Danish, *and* Humayun Nameh. Bombay 1991.

GRUBE 1991b = Grube, Ernst J.: 'The Istanbul University Library *Kalilah wa Dimnah* and other 14th-Century Persian Manuscripts', in: GRUBE (1991a: 53–77).

HACKIN 1931 = Hackin, Joseph: *La Sculpture Indienne et Tibétaine au Musée Guimet*. Paris 1931.

von HAMMER-PURGSTALL 1818 = Hammer-Purgstall von, Joseph: *Geschichte der schönen Redekünste Persiens*. Wien 1818.

HARA 1985 = Hara, Minoru: 'The Man in the Well', *The Toyo Gakuho* 66 (1985) 019–038.

HATHAWAY 1980 = Hathaway, Nancy: *The Unicorn*. Viking Press, New York 1980.

IKEGAMI 1999 = Ikegami, Keiko: *Barlaam and Josaphat, A Transcription of MS Egerton 876 with Notes, Glossary, and Comparative Study of Middle English and Japanese Versions*. New York 1999.

JACOBS 1896 = Jacobs, Joseph: *Barlaam and Josaphat*. London 1896.

JULIEN 1859–60 = Julien, Stanislas: *Contes et apologues indiens, inconnus jusqu'à ce jour, suivis de fables et de chinoises*. Vols. 1–2, Paris 1859–60.

JULIEN 1903 = Julien, Stanislas: *Die Avadānas. Indische Erzählungen und Fabeln*. Übersetzt A. Schnell, Rostock 1903. [German translation of JULIEN 1859–60].

Kalila und Dimna = Najmabadi, Seyfeddin; Weber Stefan (transl.): *Kalila und Dimna, Fabeln aus dem klassischen Persien*. München 1996.

Kamakura no Emaki 1987 = *Kamakura no Emaki* [Temple Picture-Scroll of the Kamakura Time]. Tokyo 1987.

KANTIOTES 1997 = Kantiotes, Augoustinos: *The Precious Pearl. Lives of Saints Barlaam and Ioaseph*. Melmont, Mass 1997.

KHANDALAVALA–DESAI 1991 = Khandalavala, K.; Desai, Kalpana: 'Indian Illustrated Manuscripts of the *Kalilah wa Dimnah*, *Anvar-I Suhayli*, and *Iyar-a Danish*', in: GRUBE (1991a: 128–144).

KNIPPING 1939 = Knipping, John Baptist: *De Iconographie van de Contra-Reformatie in de Nederlanden*. Hilversum 1939.

KNOX 1992 = Knox, Robert: *Amaravati, Buddhist Sculpture from the Great Stūpa*. London 1992.

KŚ = *Karma-śataka*. M.L. Feer (transl.): 'Le Karma-Çataka', *Journal Asiatique ou Recueil de Mémoires d'Extraits et de Notices Relatifs à l'Histoire, à Philosophie, aux Langues et à la Littérature des Peuples Orientaux* 9e série 17 [Paris] (1901) 53–100, 257–315, 410–486.

KÜHNE / EM = Kühne, Udo: 'Johannes von Capua', in: EM Vol. VII: cols. 580–83.

KUHN 1888 = Kuhn, E.: 'Der Mann im Brunnen, Geschichte eines indischen Gleichnisses', in: *Festgruß an Otto Böhtlingk zum Doktor-Jubiläum 3. Februar 1888 von seinen Freunden*. Stuttgart 1888: 68–76.

KUHN 1894 = Kuhn, E.: *Barlaam und Josaphat, eine bibliographisch-literargeschichtliche Studie*. Abhandlungen der Königlich Bayerischen Akademie der Wissenschaften, I. Classe, München 1894.

KÜNSTLE 1928 = Künstle, Karl: *Ikonographie der Christlichen Kunst*. Vol. 1, Freiburg 1928.

LACKNER / EM = Lackner, I.: 'Johannes von Capua', in: EM Vol. 1: cols. 1243–52.

LANG 1957 = Lang, David Marshall: *The Wisdom of Balahvar. A Christian Legend of the Buddha*. London 1957.

LANG 1966 = Lang, David Marshall: *The Balavariani (Barlaam and Josaphat). A Tale from the Christan East translated from the Old Georgian*. London 1966.

LChI = Kirschbaum, Engelbert (ed.): *Lexikon der Christlichen Ikonographie*. Rom–Freiburg–Basel / Vols. 1–8, Wien 1968–1976.

LE COQ 1909 = Le Coq von, Albert: 'Ein christliches und ein manichäisches Fragment in türkischer Sprache', in: *Sitzungsberichte der Preussischen Akademie der Wissenschaften*, Berlin 1909: 1202–1218.

LE COQ 1912 = Le Coq von, Albert: 'Türkische Manichaica aus Chotscho', *Abhandlungen der Preussischen Akademie der Wissenschaften. Philologisch-historische Klasse, Jahrgang 1911*, Berlin 1912: 1–61.

LE COQ 1923 = Le Coq von, Albert: *Die Buddhistische Spätantike in Mittelasien. Ergebnisse der Königliichen Preussischen Turfan Expeditionen, II: Manichäische Miniaturen*. Berlin 1923 [reprinted: Graz 1974].

LEBEDEVA 1985 = Lebedeva, I.: *Povest' o Varlaame i Ioasafe, pamjatnik drevnerusskoj perevodnoj literatury XI–XII v.* Leningrad 1985.

LEROY 1955 = Leroy, J.: 'Un nouveau manuscript arabe-chrétien illustré du roman de Barlaam et Josaph', *Syria* 32 (1955) 101–22.

LIEBRECHT 1860 = Liebrecht, Felix: 'Die Quellen des Barlaam und Josaphat', *Jahrbuch für romanische und englische Literatur* 2 (1860) 314–334.

LONGHURST 1938 = Longhurst, Albert Henry: *The Buddhist Antiquities of Nāgārjunikoṇḍa, Madras Presidency*. Memoirs of the Archaeological Survey of India 54, Delhi 1938.

MARZOLPH 2001 = Marzolph, Ulrich: *Narrative Illustration in Persian Lithographed Books*. Leiden 2001.

MBh = *Mahā-bhārata*. (1) V.S. Sukthankar; S.K. Belvakar; P.L. Vaidya et al. et (eds.): *The Mahābhārata for the first time critically edited*. Vol. 11, Bhandarkar Oriental Research Institute, Poona 1956. (2) James L. Fitzgerald (transl.): *The Mahabharata: Book 11: The Book of the Women, Book 12: The Book of Peace, Part One*. University of Chicago Press, Chicago 2004.

METTE 1991 = Mette, Adelheid: *Durch Entsagung zum Heil. Eine Anthologie der Literatur der Jaina*. Zürich 1991.

METTE 2010 = Mette, Adelheid: *Die Erlösungslehre der Jaina—Legenden, Parabeln, Erzählungen. Aus dem Sanskrit und Prakrit übersetzt und erläutert*. Frankfurt am Main–Leipzig 2010.

MOULE 1884 = Moule, G.E.: 'A Buddhist Sheet-Tract Containing an Apologue of Human Life', *Journal of the North-China Branch of the Royal Asiatic Society for the Year 1883*, Shanghai (1884) 94–102.

NAUMOW–KASZLEJ 2004 = Naumow, Aleksander; Kaszlej, Andrzej: *Rękopisy cerkiewnosłowiańskie w Polsce*. Kraków 2004.

Nj = Nanjio, Bunyiu: *A Catalogue of the Chinese Translation of the Buddhist Tripiṭaka, the Sacred Canon of the Buddhists in China and Japan*. Oxford 1883.

NORTH 2003 = North, Thomas: *The Moral Philosophy of Doni, popularly known as The Fables of Bidpai*. Edited by Donald Beecher, John Butler, and Carmine di Biase. Dovehouse, Ottawa 2003 (1570).

Nowak 1999 = Nowak, Janusz Tadeusz et al. (ed.): *Katalog Rekopisów Biblioteki Czartoryskich w Krakowie. Sygnatury 2001–2300.* Muzeum Narodowe w Krakowie, Kraków 1999.

Nurul Hasan / EI = Nurul Hasan: 'Abu>l-Faḍl (Faẓl) <Allāmī (Shaykh)', in: EI Vol. I: 117–18.

O'Kane 2003 = O'Kane, Bernard: *Early Persian Painting.* Kalila and Dimna *Manuscripts of Late Fourteenth Century.* London–New York 2003.

Odenius 1972–73 = Odenius, Oloph: 'Der Mann im Brunnen und der Mann im Baum', *Schweizerisches Archiv für Volkskunde* [Basel] 68–69 (1972–73) 477–86.

Olschi 1928 = Olschi, L.: *Die Romanischen Literaturen des Mittelalters.* Wildpark-Potsdam 1928.

Peri 1959 = Peri, H.: *Der Religionsdisput der Barlaam-Legende, ein Motiv abendländischer Dichtung.* Acta Salamanticensia 14.3, Salamanka 1959.

Poeschke 1998 = Poeschke, J. (ed.): *Die Skulptur des Mittelalters in Italien. Romanik.* Vol. 1, München 1998.

PP = Hemacandra-sūri: *Pariśiṣṭa-parvan.* (1) Hermann Jacobi (ed.): *Sthavirāvalīcarita or Pariśiṣṭaparvan, being an Appendix of the Triṣaṣṭiśalākāpuruṣacarita by Hemacandra.* Calcutta 1883 [2nd edition: Calcutta 1932]. (2) Johannes Hertel (transl.): *Ausgewählte Erzählungen aus Hemacandras Pariśiṣṭa-pārvan.* Leipzig 1908: 64–68.

Raby 1991 = Raby, J.: 'The Earliest illustrations to *Kalilah wa Dimnah*', in: Grube (1991a: 16–31).

Rao 1956 = Rao, P.R. Ramachandra: *The Art of Nāgārjunikoṇḍa.* Madras 1956.

Rao 1984 = Rao, P.R. Ramachandra: *Andhra Sculpture.* Hyderabad 1984.

RDK = Schmitt, Otto et al. (eds.): *Reallexikon zur Deutschen Kunstgeschichte.* Verlag C. H. Beck, Stuttgart–München 1937–.

Réau 1958 = Réau, L.: *Iconographie de l'art chrétien* 3.1. Paris 1958.

Rehatsek 1890 = Rehatsek, E.: 'Book of the King's Son and the Ascetic', *Royal Asiatic Society* N.S. 12 (1890) 1119–1155.

Roesler 2011 = Roesler, Ulrike: *Fruehe Quellen zum buddhistischen Stufenweg in Tibet. Indische und tibetische Elemente im dPe chos des Po-to-ba Rin-chen-gsal.* Reichert Verlag, Wiesbaden 2011.

Rogers 1986 = Rogers, J.M. (ed.): *Das Topkapi Saray Museum: Manuskripte.* Bulfinch Druck, Zürich 1986.

Rosen Stone 1980 = Rosen Stone, Elisabeth: 'Buddhist architecture and lay patronage at Nāgārjunakoṇḍa', in: Anna Libera Dallapiccola; Stephanie Zingel-Avé Lallemant (eds.): *The Stūpa: Its Religious, Historical and Architectural Significance.* Beiträge zur Südasienforschung 55, Franz Steiner Verlag, Wiesbaden 1980: 112–26.

Rosen Stone 1994 = Rosen Stone, E.: *The Buddhist Art of Nāgārjunakoṇḍa.* Buddhist Tradition Series 25, Delhi 1994.

SARKAR–MISRA 1966 = Sarkar, H.; Misra, B.N.: *Nagarjunikonda*. New Delhi 1966 [reprinted: 1972, 1980].

SCHOTTENHAMMER 1998 = Schottenhammer, Angela: 'A Maritime Trade of Quanzhou (Zaitun) from the Ninth through the Thirteen Centuries', in: Stefan Conermann (ed.): *Der Indische Ozean in historischer Perspektive*. Vol. 1, Asien und Afrika, Beiträge des Zentrums für Asiatische und Afrikaische Studien (ZAAS) der Christian-Albrechts-Universität zu Kiel, Kiel 1998: 89–108.

SCHRAMM 1923 = Schramm, Albert: *Der Bilderschmuck der Frühdrucke*. Vol. 7, Leipzig 1923.

SCHWARZBAUM 1979 = Schwarzbaum, Haim: *The Mishlé Shu'alim (Fox Fables) of Rabbi Berechiah Ha-Nakdan. A Study in Comparative Folklore and Fable Lore*. Kiron 1979.

SILVESTRE DE SACY 1816 = Silvestre de Sacy, Antoine Isaac: *Calila et Dimna ou Fables de Bidpai, en Arab; précédées d'un mémoire sur l'origine de ce livre, et sur les diverses traductions qui en ont été dans l'orient…* Paris 1816.

SIMSON 2010 = Simson von, Georg: 'Zur Bedeutung des Kamels im Saṁsāracakra von Ajanta und in der persischen Fassung der Parabel vom Mann im Brunnen', in: Eli Franco, Monika Zin (eds.): *From Turfan to Ajanta, Festschrift for Dieter Schlingloff on the Occasion of his Eightieth Birthday*. Lumbini International Research Institute, Lumbini 2010: 937–950.

SIVARAMAMURTI 1975 = Sivaramamurti, Calambur: *Indien, Kunst und Kultur*. Freiburg 1975 [reprinted: 1981, 1987].

SJÖBERG 1962 = Sjöberg, Lars Olof: *Stephanites und Ichnelates, Überlieferungsgeschichte und Text*. Stockholm–Göteborg–Uppsala 1962.

SK = Haribhadra: *Samarāicca-kahā* (*Samarāditya-kathā*). (1) Hermann Jacobi (ed.): *Haribhadra: Samarāïcca-kahā—A Jaina Prakṛta Work*; Volume I & II. Bibliotheca Indica, Calcutta 1926 [first edition: Calcutta 1908–1923]. (2) Johannes Hertel (transl.): *Ausgewählte Erzählungen aus Hemacandras Pariśiṣṭa-pārvan*. Leipzig 1908: 225–28. (3) Sanskrit translation: Pradyumna: *Samarāditya-saṁkṣepaḥ*, in Johannes Hertel (transl.): *Ausgewählte Erzählungen aus Hemacandras Pariśiṣṭa-pārvan*. Leipzig 1908: 320–344.

SMINÉ 1993 = Sminé, R.E.: 'The Miniatures of a Christian Arabic *Barlaam and Josaphat*: Balamand 147', *Parole de l'Orient* 18 (1993) 171–229.

SONET 1949–52 = Sonet, J.: *Le Roman de Barlaam et Josaphat I, II 1,2*. Namur-Paris 1949–52.

SOUNDARARAJAN 2006 = Soundararajan, Kodayanallur (ed.): *Nagarjunakonda (1954–60), Volume II (The Historical Period)*. Memoirs of the Archaeological Survey of India 75, New Delhi 2006.

STAMMLER 1962 = Stammler, Wolfgang: *Wort und Bild, Studien zu den Wechselbeziehungen zwischen Schrifttum und Bildkunst im Mittelalter*. Berlin 1962.

STERN–BÉNISTI 1961 = Stern, Philippe; Bénisti, Mirelle: *Évolution du style indien d'Amaravati*. Recherches et documents d'art et d'archéologie 7, Publications du Musée Guimet, Paris 1961.

SUGITA 2007 = Sugita, Hideki: 'Chutosekai ni okeru "nisohiyatan"' [The parable of "The Man in the Well" in Arabic and Persian Literature: Transmission and Transformation of a Buddhist Legend in Middle East], *Hikaku Bungaku Kenkyu* (*Studies of Comparative Literature*) [Tokyo] 39 (2007) 68–101.

T 208 = *Tchong king siuan tsa p'i yu* (Nj 1366: Saṁyukāvadāna-sūtra, selected from various Sūtras, Kumārajiva, 405 CE; Mahāyāna-sūtra), ed. Vol. 4, ch. 1, p. 533; trad. Julien 1859–60, No. 53, pp. 190–93; übers. Julien 1903, pp. 97–99; trad. Chavannes 1910–1934, No. 205.

T 1690 = *P'in t'eou lou t'ou lo chö wei yeou t'o yen wang chouo fa king* (Nj. 1347: Sūtra on the cause [Nidāna] of the preaching of the law by Piṇḍola Bharadvāja to the King Udayana, Guṇabhadra, 435–443 CE; Hīnāyāna-sūtra), ed. Vol. 32, p. 787. *T 2121*, *King liu yi siang* (Nj. 1473: [A collection of extracts] on different subjects from Sūtras and Vinaya works, comp. Saṅ-min, 516 CE), ed. Vol. 53, ch. 45, pp. 223c-224a; trad. Chavannes 1910–1934, No. 469.

T 2122 = *Fa yuan tchou lin* (Nj. 1482: "Pearl-grove of the garden of the law"), compiled by Tao shi, 668 CE, ed. Vol. 53, ch. 44, ed. p. 626a-b.

T 2131 = *Fan yi ming yi tsi* (= Mahāvyutpatti, Nj. 1640: A collection of the meanings of the [Sanskrit] names translated [into Chinese]), by Fa yun, 1151 CE, ed. Vol. 54, p. 1141c.

T 217 = *P'i yu king* (Nj. 735: Sūtra spoken by Buddha on [eight] comparisons), ed. Vol. 4, p. 801; trad. Julien, 1859–60, No. 32, pp. 131–34; übers. Julien, 1903, pp. 69–70; trad. Chavannes 1910–1934 Vol. 4: 236–37 (in the commentary on No. 469).

T = *Taishō*. Takakusu, Junjirō; Watanabe, Kaigyoku; Ono, B. (eds.): *Taishō Shinshū Daizōkyō*. Taishō Issaikyō Kankōkai, Tokyo 1924–1934.

TAGLIATESTA 2007 = Tagliatesta, F.: 'Iconography of the Unicorn from India to the Italian Middle Ages', *East ad West* 57 (2007) 175–191.

TAUSCHNER 1959 = Tauschner, Rudolf: *Volksmärchen aus dem Jeyporeland*. Berlin 1959.

TAWNEY–PENZER 1924 = Tawney, C.H.; Penzer, N.M.: *The Ocean of Story being C.H. Towney's Translation of Somadeva's Kathā Sarit Sāgara (or Ocean of Streams of Story)*... Vols. 1–10, London 1924.

VASIL'KOV 1995 = Vasil'kov, Yaroslav Vladimirovich: 'Parable of a Man, Hanging in a Tree, and its Archaic Background', N.V. Gurov, Y.V. Vasilkov (eds.): *Sthāpakaśrāddham, Professor G. A. Zograph Commemoration Volume*. St. Petersburg 1995: 257–69.

VETTER 1960 = Vetter, E.M.: 'Media Vita', *Gesammelte Aufsätze zur Kulturgeschichte Spaniens* [Münster] 16 (1960) 189–227, 217–227.

VH = Saṅghadāsa-gaṇin: *Vāsudeva-hiṇḍī*. (1) Muni Caturvijaya; Muni Punyavijaya (eds.) *Vasudevahiṇḍi-prathama-kaṇḍaṁ*. 1–2, Ātmānand Sabhā, Bhāvanagar 1930–31. (2) Jagdishchandra Jain (transl.): *The Vāsudevahiṇḍī. An Authentic Jain Version of the Bṛhatkathā*. L.D. Series 59, Bharatiya Sanskrit Vidyamandir—L.D. Institute of Indology, Ahmedabad 1977.

VOGEL 1929 = Vogel, Jean Philippe: 'Further Discoveries on the Site of Nāgārjunikoṇḍa', *Annual Bibliography of Indian Archaeology for 1927* [Leyden] (1929) 11–14.

VOGEL 1932 = Vogel, Jean Philippe: 'Excavations at Nāgārjunikoṇḍa', *Annual Bibliography of Indian Archaeology, for the year 1930* [Leyden] (1932) 1–6.

VOGEL 1933 = Vogel, Jean Philippe: 'Unidentified Sculptures from Nāgārjunikoṇḍa', *Annual Bibliography of Indian Archaeology, for the year 1931* [Leyden] (1933) 14–16.

VOGEL 1937 = Vogel, Jean Philippe: 'The Man in the Well and some Other Subjects Illustrated at Nāgārjunikoṇḍa', *Revue des Arts Asiatiques* [Paris] 11 (1937) 109–121.

VOLK 2003 = Volk, Robert: 'Das Fortwirken der Legende von Barlaam und Ioasaph in der byzantinischen Hagiographie, insbesondere in den Werken des Symeon Metaphrastes', *Jahrbuch der Östereichischen Byzantinistik* [Wien] 53 (2003) 127–169.

VOLK 2006 = Volk, Robert: 'Medizinisches im Barlaam-Roman. Ein Streifzug durch den hochsprachlichen griechischen Text. Seine Vorläufer, Parallelen und Nachdichtungen', *Byzantinische Zeitschrift* [München] 99.1 (2006) 145–93.

VOLK 2009 = Volk, Robert: *Die Schriften des Johannes von Damaskos. Herausgegeben vom Byzantinischen Institut der Abtei Scheyern* 6.1, *Historia animae utilis de Barlaam et Ioasaph (spuria)*. Einführung von Robert Volk. Berlin–New York 2009.

WEHRHAHN-STAUCH / RDK = WEHRHAHN-STAUCH, L.: 'Einhorn', in: RDK Vol. 4: cols. 1504–44.

WEIZSÄCKER 1899 = Weizsäcker, Paul: 'Mittelalterliche Bildwerke von „Mann im Brunnen"', *Zeitschrift für den deutschen Unterricht* [Leipzig] 13 (1899) 736–40.

WINTERNITZ 1909 / 1927 = Winternitz, Moriz: *Geschichte der Indischen Literatur*, Vol. 1. Leipzig 1909 / English translation: *A History of Indian Literature*. Calcutta 1927.

WOLFF 1837 = Wolff, Philipp: *Calila und Dimna oder die Fabeln Bidpai's*. Morgenländische Erzählungen 1, Stuttgart 1837.

WRIGHT 1884 = Wright, William: *The Book of Kalilah and Dimnah translated from Arabic into Syriac*. Oxford–London 1884.

YANASE 1987 = Yanase, Mutsuo: 'Tsuki-no-Nezumi Hi-no-Nezumi', *Sophia* 36–II (1987) 163–177.

ZIN 2004	= Zin, Monika: 'The Mūkapaṅgu Story in the Madras Government Museum: The Problem of the Textual Affiliations of the Narrative Reliefs in Amaravati and Nagarjunikonda', *Annali dell' Istituto Universitario Orientale*, 64 [Napoli] (2004).157–180.
ZIN 2006	= Zin, Monika: *Mitleid und Wunderkraft. Schwierige Bekehrungen und ihre Ikonographie im indischen Buddhismus*. Wiesbaden 2006.
ZIN–SCHLINGLOFF 2007	= Zin, Monika; Schlingloff, Dieter: *Saṁsāracakra, Das Rad der Wiedergeburten in der indischen Überlieferung*. Düsseldorf 2007.
ZOTENBERG 1886	= Zotenberg, M.H.: *Notices sur le livre de Barlaam et Josaphat*. Paris 1886.

The Body and the Cosmos in Jaina Mythology and Art

PIOTR BALCEROWICZ
(University of Warsaw)

1. This paper is an attempt to trace down the historical and conceptual background of an image of 'the cosmic man' (*loka-puruṣa*) frequently found in Jaina art, especially reoccurring in recent centuries.[1] The idea of 'the cosmic man', closely linked to Jaina cosmography, sees the universe in the shape of a human being, usually male, in an upright position, with his leg spread out in support and his hands resting on his hips. The question is how and when the idea developed.

2.1. An alternative and probably, for centuries, most typical image of the Jaina universe is found, e.g., in a classical work on Jaina cosmology *The Structure of the Universe* (*Loka-vibhāga*) by the Digambara Siṁha-sūri (ca 11th/12th century):

> 'Fixed in the middle of infinite empty space [surrounding it] from all directions there stands a tripartite world. In its median section there is the middle world. The middle [world] resembles a thin frame drum (*jhallarī*). The lower [world] is like an oblong reed stool. The upper [world] has a form of the *mr̥d-aṅga* drum. In such a way was the world described by the Noble One [i.e. by the Mahāvīra].'[2]

---

[1] For a description of the image, see e.g. KIRFEL (1920: 209–210), SCHUBRING (1962: 204–206, § 103), CAILLAT–KUMAR (1981: 19–21), CORT (2009), JSK, III: entry *Loka*. See also useful entries on the notion of *puruṣa* and *loka*, respectively, in Indian tradition in KTK: BÄUMER (2001) and MISRA–SHARMA (2001).

[2] LVi 1.3, 6:

samantato 'py anantasya viyato madhyāmâśritaḥ /
tri-vibhāga-sthito lokas tiryag-loko 'sya madhyagaḥ //
jhallarī-sadr̥śo madhyo vetrâsana-samo 'dharaḥ /
ūrdhvo mr̥d-aṅga-saṁsthāna iti loko 'rhatôditaḥ //

Art, Myths and Visual Culture of South Asia
Warsaw Indological Studies 4 (2011) 95–151.

In its imagery, the shape of the universe, the base of which is apparently circular, goes back to a centuries-old tradition, which is recorded as early as in the *Viyāha-pannatti* (*Bhagavatī-sūtra*). The relevant passage contains a dialogue between a senior monk follower of Pārśva and Mahāvīra on the structure and infinity of the world. In the dialogue, Mahāvīra recalling the authority of Pārśva, the earliest strand of Jaina tradition, explains the tripartite structure of the world as follows:

> 'The venerable Pārśva, the one to be accepted by the people, described the world as eternal, without a beginning or end, limited (i.e. of definite size), surrounded [by the non-world]. In the lower part it is expanded, in the middle it is tight, in the upper part it is wide: below it has a form of a pallet, in the middle [it is like] a narrow grip of an excellent thunderbolt weapon, in the upper part it is placed upwards in the shape of a *mr̥d-aṅga* drum.'[3]

The Śvetāmbara Umāsvāti (ca. 400–500 CE) describes the shape of the world (*loka*) in a similar style:

> 'The two fundamental masses of the medium of motion and of the medium of rest are the causes of the extensive structure of the world. On account of their particular extension which [sets] the fixed rule [limiting] the external manifestation of the world, the world has the shape of an hourglass-shaped stand[4] or of a thunderbolt weapon (*vajra*). The lower world has the shape of the lower half of a cow's neck. ... The

[3] Viy$_2$ 5.9.2, p. 228.3–6: [2] *pāseṇam arahayā purisâdāṇīeṇaṁ sāsate loe aṇādī aṇavadagge paritte parivuḍe, heṭṭhā vitthiṇṇe, majjhe saṁkhitte, uppiṁ visāle, ahe paliyaṁka-saṁṭhite, majjhe vara-vaira-viggahite, uppiṁ uddha-muiṁgâkāra-saṁṭhite.* Cf. Viy$_2$ 11.10.10, p. 527.17–19: *supaiṭṭaka-saṁṭhie loe pannatte, taṁ jahā—heṭṭhā vitthiṇṇe, majjhe saṁkhitte jahā satta-masae paṭhame uddesae jāva aṁtaṁ karei.*—'The structure of the world is expounded as firmly established, namely in the lower part it is expanded, in the middle it is tight etc.'

Albeit the passage is assigned to the fifth canonical period by OHIRA (1994: 77, § 150), i.e. the second half of the fifth CE (OHIRA (1994: 35–37, § 111–119)), this dating seems rather questionable and arbitrary, and the image itself is certainly much earlier, although the passage occurs in a later textual strata.

[4] The stand is apparently constructed of reeds placed obliquely upward, tied in the middle, so that they form two flat circles, upper and lower, at their ends. The structure is explained in TṬ 3.6, p. 247.18–19, as follows: ***supratiṣṭhakaḥ*** *śara-yantrakaṁ yatra vyavasthapya vāsāṁsi dhūpyante, tat kila bahv anuharati loka-sanniveśasya.*—'An hourglass-shaped stand is a tool made of reed placed on which clothes are perfumed [with incense]. That is resembled, as they say, by the composition of the world.'

middle world has the shape of a thin frame drum (*jhallarī*). The upper world has the shape of a *mṛd-aṅga* drum.'[5]

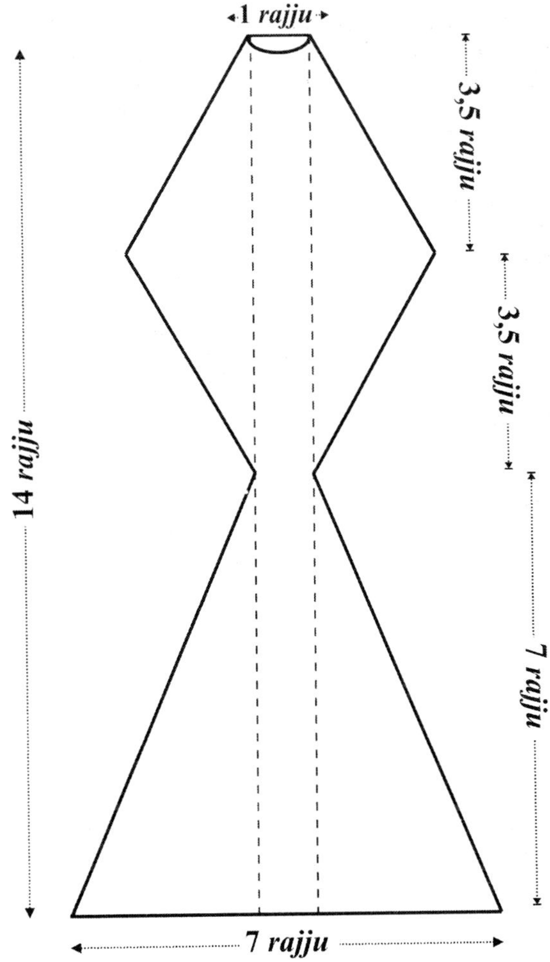

Fig. 1. Jaina world (*loka*) and its dimensions

[5] TBh$_1$ 3.6, p. 77.14–78.5: *dharmâdharmâsti-kāyau loka-vyavasthā-hetū. tayor avagāha-viśeṣāl lokânubhāva-niyamāt supratiṣṭhaka-vajrâkṛtir lokaḥ. adho-loko go-kandharâdharârdhâkṛtiḥ*[a]. ... *tiryag-loko jhallary-ākṛtiḥ. ūrdhva-loko mṛd-aṅgâkṛtir iti.*

[a] TṬ *ad loc.*, p. 146.26–27 and 247.27: *go-kandharârdhâkṛtiḥ.*

The descriptions roughly refer to a classical well-known structure, measured with immensely long units called 'cords' (*rajju*)[6] (fig. 1), the topmost semicircular shape representing the world of the liberated beings (*siddha-loka*).[7]

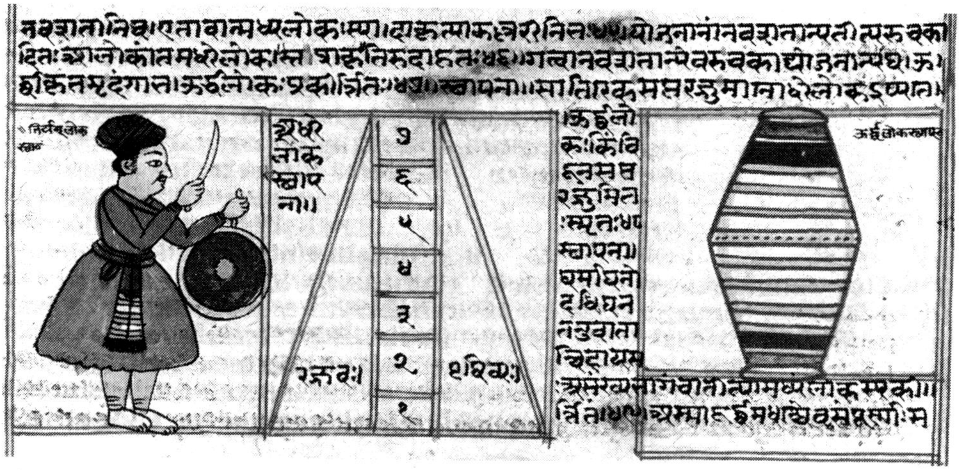

Fig. 2. Reproduced after CAILLAT–KUMAR (1981: 51). The original description of the drawing, CAILLAT–KUMAR (1981: 50): '8. The World (loka). The world has three main parts. They are shown here side by side, and not one above the other, as is more usual. In the figure on the left, a man is holding the cymbal which symbolises the middle world. It is a disc which is theoretically horizontal (*tiryag-loka*), but is always represented as seen from above. The illustration in the centre shows, without paying too much attention to proportion, the pyramid of the seven hells which make up the lower world (*adho-loka*); the picture on the right shows, in the form of a drum (*mṛdaṅga*) standing on end, the upper world (*ūrdhva-loka*) with its various levels of heavens.'

2.2. The building blocks of the universe frequently mentioned are solids in the shape of two musical instruments: *mṛd-aṅga* and *jhallarī*, well-known in mediaeval times and traditionally classified as membranophones (*avanaddha-vādya*)[8], or optionally an hourglass-shaped stand. Both the musical instruments are mentioned by Śāraṅgadeva (1210–1247) in his classical exposition of music *Saṅgīta-ratnâkara*

---

[6] See the often-quoted explanation by COLEBROOKE (1837: II, 221): 'This is explained to be a measure of space, through which the gods are able to travel in six months at the rate of 2,057,152 *yojanas* (of 2000 *crośa* each) in the twinkling of an eye.'

[7] For a good drawing that depicts all the proportions and dimensions, see JSK, III: 439 (*Tīn Lok*), vide infra p. 100. Comp. also the respective comprehensive entry on *loka*, JSK, III: 428–491.

[8] Cf. SINGH (1995: 61) and BANERJI (1976: 37).

(SRĀ 3.216c–220b), in a section describing the *kutapa* ensemble. The names of drums are also said to be allegedly mentioned earlier in the *Naṁdi-sutta* (*Nandī-sūtra*).[9] The *jhallarī* drum is known to Siddhasena-gaṇin (seventh century, perhaps the same as Siddhasena Gandhahastin, a pupil of Bhāsvāmin), who explains in his commentary on Umāsvāmin's *Tattvârtha-sūtra* (ca. 350–400):

> 'The thin frame drum (*jhallarī*) is a particular instrument which has a flat surface on its all sides and is of equal breadth of the outside frame.'[10]

Of course, what remains unchanged in the descriptions are the names of the instruments, which does not have to suggest that the instruments themselves remained the same throughout the centuries: we know that the construction of instruments may change over time although the names themselves remain the same. The tripartite structure of the universe finds its unusual graphic image in a sixteenth-century illustration, in which the three sections are displayed horizontally side by side, not vertically (fig. 2).

A variant of the shape of the universe was that of a rectangular or oblong base (fig. 3). This was most typical structure epitomised in the modern symbol of Jainism, adopted by various Jaina groupings in 1975 on the occasion of the commemoration of 2500th year of the *nirvāṇa* of Mahāvīra Vardhamāna (fig. 4).

3. However, that was not the only depiction of the universe. A rival image was that of 'the cosmic man' (*loka-puruṣa*), which inscribes the whole universe within the shape of a human being. CAILLAT–KUMAR (1981: 20) in their monograph on Jaina art and cosmology express the conviction that the idea occurs first in the later mediaeval period, or even later:

> 'Measurements are given in units of length which baffle the mind: the compilers of the Middle Ages employed the "rope" (*rajju*), which is defined as the distance covered by a god flying non-stop for six months at a speed of 1,057,152 yojanas (say 10,000,000 miles) a second. … At a later period the loka was represented in the form of a "cosmic man" (*loka-puruṣa*), who is frequently illustrated with a total height of fourteen rajjus' (emphasis—P.B.).

---

[9] See SINGH (1995: 21). This would be a rather early reference to the instruments. However, I have failed to spot the passage in printed editions.

[10] TṬ 3.6, p. 248.6–8: ***jhallary-ākṛtis tiryag-lokaḥ***. *jhallarī sarvatra sama-talā tulya-viṣkambhâyāmā vāditra-viśeṣaḥ*.

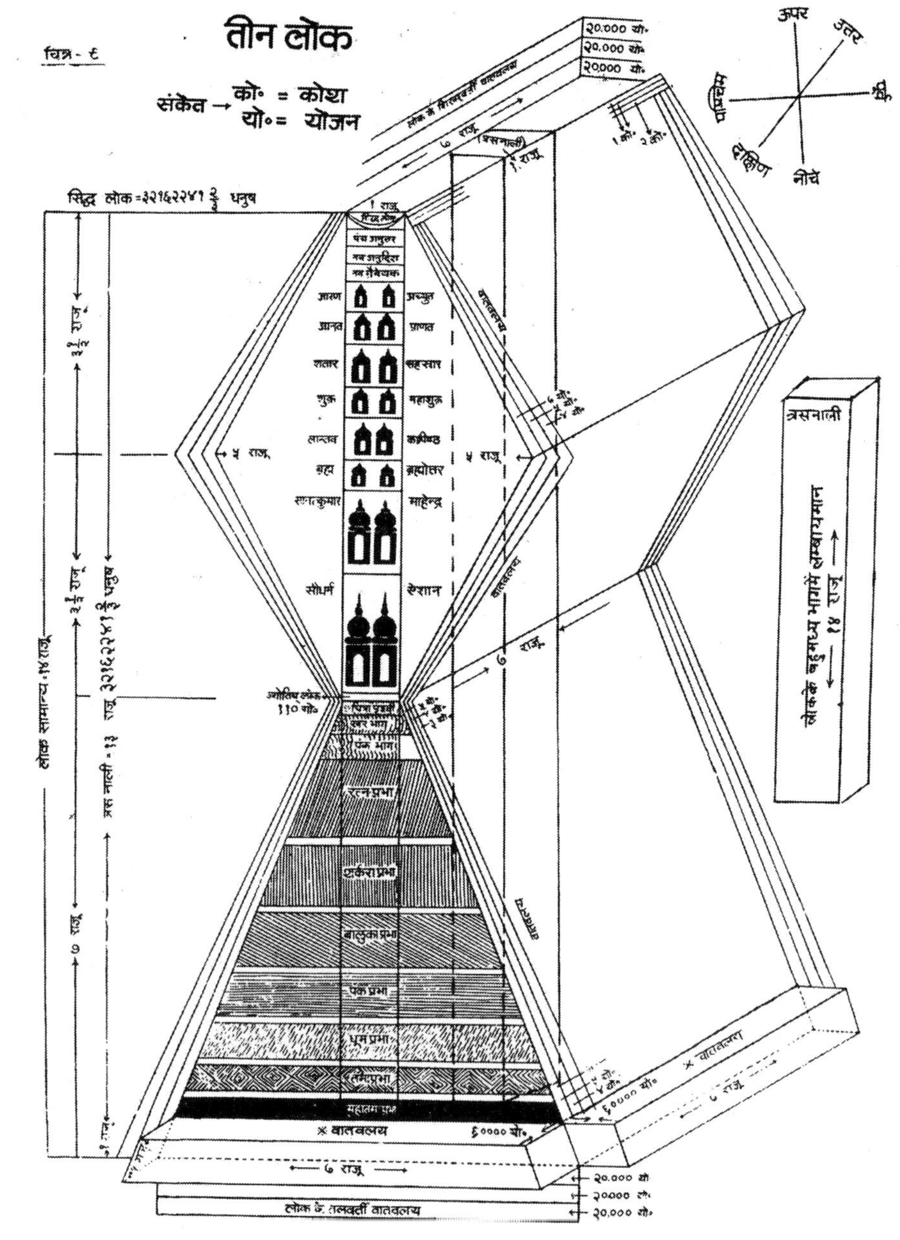

Fig. 3. Jaina world (*loka*) and its dimensions. After JSK, III: 439 (*Tīn Lok*).

The opinion is echoed by Paul DUNDAS (2002: 90)[11]:

> 'Early Jain cosmography, as found in the Śvetāmbara scriptures, provides only sketchy information about the dimensions of the *loka*. Totally absent is any reference to the "rope" (*rajju*), the unit of measurement found in the later cosmographical treatises, which is the distance travelled by a god flying for six months at a speed of ten million miles a second. Nor is there any mention of the *loka-puruṣa*, the universe in the shape of a giant man (*puruṣa*), or sometimes woman, measuring fourteen ropes from head to food, which is frequently depicted in Jain art from about the sixteenth century onwards' (emphasis—P.B.).

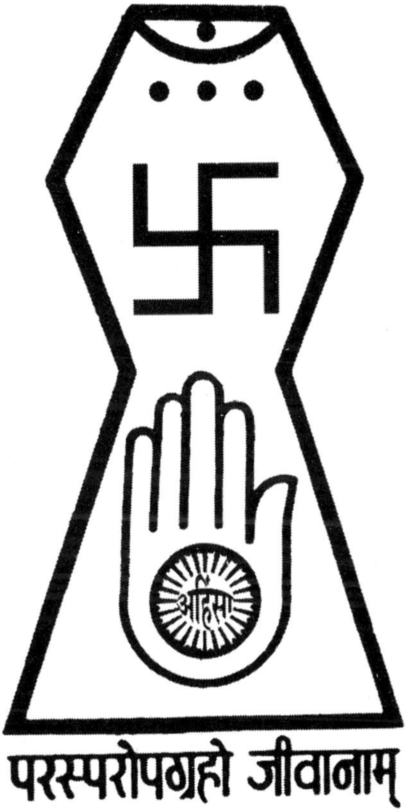

Fig. 4. Modern symbol of Jainism, adopted in 1975, with the shape of the Jaina world (*loka*).

[11] Who does not consider it necessary to mention the source of his remark, which is, in part, almost a quotation.

Figs. 5–7 are standard exemplifications of such images, which have indeed been quite popular. The images were usually made either on paper or cloth, and can be found in several collections, in India and outside, one of less known being a few cloth images at the Museu do Oriente and Fundação Oriente in Lisbon. Or particular interest is Fig. 7, where instead of 'the cosmic man', we find 'the cosmic woman', a representation which is very rare, but not unique.

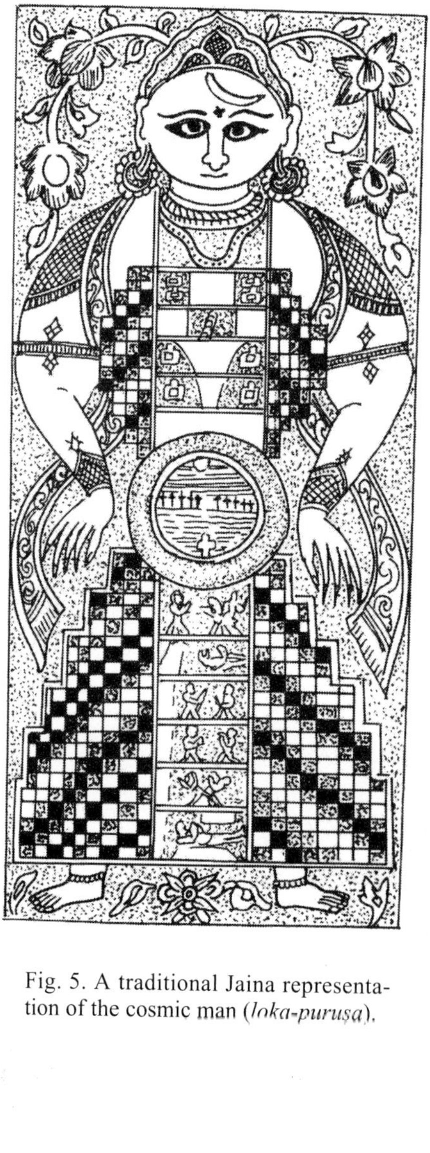

Fig. 5. A traditional Jaina representation of the cosmic man (*loka-puruṣa*).

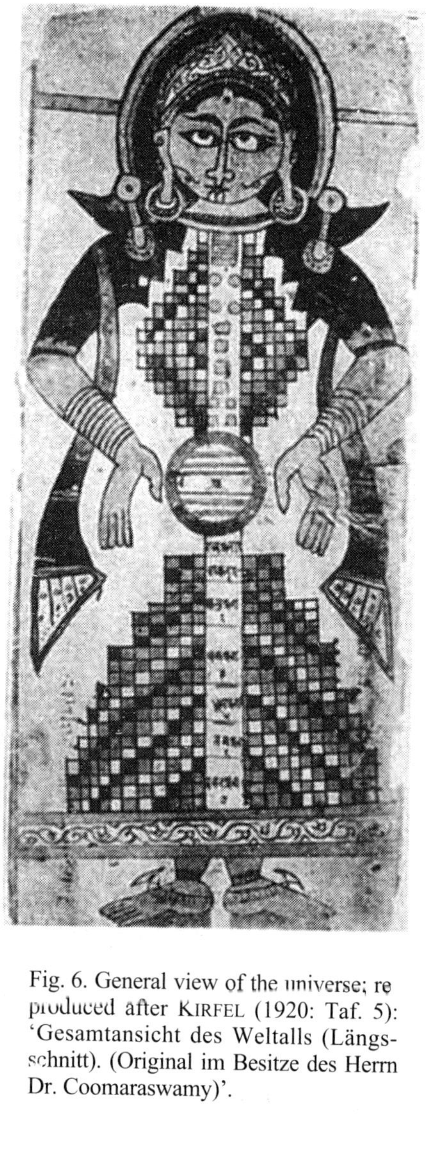

Fig. 6. General view of the universe; reproduced after KIRFEL (1920: Taf. 5): 'Gesamtansicht des Weltalls (Längsschnitt). (Original im Besitze des Herrn Dr. Coomaraswamy)'.

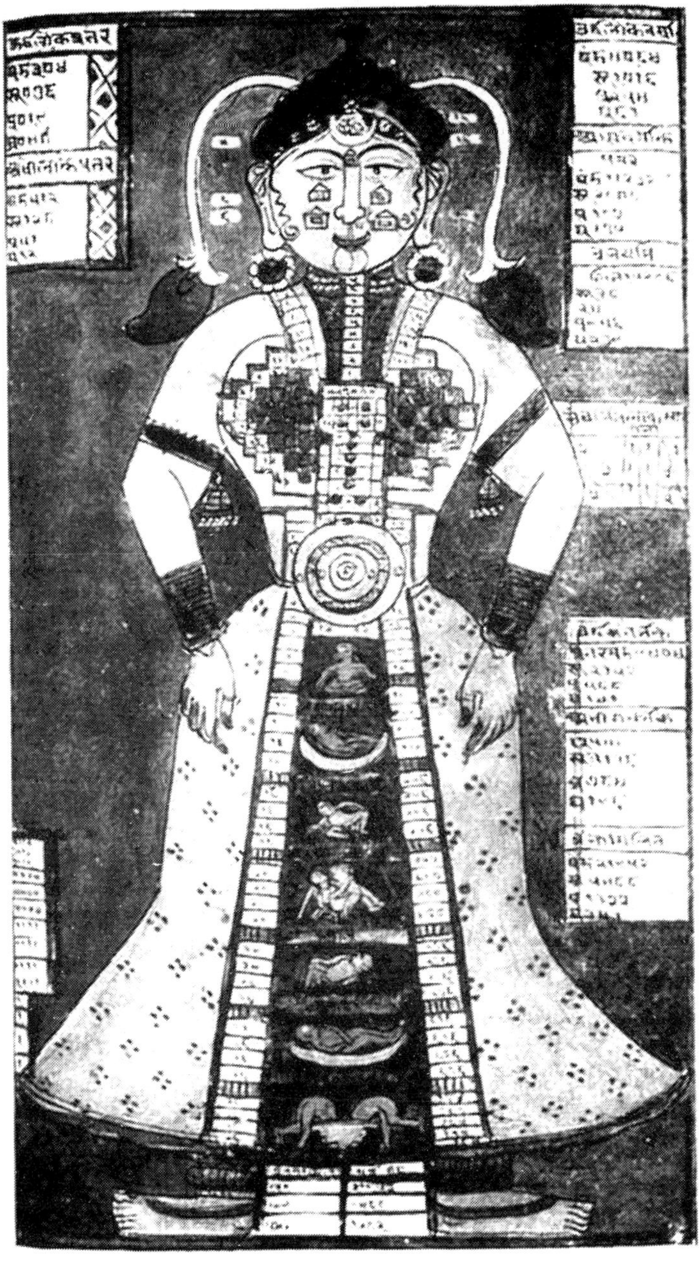

Fig. 7. The cosmic man (*loka-puruṣa*). Reproduced after GLASENAPP (1925: Tafel 15): 'The World in the Form of a Woman'.

Colette CAILLAT and Ravi KUMAR reproduced a few more images to illustrate the emergence of the idea of 'the cosmic man' in Jaina art that are said to have occurred around the sixteenth and seventeenth centuries, most notably nos.: '9. The World. [Gouache on paper, XVIth century, Gujarat].' It is also reproduced as a drawing in MISRA–SHARMA (2001: 139): 'Figure 1: Jaina Lokaprusa, XVI cent. Gujarat' (1981: 52–53); '10. The length and dimensions of the cosmic man (*loka-puruṣa*). [Gouache on paper, XVIIth century, Gujarat]' (1981: 54–55).

Other illustrations of the *loka-puruṣa* can be found e.g. in: KIRFEL (1920: Taf. 5) reproduced here; GLASENAPP (1925: Tafel 15) reproduced here; Umkant P. SHAH (1978): 'Vastrapaṭa (Cloth Painting) showing Lokapuruṣa (cosmos) and hells. Saṁvegī Upāśraya, Ahmedabad, c. 17th cent. A.D' (plate 93), 'From Paṭa (paper) of Lokapuruṣa, d.V.S. 1858 = 1801 AD. L.D. no. 27824' (plate 156; the section shows the upper middle part of the universe); ALPHEN (2000: 50, photo: Hugues Servé); MISRA–SHARMA (2001: 139): 'Figure 1: Jaina Lokapruṣa, XVI cent. Gujarat'; GRANOFF (2009: 34, 54, 60–61, 71).

The ample sources that emerge after the sixteenth century may easily suggest that the idea of the cosmic man appeared first around that time, and this is the conviction shared by the scholars quoted above.

4.1. However, a closer examination of textual sources will easily reveal that the idea of *loka-puruṣa* was much earlier. For instance, Siddhasena-gaṇin alias Gandhahastin, already referred to, describes the shape and structure of the world as follows:

> 'In this [passage] before, to begin with, the structure of the lower world as such is described. ... Subsequently, the structure of the middle world [is described] step by step, beginning with the Rose Apple Island and the Salty Ocean. Later, in the fourth [chapter], the structure of the upper world [is described]. In such a way [we have] the tripartite world, which occurs as an assemblage of the five fundamental masses, which is characterised as a place that holds living beings and lifeless elements, which has a form of a man who stands in a posture of spread-out legs and with the pair of his arms resting on the hips...'[12]

There is no doubt that what Siddhasena Gandhahastin has in mind is a well-developed image of the cosmic man (*loka-puruṣa*). We can still go at least two centuries

[12] TṬ 3.1, p. 229.10–13: *tatra prāk tāvad adho-loka-svarūpam eva pr̥thivī-bhedenôcyate. ... tatas tiryag-loka-svarūpaṁ jambū-dvīpa-lavaṇâdi prakrameṇa, paścāc caturthe urdhva-loka-svarūpam iti, evam ayaṁ tri-vibhāgaḥ pañcâsti-kāya-samudaya-vr̥ttir jīvâjīvâdhāra-kṣetra-lakṣaṇo vaiśākha-sthāna-sthiti-kaṭi-stha-kara-yugma-puruṣâkr̥tir lokaḥ...*

back to Umāsvāti, the author of the *Dissertation on the delight derived from tranquillity* (*Praśama-rati-prakaraṇa*). In the section on the six fundamental masses, he states that all of them together constitute the cosmic man (*loka-puruṣa*):

> 'Living beings and lifeless elements [constitute] what is known as six-fold substance[13]. That is the cosmic man. He stands in a posture of spread-out legs and with the pair of his arms resting on the hips.'[14]

Commenting on the passage, a certain Haribhadra-sūri (first half of the twelve century) explains the image of this verse:

> '[Now we comment on the phrase:] **The cosmic man**. "The cosmic man" means [the world that looks] like a man, because it [stands] in such a peculiar position. [Next phrase to comment on is]: **a posture of spread-out legs**. It is a posture of an archer with spread-out legs: viz. it is a man standing upright with his two legs (lit. shanks) wide apart. His two hands are bent and rest on hips.'[15]

The term 'posture of spread-out legs' (*vaiśākha-sthāna*), occurring in TṬ 3.1 and PRP 210, is a direct allusion to the tree and its branches, for the term is explained to derive from *viśākha*, i.e. 'having spread-out branches (*śākhā*).'[16]

---

[13] The six substances, made up of the five fundamental masses (*asti-kāya*)—living beings, medium of motion, medium of rest, space and matter—as well as of time as the sixth substance are enumerated by Umāsvāmin in TS, see $TS_{śvet}$ 5.1–2, 38: [1] *ajīva-kāyā dharmâdharmâkāśa-pudgalāḥ.* [2] *dravyāṇi jīvaś ca.* [38] *kālaś ca ity eke.* = TS_{dig} 5.1–3, 39: [1] *ajīva-kāyā dharmâdharmâkāśa-pudgalāḥ.* [2] *dravyāṇi.* [3] *jīvaś ca.* [39]. *kālaś ca.* There was a dispute among the Śvetāmbaras as to whether to include time among the substances: we can see that Umāsvāti, the author of PRP and TBh, was of the opinion, as the Digambaras unanimously were, that also time is a substance (*dravya*). However, the reading of $TS_{śvet}$ 5.1–2, 38 ('Some [philosophers maintain] that also time is [a substance]') indicates that Jaina thinkers were not so unanimous. However, compare Umāsvāti's description of the world consisting of *five* fundamental masses in TBh_1 3.6, p. 66.12: *pañcâsti-kāya-samudāyo lokaḥ.*—'The world is a combination of the five fundamental masses,' which stands in contradiction with the above quoted passage of PRP 210, a text traditionally ascribed to the same author.

[14] PRP 210:

jīvâjīvā dravyam iti ṣaḍ-vidhaṁ bhavati loka-puruṣo 'yam /
vaiśākha-sthāna-sthaḥ puruṣa iva kaṭi-stha-kara-yugmaḥ //

[15] PRṬ 210: ***loka-puruṣaḥ*** *puruṣa iva loka-puruṣaḥ prativiśiṣṭa-sthānatvāt.* ... ***vaiśākha-sthāna*** *iti. vaiśākhaṁ dhānuṣkasya sthānakam. ūrdhvam avasthitaḥ puruṣo vikṣipta-jaṅgā-dvayaḥ* (recte: °*-jaṅghā-*°) *kaṭyāṁ vyavasthāpitā-kuñcita-hasta-dvayo yathā tadval loka-puruṣa iti.*

[16] Cf. Cf. BṛS 94.02ab: *vaiśākhe nirupahate vṛkṣe.*

Interestingly, the *vaiśākha-sthāna* position resembles the posture of *kāyôtsarga* (Pkt. *kāussagga*), the earliest ascetic and meditative position practised by Jaina mendicants, which belongs to the six fundamental obligatory rites (Pkt. *āvassaya*, Skt. *āvaśyaka*, see ĀvS 5).

Further, immediately after the description of the universe in the form of the cosmic man (PRP 210), Umāsvāti proceeds to give a detailed description of the three sections of the universe, which either may be interpreted an explication of what the cosmic man looks like or is an explicit reference to an alternative model of the universe, current in the fifth century, in the shape of three vessel-like or bucket-like solids:

> 'As regards this [universe in the shape of a cosmic man, people] describe the lower world as having the shape of a bucket facing down (sc. upside down), the [middle] traverse world as a plate, and the upper [world] as an upward structure [in the shape] of a bucket.'[17]

What we find here is a more or less a traditional description of the universe, i.e. the universe conceived in the form of two vessels, or solids, placed on top of each other. Interestingly, Umāsvāti treats the image of the *loka-puruṣa* as primary not only because he mentions it first, but also because he explicitly states that 'people describe' (*varṇayanti*) the cosmic man as having a form of two buckets with a plate in-between.

There can be no doubt that the idea of the cosmic man (*loka-puruṣa*) was already developed in the fifth century. A similar conclusion, albeit adopted for different reasons (*vide infra*, p. 109), is also expressed by Suzuko OHIRA (1994: 79, § 160), who seems to suggest that the 'profile of the World-man', i.e. *loka-puruṣa*, 'must have occurred when the Jaina-centred world view was established,' viz. 'the late fifth century.'[18]

4.2. The opinion expressed by Suzuko OHIRA will have to be reconsidered though. A closer analysis of the terminology occurring in Jaina cosmography of the period prior to the fifth century also reveals that it must have derived from the idea of the cosmic man. Accordingly, there are at least the following 'body parts' of the universe (*loka*):

---

[17] PRP 211:

tatrâdho-mukha-mallaka-saṁsthānaṁ varṇayanty adho-lokam /
sthālam iva tiryag-lokam ūrdhvam atha mallaka-samudgam //

The verse is also quoted in TṬ 3.6, p. 247.22–25.

[18] See OHIRA (1994: 37, § 119).

— The 'neck' (*grīvā*): it is reflected in the class of divine beings called *graiveya* / *graiveyaka* / *gevijja* ('neck-gods') and their abodes called *gevijja-vimāṇa-patthaḍā* ('layers of the abode of the "neck-gods"')[19]. the connection between the name of the 'neck-gods' and the 'neck' of cosmic man is highlighted by Umāsvāti at a later period: 'Further, neck-gods are located in the spatial units of the neck of the cosmic man, being the support of the neck, [and therefore they are also called]: "neckish", "neck-like", "neck-born", "neck-based".'[20] Such a detailed explanation, approximating an etymologising attempt, shows that the name was not coincidental and the author was aware of its relation to the concept of the cosmic universe.

— The 'artery' or 'vein' of the world (*loka-nāḍī*). This is the middlemost vertical artery of the universe, a kind of 'vertebral column' of the cosmos which also serves as a transport stretch for the transmigrating souls between death and new birth as well as for souls that move up to the world of the liberated beings (*siddha-loka*) after shedding all karmic matter. Also Umāsvāti makes a clear reference to the cosmic 'vein': '[Divine beings] inhabiting the highest abode [of the world] can see the whole artery of the world.'[21]

— The navel of the world (*nābhī*), which is Mount Meru (*meru-parvata*). We find a reference to Meru as the navel of the world in the Canon, where Meru is referred to by a number of other names, such as Mandara etc., but where it is also explicitly said to 'the navel of the world in the middle [of the world].'[22] Also Umāsvāmin mentions Meru in the same context: 'In the centre of these [concentric continents and oceans] there is located [the continent] Jambudvīpa, 100,000 miles in diameter, with the [Mount] Meru as its navel.'[23] His commentator Umāsvāti explains: 'Likewise, the [Mount] Meru is placed like a navel in the shape of a golden cone, immersed with 1,000 miles below the surface of the earth, risen

---

[19] See Ṭhāṇ 232, p. 90.1–9, and TS/TBh 4.20.

[20] TBh 4.20, p. 106.15–17: *graiveyās* {TṬ: *graiveyakās*} *tu loka-puruṣasya grīvā-pradeśa-viniviṣṭā grīvā-bharaṇa-bhūtā graivā grīvyā graiveyā graiveyakā iti.*

[21] TBh 4.21, p. 108.5–6: *anuttara-vimāna-vāsinas tu kṛtsnāṁ loka-nāḍīṁ paśyanti.* The commentator Siddhasena-gaṇin leaves no doubt that 'the divine beings that inhabit the five highest abodes [of the world] can see the whole vein of the world, located in the very centre of the world, but not the whole world [as such]' (TṬ *ad loc.*: ***anuttara-vimāna**-pañcaka-**nivāsinas tu** samastām **loka-nāḍīṁ paśyanti** loka-madhya-vartinīṁ, na punar lokam iti.*). For a wider context of the *nāḍi* / *nāḍī* see p. 127 and n. 84.

[22] Samav 16 [1], p. 356.2–3: *maṁdara meru ... majjhe lokassa nābhī.* See also KIRFEL (1920: 233) makes a reference to *Jambū-dvīpa-prajñapti* Bl. 269 and *Loka-prakāśa* p. 610, where likewise Mount Meru is said to be the navel of the world (*nābhī lokasya*).

[23] TS 3.9: *tan-madhye meru-nābhir vṛtto yojana-śata-sahasra-viṣkambho jambū-dvīpaḥ.*

99,000 [miles above the surface] and the upper [part above the surface] is spread 10,000 [miles in all directions (sc. thick at the base)].'[24]

— The skin, or the outer limit, set to the extension of the cosmic body. The idea of the space limited by the skin is explicitly expressed, at a slightly later period, by Siddhasena Gandhahastin, while referring to a uniquely Jaina idea: 'The contraction and expansion of the soul [takes place] only within the limits of the inflated expanse of the skin [of the cosmic body].'[25] The soul consists of innumerable spatial units, just as the world (*loka*) does, but it can eventually occupy a space delimited by an external boundary of the skin. Therefore, the actual size of the embodied soul is determined by its body and can be as little as the size of atom or as big as the size of the world. In the latter case the boundary that sets limits to the expansion of the soul is the 'skin' of the world. Behind Siddhasena Gandhahastin's statement lies the belief that the soul, a while before the final moment of liberation, first expands in size till it reaches the boundary of the world (*loka*) and then immediately shrinks in order to shake off karmic matter that envelops it, a process which is called *samudghāta* (*vide infra* p. 129). Although the 'skin' (*carman*) of the world in not mentioned explicitly by Umāsvāti, the idea of a boundary of such a kind is implicit in what he says: 'An lamp burning due to the material cause of fire immersed in oil can illuminate even a large space of an attic, but [can] also [illuminate]: a tiny [space of the size of] a casket [when] covered by the casket, a tiny [space of the size of] a bushel [when] covered by a bushel, a tiny [space of the size of] a trough [when] covered by a trough, a tiny [space of the size of] a bucket [when] covered by a bucket, a tiny [space of the size of] a palm [when] covered by a palm. Exactly in the same way, due to contraction and expansion of [its] spatial units, the living being pervades, or penetrates, the five-fold aggregate of the body, either a gigantic or infinitesimal, which is an accumulation of spatial units of the medium of motion, the medium of rest, space, matter and souls.'[26] The comparison of the soul filling the body to the light of a lamp filling the space, probably of Upaniṣadic origin, is quite significant as we shall see later (p. 126 f.). The larger space pervaded by the body referred to with the phrase 'a gigantic … aggregate of the body, which is an accu-

---

[24] TBh 3.9, p. 80.8–10: *merur api kāñcana-sthāla-nābhir iva vr̥tto yojana-sahasram adho-dharaṇi-talam avagāḍho nava-navaty-ucchrito daśādho vistr̥taḥ sahasram uparîti.*

[25] TṬ 5.16: *carma-maṇḍalasyêva saṁhāra-visargāv iti.*

[26] TBh 5.16, p. 124.3–8: *taila-varty-agny-upādāna-pravr̥ddhaḥ pradīpo mahatīm api kūṭâgāra-śālāṁ prakāśayaty aṇvīm api māṇikâvr̥taḥ māṇikaṁ droṇâvr̥to droṇam āḍhakâvr̥taś câḍhakaṁ prasthâvr̥taḥ prasthaṁ pāṇyâvr̥to pāṇim iti. evam eva pradeśānāṁ saṁhāra-visargābhyāṁ jīvo mahāntam aṇuṁ vā pañcavidhaṁ śarīra-skandhaṁ dharmâdharmâkāśa-pudgala-jīva-pradeśa-samudāyaṁ vyāpnotîty avagāhata ity arthaḥ.*

mulation of spatial units of the medium of motion, the medium of rest, space, matter and souls' (*mahāntam ... śarīra-skandhaṁ dharmâdharmâkāśa-pudgala-jīva-pradeśa-samudāyaṁ*) is nothing but the whole world, for the five elements that constitute the larger body, mentioned in the passage, are the five fundamental masses (*asti-kāya*)[27], and these make up the whole world.[28] Accordingly, during the *samudghāta* process, the soul expands until it reaches the boundary of the world and thereby permeates the whole world for a single time unit.

Such a 'corporeal' terminology—neck (*grīvā*), vein (*nāḍī*), navel (*nābhī*), skin (*carman*)—that is both so closely embedded in cosmological beliefs and establishes a correlation between the world structure and body parts must have been established some time earlier than the period of Umāsvāti, later strata of the *Ṭhāṇaṁga-sutta* and the *Samavāyaṁga-sutta*, for the cosmology in question is clearly not a product of the fifth century. And that would push the idea of the cosmic man even much earlier.

4.3. The list of body parts of the universe, or of the parts of the universe that derive their names from respective parts of human body, elaborated in § 4.2., can still be augmented. Suzuko OHIRA (1994: 78–79) draws our attention to an interesting passage of the *Bhagavatī-sūtra* (Viy$_1$ 6.5 *sū* 240–241) which describes certain peculiar cosmic structures that enfold a part of the universe in unfathomable darkness. The first of them is 'the body of darkness' (Skt. *tamo-kāya*, Pkt. *tamu-kkae*):

> 'This body of darkness rises here upwards in a line, one space-unit thick, from the water surface, extending for 42.000 miles beyond Tawny-watered Ocean (Aruṇôdaka), which lies beyond the island of Aruṇavara, striding over [circular] islands and oceans [that extend] endlessly in the horizon outside of the Island of Jambudvīpa. It goes 17.210 miles upwards, then from there it spreads on both sides, envelops all four lower heavens (*kalpa*): Saudharma, Aiśana, Sānatkumāra and Māhendra; this body of darkness contracts, when it reaches the plane of the abode of the Ṛiṣṭa heaven in the heaven of Brahmā.'[29]

---

[27] See TS 5.1–2 (see n. 13).

[28] See TBh 3.6, p. 66.12: *pañcâsti-kāya-samudāyo lokaḥ.*—'The world is a combination of the five fundamental masses.' For the world (*loka*) as an aggregate of the five fundamental masses (*asti-kāya*) see also TṬ 3.1, p. 229.10–13, quoted in n. 12, for the translation see p. 104.

[29] Viy$_2$ 6.5.2: *jaṁbu-ddīvasa dīvassa bahiyā tiriyam asaṁkhejje dīva-samudde vītivaittā aruṇavarassa dīvassa bāhirillāo vetiyaṁtāo aruṇôdayaṁ samuddaṁ bāyālīsaṁ joyaṇa-sahassāṇi ogāhittā uvarillāo jal'aṁtāo eka-padesiyāe seṭhīe ittha ṇaṁ tamu-kkāe samuṭṭhie; sattarasa ekkavīse joyaṇa-sate uḍḍhaṁ uppatittā tao pacchā tiriyaṁ pavittharamāṇe*

The other is the eight black fields (Skt. *aṣṭa-kṛṣṇa-rājī*, Pkt. *aṭṭha kaṇha-rāī*), connected with the body of darkness:

> 'These eight black fields, shaped in a quadrangular form of a platform, are attested to be there towards the plane of the abode of the Riṣṭa heaven in the heaven of Brahmā, above the heavens of Sanatkumāra and Māhendra, namely: there are two from the eastern side, there are two from the western side, there are two from the southern side, there are two from the northern side. The innermost eastern black field touches a southern outermost black field. The southern innermost black field touches western outermost black field. The western innermost black field touches northern outermost black field. The northern innermost black field touches the eastern outermost black field. Both eastern and western outermost black fields are hexagonal. Both northern and southern outermost black fields are triangular. Both eastern and western innermost black fields are quadrangular, both northern and southern innermost black fields are [likewise] quadrangular.'[30]

The arrangement of the black fields would be approximately as the one shown in Fig. 8. This peculiar arrangement of the cosmic regions—i.e. of the body of darkness, which emerges vertically like an impregnable screen, and of the eight black fields, connected to it, which cover the enclosure from the top, and jointly form a spatial structure impenetrable to light—does not seem to perform any function. The structure is placed directly on the uppermost section of the hellish regions, which all are immersed in absolute darkness. The interior of the structure must therefore remain eternally dark, too, because the light does not enter there from any side. The text emphasises that the region inside is empty and not inhabited by any beings, there are no houses, villages etc. there. Thus the role of this dark solid, of a rather

pavittharamāṇe sohammīsāṇa-saṇaṁ-kumāra-māhilaṁde cattāri vi kappe āvarittāṇaṁ uḍḍhaṁ pi ya ṇam jāva baṁbha-loke kappe riṭṭha-vimāṇa-patthaḍaṁ saṁpatte, ettha ṇam tamu-kkāe sanniṭṭhite.

[30] Viy$_2$ 6.5.18: *uppiṁ saṇaṁkumāra-māhiṁdāṇaṁ kappāṇaṁ, havviṁ baṁbha-loge kappe riṭṭhe vimāṇa-patthaṭe, ettha ṇaṁ akkhāḍaga-samacauraṁsa-saṁṭhāṇa-saṁṭhiyāo aṭṭha kaṇha-rāīo paṇṇattao, taṁ jahā—puratthimeṇam do, paccatthimeṇaṁ do, dāhiṇeṇaṁ do, dāhiṇeṇaṁ do, uttareṇaṁ do. puratthim'abbhaṁtarā kaṇha-rāī dāhiṇa-bāiraṁ kaṇha-rāī puṭṭhā, dāhiṇ'abbhyaṁtarā kaṇha-rāī paccatthima-bāhiraṁ kaṇha-rāī puṭṭhā, paccatthim'abbhaṁtarā kaṇha-rāī uttara-bahiraṁ kaṇha-rāī puṭṭhā, uttara'bbhaṁgtarā kaṇha-rāī puratthima'bāhiraṁ kaṇha-rāī puṭṭhā. do puratthima pacchatthimāo bāhirao kaṇha-rāīo chal'aṁsao, do uttara-dāhiṇa-bāhirāo kaṇha-rāīo t'aṁsāo, do puratthima-paccatthimāo abbhiṁtarāo kaṇha-rāīo caur'aṁsāo, do uttara-dāhiṇao abbhitarāo kaṇha-rāīo caur'aṁsāo.*

irregular, indefinite form, cannot be functional but structural, in the sense of its being merely there as an important part of the structure of the universe. As OHIRA (1994: § 160) correctly, in my opinion, explains, 'Taking the Jaina *loka* in a profile of the World-man, Tamaskāya is situated in the position of a womb with Kr̥ṣṇarāji (a strange name) on top which assumes a symbolic form of *swastika* or *śrivatsa*. ... These dark regions thus seem to signify the cosmic *garbha*, the innermost shrine of the Jainas. ... These regions are thus placed above the profane lower world.'

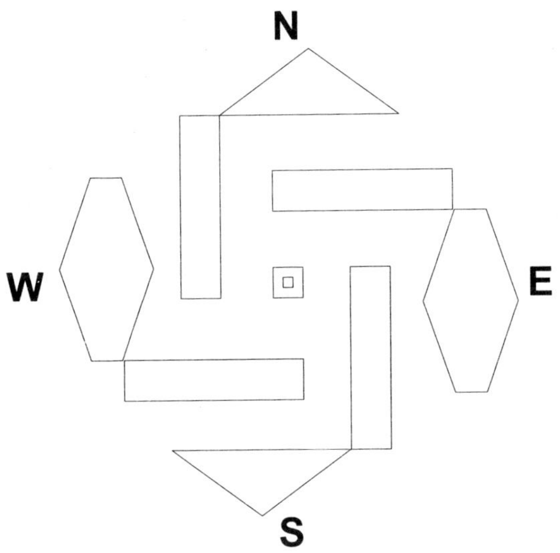

Fig. 8: The spatial arrangement of the eight black fields. Comp. also the chart 'The Black Fields' in DELEU (1970: 125).

Thus, next to the 'neck' (*grīvā*), the 'artery' (*nāḍī* / *nāḍi*), the navel (*nābhī*) and the skin (*carman*) of the world, we can also distinguish the womb (*garbha*), enveloped in eternal darkness, a concept that may have developed in the fifth century, or even earlier.[31] This further confirms that the idea of the cosmic man was already an accepted concept well-rooted in the Jaina cosmology of the fifth century. What is important is that the image of the universe in the shape of the cosmic man had its thoroughgoing implications not only for a general outline of the world structure but it was reflected in a few world regions of the universe that derived their names from body parts.

---

[31] Suzuko OHIRA (1994: 79, § 158) assigns the 'idea of the dark cosmic regions' to 'the fifth canonical stage after the completion of the Dvipasāgara p.'.

4.4. Furthermore, we find some evidence attesting to the existence of such a concept as early as the beginning of the third century CE at the very latest. This is, namely, the following image of the world structure we come across as interwoven in a dialogue between Mahāvīra and his disciple Gautama in the *Viyāha-pannatti* (*Bhagavatī-sūtra*):

> '[2. Gautama asks Mahāvīra:] On what basis, O Lord, has it been said [earlier] that [the world] is eight-fold etc. up to that the living beings are bound by *karman*? [Mahāvīra replies to Gautama:] O Gautama, suppose somebody expands a leather bag (lit. "bladder" or "belly") [by blowing air inside]. Having expanded the leather bag, he ties it tight from the upper end. Having bound [it from the upper end], he binds it with a knot in the middle. Having bound [it] with a knot in the middle, he unties the upper knot. Having untied it, he empties the upper section (sc. removes the air from it). Having emptied the upper section, he fills the upper section with a mass of water (lit. "with the body of water", considered sentient!). Having filled [it with water], he ties it tight from the upper end [again]. Having tied [it], he unties the knot in the middle. Now, say, Gautama: will the mass of water remain in the upper layer above this [lower] mass of air?—Indeed, it will. (sic!)—On this basis [it has been said that the world is eight-fold] … up to … that living beings are bound by *karman*. [3] Now, suppose, someone expands a leather bag [by blowing air inside]. Having expanded [it], he ties it around the waist (hips, *kaṭi*). Having tied [it], he would plunge very deep into the waters which are impossible for a man to cross over [with the inflated leather bag]. Now, say, Gautama, will that man remain on the surface (lit. "in the upper layer") of this mass of water? —Indeed, he will.—So, in such a way, the structure of the world is expounded to be eight-fold … up to … living beings are [expounded to be] bound by *karman*.'[32]

[32] Viy$_2$ 1.6.2–3, p. 48.1–11: [2] *se keṇa'ṭṭheṇaṁ bhaṁte evaṁ vuccati aṭṭha-vihā jāva jīvā kamma-saṁgahitā? goyamā! se jahā-nāmae kei purise vatthim āḍoveti, vatthim ādovittā uppiṁ sitaṁ baṁdhati, badhittā majjhe ṇaṁ gaṁṭhiṁ baṁdhati, majjhe gaṁṭhiṁ baṁdhitā uparilaṁ gaṁṭhiṁ muyati, muittā uparillaṁ desaṁ vāmeti, uparillaṁ desaṁ vāmettā uvarillaṁ desaṁ āu-yāyassa pūreti, pūrittā uppiṁ sitaṁ baṁdhati, baṁdhittā, majjhillaṁ gaṁṭhiṁ muyati. se nūṇaṁ gottamā! se āu-yāe tassa vāu-yāyassa uppiṁ uvari-tale ciṭṭhati? haṁtā, ciṭṭhati. se teṇa'ṭṭheṇaṁ jāva jīvā kamma-saṁgahitā.* [3] *se jahā vā kei purise vatthim āḍovetti, āḍovittā kaḍīe baṁdhati, baṁdhittā atthāham atārama-porusiyaṁsi udakaṁsi ogāhejja. se nūṇaṁ gotamā! se purise tassa āu-yāyassa uvarima-tale ciṭṭhati? haṁtā, ciṭṭhati. evaṁ vā aṭṭha-vihā loya-ṭṭhitī paṇṇattā jāva jīvā kamma-saṁgahitā.*

The passage is assigned to the early third canonical period by OHIRA (1994: 75–76, § 146), i.e. the beginning of the third century CE[33], and such dating seems quite plausible.

To understand the image evoked in the passage properly and the gist of the 'experiment' described above, which patently goes against our experience, we should recall what these eight layers are conceived to represent in an early structure of the universe:

> 'The cosmos has an eightfold articulation (*aṭṭhavihā loga-ṭṭiī pannattā*): [1] wind rests (*paiṭṭhiya*) on space, [2] water rests on wind, [3] earth rests on water, [4] living being rest on earth, [5] inanimate matters rest on the souls, [6] the souls rest on karman; moreover, [7] inanimate matters are 'caught' (*saṁgahiya*) by scil. are in the grasp of the souls and [8] the souls are "caught" by karman.'[34]

The description of the inflated leather bag—apparently in a human shape—evokes, beyond doubt, an image of a leather hull that covers a body that is filled with the elements of space, wind, water, earth etc. and with the soul. That neatly corresponds to the image of the world as amassment of all entities, or all 'fundamental masses' (*asti-kāya*) in later terminology[35]. The world is a macrocosm that resembles a microcosm of a human body: both are filled with matter (wind, air, water, earth, inanimate elements, soul and *karman*) and both have waist that divides it into two parts, upper and lower. The 'waist' of the world is in the middle of it where it is bound with a knot (*majjhe ... gaṁṭhiṁ baṁdhati, majjhe gaṁṭhiṁ baṁdhitā*, see n. 112).

We find a reference to such an image of the contraction and inflation of a leather bag, filled in by air also in later literature. While discussing the process of the expansion of the soul's spatial units, Siddhasena-gaṇin Gandhahastin makes use of three popular metaphors, one of them being the leather ball (ball): '…the contraction and expansion of the soul's spatial units is [an] accepted [fact], just like the fact of the spreading out of a folded piece of cloth, just like the reduction and extension of the light of a lamp, just like shrinking and inflation of a leather ball.'[36]

---

[33] OHIRA (1994: 22, § 69).

[34] DELEU (1970: 81, § I 6 [5]).

[35] See p. 109 and n. 28.

[36] TṬ 5.16, p. 335.1–10: *yasmāj jīvasya* ***pradeśānāṁ*** *saṅkoca-vikāsāv iṣyete, paṭasyêva piṇḍita-vitatâvasthāyitā, pradīpa-prakāśasyêva saṅkucana-prasāraṇe, carma-maṇḍalasyêva* ***saṁhāra-visargāv*** *iti.…*

4.5. Still another canonical text attests to the existence of a well developed image of the cosmic man (*loka-puruṣa*), and that is the *Naṁdi-sutta* and the commentary *Naṁdi-cūrṇi* thereon, which presuppose such an image in order to develop it further. There, we find an image of the man of twelve limbs, consisting of a pair of feet, two lower legs and two thighs, two halves of the torso and two arms, the neck and the head. That man is metaphorically called as testimonial cognition (*śruta-jñāna*), which is the Jaina Canon. Out of these twelve limbs, the feet are the *Āyāraṁga-sutta* (*Ācārâṅga-sūtra*) and *Sūya-gaḍaṁga* (*Sūtra-kṛtâṅga*), the successive main canonical works—enumerated in NaṁS 68- –form the remaining body parts, up to *Vivāga-sūtaṁ* (*Vivāga-sūyaṁ*; *Vipāka-śruta* / *Vipāka-sūtra*) and *Ditthi-vāo* (*Dṛṣṭi-vāda*) being the neck and the head respectively'[37].[38] To have such an image—most probably developed around the fifth century[39]—of the 'scriptural man' consisting of twelve limbs (*aṅga*) which correspond to the twelve limbs (*aṅga*) of the Jaina Canon, is based on and presupposes an earlier cosmological image of 'the cosmic man' (*loka-puruṣa*).

---

[37] NaṁCū 77, p. 57.1: "*pāya-dugaṁ jaṁghôrū gāta-dugaddhaṁ tu do ya bāhūyo / gīvā siraṁ ca puriso bārasa-aṁgo suta-visiṭṭho //*" *icc'etassa suta-purisassa jaṁ sutaṁ aṁga-bhāva-bhāga-ṭṭhitam taṁ aṁga-paviṭṭhaṁ bhaṇṇati. jaṁ puṇa etass'eva suta-purisassa vairega-ṭṭhitaṁ taṁ aṁga-bāhiraṁ ti bhaṇṇati. ahavā*—"*gaṇa-hara-katam aṁga-gataṁ jaṁ kata therehiṁ bāhiraṁ taṁ ca / ṇiyataṁ vaṁga-paviṭṭhaṁ aṇiyata suta bāhiraṁ bhaṇitaṁ //*"—'"A pair of feet, [two] lower legs and [two] thighs, two halves of the torso and two arms, the neck and the head—[these constitute] the man of twelve limbs who is characterised as testimonial cognition (i.e. the Scriptural Canon)." The testimonial cognition of this "testimonial man" which is established as the parts of the body in the form of the limbs is called primary canonical texts (*aṅga-praviṣṭa*). The testimonial cognition of this "testimonial man" which is established as other than this is called secondary canonical texts (*aṅga-bahya*). Alternatively, "what has been phrased by Mahāvīra's immediate disciples (*gaṇa-dhara*) belongs to primary canonical texts (*aṅga-gata*), whatever is composed by ancient teachers belongs to secondary canonical texts (*aṅga-bahya*). Still another alternative: whatever is eternal is called primary canonical texts, whatever is not eternal is called secondary [canonical texts]."'

[38] See also KAPADIA (2000: 20), who however mentions as *Sūya-gaḍaṁga* the neck of the *suta-purisa* (*śruta-puruṣa*), i.e. the Scripture-Man: 'These 12 *Aṅgas* are looked upon as the 12 limbs (*aṅgas*) of a *śruta-puruṣa* or the *śruta* personified. They are: 2 Pādas (feet), 2 *jaṅghās* (lower legs), 2 ūrus (thighs), 2 *gātrārdhas* (back and belly), 2 *bāhus* (hands), 1 *grīvā* (neck) and 1 *śiras* (head). *Āyāra* and *Sūyagaḍa* stand for the feet of the *śruta-puruṣa*, whereas *Diṭṭhivāya*, for the head. On the other hand, so far as *anaṅga-paviṭṭha suya-nāṇa* is concerned, it does not form a part and parcel of this *śruta-puruṣa*; for it comprises such wcriptures as are not included in the *dvādaśāṅgī*.' Cf. OHIRA (1994: 31, § 101) who follows KAPADIA.

[39] See also OHIRA (1994: 79, § 160), who seem to suggest that the 'profile of the World-man', i.e. *loka-puruṣa*, 'must have occurred when the Jaina-centred world view was established,' viz. 'the late fifth century' (see OHIRA (1994: 37, § 119).

5.1. We might ask what the origin of such a concept of the world in a human shape may have been, a question to which we will probably never receive a satisfying reply. We can however attempt to partially trace the background of the image, i.e. certain conceptual building blocks that lay at its background. This does not have to mean that the concepts referred to below were direct sources of the concept of the *loka-puruṣa*. The most we can say is that these conceptual building blocks were certain ideas that were circulated in ancient India in various religious milieux, and even those which were somehow related to Vedic ideas and images do not imply that the Jainas derived them from Vedic Ārya culture. The echo of such Vedic concepts may only indicate either that similar ideas were circulated independently in the territories where Jainism originally developed or that such ideas, which indeed go back to the Vedic culture in their origins, were secondarily taken up by non-Vedic religious groups in a loose manner and occasionally referred to as a model or inspiration free of its original Vedic background and roots. Those who practically recycled or creatively used such ideas in the cosmology may not even have been aware of their real origins: had they been aware, they would most probably have rejected them outright. In other words, I will try to identify certain ideas there in the cultural mileu of Ancient India where the concept of the *loka-puruṣa* gradually developed.

One of the tracks will indeed lead us back to Vedic times, to the *Puruṣa-sūkta* to be exact. There, we read of the intermediate regions of the world that have come into existence form the navel (*nābhī*) of the primeval man (*puruṣa*):[40]

> 'The intermediate regions came into being from the navel [of the primeval man (*puruṣa*)]; from his head the sky emerged, from his feet the earth, from his ear the directions—in such a way [the sacrificers] fashioned the worlds.'[41]

This establishes a connection between the navel and the middle regions of the world in a way similar to the middle world of Jainas with the Mount Meru located in the middle of it as its navel[42].

Moreover, the Ṛg-vedic hymn also establishes a link between the primeval man and the universe:

---

[40] Cf. See p. 129, but also n. 86.

[41] Ṛ̥V 10.90.14:
nā́bhyā ā̱sīd ant̤árikṣaṁ śīrṣṇó dyaúḥ sám a̱vartata /
padbhyā́m bhū́mir díśaḥ śrótrāt táthā lokā́m̐ akalpayan //

[42] On mythological, ritual and cosmological ramifications of the Jaina image of Mount Meru see HEGEWALD (2010).

> 'It is the primeval man who is all this [what exists],[43] all that has come into existence and all that is to come into existence. Indeed [he is] the lord of immortal state, [he is] what grows from nourishment.'[44]

Just as the primeval man (*puruṣa*) of the Vedic hymn embraces all that exists in the three times, the *puruṣa* of the Jaina world spatially incorporates and gives room to practically all entities that exist: beyond him there is just a void space (*alokâkaśa*), where even no movement is possible. Everything that comes into existence or perishes, or moves around exists within the *loka-puruṣa*. As indicated above, these parallels do not imply that the Jainas borrowed their cosmological image for the repository of Vedic ideas: the similarities, either here or in the cases mentioned below, may be either coincidental or adopted as a mere image of anthropomorphic world without any consciousness that it had its origins in Vedic literature.

We find an interesting and important trait in the *Atharva-veda* as well:

> 'The man (*puruṣa*) materialised as all the directions [of the world], those which are spread upright, those which are spread horizontally. The one who knows the stronghold of Brahman is called the man (*puruṣa*).'[45]

Clearly, 'the stronghold' of the passage is the body, either human or cosmic, or divine. The man who materialised is also the source of all the directions. This is also the 'spirit' which fills in all the accessible space. Interestingly, all directions, those which are spread upright, those which are spread horizontally', stem from it, just like all the directions of the Jaina universe stem from the centremost sphere of the cosmic man (*vide infra*, p. 139 f.).

5.2. Secondly, a traditional etymology of the term *puruṣa* offered by Yāska (c. 5th century BCE), who incidentally quotes a verse of the *Śvetâśvatarôpaniṣad* (ŚvU 3.9), etymologises it in a quite a revealing manner that offers a crucial backdrop to the image of the inflated leather hull of the *Viyāha-pannatti* 1.6.2–3 quoted above:

---

[43] See n. 46.

[44] RV 10.90.2:

púruṣa evédáṁ sárvaṁ yád bhūtáṁ yác ca bhávyam /
utāmṛtatvásyéśāno yád ánnenâtiróhati //

[45] AV 10.2.28:

ūrdhvó nu sṛṣṭā́s tiryáṅ nú sṛṣṭā́ḥ sárvā díśaḥ púruṣa ā́ babhūvā́m̐ /
púraṁ yó bráhmaṇo véda yásyāḥ púruṣa ucyáte //

'[The term] "man" (*puruṣa*) [means] "the one who resides in the stronghold" (*puri-ṣāda*), [or] "the one who sleeps in the stronghold" (*puri-śaya*), or [the term is derived] from the verbal root "to fill", viz. "he fills" [in the sense] "he pervades the interior"—[said] with respect to the inner person (i.e. soul).
"All this [that exists][46] is filled by this man, to whom there is nothing anterior nor posterior, with respect to whom there is nothing smaller and nothing greater, who is immovable like a tree, who alone abides in heaven".'[47]

What is important for us in this short etymological note is, first, the meaning of the process of 'filling / pervading the interior' itself, which Yāska relates directly to

---

[46] For paralles to *idaṁ sarvam* see, e.g., RV 10.90.2: *púruṣa evédáṁ sárvaṁ*; ChU 3.14.1: *sarvaṁ khalv idaṁ brahma*; MāU 1, 2: *om ity etad akṣaraṁ idaṁ sarvam. … sarvaṁ hy etad brahma*; ŚvU 3.9: *idaṁ pūrṇaṁ puruṣeṇa sarvam*. Interestingly, the famous hymn about the *Puruṣa*, esp. the verse RV 10.90.2, is quoted in ŚvU 3.15.

[47] Nir 2.3: ... *puruṣaḥ puri-ṣādaḥ puri-śayaḥ pūrayater vā pūrayaty antarity antara-puruṣam abhipretya.*

yasmāt paraṁ nâparam asti kiṁcid yasmān nâṇīyo na jyāyo 'sti kaścit /
vṛkṣa iva stabdho divi tiṣṭhaty ekas tenêdaṁ pūrṇaṁ puruṣeṇa sarvam // ŚvU 3.9 //

The ideas (esp. the 'residing in…') expressed in this and other passages (MBh 12.203.35: *puraṁ ... śete*, p. 118; ŚatBr 13.6.2.1: *puri śete*, p. 118) are in the background for Jaina etymology of the term *puruṣa* found in Candrarṣi's *Pañca-saṁgraha* and Vīrasena's *Dhavalā-ṭīkā*:

PSaṁ 1.106:

puru-guṇa-bhoge sede karedi loyamhi puru-guṇaṁ kammaṁ /
puru uttamo ya jamhā tamhā so vaṇṇido puriso // 106 //

'Because he is the one who resides in plentiful qualities and pleasures, who performs the deeds of plentiful qualities in this world, who is plentifully excellent, that is why he is called the man.'

DhṬ vol. 1, p. 343.3–5, ad ṢKhĀ 1.1.101: *puru-guṇeṣu puru-bhogeṣu ca śete svapitîti puruṣaḥ. suṣupta-puruṣavad anugata-guṇo 'prāpta-bhogaś ca yad-udayāj jīvo bhavati sa puruṣaḥ aṅganâbhilāṣa iti yāvat. puru-guṇaṁ karma śete karotîti vā puruṣaḥ.*—'One is the man (*puruṣa*) because he resides, or reclines (*-su* / *svapiti*), in plentiful (*puru-*) qualities and in plentiful (*puru-*) pleasures, which is tantamount to saying the following: that from the rise of which the living being cannot attain good qualities or experience pleasures, like a person in deep sleep, is the man, i.e. the one who desires women. Alternatively, one is the man because he resides in, or accomplishes, the deeds (*karman*) of plentiful (*puru-*) qualities.'

Interestingly, the above Jaina etymology of the term does not contain the idea of 'filling the body' or 'residing in the stronghold', the concept of *pur* / *puri* is replaced in this etymology by the term *puru*.

the term *puruṣa*, second, the conviction that *puruṣa* is located in a human body, called the 'stronghold' (*pur*), and third, the idea that the *puruṣa* fills, or pervades, everything that exists. Clearly, the *puruṣa* assumes in this short note of etymology a cosmic dimension. These three elements combined easily yield an image of the universe pervaded in its totality by the *puruṣa* ('the man') the way a human body is pervaded by the soul. And this image incorporates two Jaina metaphors: the world in the human shape as well as the world in the form of a tripartite leather bag filled with air or with other elements.

That this was not just a singular association which Yāska happened to conjure up *ad hoc* is testified both by the reference he makes to the Upaniṣadic tradition as well as by the fact that we come across the same idea much earlier in the *Śata-patha-brāhmaṇa*:

> 'The stronghold (*pur*) is undeniably these worlds. This very [stronghold] is the man (*puruṣa*), who is that which blows (sc. the wind). He resides in this stronghold. Hence he is *puruṣa*.'[48]

These passages undeniably establish an equivalence of the man (*puruṣa*) and the universe by taking recourse to the belief that the 'stronghold', i.e. his body which he fills, is the whole universe (*ime lokāḥ*) filled by him.

5.3. Further, the idea of the primeval man (*puruṣa*) and its microcosmic reflection in the form of the soul pervading the body is found also in the *Mahā-bhārata*, which clearly is a newly elaborated extension of the earlier motif:

> 'The immense soul pervades and resides in the pure stronghold of the nine doors (i.e. the body), endowed with these faculties. Therefore the [soul] is called the man (*puruṣa*).'[49]

First, what we find in the verse is a conviction that the soul pervades the physical body precisely in the manner etymologised by Yāska above as the entity 'that resides in a stronghold' (Nir: *puri-ṣādaḥ*, MBh: *puraṁ ... śete*), but what is rather unusual is the attribute of the soul, i.e. its immensity (*mahān ātman*), which connotes the idea that the actual size of the soul is much larger than the body it fills and that the boundary of the body, like a wall of a stronghold, sets the limits to the embodied soul. That

---

[48] ŚatBr 13.6.2.1: ... *ime vai lokāḥ pūr ayam eva puruṣo yo 'yam pavate so 'syām puri śete tasmāt puruṣas*...

[49] MBh 12.203.35:

> *nava-dvāraṁ puram puṇyam etair bhāvaiḥ samanvitam /*
> *vyāpya śete mahān ātmā tasmāt puruṣa ucyate //*

attribute serves as a direct link to connect the idea of the soul with the concept of the primeval man (*puruṣa*), who is, traditionally from Vedic times, understood not only to pervade or to be at least coextensive with the world but also to extend beyond its limits by far. In fact, the primeval man sets the limits of the manifest, perceivable world, being himself much larger than the world one can fathom:

> '[1] The primeval man is thousand-headed, thousand-eyed, thousand-footed. Having occupied the whole earth, he still stood out for 10 thumbs. ... [3] Such is the greatness of this [world], albeit the primeval man is greater. Just one his quarter is all the beings; his [remaining] three quarters is the immorality in heaven.'[50]

The *puruṣa* contains in himself the criterion whereby all that manifestly exists (one quarter consisting of all the beings) is distinguished from all that is beyond perception and manifestation (the remaining three quarters). One could say that is it the *puruṣa* himself that sets the boundary of the visible world.

A similar idea of the *puruṣa* as the source of the universe is expressed elsewhere in the *Mahā-bhārata*:

> 'Since he both pervades and resides [in everything that exists], he is [called] the highest man, and also because he the source and end of everything that exists and does not exist.'[51]

Of course, both verses of the *Mahā-bhārata* principally intimate the Upaniṣadic idea of the absolute that pervades all that exists and the equivalence of the macro- and microcosm, i.e. the absolute (*brahman*), understood either in a theistic or non-theistic way, and the individual soul (*ātman*). What does stand out in both verses is a clear mention of the ultimately anthropomorphic aspect of this relation that is projected onto the world.

This tradition which was once articulated in the *Puruṣa-sūkta* and etymologised by grammarians, which understood the *puruṣa* as that which fills the universe, or 'pervades the interior' of the world, which sets the boundary of the manifested world, may perhaps have been the first point of reference of, or inspiration for the

---

[50] RS 10.90.1,3:
sahásra-śīrṣā púruṣaḥ sahasrâkṣáḥ sahásra-pāt /
sá bhūmiṁ viśváto vṛtvā́ty atiṣṭhad daśâṅgulám // 1 // ...
etā́vān asya mahimā́to jyā́yāṁś ca pū́ruṣaḥ /
pā́do 'sya víśvā bhūtā́ni tripā́d asyâmṛ́taṁ diví // 3 //

[51] MBh 5.6.10:
pūraṇāt sadanāc câiva tato 'sau puruṣôttamaḥ /
asataś ca sataś câiva sarvasya prabhavâpyayāt //

Jaina idea of the cosmic man, i.e. the anthropomorphic world filled with souls—no more with one universal soul or absolute (*brahman*)—and 'all that exists, all that has come into existence and all that is to come into existence,' as the author of the *Puruṣa-sūkta* verbalised it.

6. As I have pointed out, the compound 'posture of spread-out legs' (*vaiśākha-sthāna*), used by Siddhasena Gandhahastin, is a clear allusion to a tree with spread-out branches (*vide supra*, p. 105), albeit apparently standing upwards. This brings us to another point or reference that may stand behind the idea of the cosmic man, and this is the image of the tree, broadly understood.

As it is well-known, in the Vedic literature we come across an idea of the man being compared to the *skambhá*, or (personified) sacrificial pole being the universal tree, or the *axis mundi* and the pole supporting the world, most unequivocal examples perhaps being two hymns of *Atharva-veda* 10.7 and 10.8.[52] In addition, the hymns establish the equivalence between the sacrificial pole and the human being on a cosmic level, and the *skambhá* assumes anthropomorphic dimension. This happens on at least two levels. First, the sacrificial pole in its cosmic dimension is directly referred to as a human being:

> 'You (the sacrificial pole) are the woman, you are the man, you are the boy, you are the girl. Grown old, you totter with a stick. Newly born, you face the whole world.'[53]

Secondly, the world structure that derives from the structure of the sacrificial pillar corresponds to body parts, which is exemplified by the selection of verses below[54]:

> '[2] Out of which member of his [body] does the fire glow? Out of which member does the air blow? Out of which member does the moon traverses high, passing over the trunk of the mighty sacrificial pole? [3] In which member of his [body] does the earth reside? In which member does the intermediate space reside? In which member does the heaven reside firmly fixed? In which member does the highest paradise reside? … [8] To what degree did the sacrificial pole penetrate all the universe that Prajāpati created, with its higher, lower and

---

[52] Cf. e.g. HORSCH (2004: 433), SRINIVASAN (1978: 14 ff.).

[53] AV 10.8.27 speaks of the sacrificial pole as the human being:
tvaṁ strī tvaṁ pumān asi tvaṁ kumāra uta vā kumārī /
tvaṁ jīrṇo daṇḍena vañcasi tvaṁ jāto bhavasi viśvato-mukhaḥ //

[54] See also See RENOU (1955: 46), SRINIVASAN (1978), PARPOLA (2005: 49 f.).

middle segments? How large was that [part] which he did not penetrate? [15] Tell me about this sacrificial pole in whom both immortality and death are conjoined in man, whose expanse [and] whose veins are conjoined in man: which one is he? [16] Tell me about this sacrificial pole whose four quarters stand as primary veins, in whom the sacrifice advances: which one is he?'[55]

The mapping of the world structure onto the parts of a human body, as we have it e.g. in AV 10.7, imitates to a certain degree the structure of the *Puruṣa-sūkta* (RV 10.90): in AV 10.7, it is the personified sacrificial pole—instead of the *puruṣa*—that is the source of the universe and of all its spatial sections (2–3, 8, 12, 16, 27), celestial bodies (18), time divisions (5,6), the *Veda*s (10, 14, 19–20), creatures, divine beings and humans (10, 22, 24) etc. As Doris SRINIVASAN (1978: 223) observes, 'The AV demonstrates that when multiple body parts and forms are ascribed to the divine, that deity, in nearly every case, is associated with creation on a cosmic scale,' and a very special case is the equivalence between the personified sacrificial pole (*skambhá*), treated as the *axis mundi*, and the cosmic body.

The upright sacrificial pole, which is a reference to a tree and functions as the axis of the world, undergoes a process of anthropomorphisation and has its counterpart in the imagery of the *Upaniṣad*s. A similar kind of equivalence is found in a well-known image which we find in the *Bṛhad-āraṇyakôpaniṣad*:

'Man (*puruṣa*) is like an immense tree—that is the truth.'[56]

This equivalence will be reinforced in a peculiar aspect of Jaina salvific doctrine of the *samudghāta* process (*vide infra* p. 129).

---

[55] AV 10.7.2–3, 8, 16:
kasmād aṅgād dīpyate agnir asya kasmād aṅgāt pavate mātari-śvā /
kasmād aṅgād vi mimīte 'dhi candramā maha skambhasya vimāno aṅgaṁ // 2 //
kasminn aṅge tiṣthati bhūmir asya kasminn aṅge tiṣṭhaty antarikṣam /
kasminn aṅge tiṣṭhaty āhitā dyauḥ kasminn aṅge tiṣṭhaty uttaraṁ divaḥ // 3 //
yat param avamaṁ yac ca madhyamaṁ prajāpatiḥ sasṛje viśvra-rūpam /
kiyatā skambhaḥ pra viveśa tatra yan na prāviśat kiyat tad babhūva // 8 //
yatrâmṛtaṁ ca mṛtyuś ca puruṣe 'dhi samāhite /
samudro yasya nāḍyaḥ puruṣe 'dhi samāhitāḥ skambhaṁ taṁ brūhi katamaḥ svid eva saḥ // 15 //
yasya catasraḥ pradiśo nāḍyas tiṣṭhanti prathamāḥ //
yajño yatra parākrāntaḥ skambhaṁ taṁ brūhi katamaḥ svid eva saḥ // 16 //
See also SRINIVASAN (1978: 210 ff.).

[56] BĀU 3.9.28:
yathā vṛkṣo vanaspatis tathâiva puruṣo 'mṛṣā / …

Also the *Śvetâśvatarôpaniṣad*, in the verse which Yāska cites (*vide supra*, p. 117), evokes the anthropomorphic structure of the world which assumes the form of the unshakeable *axis mundi*:

> '[8] I know this immense man (*puruṣa*), who has the colour of the sun, [who is] beyond darkness. Only when one has recognised him does one transcend death. There is no other path to get there. [9] All this [that exists] is filled by this man, to whom there is nothing anterior nor posterior, with respect to whom there is nothing smaller and nothing greater, who is immovable like a tree, who alone abides in heaven.'[57]

The supreme being (*puruṣa*), who in his cosmic dimension fills the whole universe, is likened here to a tree and as such he marks out the axis of the world in the same manner as the sacrificial pole does. That closely corresponds to the general tendency of the Vedic, especially Atharva-Vedic period, during which 'for all its abstract tendencies, Skambha still retains traces of anthropomorphism.'[58] In the Upaniṣadic passage the *puruṣa* remains 'immovable' (*stabdha*), a participle derived from the root √*stambh*, a variant of which is √*skambh*, and typifies a sacrificial pole.[59]

7. Another point of reference, albeit much less obvious, that may prove relevant for establishing the history and conceptual background of the image of 'the cosmic man' is the equivalence of the temple and the human(-like) body. It seems that the design of the main building of the Indian temple as such reflected a god, or emulated the structure of the body of an anthropomorphised god, or the universal *puruṣa*. It is an additional association of the imagery of the temple, apart from the more common that of the mountain and the cavern.[60]

Referring to a concrete example of Southern India, i.e. to the Viṣṇu-gṛha temple in Kāñchīpuram, or Paramēcchura Viṇṇagaram, known today as Vaikuṇṭha Perūmal Temple, built by Nandivarman Pallavamalla in ca. 770–775, D. Dennis HUDSON

---

[57] ŚvU 3.8–9:

> *vedâham etaṁ puruṣaṁ mahāntam āditya-varṇaṁ tamasaḥ parastāt /*
> *tam eva viditvâti mṛtyum eti na anyaḥ panthā vidyate 'yanāya //*
> *yasmāt paraṁ nâparam asti kiṁcid yasmān nâṇīyo na jyāyo 'sti kaścit /*
> *vṛkṣa iva stabdho divi tiṣṭhaty ekas tenêdaṁ pūrṇaṁ puruṣeṇa sarvam //*

[58] SRINIVASAN (1978: 210). See also VATSYAYAN (2003: 9–10): 'Several Hymns in the *R̥gveda* are devoted to the *stambha* or the *skambha* where the supreme being is seen as a great Cosmic Pillar.'

[59] Cf. PARPOLA (2005: 49): 'The Vedic concept of "world pillar" or "axis mundi" is associated with the verb *sta(m)bh* and its variant *ska(m)bh-*.'

[60] See Stella KRAMRISCH (1976: 161–174).

(2008: 6) expressly establishes the link between god and his temple: 'The Emperor's Vishnu-house is the entire mandala arena defined by the enclosing prakara, but God is believed to live at its center. He does so in two ways: the vimana palace is His body; and He lives inside the vimana as three black stone icons.'

That this was not a incidental phenomenon, limited to the South, is confirmed by other examples taken from other parts of India, as Bettina BÄUMER (2001: 46) points out, referring to the tradition of Orissa reflected in the *Śilpa-ratna-kośa* by Sthapānaka Nirañjana Mahāpātra, 'composed in 1620'[61]: 'The elevation of a temple (*śikhara* above the *garbhagṛha* or *sanctum*) is also likened to the body of *puruṣa*, and the different parts of the temple are named after the limbs of the body ..., the soul being the consecrated image in the *sanctum* (ŚiRaKo 6–14).' This correspondence was noticed already by Stella KRAMRISCH (1976: 303), who drew the attention to the *sanctum* (*garbha-gṛha*) as a central section of both the temple and god's body: 'The static perfection of the dark Garbhagṛha with its plain walls is translated into the body of the temple, the "body of God"...'

Indeed, the peculiar name *garbha-gṛha* for the central section of the temple stands out and immediately evokes associations with the body and the womb. In an often-quoted passage of the same work, Stella KRAMRISCH (1976: 163) referring to the idea of the name of the *garbha-gṛha*, writes: 'The name refers also to the human body and to the inception of life. ... The Garbhagṛha is not only the house of the Germ or embryo of the Temple as Puruṣa; it refers to man who comes to the Centre and attains his new birth in its darkness.'

A contrary view as regards the derivation of '*garbha-gṛha*' from semantics of the womb is voiced by Anna Aleksandra ŚLĄCZKA (2006: 176, n. 12) who argues that '...the comparison of the temple's cella to a womb, often encountered in secondary literature, is not based on any textual source. The term was popularised by Kramrisch...', and '... the interpretation of *garbhagṛha* as "womb-chamber" is misleading as it implies unnecessary symbolism. The translation "inner chamber" seems thus more appropriate.'

Whether it is justified to directly relate '*garbha-gṛha*' to 'the womb' or merely to 'the inner part', ŚLĄCZKA's disagreement ultimately concerns merely the theory that *garbha-gṛha* derives its name form the direct association with the womb; it does not, however, speak against the idea that the temple is a body of a divine being. Her suggestion to understand *garbha-gṛha* as 'inner chamber' may indeed seem justified in the light of references found e.g. in the *Caraka-saṁhitā*:

[61] ŚiRaKo, p. 1 ('Introduction').

> '[In winter], one shoud spend time in a warm underground chamber or in a warm inner chamber [of a house];'[62]

or

> '[When sick, a person] well-anointed should sweat thoroughly in underground chambers, in dry saunas or in warm inner chambers heated with charcoal that does not emit smoke.'[63]

These are early (i.e. roughly first half of the first millennium CE) 'architectonic' references to housing structures in a text on medicine and there can be no doubt that the *garbha-gṛha* in these passages is an inner chamber of a house, apparently sealed off from the outside, i.e. without windows or large entrances, to keep heat inside the chamber. Clearly, these passages allute to the protective role of the chamber or room, which envelops the person in warmth and safety just like the womb protects the foetus. Perhaps, therefore, the better and more accurate understanding of the term *garbha-gṛha* would be that of 'inner, womb-like protective chamber'.

However, we also find quite a different association in the above-cited text on architecture by Nirañjana Mahāpātra, of relative late origin though, who maps the body of the *puruṣa* onto the temple, and also twice draws a direct correspondence between 'the belly' (*udara*) and the 'inner chamber' (*garbha-gṛha*):

> 'Further above there is the belly which is the place of the womb and the vertical projection corresponds to the heart.'[64]
> 'Just as the upper wall is a thigh, so is the wall junction the hip. [Just as] the belly is the inner [chamber] so is the place of the vertical projection the heart of the temple.'[65]

The same texts claims both that belly of the temple is the place of the womb, and the belly is at the same time the inner chamber of the temple. We thus clearly see that the 'inner chamber' is indeed related to the belly and, apparently, the only conceivable reason for this cannot but be the association of the *garbha-gṛha* with the womb. Despite the relative recent origin of the text itself, we can safely assume that it view on the relation of the inner chamber and the womb expressed in it was of much earlier

---

[62] CarS 1.6.14cd: *bhajed bhūmi-gṛhaṁ côṣṇam uṣṇaṁ garbha-gṛhaṁ tathā //*

[63] CarS 1.14.28:

bhū-gṛheṣu ca jentākeṣûṣṇa-garbha-gṛheṣu ca /
vidhūmâṅgāra-tapteṣu svabhyaktaḥ svidyate sukham //

[64] Śirako 9bd: … *tathôpari / udaraṁ garbha-bhāgaś ca rāhā hṛdaya-saṁnibhā //*

[65] ŚiRaKo 12:

ūrdhva-jāṅghaḥ yathā jāṅghaḥ bāḍāntaḥ kaṭir eva ca /
garbhôdaraṁ rāhā-deśaḥ prāsāde hṛdayaṁ tathā //

origin, for the text in not revolutionary in its approach in any way. Further, the association of the structure of the temple with the body is underscored by a ritual which ŚLĄCZKA (2006: 188) herself recalls quoting the opening verse of the *Kāśyapa-śilpa*:

> 'Now I will describe the rules of placing the consecration deposit as the main topic. The temple is said to be the body. The consecration deposit is the vital force of the [temple].'[66]

Temple consecration ritual known as 'the placing of the consecration deposit' (*garbha-nyāsa*), or the depositing of 'the soul' (*jīva*), as the *garbha* (or *garbhaka*) is sometimes called, is a symbolic conception of the temple body, similar to the conception of a child,[67] and could be interpreted as an insemination of the temple ground.

We are justified, it seems, to conclude that the temple was thought of also as a projection of the body of god or *puruṣa* at least from the later second half of the first millennium CE. It is not impossible that the parallelism between the temple structure and the body of god or the universal *puruṣa* as exemplified by the Viṣṇu-gṛha temple in Kāñchīpuram, analysed by D. Dennis HUDSON, had its much longer history: such a complex and sizeable temple structure with a well-thought design must have had its predecessors, albeit in a much more modest form. The idea of the *puruṣa* underlying the symbolic structure of the temple may even go back to the Vedic tradition. As Bettina BÄUMER (2001: 47) observes, the origin of the archetype of the anthropomorphic image 'is probably to be found in the golden figure of the *puruṣa* which was built into the Vedic fire-altar, much before any anthropomorphic images of gods were known.' She further notes that 'Some Śilpaśāstras derive the anthropomorphic form from the *yūpa* (the sacrificial pole—P.B.) with which it shares its verticality and the round head' (2001: 47), and as an example adduces the following passage from the commentary on the *Vastu-sūtrôpaniṣad*:

> 'The nature of the man (*puruṣa*) of the size of a thumb manifests itself; by imagination, [his] size [conceived] as light [is said to be] "the thumb". [Further], the [man] is like the shaft of a sacrificial pole.'[68]

---

[66] *Kāśyapa-śilpa* 1 (ŚLĄCZKA (2006: 73)):
atha vakṣye viśeṣeṇa garbha-nyāsa-vidhiṁ param /
prāsādaṁ deham ity uktaṁ tasya prāṇas tu garbhakam //
ŚLĄCZKA (2006: 73) herself also refers to KRAMRISCH (1946: 163) and RASTELLI (2003) to support the claim that the temple represents the body.

[67] Cf. ŚLĄCZKA (2006: 176–177).

[68] *yathā aṅguṣṭha-mātra-puruṣasya bhāvaḥ prabhavati vikalpena aṅguṣṭham iti jyotir mātram. sa yūpasya daṇḍa iva.* Sanskrit text quoted after BÄUMER (2001: 47).

Interestingly, this image recalls the famous Upaniṣadic idea known from *Kaṭhôpaniṣad* and the *Śvetâśvatarôpaniṣad*:

> 'The man (*puruṣa*) of the of the size of a thumb dwells in the body;'[69]

and

> 'The man (*puruṣa*) of the of the size of a thumb, the inner self, always resides in the heart of people.'[70]

The same idea is found to also in the well-known passage of the *Maitrāyaṇīyôpaniṣad*:

> 'Having meditated on the one who is of the size of the thumb within the body, who is smaller than atom, one attains the highest state. … That [man (*puruṣa*)] who is of the size of the thumb within the body, [who] like the light of a lamp is twice and threefold, is extolled as Brahman. [This] great god has entered into the [three] worlds[71].'[72]

This reference to the *puruṣa* conveys also two other important traits. The first is the belief that the *puruṣa* fills the whole space of the body the way the light of a lamp grows bigger depending on the outer limits to the expansion, e.g. set by the skin. Precisely this image was later employed by Umāsvāti to demonstrate how the soul fills the whole space of the universe during the process of *samudghāta* (*vide supra*, p. 108)! For the Jaina, however, the *puruṣa* is replaced by the *jīva*, but the structural correlation remains the same. The obscure picture of the cosmic man's size imagined as light (*vikalpena aṅguṣṭham iti jyotir mātram*) painted by the author of the *Vastu-sūtrôpaniṣad* (*vide supra*, p. 125) now becomes a rather unambiguous reference to such a light that can expand, even though it can be as small as the thumb. Further, in the *Maitrāyaṇīyôpaniṣad* the *puruṣa*, in the form of Brahman, ultimately pervades the three worlds, similar to the picture of the soul undergoing the *samudghāta* process.

No doubt the *Śilpa-śāstra*s knew the idea of the *puruṣa* and applied its multidimensional symbolism, including the light metaphor, to the structure of the temple.

---

[69] KU 4.12: *aṅguṣṭha-mātraḥ puruṣo madhya ātmani tiṣṭhati* /

[70] KU 4.12 = ŚvU 3.13ab: *aṅguṣṭha-mātraḥ puruṣo 'ntar-ātmā sadā janānāṁ hṛdaye saṁniviṣṭaḥ* /

[71] The expression *bhuvanāni* probably means *tri-bhuvanāni*.

[72] MaiU 6.38: *śarīra-prādeśâṅguṣtha-mātram aṇor apy aṇuṁ dhyātvâtaḥ paramatāṁ gacchati. ...*

> *aṅguṣṭha-prādeśa-śarīra-mātraṁ pradīpa-pratāpavat dvis tridhā hi / tad brahmâbhiṣṭūyamānaṁ maho devo bhuvanâny āviśesa //*

Further, as the *Vastu-sūtrôpaniṣad* quotation above testifies, Indian architects treated the *puruṣa* as the shaft of a sacrificial pole that apparently played the role of the *axis mundi* within the temple. This closely corresponds to the symbolism of the tree discussed above (§ 6). It is therefore no longer surprising that an early mediaeval (between 9th and 12th centuries CE) treatise on the science of dwelling (*vastu-śāstra*), the *Maya-mata* mentions '*puruṣa*' as a variety of tree (MM 15.64a), the wood of which is most suitable for the supporting pillars (*ūrdhva-bhūruha*, MM 15.67d)—an obvious application, by way of referring to the whole by means of its component, of the idea that the temple is the body of god or the cosmic man and that the cosmic man is the sacrificial pole symbolically present in the temple structure.

The equivalence of the temple and the *puruṣa* or of the temple and god's body, or—to express it in more universal terms: of the sacral edifice and a divine, supernatural being—had its counterpart in Buddhist tradition, replaced by the assimilation of the Body of the Buddha and the *stūpa*,[73] and there is ample evidence that attests to it.[74] The idea that the *stūpa* was not merely a symbol of the Buddha but the Buddha himself was plainly stated by André BAREAU (1962: 269): 'la participation du stūpa au caractère sacré des reliques et de la personne du Bouddha ou du saint tend à personnaliser le monument. ... Dès avant notre ère, donc, le stūpa est plus que le symbole du Bouddha, c'est le Bubddha lui-même... [emphasis—P.B.],'[75] and much later succinctly rephrased by Adrian SNODGRASS (1985: 362 f.): 'The stupa is the body of the Buddha.'[76]

An additional support to the claim is lent by the discovery that the Buddhists held that the *stūpa*, which was believed to contain the relics of the Buddha, actually was not only a legal person *per se*,[77] but was also treated as a living body of the Buddha[78]:

> 'There is also a whole series of epigraphical and literary documents that prove that the physical relic of the Buddhas was thought to be possessed of "life" or "breath", and to be impregnated with the characteristics that defined and animated the living Buddha, that show that the relic or the reliquary that contained it had and exercised the right to

[73] See MUS (1935: 105), SNODGRASS (1985).

[74] On certain similarities in approach to god's body–temple equivalence in Hinduism and the Buddha–*stūpa* equivalence in Buddhism see SCHOPEN (1994) and on certain possible historical links: BRONKHORST (2005).

[75] Quoted also in SCHOPEN (1994: 363) and BRONKHORST (2005: 68, § 2.5).

[76] See also STRONG (2004: 32): '... a stūpa "is" a living Buddha'.

[77] SCHOPEN (1987: passim, esp. 128–131).

[78] SCHOPEN (1987: passim, esp. 131–133).

> own personal property—that it was legally a person—and that it was cognitively classified with living persons of rank,'[79] and 'that it was—like the Hindu image—a "juristic personality" and owned property; that, finally, the Indian Buddhist community practised a form of what in the West was called "burial *ad sanctos*" and that this can only be accounted for by the belief that the *stūpa* contained a living presence.'[80]

The conceptual mapping of the structure of god or the Buddha or the *puruṣa* on an architectonic physical structure is further confirmed by that fact that, in the structure of the temple or the *stūpa*, the 'breath structure' (*prāṇa-rūpa*) of, or the configuration of the vital forces within, the body of the cosmic man (*puruṣa*) coincides with the 'breath lines' (*prāṇa-sūtra*), i.e. the gridwork drawn on the surface of the *maṇḍala*, on which the *stūpa* rests.[81] Furthermore, as Adrian SNODGRASS (1985: 115) further observes, 'the intersections of the gridlines define vulnerable points or tender spots (*marman*) within the body of Puruṣa, corresponding to breath-knots and centres within the macrocosmic and microcosmic pneumatic bodies.[82] In the laying out of the plan of the Hindu temple and also that of the stupa the location of these *marman*s affect the positions of the building's elements…' These are the associations that underlie an idea that is common for both types of structures, i.e. the idea of *vastu-puruṣa*, well known from Indian *Śilpa-śāstra*.[83]

The exact structural correspondence of an architectonic structure (say, a temple or a *stūpa*) and of a body (say, of god, the Buddha or the cosmic man) highlights an important idea that the structure is actually pervaded or filled—also through the vital forces or breaths[84]—by its 'inhabitant' whose body it represents or with whose body it is actually identical. That corresponds exactly to etymology recorded by Yāska and reflected in the *Śvetâśvatarôpaniṣad* 3.9 (*vide supra*, § 5.2) and strikingly resembles the way the cosmic man in Jainism pervades the whole universe.

---

[79] SCHOPEN (1987: 134).

[80] SCHOPEN (1976: 161); cf. SCHOPEN (1990).

[81] See SNODGRASS (1985: 115).

[82] SNODGRASS refers here also to KRAMRISCH (1976: 51–53, 55–57, 51 n. 87).

[83] See Bettina BÄUMER (2001: 46 ff.).

[84] See SNODGRASS (1985: 111): 'The lines that subdivide the mandala plan have more than a merely geometric significance. They are lines of Breath (*prāṇa*), having symbolic reference to pneumatic structure of the world and man. The body of man and the body of the cosmos are suffused with Breath; they are held together by pneumatic net. The "ground" or "field" of the world is criss crossed with lines of Breath; and the psycho-physical "field" of man is a network of subtle, pneumatic arteries (*nāḍi*). The macrocosmic and microcosmic worlds are "measured out" by these lines of Breath. Hence *prāṇa* is a prototypic measure, the width of the line (*sūtra*) used to lay out the mandala.'

The structural correspondence of the animate being and the inanimate architectonic structure it pervades is much closer and it even comprises such elements of the body as the main 'artery' or 'vein' along the spinal bone (*nāḍī* / *nāḍi*)[85] and the navel (*nābhi*), which is centrally located in the body or in the temple, at the level of the womb (*garbha*), from which the whole space and all its directions emanate[86].

In the above, we can notice an underlying common element: that of the animate entity (*deva*, *buddha*, *puruṣa*, *jīva* etc.) that fills the space he is located in, be it a physical body, a temple, a *stūpa* or the anthropomorphic world, and the centre of it being the womb (*garbha*). The above discussion also leads us to a conclusion that the development that mapped the human-like body onto the design of an architectonic edifice 'inhabited' by its dweller paralleled a similar process of laying out the structure of the universe after the shape of the cosmic man. The universe was thus treated in a quite similar manner as the temple, being merely one more sort of space filled or pervaded by the animate being which inhabited it. What is still puzzling is the following: We can see that the structures of the Buddhist *stūpa*, the Hindu temple etc. corresponded to the standard set-out of the form of their dwellers (the Buddha, god, *puruṣa*). But who *mutatis mutandis* was supposed to be the dweller of the Jaina universe (*loka*) whose task or role would be to fill the whole space and whose bodily structure would the universe ultimately display? The early Jaina literature supplies, in my opinion, the answer to the query.

8. My thesis is that what actually fills the space of the universe (*loka*) and what moulds its structure after its shape is, potentially, every individual soul (*jīva*) that accomplishes this task at a very specific moment of its 'career' in the *saṁsāra*. To wit, this happens during a process of the shaking-off of the karmic matter called *samudghāta* (Pkt.: *samugghāya*):[87] it is precisely in the process that the soul's spatial units expand up to the limits of the universe and then contract.

---

[85] See p. 127 and n. 84.

[86] See Adrian SNODGRASS (1985: 21): 'The concept of the genesis of space as an expansion or radiation from a point is reflected in language. The Sanskrit word *nābhi*, "the hub or nave of a wheel" and also "centre" and "navel", derives from the root *nabh*, "to expand". With reference to the human body, the navel corresponds to space, and in the *Ṛg Veda* the cosmos is frequently spoken of as "expanded" from a chthonic navel. Also, in the *Vedas* space is often designated by the word *diś*, which is literally "cardinal point" or "direction".'

[87] For a succinct and informative description of the process known as *samudghāta* (*samugghāya*) see SCHUBRING (1962: 183–184, § 89): 'By being annihilated several kinds of Karman suffer a special fate by being subjected to the *samugghāya*, i.e. the "ejection" of their particles. ... There are seven cases of *s*. (Ṭhāṇ. 409 b; Samav. 12 b), the last of which being reserved to the Kevalin, so that the remaining six are comprised

At the time of Umāsvāmin (ca 350–400) the idea of the soul which can expand in size up to the spatial limits of the universe and contract down to a minute size seems to be well established. The author of the *Tattvârtha-sūtra* avails himself of the popular picture of the light emitted by a lamp which completely fills any space it happens to occupy:

> '[The souls can pervade] an innumerably small part [of the world] and more [up to the whole world]. [It is] due to contraction and expansion [respectively] of [their] spatial units, just like a lamp [can fill a space with its light].'[88]

There can hardly be any doubt that what the maximum expansion up to the limits of the universe may refer to is precisely the *samudghāta* process.

Śvetāmbara Umāsvāti, the author of the *Praśama-rati-prakaraṇa*, traditionally assumed to be also the commentator on the *Tattvârtha-sūtra* (which seems rather doubtful), describes this peculiar process in quite a detail. The soul of a person who has attained perfect cognition, or omniscience (*kevala*), and is ready to accomplish the ultimate emancipation (*mokṣa*), expands its size and fills the complete universe (*loka*) in the first four instants, known as smallest time units (*samaya*), and the in subsequent four instants it shrinks back to its original size. During these eight instants the soul gets rid of all the remaining karmic matter, which has been veiling it since times immemorial up to this moment:

---

as *chaumattiya* s. (e.g. Samav 11 b). This does not mean, however, that it were within the power of monks only to attain it, the fact is, rather, that all beings share in it correspondingly (Pannav. 561 b). For they all have a certain sense of karman (*veyaṇā*), have passion (*kasāya*), suffer death (*maraṇa*) and thus are in possession of the accordingly called *samugghāya* (1 to 3), in the third case the *māraṇ'antiya s.* As far as they have a fiery body they are given the possibility of also attaining the corresponding *samughāya* (4 to 6) (cmop. Ṭhāṇ. 288 a). As to the process concerning the *kevali-s.* we are advised by Uvav. § 141 ff.; Ṭhāṇ. 422 a. To put it briefly, the Kevalin projects his soul atoms still infected with Karman from the vertex and the footpoint from the right and the left side, from the chest and the back in the shape of columns each reaching to the end of the world and the retracts them again. During the time of the 8 *samaya* it takes to accomplish this process, the Karman particles—as must be added logically—disengage from the soul. The *samugghāya* of other beings take a longer time, i.e. ¿ *samaya* within a *muhutta* (Pannav. 561 b),and the space filled up by them is, in proportion, infinitesimally small, i.e. equal to the body of the resp. being, though in the case of the last of these *samugghāya* columns we have to add up to ¿ *joyaṇa* in one direction. The ejected (*nicchūḍha*) *poggala* dissipate in the world ...'

[88] TS 5.15–16: *asaṁkhyeya-bhāgâdiṣu. pradeśa-saṁhāra-visargābhyāṁ pradīpavat.*

> '[273] Whatever karmic matter[89] the omniscient [being still] possesses, [and] which exceeds his life span [to be experienced as determined by his *karman*], the [omniscient] lord then undertakes [the process of] the shaking-off of this [karmic matter].
> [274] In the first instant [the omniscient emanates the remaining karmic matter in the form of] an [upright] pole.[90] And, similarly, in the next instant [he flings it open as] a [two-panel] door [sidewise].[91] Further, in the third [instant he transforms it into] a churning-stick, whereas in the fourth [instant he fills the gaps] and pervades the [whole] universe.
> [275] Next, in the fifth [instant], he retracts the intermediate [spatial units of the soul that filled in the gaps in the universe], and subsequently, in the sixth [instant he transforms them back into] a churning-stick. Then, in the seventh [instant], he retracts [these spatial units in the form of a churning-stick into] a [two-panel] door. Finally, in the eighth [instant, he retracts these into a form of] an [upward] pole.'[92]

The process of *samudghāta* is undertaken by any soul that has already eliminated all negative, morally relevant and harmful karmic matter, and has attained omniscience. However, even in such a perfect condition the soul, or actually its body, is still under the influence of the *karman* that determines its life span, physiological processes etc. It is further believed that it is necessary to eliminate even these, seemingly innocuous kinds of *karmic* matter before one can attain full-fledged lib-

---

[89] The commentator indicates that what is meant is the remaining 'non-harmful' karmic matter that determines experience, individuality and social status, and has to be experienced: PRṬ 273, p. 186.23: *karma vedya-nāma-gotrâkhyam*.

[90] Cf. PRṬ 274 ad loc.: *sva-śarīra-pramāṇa-daṇḍa-bāhulyenôrdhvam adhaś câtma-pradeśān vikṣipaty ā lokântāt.*—'He discharges the spatial units of his soul upwards and downwards, up to the end of the world, so that its vastness is that of a pole of the size (diameter) of his own body.'

[91] Cf. PRṬ 274 ad loc.: *dvitīya-samaye tu kapāṭī-karoti dakṣiṇôttarato vistārayaty ā lokântāt.*—'But in the second instant he transforms [the pole] into a [two-panel] door, [then] he extends it southwards and northwards, up to the end of the world.'

[92] PRP_2 273–275 = PRP_3 272–274:

yasya punaḥ kevalinaḥ karma bhavaty āyuṣo-'tirikataram /
sa samudghātaṁ bhagavān atha gacchati tat samīkartum //
daṇḍaṁ prathame samaye kapāṭam atha côttare tathā samaye /
manthānam atha tṛtīye loka-vyāpi caturthe tu //
saṁharati pañcame tv antarāṇi manthānam atha punaḥ ṣaṣṭhe /
saptamake tu kapāṭam saṁharati tato 'ṣṭame daṇḍam //

eration (*mokṣa*) and traverse to the highest abode of the whole universe, or the world of the liberated beings (*siddha-loka*), because even a minute remnant of karmic matter hampers liberation. The idea of the process of *samudghāta* is that the soul expands to the maximum and then shrinks immediately within a very short time so that, it seems, the karmic matter enveloping the soul has, in its inertia, no time and capability to contract accordingly and remains scattered all over the universe: the living soul moves and contracts faster than the lifeless matter.

To understand the mechanism of the process[93], one should first remember that the soul in Jainism, being a kind of substance, is understood as a sort of spatially extensive body, composed of spatial units, like all other substances. Further, the number of spatial units of the soul (*jīva*) is innumerable (i.e. extremely large but still limited in number), as is the number of spatial units of the medium of motion (*dharma*) and of the medium of rest (*adharma*).[94] This synchronism is quite important because the space (*ākāśa*) within which the soul can expand is limited by the existence of the media of motion and rest, and these occur only within the anthropomorphic universe (*loka*), filled by space. The rest of the space that limitlessly extends beyond the boundary of the universe is called 'non-world' (*aloka*).[95] In other words, the spatial

---

[93] For its relevant description see also RVār 1.20, p. 77.12 ff.: *hanter gami-kriyātvāt saṁbhūyâtma-pradeśānāṁ ca bahir-ud-hahanaṁ* (recte: °*-uddhananaṁ*) *samudghātaḥ. sa sapta-vidhaḥ.* ... [comp. GSKVṛ 583, p. 735.13–15; Paṇṇ 36, 2085–6 ff., p. 439] *vedanīyasya bahutvād alpatvāc câyuṣo 'nābhoga-pūrvakam āyuḥ-samakaraṇârthaṁ dravya-svabhāvatvāt surā-dravyasya phena-vega-budbudâvir-bhāvôpaśamanavad deha-sthâtma-pradeśānām bahiḥ-samudghātanaṁ kevali-samudghātaḥ. ... śeṣāḥ pañca samudghātāḥ ṣaḍ-dikkāḥ. yato vedanâdi-samudghāta-vaśād bahir-niḥsṛtānāṁ ātma-pradeśānāṁ pūrvâpara-dakṣiṇôtttarôrdhvâdho-dikṣu gamanam iṣṭaṁ śreṇi-gatitvād ātma-pradeśānām. ... kevali-samudghātaḥ aṣṭa-samayikaḥ—daṇḍaka-vāṭa-pratara-loka-pūraṇāni caturṣṣu samayeṣu punaḥ prataraka-pāṭa-daṇḍa-sva-śarīrânupraveśāś caturṣu iti.*

[94] TS_{dig} 5.8: *asaṁkhyeyāḥ pradeśā dharmâdharmâika-jīvānām.* / $TS_{śvet}$ 5.7–8: *asaṁkhyeyāḥ pradeśā dharmâdharmayoḥ. jīvasya.*—'Spatial units of motion, rest and souls are innumerable' / 'Spatial units of motion and rest are innumerable. [Likewise the number of spatial units] of the soul [is innumerable]'. See below p. 137.

[95] See SSi.5.12, § 549, p. 210.9, 211.5–6: *uktānāṁ dharmâdīnāṁ dravyāṇāṁ lokâkāśe 'vagāho na bahir ity arthaḥ. ... sa yatra tal lokâkāśam. tato bahiḥ sarvato 'nantam alokâkāśam.*—'The meaning [of the *sūtra*] is that the above-mentioned [substances] such as the medium of motion etc. have their location in the space of the universe, not outside. ... Where this [universe] is [located] there is the space of the universe. Outside of it there is absolutely infinite space of the non-world.' See also PSā 2.44:

> *logâlogesu ṇabho dhammâdhammehi ādado logo /*
> *sese paḍucca kālo jīvā puṇa poggalā //*

units of soul can move as far as the medium of motion exists and the number of the soul's spatial units, soiled with *karmic* matter, accord with the number of the spatial units of the medium which enables the soul's movements, including its expansion. Therefore the soul's spatial units can expand till they overlap with spatial units of the space of the world (*lokâkāśa*). The idea is plainly stated by Pūjyapāda Devanandin, who adds some more important details:

> 'Motion, rest and souls have equally innumerable number of spatial units. ... Even though the soul, to begin with, [can be of the size of] a spatial unit—because it has a nature which can contract and expand—it acquires a body, developed from karmic matter, [of the size of] an atomic particle or [of the] large [size and], having extended itself accordingly, dwells. However, when [it's karmic body] assumes [the size] filling the world [completely, i.e. during the *samudghāta* process], then the soul's eight central spatial units locate themselves as the central spatial units below Mandara mountain (i.e. Mount Meru) in the middle of [the region called] Varigated Dimond Nether Layer (*citra-vajra-paṭala*). The remaining spatial units [move] upwards, downwards and horizontally, [and] penetrate the whole space of the world.'[96]

The soul is, by nature, capable of filling the whole space of the body it inhabits by adjusting its flexible size and it happens to take place exactly the way god occupies a temple, or the Buddha inhabits the *stūpa* etc. (see § 7): '[The size and the shape of the soul] adjusts itself to the size [and shape] of its body.'[97] Although Devanandin does not refer to the *samudghāta* process explicitly in this passage, it is quite obvious in the context that when the soul assumes its maximum size, while filling the whole space of the universe (*loka-pūraṇa*), it happens precisely during the process of shaking off the karmic matter, for we read of no other occasion when such expansion and contraction could take place.

> 'The space (*nabho* = *ākāśa*) [extends] in the universe and non-universe. The universe is penetrated with the medium of motion and the medium of rest, with time, which depends on the remaining [two substances], with souls and matter.'

[96] SSi 5.8, p. 208.9–13: *dharmâdharma-jīvās tulyâsaṁkhyeya-pradeśāḥ. ... jīvas tāvat pradeśo 'pi san saṁharaṇa-visarpaṇa-svabhāvatvāt karma-nirvartitaṁ śarīram aṇu mahad vâdhitiṣṭhaṁs tāvad avagāhya vartate. yadā tu loka-pūraṇaṁ bhavati tadā mandarasyâdhaś citra-vajra-paṭala-madhye jīvasyâṣṭau pradeśā madhya-pradeśā vyavatiṣṭhante. itare pradeśā ūrdhvam adhas tiryak ca kṛtsnaṁ lokâkāśaṁ vyaśnuvate.*

[97] RVār 5.16, p. 459.27: *śarīra-pramāṇânuvidhānāt.*

Devanandin takes up the issue of the process of *samudghāta* in a subsequent portion of his work, where he describes it as follows:

> 'When, however, [the monk in the third stage of meditation], whose life span [determined by the remaining *karman*] is one interim moment[98] [or less], has become the [so-called omniscient] with residue operations[99], then he—since he is someone who [has achieved] the highest degree of his own cognitive faculties, who is accompanied by inner equanimity (*sāmāyika*), who is [himself] a pre-eminent factor, who [has embarked on] enormous restraint [and] who has brought to maturity the lesser *karman* has by his own nature the power to expunge the dust of the remaining karmic matter—pervades the world with its [karmic matter particle]s as an [upright] pole, as a [two-panel] door and as an oblong by spreading spatial units of his own soul within four instants; then, again, within the same number [of four] instants the process of drawing the contracted spatial units back takes place, the duration of the four remaining types of *karman* is made equal [and his soul returns to] the original size of his body; subsequently, he embraces meditation which counteracts subtle operations initiated through the activity of his subtle body.'[100]

What is, perhaps, not immediately manifest but what seems quite intriguing in these descriptions are two elements: the mention of 'the eight spatial units of the soul' (*jīvasyâṣṭau pradeśāḥ*) and the reference to the expanding and contracting soul which 'pervades the world' with particles of its karmic matter in a form of 'an [upright] pole' and of 'a [two-panel] door' (*daṇḍa-kapāṭa-°*).

---

[98] I.e. approx. 48 minutes.

[99] *Sayogin*, lit. 'the one possessing operations', i.e. the adept at the thirteenth level of spiritual development (*guṇa-sthāna*, lit. 'degree of good qualities'), out of fourteen: he has already become omniscient, but due to the presence of some residue karmic matter that binds him in the world (*saṁsāra*), he is not yet fully liberated, even though actual final liberation is a matter of time. On the fourteen *guṇa-sthāna*s see e.g. GLASENAPP (1942: 75–92), TATIA (1951: 268–280).

[100] SSi 9.44, p. 360.12–361.3: *yadā punar antar-muhūrta-śeṣâyuṣkas tato 'dhika-sthiti-śeṣa-karma-trayo bhavati sayogī tadâtmôpayogâtiśayasya sāmāyika-sahāyasya viśiṣṭa-karaṇasya māhā-saṁvarasya laghu-karma-paripācanasyâśeṣa-karma-reṇu-pariśātana-śakti-svabhāvyād daṇḍa-kapāṭa-pratara-loka-pūraṇāni svâtma-pradeśa-visarpaṇataś caturbhiḥ samayaiḥ kṛtvā punar api tāvadbhir eva samayaiḥ samupahṛta-pradeśa-visaraṇaḥ samī-kṛta-sthiti-śeṣa-karma-catuṣṭayaḥ pūrva-śarīra-pramāṇo bhūtva sūkṣma-kāya-yogena sūkṣma-kriyā-pratipāti-dhyānam dhyāyati.*

The idea of these eight spatial units of the soul is not an invention of Pūjyapāda Devanandin but is found also in earlier canonical literature, as noticed and explained by SCHUBRING (1962: 130, § 58):

> 'The number of units (*paesa* / *pradeśa*—P.B.) is ∞ (i.e. infinite—P.B.) with the total space as well as with souls and mater, and s˙(i.e. innumerable—P.B.) with motion and rest (148a) and with the space of the world (421a, 610a, 873b). Moreover there are 8 centremost units (*majjha-paesa*), which, each with motion, rest and space are supposed (acc. to comm.) to exist in the centre of the upper regions of the world, called the Ruyaga, in Rayaṇappabhā (§107), with the souls within their resp. bodies. They will occupy 1–6 or either 8, but *vastu-svabhāvāt* not 7 units of space (Viy. 886a, 395b). In the realm of space we meet the 4 main and the 4 intermediate directions (*disā* or *vidisā*) in addition to zenith (*uḍḍhaṁ*) and nadir (*aho*). ... Acc. to comm. they are of two- resp. one dimensional shape. The pole from which they start (Viy. 606a, Thān, 77b) is a square cube of 8 *paesa*.'

An indirect reference to the eight spatial units of the soul is found also in a slightly ambiguous passage in Puṣpadanta and Bhūtabali's (ca. 200 CE) work called the *Cha-kkhaṁḍâgame* (*Ṣaṭ-khaṇḍâgama*, ṢKhĀ):

> 'The one who is known to be bound as an embodied being from beginningless times, like someone who is bound with [all] his spatial units in dependence on the eight central spatial units of the soul, such [a person] is completely bound as an embodied being from beginningless times.'[101]

The eight central spatial units are apparently the only immovable units of the soul throughout its mundane existence, especially during the process of *samudghāta*, and that condition is contrasted with the liberated soul, with all its spatial units located in the world of the liberated beings (*siddha-loka*) at the top of the universe.

A reference to the process of *samudghāta* can be found also in the canonical literature, for instance in the *Viyāha-pannatti* which describes how a homeless monk, the moment when he enters death, spreads all the remaining subtle particles of karmic matter over the whole universe in order to rid of them.[102]

---

[101] ṢKhĀ 5.6 *sū* 63 (vol. 14, p. 46.1–2): *jo aṇādiya-sarīri-baṁdho ṇāma yathā* <recte: *jahā*> *aṭṭhaṇṇam jīva-majjha-padesāṇaṁ aṇṇoṇṇa-padesa-baṁdho bhavadī so savvo aṇādiya-sarīri-baṁdho ṇāma*.

[102] Viy$_2$ 18.3.8, p. 805.6–13: *aṇagārassa ṇaṁ bhaṁte! bhāviyappaṇo savvaṁ kammaṁ vedemāṇassa, savvaṁ kammaṁ nijjaremāṇassa, savvaṁ māraṇaṁ maramāṇassa, savvaṁ*

Brief references to the process, in particular to the idea of the expansion and contraction of the soul's spatial units, are also found in the Digambara commentary on the *Cha-kkhaṁḍâgame*:

> '[The *sūtra*:] The experience of experiential *karman* [responsible for pleasure and pain] is in a certain sense established. [The commentary:] Why? Because one apprehends the state of spatial units of the soul by way of contraction and expansion in an omniscient being, who is bereft of all activity, whose all operations [of mind, speech and body] have been completely destroyed.'[103]

In another passage, the commentator Vīrasena takes for granted that the soul may be either of a size of the whole universe (when inflated to the maximum) or of a size of an infinitesimal fraction of a thumb understood as a length unit (when contracted to the maximum):

> 'As for the [types of sense organs of souls endowed with various number of sense organs,] internal receptors such as the eye and other sense organs are the disposition of the spatial units of the self which are of the size of the universe and purified or [the disposition of the spatial units] which are of the size of an innumerable portion of a thumb being a length unit.'[104]

In addition, the same text makes explicit the mention of the eight central spatial units of the soul, while discussing three different kinds of karmic bonds (*baṁdha*), one of them being prompted by an impulse (*prayoga*).[105] These make up the central 'hub' of the karmic bondage. In another passage, the work records the following (imaginary) discourse between Mahāvīra and his disciple Gautama:

---

sarīraṁ vippajahamāṇassa, carimaṁ kammaṁ vedemāṇassa, carimaṁ kammaṁ vijjaremāṇassa, carimaṁ māraṁ maramāṇassa, carimaṁ sarīraṁ vippajahamāṇassa, māraṇaṁtiyaṁ kammaṁ vedemāṇassa, māraṇaṁtiyaṁ kammaṁ nijjaremāṇassa, māraṇaṁtiyaṁ māraṁ maramāṇassa, māraṇaṁtiyaṁ sarīraṁ vippajahamāṇassa je carimā nijjarā-poggalā, suhumā ṇaṁ te poggalā paṇṇattā samaṇāuso! savvaṁ logaṁ pi ṇaṁ te ogāhittāṇaṁ ciṭṭhaṁti? haṁtā, māgaṁdiya-putto! aṇagārassa ṇaṁ bhāviyappaṇo jāva ogāhittāṇaṁ ciṭṭhaṁti.

[103] ṢKhĀ 4.2.11, *sū* 5 and DhṬ ad loc. (vol. 12, p. 367.11–13): ***veyaṇī-veyaṇā siyā ṭṭhidā***. *kudo? ajogi-kevalimmi ṇaṭṭhâsesa-jogammi jīva-padesāṇaṁ saṁkoca-vikocâbhāveṇa avaṭṭhāṇ-'uvalaṁbhādo.*

[104] DhṬ ad ṢKhĀ 1.1.33, vol. 1/1, p. 234.11-3: *tatra loka-pramitānāṁ viśuddhānām ātma-pradeśānāṁ pratiniyata-cakṣur-adiindriya-saṁsthānenâvasthitānām utsedhâṅgula-syâsaṁkhyeya-bhāga-pramitānāṁ vā vṛttir abhyantarā nirvṛttiḥ.*

[105] Viy_2 8.9.12, p. 380.18: *aṭṭhaṇhaṁ jīva-majjha-paesāṇaṁ.*

> '[246] O Lord, how many central spatial units are expounded to be there of the fundamental mass of the medium of motion (*dharmâsti-kāya*)? O Gautama, there are eight central spatial units of the fundamental mass of the medium of motion. [247] O Lord, how many central spatial units are expounded to be there of the fundamental mass of the medium of rest (*adharmâsti-kāya*)? [Reply:] Exactly as above. [248] O Lord, how many central spatial units are expounded to be there of the fundamental mass of space (*ākāśâsti-kāya*)? [Reply:] Exactly as above. [249] O Lord, how many central spatial units are expounded to be there of the fundamental mass of soul (*jīvâsti-kāya*)? [Reply:] O Gautama, there are eight central spatial units of the fundamental mass of the soul. [250] O Lord! And how many spatial units of space do these eight central spatial units of the fundamental mass of soul occupy? [Reply:] O Gautama! They [coincide] with minimum one or two, or three, or four, or five, or six, or with maximum eight, but in no case with seven [spatial units of space].'[106]

Thus, in all the fundamental masses, including the soul and matter, one can distinguish the eight central spatial units, which are 'spatially synchronised' or co-extensive. A similar idea is also mentioned in the *Ṭhāṇaṁga-sutta* in a respective portion on the middle section of the universe (*madhya-pradeśa-pāda*):

> 'There are eight central spatial units of the medium of motion (*dharma*). There are eight central spatial units of the medium of rest (*adharma*). There are eight central spatial units of space (*ākāśa*). There are eight central spatial units of the soul (*jīva*).'[107]

These descriptions suggest that the eight central spatial units of each of the fundamental masses (*asti-kāya*) respectively overlap, since they must all be centrally lo-

[106] Viy$_2$ 25.4 §§ 246–250, p. 1011.16–1012.2: [246] *kati ṇaṁ bhaṁte! dhamma'tthi-kāyassa majjha-paesā pannattā? goyamā! aṭṭha dhamma'tthi-kāyassa majjha-paesā pannattā.* [247] *kati ṇaṁ bhaṁte! adhamma'tthi-kāyassa majjha-paesā pannattā? eva cêva.* [248] *kati ṇaṁ bhaṁte! āgāsa'tthi-kāyassa majjha-paesā pannattā? eva cêva.* [249] *kati ṇaṁ bhaṁte! jīva'tthi-kāyassa majjha-paesā pannattā? Gotama! aṭṭha jīva'tthi-kāyassa majjha-paesā pannattā.* [250] *ee ṇaṁ bhaṁte! aṭṭha jīva'tthi-kāyassa majjha-paesā katisu āgāsa-paesesu ogāhiṁti? Goyamā! jahanneṇaṁ ekkaṁsi vā dohi vā tīhi vā cauhiṁ vā paṁcahiṁ vā chahiṁ vā, ukkoseṇaṁ aṭṭhasu, no cêva ṇaṁ sattasu.*

[107] Ṭhāṇ 8 § 626, p. 255.10–13: *aṭṭha dhamma'tthi-gāta-majjha-padesā pannattā, aṭṭha adhamma'tthi-gāta-majjha-patesā pannattā, eva c'evaṁ aṭṭha āgāsa'tthi-majjha-patesā pannattā, evaṁ c'eva aṭṭha jīva-majjha-patesā pannattā.*

cated. The text also specifies that the central spatial units of the soul are located centrally in the world and they can either be compressed to such a degree that they would occupy just a single unit of space or extend as much as to occupy maximum eight adjacent units of space.

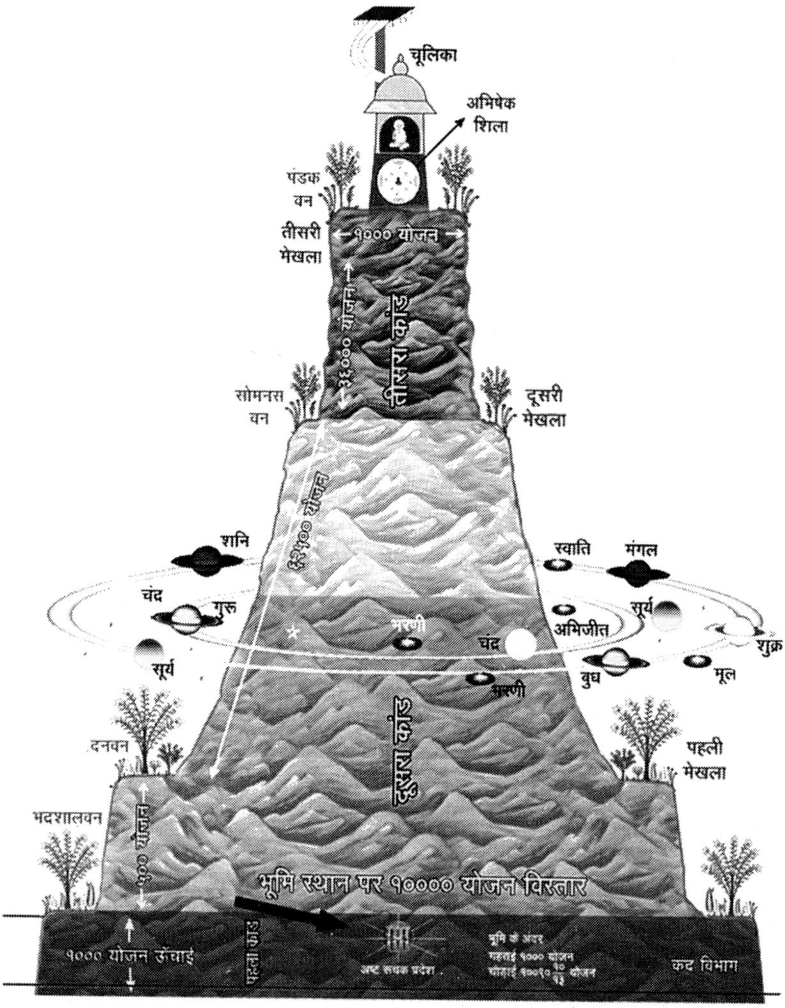

Fig. 9. Mout Meru (*meru-parvata*). Reproduced after SŪRĪŚVAR (2008: 32). The black arrow indicates the position of the eight-pointed crystal cube (*aṣṭa pradeśika rucaka*), erroneously named by *aṣṭa-rucaka-pradeśa* by SŪRĪŚVAR.

Incidentally, what is the spatial centre of an individual soul, including its eight-fold structure, turns out to coincide with the centremost point of the universe, called the crystal cube (*rucaka*), from which, as it is repeatedly said, all cardinal directions and intermediate directions commence:[108]

> 'Indeed, these cardinal directions have their beginning in the crystal cube (*rucaka*), they stem from the crystal cube (*rucaka*), they begin with two spatial units, they have more than two spatial units. With respect to the universe, their [length is of] innumerable spatial units (sc. are limited in length). With respect to the 'non-universe', their [length is of] infinite spatial units…'[109]

The position of the crystal cube from which all directions stem is occasionally reproduced in Jaina art or popular literature (fig. 9).
It is not merely an incidental remark in the text but the image of the central eight-unit cube of the universe is a recurrent theme in Jaina canonical literature:

> '[Gautama asks Mahāvīra:] O Lord, where is the central section of the expanse of the middle section of the middle world expounded to be? [Mahāvīra replies to Gautama:] O Gautama, inside upper and nether tiny layers inside this land [called] Ratnaprabhā within the section of the extensive middle part of Mandara (sc. Meru) Mountain in the Island of Jambudvīpa, there, in the centre of the middle world a crystal cube (*rucaka*) consisting of eight spatial units is expounded to be [located], from which these ten cardinal directions stem.'[110]

This idea as it was expressed by the authors of the *Viyāha-pannatti* is echoed by the commentators of the *Āyāraṁga-sutta*:

---

[108] For a closer description of the cube, or eight *pradeśa*s of the Ratnaprabhā (Rayaṇa-ppabhā), see OHIRA (1994: 80, § 163).

[109] Viy_2 13.4 § 16, p. 629.17–19: *iṁdā ṇaṁ disā ruyagâdīyā ruyaga-ppavahā du-padesâdīyā du-pades'uttarā, logaṁ paḍucca asaṁkhejja-paesiyā, alogaṁ laḍucca aṇaṁta-padesiyā…* See also Viy_2 13.4.21, p. 630.5–6: *vimalā ṇaṁ disā ruyagâdīyā ruyaga-ppavahā …*

[110] Viy_2 13.4 § 15, p. 629.9–12: *kahi ṇaṁ bhaṁte! tiriya-logassa āyāma-majjhe pannatte? goyamā! jaṁbu-ddīve dīve maṁdarassa pavvayassa bahu-majjha-desa-bhāe imīse rayaṇa-ppabhāe puḍhavīe uvarima-heṭṭhillesu khuḍḍaga-payaresu, ettha ṇaṁ tiriya-loga-majjhe aṭṭha-paesie ruyae pannatte, jao ṇaṁ imāo dasa disāo pavahaṁti…* See also Viy_2 13.4 § 67, p. 638.17–19: *kahi ṇaṁ bhaṁte! loe bahusame? kahi ṇaṁ bhaṁte! loe savva-viggahie pannatte? goyamā! imīse rayaṇa-ppabhāe puḍhavīe uvarima-heṭṭhillesu khuḍḍaga-payaresu, ettha ṇaṁ loe bahu-same, ettha ṇaṁ loe savva-viggahie pannatte.*

> 'The crystal cube (*rucaka*) consisting of eight spatial units is [located] centrally in the middle section of the world. It is the source of cardinal directions [of the space], and it is really the origin of intermediate directions.'[111]

Just as the eight-pointed crystal cube (*aṣṭa-pradeśika-rucaka*) consisting of eight spatial units (*pradeśa*) is, metaphorically speaking, the source of all the space, or—to be more exact—as it is the sphere from which all the spatial cardinal directions commence and radiate in the expanse of the whole universe, similarly the central 'eight spatial units of the soul' (*jīvasyâṣṭau pradeśāḥ*) is the area from which the soul expands during the process of the shaking-off of the karmic matter (*samudghāta*).

The structural similarity between the shape of the anthropomorphic soul and that of the anthropomorphic universe is so striking that it can hardly be coincidental. That it is a conscious overlap and not a matter of mere coincidence is highlighted by Pūjyapāda Devanandin who explicitly establishes a direct link between both spatial structures: that of the soul in the apogee of the *samudghāta* process and that of the anthropomorphic universe:

> '...the soul's eight spatial units locate themselves as the central spatial units below Mandara mountain (i.e. Mount Meru) in the middle of [region called] Varigated Dimond Nether Layer (*citra-vajra-paṭala*).'[112]

That the structural similarity between the soul and the world, at least as far as the centremost position of the eight central spatial units is concerned, is indisputable and not merely coincidental is confirmed also by two separate descriptions of spatial units of the soul and of the world provided by one and the same author Akalaṅka two centuries later.

The first passage describes the structure of the world with its centremost eight spatial units:

> 'The scope of [all] these [disciplines of knowledge] is the world. [Its] location, which is the space, consists in countless cardinal lines of the units of space drawn systematically—like threads of a piece of cloth or

---

[111] ĀyārN 1.42, p 4:
attha-paeso ruyago tiriyaṁ loyassa majjhayāruṁmi /
esa pabhavo disāṇaṁ es'eva bhave aṇudisāṇaṁ //

[112] SSi 5.8, p. 208.12: ...*mandarasyâdhaś citra-vajra-paṭala-madhye jīvasyâṣṭau pradeśā madhya-pradeśā vyavatiṣṭhante*, quoted above in n. 96.

like filaments of leather—upwards, horizontally and downwards, which are called "straight lines".[113]
In the sizeable central part of the space of the infinite non-world there is the world which resembles an [hourglass-shaped][114] stand. In its upper, lower and middle [sections the world] bears the shape of the *mṛd-aṅga* drum, an oblong reed stool and the thin frame drum (*jhallarī*);[115] [it has a form of] circular cylinder extending in its upper, lower and middle [sections] enveloped with a layer of the rarefied air, [it is] fourteen 'cords'[116] in expansion (i.e. height). The centre of the word are eight units of space fixed in the crystal cube inside [the region called] Dimond Gem Nether Layer at the base of Meru[117].'[118]

What is interesting in the passage is a comparison of the spatial grid of the world, based on the straight lines (*śreṇi*), to filaments (lit. 'pieces') of leather (*carmâvayava*) which extend in all cardinal directions. This image corresponds to a number of earlier references to leather or skin (*carman*) of the world, such as a leather bag (*vatthi*) referred to in the *Viyāha-pannatti*[119] or 'the inflated expanse of the skin [of the cosmic body]' found in Siddhasena Gandhahastin's *Tattvârthâdhigama-ṭīkā*[120]. It would indeed be quite peculiar—on the part of a Jaina thinker who by nature abhors leather products, which involve killing of animals, and for whom a reference to making use of pieces of skin / leather is rather a taboo inasmuch as it may involve

[113] This goes back to a passage found in SSi 2.26: *loka-madhyād ārabhya ūrdhvam adhas tiryak ca ākāśa-pradeśānāṁ krama-sanniviṣṭānāṁ paṅktiḥ śreṇir ity ucyate.*— 'Cardinal lines of the units of space that are arranged in a sequence, which extend upwards, horizontally and downwards, commencing from the middle of the world, are [technically] called "straight lines".'

[114] See n. 4.

[115] See LVi 1.3, 6 (n. 2 above).

[116] See n. 6 and Illustration 1 (p. 97).

[117] Cf. SSi 5.8: *citra-vajra-paṭala-madhye jīvasyâṣṭau pradeśā madhya-pradeśā vyavatiṣṭhante*, n. 96 above.

[118] RVār 1.20, p. 76.9–11: *teṣāṁ viṣayo lokaḥ. kṣetram ākāśaṁ paṭa-sūtravac carmâvayavavad vā ānupūrvyeṇa ūrdhvâdhas-tiryag-vyavasthitā asaṁkhyātā ākāśa-pradeśa-paṅktayaḥ śreṇaya uktāḥ.*

alokâkāśasyânantasya bahu-madhye supratiṣṭhaka-saṁsthāno lokaḥ, urdhvam adhas tiryaṅ mṛd-aṅga-vetrâsana-jhallary-ākṛtiḥ, tanu-vāta-valaya-parikṣipta ūrdhvâdhas-tiryakṣu pratara-vṛttaś catur-daśa-rajjv-āyāmaḥ. meru-pratiṣṭha-vajra-vaiḍūrya-paṭalântara-rucaka-saṁsthitā aṣṭāv ākāśa-pradeśā loka-madhyam.

[119] See n. 32.

[120] See n. 25.

causing suffering to living beings—to refer to *pieces* or filaments of leather (skin), unless such reference was dictated by some special reason. The justification would in this case be both historical and cosmological: this reference is made against a backdrop of a particular historical image of a universe in human shape, already referred to as having the form of the leather hull (*vide supra*, p. 113).

If we compare the above passage with another one, quoted by Akalaṅka from an unidentified older source, the similarity of the world structure and of the soul, at least as far as the overlapping of the eight central spatial units, becomes manifest:

> 'In the case of all souls the soul's eight central spatial units, being flawless, are completely immovable at all times. Similarly, in the case of omniscient beings and liberated beings, who are free of any activity, all spatial units are completely immovable. In the case of souls which are subject to predominance of struggle, suffering and sorrow, all other spatial units, except for the above-mentioned eight central spatial units, are indeed not immovable. In the case of the remaining living beings, [spatial units] are both immovable and movable'...[121]

The passage, a little unclear at first, mentions three kinds of cases when the souls' eight central spatial units are either motionless or not. The first case is that of the soul undergoing the *samudghāta* process, whose eight central spatial units are the same as those of the crystal cube (*rucaka*) located in the very centre of the universe at the bottom of Mount Meru. In that case, the soul's central spatial units overlap with the units of the world. The liberated beings are eternally immovable, spatially located at the top of the universe, hence all their spatial units are likewise immovable. The structural match between the world and the soul is nothing novel: it only emphasises what we have observed in earlier strata of Jaina literature.

The fixed position of the soul's 'cube' is also well-attested in later Digambara tradition, e.g. in Vīrasena's *Dhavalā* commentary on the *Ṣaṭ-khaṇḍâgama*:

> 'Since certain spatial units of the soul of a person in the state of bondage (*chadma-stha*), who is devoid of afflictions such as distress, pain, fear etc., are immovable, that is why the fixed accumulations of *karman* remain fixed, and since in the same way certain spatial units of

[121] RVār 5.8, p. 451.13–16: "*sarva-kālaṁ jīvâṣṭa-madhya-pradeśā nirapavādāḥ* (fn. 4: *nirdoṣāḥ spanda-rahitatvāt*—editor) *sarva-jīvānāṁ sthitā eva, kevalināṁ api ayogināṁ siddhānāṁ ca sarve pradeśaḥ sthitā eva, vyāyama-duḥkha-paritāpôdreka-pariṇatānāṁ jīvānāṁ yathôktâṣṭa-madhya-pradeśa-varjitānām itare* (recte °*-varjitā itare*) *pradeśāḥ asthitā eva, śeṣāṇāṁ prāṇināṁ sthitāś câsthitāś ca*" *iti vacanān mukhyā evâtma-pradeśāḥ*.

the soul are in motion, the accumulations of *karman* which are movable remain in motion; for precisely this reason the are known as not immovable.'[122]

Apparently, this particular soul who is, at the same time, both in the state of bondage and is devoid of afflictions such as distress, pain, fear etc., is a soul on the verge of final liberation: all its karmic afflictions (*kleśa*) have been eliminated, but it continues to remain in the *saṁsāra* as long as its residue karmic particles are eliminated. This passage refers to the *samudghāta* process, during which some of its spatial units remain fixed an immovable (in the centre of the universe), whereas most of its spatial units expand up to the confines of the universe and eventually contract, to discard the residue karmic matter.

We can see that the idea of the *samudghāta* process, in which the soul expands and completely fills the cosmic space up to the limits where the movement of its spatial units is possible, was instrumental in shaping and justifying the image of the cosmic man. When the soul thus expanded, the world resembled a human being. Additional elements of cosmology were also employed whereby the centre of the universe and the centre of the expanded soul overlapped, that centremost area being the crystal cube (*rucaka*) at the bottom of Mount Meru and the navel of the soul respectively. In fact, these centremost areas were one and the same point: the navel of the expanded soul and the navel of the world (*nābhī*), i.e. the navel of the *loka-puruṣa*.

10. From the above we may draw a few conclusions.

First, the image of the cosmic man was already present in Jainism already in a full-fledged form at least in the middle canonical period (ca. 1–2 centuries CE), but there are traces of it that date back to the earliest strata of the Jaina literature, e.g. to the time of the composition of *Isi-bhāsiyāiṁ* (*Ṛṣi-bhāṣitāni*). Although we do not, as it seems, come across any detailed description of the concept of the *loka-puruṣa* or the term itself (e.g. *loya- / loga-purisa*), some cosmological terminology that derives from the parts of human body (e.g. veins, navel, neck, womb) and the concept of tripartite composition of the universe must have presupposed the image of the world resembling the structure of the human body.

Second, the idea of the *loka-puruṣa* in Jainism has the idea of the cosmic man (*puruṣa*) of the Vedic and early Hindu tradition in the background. It would, however, be too far-fetched to claim that such Vedic and early Hindu concepts were the

[122] DhṬ ad ṢKhĀ 4.2.11.3 (Vol. 12, p. 366.5–7): *vāhi-veyaṇā-sajjhasâdi-kilesa-virahiyassa chadumatthassa jīva-padesāṇam kesiṁ pi calaṇâbhāvādo tattha ṭṭhida-kamma-kkhaṁdhā vi ṭṭhidā c'eva hoṁti, tatth'eva kesiṁ jīva-padesāṇaṁ saṁcāl-'uvalaṁbhādo tattha ṭṭhida-kamma-khaṁdhā vi saṁcalaṁti, teṇa te aṭṭhidā tti bhaṇṇaṁti.*

source of the Jaina notion of the cosmic man (*loka-puruṣa*). Jaina cosmology was not modelled after some cosmological or cosmogonic ideas preserved in the *Veda*s, *Upaniṣad*s or the Epic, albeit it does derive certain inspiration from such ideas which undoubtedly permeated to some degree relatively wide strata of ancient Indian society. Accordingly, manifold and pregnant layers of meanings and semantic or cosmological ramifications attached to the word and to the concept of *puruṣa* in the Vedic and early Hindu traditions were effectively utilised by Jaina thinkers in 'strengthening' the anthropomorphic world structure that had already existed in the cosmology. Such inspiration or borrowings were, it should be emphasised, occurred without any conscious effort or awareness of the real Vedic source: had the Jainas sensed that the motives they adopted either historically go back to or 'ideologically' pertain to the Vedic tradition, such inspirations would have been rejected outright. It is also quite probable that the resemblance of certain cosmological traits underlying the Jaina idea of the cosmic man to some Vedic motives is coincidental or both Jaina and Vedic go back to some other source of which we no longer know anything.

Third, the belief in the expansion of the soul during the process of 'the shaking off the karmic matter' (*samugghāya* / *samudghāta*), which seems to be a very early idea, must have been instrumental in formulating the anthropomorphic image of the world. The cosmos is, so to say, the inflated human soul, which subsequently shrinks back to its original size. However, the expansion process of the soul's personal space draws the limits of the universe. What is primary, therefore, is the *puruṣa* which draws the boundary of the world. It is not the tripartite world which is already there to be filled by the *puruṣa*.

Fourth, that anthropomorphic image coexisted, at least from a certain point of time, side by side with another, purely geometric image, that of a tripartite world consisting of two solids, or slanting oblongs, placed one on top of each other and separated by a flat disc. It is however extremely difficult to say which of them was earlier. The simplicity of the geometrical would speak in favour of its temporal precedence. However, it is impossible to account for reasons that would lead early Jaina thinkers to accept such an image.

Fifth, as far as cosmological dimension is concerned, Mount Meru, also known as Mandara mountain, was believed to be located in the centre of the universe, not only spatially but also symbolically: through its crystal cube space (*rucaka*), it symbolically connects the image of the universe (*loka*) with the image of the soul, and with the idea of the latter's expansion and retraction (*samudghāta*). In fact, the crystal cube, which splits the nether worlds from the middle world, inhabited among others by humans, is the focal point, or hub, jointly of Mount Meru, the universe and the soul, understood in its two aspects: as an individual soul (*jīva*) and as the 'world soul' (*loka-puruṣa*).

BIBLIOGRAPHY

ALPHEN 2000 = Alphen, Jan Van: *Steps to Liberation. 2,500 Years of Jain Art and Religion*. Etnografisch Museum Antwerpen, Indian Study Centre Universiteit Antwerpen, Antwerp Indian Association, Antwerp 2000.

AV = *Atharva-veda*. Sātvalekar (ed.): *Atharva-veda-saṁhitā*. Svādhyāya-maṇḍala, Pāraḍī, Vi. Surat 1957.

ĀvS = *Āvassaya-sutta* [*Āvaśyaka-sūtra*]. Muni Puṇyavijayaji and Pt. Amritlāl Mohanlāl Bhojak (ed.): *Dasaveyāliyasuttaṁ, Uttarajjhayaṇāiṁ and Āvassayasuttaṁ*. Jaina-Āgama-Series 15, Śrī Mahāvīra Jaina Vidyālaya, Bombay 1977.

ĀyārN = *Āyāraṁga-nijjutti* [*Ācārâṅga-niryukti*]. Willem B. Bollée: *The Nijjuttis on the Seniors Of the Śvetâmbara Siddhânta: Āyāranga, Sasaveyāliya, Uttarajjhāyā and Sūyagaḍa. Text and Selective Glossary*. Beiträge zur Südasienforschung 169, Südasien-Institut der Universitat Heidelberg, Franz Steiner Verlag, Stuttagart 1995.

BANERJI 1976 = Banerji, Sures Chandra: *Fundamentals of Ancient Indian Music and Dance*. L.D. Series 57, L.D. Instittue of Indology, Ahmedabad 1976.

BAREAU 1962 = Bareau, André: 'La construction et le culte des stūpa d'après les *Vinayapiṭaka*', *Bulletin de l'École Française d'Extrême-Orient* 50 (1962) 229–274.

BĀU = *Bṛhad-āraṇyakôpaniṣad*. OLIVELLE (1998: 29–165).

BÄUMER 2001 = Bäumer, Bettina: 'Puruṣa', in KTK, vol. 1: 29–50.

BṛS = Varāhamihira: *Bṛhat-saṁhitā*. Avadha Vihāri Tripāṭhī: *Bṛhat-saṁhitā of Varāhamihira*. Varanaseya Sanskrit Vishvavidhyalaya, Varanasi 1968.

BRONKHORST 2005 = Bronkhorst, Johannes: 'Les reliques dans les religions de l'Inde', in: Lars Göhler (ed.): *Indische Kultur im Kontext. Rituale, Texte und Ideen aus Indien und der Welt. Festschrift für Klaus Mylius*. Beiträge zur Indologie 40, Otto Harrassowitz Verlag, Wiesbaden 2005: 49–85.

CAILLAT–KUMAR 1981 = Caillat, Colette; Kumar, Ravi: *The Jain Cosmology*. Bombay–Delhi–Bangalore 1981.

CarS = *Caraka-saṁhitā*. Narendra Nātha Senagupta, Balāicandra Senagupta (eds.): *The Carakasaṇhitā of Mahāmuni Agniveśa. Revised by Charaka. With the 'Āyurveda-Dīpikā' Commentary of Cakrapāṇidatta and 'Jalpakalpataru' by Gaṅgadhara*. Calcutta 1927 [reprinted: Vidya Vilas Press, Varanasi 1983].

ChU = *Chāndogyôpaniṣad*. See: OLIVELLE (1998: 166–287).

COLEBROOKE 1837 = Colebrooke, Henry Thomas: *Miscellaneous Essays*. 2 Vols., W.H. Allen & Company, London 1837.

CORT 2009 = Cort, John: 'The Cosmic Man and the Human Condition', in: GRANOFF (2009: 34–47).

DELEU 1970 = Deleu, Josef: *Viyāhapannatti <Bhagavai>, the Fifth Aṅga of the Jaina* Canon, Introduction, critical analysis, commentary, indexes. „De Tempel", Brugge 1970.

DhṬ = Vīrasena: *Dhavalā-ṭīkā*. Commentary of *Ṣaṭ-khaṇḍâgama*. See: ṢKhĀ.

DUNDAS 2002 = Dundas, Paul: *The Jains*. Second edition, Routledge, London–New York 2002 [first edition: 1992].

GLASENAPP 1925 = Glasenapp, Helmuth von: *Der Jainismus. Eine indische Erösungs-religion*. Alf Hager Verlag, Berlin 1925 [2. edition: Hager, Berlin 1964; English translation: *Jainism—An Indian Religion of Salvation*. Translated by Shridhar B. Shrotri, Lala Sundar Lal Jain Reserach Series Vo. XIV, Motilal Banarsidass, Delhi 1999].

GLASENAPP 1942 = Glasenapp, Helmuth von: *The Doctrine of Karman in Jain Philosophy*. English translation from German by G.B.Gifford, edited by H.R.Kapadia, Bombay 1942.

GRANOFF 2009 = Granoff, Phyllis (ed.): *Victorious Ones. Jain Images of Perfection*. Rubin Museum of Art / Mapin Publishing, New York–Ahmedabad 2009.

GRANOFF 2009 = Granoff, Phyllis (ed.): *Victorious Ones. Jain Images of Perfection*. Rubin Museum of Art / Mapin Publishing, New York–Ahmedabad 2009.

GS = Neminātha: *Gommaṭa-sāra*. Ādinātha Neminātha Upādhye, Pt. Kailāśacandra Śāstrī (ed.): *Gommaṭa-sāra (Jīva-kāṇḍa) of Acharya Nemichandra Siddhanta-Chakravarti. [with the Karṇāta-vṛtti of Keśavaṇṇa, Sanskrit Ṭīkā Jīvatattvapradīpikā, Hindi Translation and Introduction*]. 2 Vols., Jñānapīṭha Mūrtidevī Jaina Grantha-mālā 14/15 (Prakrit Grantha), Bhāratīya Jñānapīṭha Prakāśana, Delhi 1978/1979.

GSKVṛ = Keśavaṇṇa: *Karṇāta-vṛtti*. See GS.

HEGEWALD 2010 = Hegewald, Julia A. B.: 'Visual and Conceptual Links between Jaina Cosmological, Mythological and Ritual Instruments', *International Journal of Jaina Studies* (Online) Vol. 6, 1 (2010) 1–20.

HORSCH 2004 = Horsch, Paul: 'From Creation Myth to World Law: The Early History of *Dharma*?', *Journal of Indian Philosophy* 32 (2004) 423–448 [originally published: 'Vom Schöpfungsmythos zum Weltgesetz', *Asiatische Studien: Zeitschrift der Schweizerischen Gesellschaft für Asiankunde* 21 (1967) 31–61].

HUDSON 2008 = Hudson, D. Dennis: *The body of God: An Emperor's palace for Krishna in eighth-century Kanchipuram*. Ed. by Margaret H. Case. Oxford University Press, New York 2008.

IsiBh = *Isi-bhāsiyāiṁ* [*Ṛṣi-bhāṣitāni*]. Schubring, Walther (ed., transl.): *Isibhāsiyāiṁ. Aussprüche der Weisen aus dem Prakrit der Jainas.*

Übersetzt nebst dem revidierten Text. Alt- und Neu-Indische Studien 14, Franz Steiner Verlag, Hamburg 1969.

JSK = *Jainendra Siddhānta Kośa.* Ed. by Jinendra Varṇī, Parts 1–5, Jñānapīṭha Mūrtidevī Jaina Grantha-mālā 38, 40, 42, 44, 48 [*Saṁskṛta Granthâṅka*], Bhāratīya Jñānapīṭha Prakāśana, Delhi 1997, 1999, 2000.

KAPADIA 2000 = Kapadia, Hiralal Rasikdas: *A History of the Canonical Literature of the Jainas.* Sharadaben Chimanbhai Educational Research Centre, Ahmedabad 2000 [first edition: Surat 1941].

KIRFEL 1920 = Kirfel, Willibald: *Die Kosmographie der Inder nach den Quellen dargestellt.* Kurt Schroeder, Bonn–Leipzig 1920. [reprinted: Georg Olms Verlag, Hildesheim–Zürich–New York 1990].

KRAMRISCH 1976 = Kramrisch, Stella: *The Hindu Temple.* 2 Vols., reprinted, Motilal Banarsidass, Delhi 1976 [first edition: the University of Calcutta, Calcutta 1946].

KTK = Bäumer, Bettina (ed.): *Kālātattvakośa. A Lexicon of Fundamental Concepts of the Indian Arts.* 4 Vols., revised edition, Indira Gandhi National Centre for the Arts and Motilal Banarsidass, Delhi 2001 [first edition: 1988, 1992, 1996, 1999].

KU = *Kaṭhôpaniṣad.* See: OLIVELLE (1998: 372–403).

LVi = Siṁha-sūri: *Loka-vibhāga.* Bālacaṁdra Siddhānta-Śāstrī (ed.): *Śrī Siṁha-sūra-ṛṣi-viracita Loka-vibhāga.* Jīvarāja Jaina Granthamālā – Solāpur 13, Jaina Saṁskṛti Saṁsrakṣaka Saṁgha, Solāpur 20001.

MaiU = *Maitrāyaṇīyôpaniṣad* [*Maitrī, Maitreya, Maitrāyaṇa, Maitrāyaṇī, Maitrāyaṇīya*]. V.P. Limaye; R.D. Vadekar: *Eighteen Principal Upaniṣads (Upaniṣadic Text with Parallels from extant Vedic Literature, Exegetical and Grammatical Notes).* Vaidika Saṁśodhaya Maṇḍala, Poona 1958: 325–357.

MāU = *Māṇḍūkyôpaniṣad.* Ābājī Śarma (ed.): *Sagauḍapādīya-kārikâtharvavedīya-māṇḍūkyôpaṇiṣat. Ānandagiri-kṛta-ṭīkā-saṁvalita-śāṁkara-bhāṣya-samapetā.* Ānandâsrama-saṁskṛta-granthâvali 10, Ānandâsrama-mudraṇâlaya, no place 1984. (2) OLIVELLE (1998: 473–477). (3) WOOD (1992).

MBh = *Mahā-bhārata.* (1) Vishnu S. Sukthankar et al. (ed.): *The Mahā-bhārata for the first time critically edited.* Bhandarkar Oriental Research Institute, Poona 1933–1966.

MISRA–SHARMA 2001 = Misra, V.N.; Sharma, P.L.: 'Loka', in KTK, vol. 2:119–156.

MM = *Maya-mata.* Bruno Dagens (ed.): *Mayamatam. Treatise on Housing, Architecture and Iconography.* Sanskrit text and Translation. 2 Vols., Indira Gandhi national Centre for the Arts, Motilal Banarsidass, Delhi 2007 [first edition: 1994].

MUS 1935 = Mus, Paul: *Barabudur. Esquisse d'une histoire du bouddhisme fondée sur la critique archéologique des textes.* 2 vols., Imprimerie d'Extrême-Orient, Hanoi 1935 [reprinted: Arno Press, New York

1977; English translation: *Barabudur. Sketch of a History of Buddhism Based on Archaeological Criticism of the Texts*. Translated by Alexander W. McDonald, Sterling Publishers, New Delhi 1998].

NaṁCū = *Naṁdi-cūrṇi*. See NaṁS.

NaṁS = *Naṁdi-sutta / Naṁdī-sutta* [*Nandi-sūtra / Nandī-sūtra*]. (Muni Puṇyavijaya (ed.): *Nandisuttaṁ by Devavācaka with the Cūrṇi by Jinadāsa Gaṇi Mahattara*. Prakrit Text Society Series 9, Ahmedabad, Vārāṇasī 1966.

Nir = Yāska: *Nirukta*. H.M. Bhadkamkar, R.G. Bhadkamkar (eds.): *The Nirukta of Yāska*. 2 Vols., Reprinted, Bhandarkar Oriental Research Institute, Poona 1985 [first edition: 1918, 1942].

OHIRA 1982 = Ohira, Suzuko: *A Study of the Tattvārthasūtra with Bhāṣya with Special Reference to Authorship and Date*. Lalbhai Dalpatbhai Series 86, Bharatiya Sanskrit Vidyamandir – L.D. Institute of Indology, Ahmedabad 1982.

OHIRA 1994 = Ohira, Suzuko: *A Study of the Bhagavatīsūtra. A Chronological Analysis*. Prakrit Text Series 28, Prakrit Text Society, Ahmedabad 1994.

OLIVELLE 1998 = Olivelle, Patrick: *The Early Upaniṣads*. Annotated Text and Translation, Oxford University Press, Oxford–New York 1998.

Paṇṇ = *Paṇṇavaṇā-sutta* [*Prajñāpanā-sūtra*]. Muni Puṇyavijaya, Dalsukh Mālvaṇiā, Amritlāl Mohanlāl Bhojak (ed.); *Paṇṇāvaṇāsuttam*. 2 vols., Jaina-Āgama-Series 9.1,2, Śrī Mahāvīra Jaina Vidyālaya, Bombay 1969, 1971.

PARPOLA 2005 = Parpola, Asko: 'The Nāsatyas, the Chariot and Proto-Aryan Religion', *Journal of Indological Studies* 16–17 (2004–2005): 1–63 [Kyoto: Association for the Study of Indian Though].

PRP = Umāsvāti: *Praśama-rati-prakaraṇa*. (1) Vijaya-jinendra-sūrîśvara, Vijaya-karpura-sūrîśvara, Viyayāmṛta-sūrîśvara (ed.): *Pūjyavara Śrīmad-Umāsvāti-vācaka-viracitaṁ Praśama-rati-prakaraṇaṁ Ṭīkā-sahitam*. Lākhābāval-Śaṁtipurī (Saurāṣṭra)—no publication date. (2) Rājakumārajī Sāhityācārya (ed.): *Śrīmad-Umāsvāti-vicarita Praśamarati-prakaraṇa*. Śrī-parama-śruta-prabhāvaka Maṇḍala, Śrīmad Rājacandra Āśrama, Agās Vīra Saṁvat 2514 = Vikrama Saṁvat 2044 [= 1983]. (3) Yajneshwar S. Shastri: *Ācārya Ūmāsvāti Vācaka's Praśamaratiprakaraṇa*. L.D. Series 107, L.D. Instittue of Indology, Ahmedabad 1989.

PRṬ = Haribhadra-sūri: *Praśama-rati-ṭīkā*. PRP_1, PRP_2.

PSā = Kundakunda: *Pavayaṇa-sāra* [*Pravacana-sāra*]. A.N. Upadhye (ed.): *Śrī Kundakundācārya's Pravacanasāra (Pavayaṇasāra), a Pro-Canonical Text of the Jainas, the Prakṛit Text critically edited with the Sanskrit Commentaries of Amṛtacandra and Jayasena*. Parama-Śruta-Prabhāvaka Mandal, Shrimad Rajachandra Ashrama, Agās–Gujarat 1984. [1. ed.: Bombay 1935].

PSaṁ = Candrarṣi Candramahāttara: *Pañca-saṁgraha*. Hiralal Jain (ed.): *Pañca-saṁgraha*. Jñānapīṭha Mūrtidevī Jaina Grantha-mālā, Bhāratīya Jñānapīṭha Prakāśana, Vāraṇāsī 1960.

RASTELLI 2003 = Rastelli, Marion: 'Der Tempel als Mythisierung der Transzendenz', in: Gerhard Oberhammer; Marcus Schmücker (eds.): *Mythisierung der Transzendenz als Entwurf ihrer Erfahrung. Arbeitsdokumentation eines Symposiums*. Österreichischen Akademie der Wissenschaften, Wien 2003: 313–348.

RENOU 1955 = Renou, Louis: 'Etudes védiques', *Bulletin de la Maison Franco-Japonaise (Nouvelle Série)* 4,1 (1955) 1–48.

RVār = Akalaṅka: *Tattvârtha-vārttika* (*Rāja-vārttika*). Mahendra Kumar Jain (ed.): *Tattvārtha-vārttika* [*Rāja-vārttika*] *of Śrī Akalaṅkadeva*. Edited with Hindi Translation, Introduction, Appendices, Variant Readings, Comparative Notes etc. Parts I–II. First edition, JMJG 10, 20 [*Sanskrit Grantha*], D 1953–1957. [2. ed.: D 1982].

Samav = *Samavāyaṁga-sutta* [*Samavāyâṅga-sūtra*]. Muni Jambūvijaya (ed.): *Ṭhāṇaṁga-suttaṁ* and *Samavāyāṁga-suttaṁ* (*Sthānâṅga-sūtra* and *Samavāyâṅga-sūtra*). Jaina-Āgama-Series 3, Śrī Mahāvīra Jaina Vidyālaya, Bombay 1985.

SCHOPEN 1976 = Schopen, Gregory: 'On the Buddha and His Bones: The Conception of a Relic in the Inscriptions from Nāgārjunikoṇḍa', *Journal of the American Oriental Society* 108 (1988: 527–537 [reprinted in / pagination after: SCHOPEN (1997: 148–164].

SCHOPEN 1987 = Schopen, Gregory: 'Burial *Ad Sanctos* and the Physical Presence of the Buddha in Early Indian Buddhism', *Religion* 17 (1987) 193–225 [reprinted in / pagination after: SCHOPEN (1997: 114–147)].

SCHOPEN 1990 = Schopen, Gregory: 'The Buddha as an owner of property and permanent resident in Medieval Indian monasteries,' *Journal of Indian Philosophy* 18 (1990) 181–217 [reprinted in / pagination after: SCHOPEN (1997: 258–289].

SCHOPEN 1994 = Schopen, Gregory: '*Stūpa* and *Tīrtha*: Tibetan Mortuary Practices and an Unrecognized Form of Burial *Ad Sanctos* at Buddhist Sites in India', *Buddhist Forum* III (1994) 273–293 [reprinted in / pagination after: SCHOPEN (2005: 350–369).

SCHOPEN 1997 = Schopen, Gregory: *Bones, Stones, and Buddhist Monks: Collected Papers on the Archaeology, Epigraphy, and Texts of Monastic Buddhism in India*. University of Hawaii Press, Honolulu 1997.

SCHOPEN 2005 = Schopen, Gregory: *Figments And Fragments Of Mahāyana Buddhism In India: More Collected Papers*. University of Hawaii Press, Honolulu 2005.

SCHUBRING 1962 = Schubring, Walter: *The Doctrine of the Jainas*. Translated from the German by Wolfgang Beurlen, Motilal Banarsidass, Delhi 1962 [reprinted: MB 1978. Revised edition: Revised Willem Bollée and Jayandra Soni, Motilal Banarsidass, Delhi 2000].

SHAH 1978 = Shah, Umkant P.: *Treasures of Jaina Bhaṇḍāras*. L.D. Series 69, L.D. Institute of Indology, Ahmedabad 1978.

SINGH 1995 = Singh, Thakur Jaideva: *Indian Music*. Sangeet-Paridarshini Series 2, Sangeet Research Academy, Calcutta 1995.

ṢKhĀ = Puṣpadanta and Bhūtabali: *Cha-kkhaṁḍâgame* [*Ṣaṭ-khaṇḍâgama*]. Hirarlal Jain, Phoolachandra Siddhanta Shastri, Balachandra Sidhanta Shastri (ed.): *Shatkhandagama of Pushpadanta and Bhootabali with the Commentary Dhavala of Veerasenacharya*, edited with Indroduction, Hindi translation, Notes and Indexes. 16 Vols., Jaina Sāhityoddhāraka Fund, Amaravati 1939–1959 [revised fourth edition: Jain Saṁskṛti Saṁrakṣak Saṅgha, Solāpur 2000].

SNODGRASS 1985 = Snodgrass, Adrian: *The Symbolism of the Stupa*. Motilal Banarsidass, Delhi 1985 / Southeast Asia Program, Cornell University, Ithaca (N.Y.) 1985 [reprinted: Motilal Banarsidass, Delhi 2007].

SRĀ = Śāraṅgadeva: *Saṅgīta-ratnâkara*. R.K. Shringy, Prem Lata Sharma (eds.): *Saṅgītaratnākara of Śāraṅgadeva. Text and English Translation*. 2 Vols., Munishiram Manoharlal Publishers, Delhi 1989.

SRINIVASAN 1978 = Srinivasan, Doris: 'The Religious Significance of Divine Multiple Body Parts in the *Atharva Veda*', *Numen* 25,3 (1978) 193–225.

SSi = Pūjyapāda Devanandin: *Sarvârtha-siddhi*. Phoolchandra Shastri (ed.): *Ācārya Pūjyapāda's Sarvārthasiddhi [The commentary on Ācārya Griddhapiccha's Tattvārtha-sūtra]*. Edited and translated [into Hindi]. Varanasi 1934 [reprint: Jñānapīṭha Mūrtidevī Jaina Grantha-mālā 13, Bhāratīya Jñānapīṭha Prakāśana, Delhi 2000]. [= Digāmbara Recension].

STRONG 2004 = Strong, John: *Relics of the Buddha*. Princeton University Press, Princeton 2004.

SŪRĪŚVAR 2008 = Sūrīśvar, Vijay Jinottam: *Suśīl Sadbodh Śatak*. Śrī Suśīl Sāhitya Prakāśan Samiti, Jodhpur 2008.

ŚatBr = *Śata-patha-brāhmaṇa* [*Mādhyanandinīya* recension]. Albrecht Weber (ed.): *The Çatapatha-brāhmaṇa, in the Mādhyandina-Çākhā with extracts from the commentaries of Sāyaṇa, Harisvāmin and Dvivedagaṅga*. Otto Harrassowitz Verlag, Leipzig 1924. [first edition: Leipzig 1855].

ŚiRaKo = Sthapānaka Nirañjana Mahāpātra: *Śilpa-ratna-kośa*. Bettina Bäumer; Rajendra Prasad Das: *Sthāpakaśri-nirañjana-mahāpātra-viracitaḥ. Śilparatnakośa: A Glossary of Orissan Temple Architecture by Sthāpaka Nirañjana Mahāpātra. Sanskrit text critically edited with English translation and illustrations.* Kalāmūlaśāstra granthamālā 16, Indira Gandhi National Centre for The Arts and Motilal Banarsidass Publishers, New Delhi 1994.

ŚLĄCZKA 2006 = Ślączka, Anna Aleksandra: *Temple Consecration Rituals in Ancient India: Text and Archaeology*. [PhD Dissertation] Proefschrift ter verkrijging van de graad van Doctor aan de Universiteit Leiden,

Leiden 4 Oktober 2006: https://openaccess.leidenuniv.nl/handle/1887/4581 [published: E.J. Brill, Leiden 2006].

ŚvU = *Śvetâśvatarôpaniṣad*. See: OLIVELLE (1998: 413–433).

TATIA 1987 = Nathmal Tatia, *Studies in Jaina Philosophy*, P.V.Research Institute, Varanasi 1987 [first edition: Varanasi 1951].

TBh = Umāsvāti: *Tattvârthâdhigama-bhāṣya*. See: $TS_{śvet}$.

Ṭhāṇ = *Ṭhāṇaṁga-sutta* [*Sthānâṅga-sūtra*]. Muni Jambūvijaya (ed.): *Ṭhāṇaṁga-suttaṁ* and *Samavāyāṁga-suttaṁ* (*Sthānâṅga-sūtra* and *Samavāyâṅga-sūtra*). Jaina-Āgama-Series 3, Śrī Mahāvīra Jaina Vidyālaya, Bombay 1985.

TS_{dig} = Umāsvāmin: *Tattvârtha-sūtra*. See: SSi. [= Digāmbara Recension].

$TS_{śvet}$ = Umāsvāmin: *Tattvârtha-sūtra*. (1) M.K. Mody (ed.): *Tattvârthâdhigama by Umāsvāti being in the Original Sanskrit with the Bhāṣya by the author himself.* Bibliotheca Indica New Series 1044, 1079, 1118, Asiatic Society of Bengal, Calcutta 1903, 1904, 1905. [= Śvetāmbara Recension]. (2) Khūbacandra (ed.): *Śrīmad-umāsvāti-viracita Sabhāṣya-tattvârthâdhigama-sūtra*. Śrī Parama-śruta Prabhāvaka Maṇḍala, Śrīmad Rājacaṁdra Āśram, Agās 1992.

TṬ = Siddhasena-gaṇin (Gandhahastin): *Tattvârthâdhigama-ṭīkā*. Hīrālāl Rasikdās Kapadia (ed.): *Tattvārthādhigamasūtra (A Treatise on the Fundamental Principles of Jainism) by His Holiness Śrī Umāsvāti Vāchaka, together with His connective verses commented upon by Śrī Devaguptasūri & Śrī Siddhasenagaṇi and His own gloss elucidated by Śrī Siddhasenagaṇi, edited with Introduction in English and Sanskrit*. 2 Vols., Sheth Devchand Lalbhai Jain Pustakoddhar Fund Series Nos. 67 and 76, Jivanachand Sakerchand Javeri, Bombay 1926 (Part I: Chapters I–V), 1930 (Part II: Chapters VI–X).

VATSYAYAN 2003 = Vatsyayan, Kapila: *The Square and the Circle of the Indian Arts*. Abhinav Publications, New Delhi 2003 [first edition: Humanities Press, Atlantic Highlands 1983].

Viy = *Viyāha-pannatti / Viyāha-paṇṇatti / Bhagavaī-viyāha-paṇṇaṭṭī* [*Bhagavatī Vyākhyā-prajñapti / Bhagavatī-sūtra*]. (1) Ghevara-candra Bāṁṭhiyā (ed.): *Bhgavatī-sūtra*. Vols. 2-7, Akhila Bhāratīya Sādhumārgī Jaina Saṁskṛti Rakṣaka Saṅgha, Sailana 1966–72. (2) Bechardas J. Doshi; Amritlal Mohanlal Bhojak (ed.): *Viyāha-paṇṇattisuttaṁ*. 3 parts, Jaina-Āgama-Series 4, Śrī Mahāvīra Jaina Vidyālaya, Bombay 1974–1982.

WOOD 1992 = Wood, Thomas E.: *The Māṇḍūkya Upaniṣad and the Āgama Śāstra. An Investigation into the Meaning of the Vedanta*. Motilal Banarsidass, Delhi 1992.

The Spread of Buddhism from India to Sri Lanka: Its Visual Representation

SILKE K. YASMIN FISCHER
(Ludwig Maximilian University of Munich)

A prominent *topos* in the literature and art of Sri Lanka is the arrival and establishment of Buddhism in the mid-3rd century BCE.[1] The *Mahā-vaṁsa* (hereafter MhV), for example, a Pāli chronicle written by the monk Mahānāma in the fifth century, reports on the spread of Indian Buddhism to Sri Lanka in ten chapters.[2] In later Sinhalese works, too, the spread and establishment of Buddhism is described in detail.[3] For several centuries these literary accounts were not only understood in literate circles, their contents were also imparted to lay Buddhists by way of public recitations.[4] On the level of visual representation these accounts are preserved for a wider audience as pictures in temples. An early 19th-century cave painting at Dambulla [fig. 1] shows the arrival of the Buddhist monk Mahinda at the mountain peak of Mihintale. Mahinda, considered to be the son of the Indian emperor Asoka (Skt. Aśoka), is meeting the Sinhalese king Devānaṁpiyatissa, who is converted to Buddhism after hearing Mahinda's sermon.[5] Mahinda's arrival in Sri Lanka has remained

---

[1] The most important topics treated are the biography of the Buddha and the Jātakas; see BANDARANAYAKE (1986: 25).

[2] See MhV 5 and 12–20. Since this paper is concerned with the Pāli tradition, personal names are given in Pāli spelling throughout.

[3] An example of a later work dealing with the establishment of Buddhism in Sri Lanka is Parākrama's *Siṁhala-thūpa-vaṁsa* (hereafter SThūp) written in the 13th century; see SThūp 108–124.

[4] Concerning recitations of the SThūp, see JAYAWICKRAMA (1971: xiv). DEGALLE (2006) shows that recitations of certain Sinhalese texts, the *baṇa-pot*s, are generally to be considered as a particular form of preaching.

[5] A similar 19th-century depiction is found in the Śailabimbarāmavihāra at Dodanduva. Here as well as in the cave at Dambulla another painting shows the arrival of the

Art, Myths and Visual Culture of South Asia
Warsaw Indological Studies 4 (2011) 153–164.

a popular motif in temple decorations of the 20th and 21st centuries.[6] In government schools Sinhalese children are introduced to Mahinda and Devānaṁpiyatissa in words and pictures through their textbooks on Buddhism.[7] The historical account of the arrival of Buddhism in Sri Lanka has been subject to change over the centuries. It is the aim of this paper to demonstrate, through a comparison of literature and art from different eras, how the presentation of these events was influenced and changed by contemporary needs. The examples of pictorial representation shown below are taken from the 19th and 20th centuries, since this is the period in which the replacement of traditional forms of painting by modern ones is particularly apparent.

The most authoritative literary account of the history of Buddhism in Sri Lanka, which still enjoys great popularity today, is the MhV.[8] In chapters 5 and 12 to 20 its author Mahānāma describes the spread of Buddhism, the *sāsana*, from India to Sri

---

Bodhi tree that the nun Saṅghamittā took from India to Sri Lanka at the behest of her brother Mahinda. According to MhV 19.1–4, King Asoka also sends artists and craftsmen along with the Bodhi tree and Saṅghamittā to Sri Lanka. Thus, the arrival of Buddhism affected not only the intellectual but also the material culture of Sri Lanka.

[6] An example of this ongoing popularity is found in the temple at Galle, where an image-house contains several sculptures depicting Mahinda's arrival. Recent Sinhalese and English publications aim to make this event and its historical circumstances widely known and easily accessible; see e.g. EDUSSURIYA (2005), RAJAPAKSE (2003), SENEVIRATNE (2007) and WETTAMUNI (2002).

[7] Compare for instance chapters 14 and 15 in the third-grade Buddhism textbook *Sadaham Maga. Te Väni Peḷa* (SM) or chapter 18 of the current first-grade textbook *Buddha Dharmaya. 1 Vana Vasaya.* Even in the late 19th century, the first Buddhist catechism in use at government-approved Buddhist schools already made reference to Asoka, Mahinda and Devānaṁpiyatissa; see numbers 289 to 302 in OLCOTT (1881).

[8] The MhV relates the history of Buddhism in Sri Lanka in 37 chapters with 2,915 verses. The plot of Chapters 1 to 6 is still based in India. It starts with the biography of the Buddha, with special reference to his three legendary visits to Lanka and the ancestry of his father Suddhodana, traced back to the mythical King Mahāsaṁmata at the beginning of this age of the world. Next are described the history and spread of Buddhism, including the three councils and the life-story of king Asoka, patron of Buddhism, and the line of descent of the Indian Vijaya, who established the Sinhalese royal lineage. From chapter 7 onwards the plot is based in Sri Lanka. After a description of the first kings, the introduction and establishment of Buddhism is related. The reader learns how the Sinhalese King Devānaṁpiyatissa and his followers were converted to Buddhism by the monk Mahinda, how under his reign the first Buddhist temples were erected, and how Buddhist relics, particularly an offshoot from the Bodhi tree in Bodhgayā, reached Sri Lanka. The chronicle finally presents the history of Buddhism under the kings subsequent to Devānaṁpiyatissa, concluding in 302 CE with King Mahāsena.

Lanka, employing a certain narrative technique that either links an event to a past event or legitimises it through predictions. The history of Buddhism thus appears as spanning several ages, it places the succession of single events in a meaningful context and evokes a multilayered soteriological process. People involved in the success of the *sāsana* act not for personal motives but through their connection with events of the past. They possess supernatural powers, and their actions are supported by *deva*s. In chapter 13 ('The Coming of Mahinda'), for example, Mahānāma explains that Mahinda's introduction of Buddhist teachings in Sri Lanka has already been predicted by the Saṁbuddha.[9] However, Mahinda who, in his twelfth year as a monk, had been instructed by his monastic community to travel to Sri Lanka, sees that the time has not yet come. The current Sinhalese king is too old and he predicts that it will be his son, King Devānaṁpiyatissa, who receives the teachings when he climbs mount Missaka on the *uposatha* day in the Jeṭṭha month.[10] When the time is ripe, the god Indra reminds the monk Mahinda of his mission and promises further help.[11] Mahinda travels to the island in the company of four other monks, a novice, and a lay person, flying through the air and landing on the Missaka rock.[12] Chapter 14 of the MhV ('The Entry into the Capital') describes how a *deva* transforms itself into a stag, so as to lure King Devānaṁpiyatissa, out hunting near the Missaka rock, close to Mahinda. When the king sees the stag browsing, being reluctant to kill the heedless animal, he strikes his bowstring. The stag escapes and Devānaṁpiyatissa takes up the chase. The arrow he shoots lands near Mahinda, and the *deva*, whose mission is complete, vanishes.[13] Mahinda, now within eyeshot of the king, first makes his fellow monks disappear, thinking that Devānaṁpiyatissa might be alarmed at the sight of them. Then Mahinda calls out the king's name, but on seeing the monk the king is afraid, believing him to be a *yakkha*.[14] Mahinda then tries to calm him down by explaining that they are Buddhist monks who have come from India out of compassion. Recalling a message received from king Asoka, King

---

[9] MhV 13.15. SThūp 110–124 relates similar events involving Mahinda and Devānaṁpiyatissa.

[10] MhV 13.1–14.

[11] MhV 13.15–16. The ordination of Mahinda had been predicted as well: the Buddhist monk Moggalliputta Tissa sees that Asoka's children will further the *sāsana* as members of the monastic community, and persuades him to have them ordained.

[12] MhV 13.18–21. Missaka is the Pāli name for the present-day mountain peak of Mihintale.

[13] MhV 14.1–5.

[14] MhV 14.6–7.

Devānaṁpiyatissa loses his fear and puts down his arms before he and his retinue join Mahinda.[15] The latter makes his fellow monks reappear and explains in reply to Devānaṁpiyatissa that in India there are many Buddhist monks, endowed with supernatural powers and the faculty of mind-reading. When the king asks how they came to Sri Lanka, Mahinda explains that they came neither by land nor water; the king realises that they must have travelled through the air. Mahinda then asks the king several questions to test his intelligence,[16] and, when satisfied, begins preaching. The king and his retinue of 40,000 men then take the three refuges.[17] The chapter continues with the king's invitation to the monks to accompany him to town. Mahinda turns down the invitation because that evening the monks intend to ordain the layman Bhaṇḍu.[18] Only after a conversation with Bhaṇḍu is the king convinced that the monks, too, are human beings. Thus reassured, he travels back to town.[19] Once the ordination has taken place, Mahinda asks the novice Sumana to announce far and wide that he will give a sermon. After this sermon countless numbers of *devas*, *nāgas*, and other beings take the three refuges.[20] Next morning, the monks fly to town through the air; the place where they land will become the location of the *thūpa* Paṭhamacetiya.[21] They are appropriately received and entertained in the palace, and seers predict that from now on the monks will be the new rulers of the island.[22] Queen Anulā along with five hundred women and innumerable residents of the town listen to Mahinda's sermons.[23] The following six chapters describe the king's donations to the monks and his erection of *thūpas*, as well as the arrival of the Bodhi tree from India and the establishment of an order of nuns by Mahinda's sister, the nun Saṅghamittā.

The early 19th-century painting found at Rangiri Dambulla Rājamahāvihāra [fig. 1] makes it clear that the narrative of the monk Mahinda and King Devānaṁ-

---

[15] MhV 14.8–10. The SThūp 112 f. generally follows the MhV but uses the term *amanuṣya* ('non-human', SThūp 112.4) instead of *yakkha* (MhV 14.7).

[16] MhV 14.11–21.

[17] MhV 14.22–23.

[18] MhV 14.24–28.

[19] MhV 14.29–31.

[20] MhV 14.32–41.

[21] MhV 14.42–45.

[22] MhV 14.46–55.

[23] MhV 14.56–65.

piyatissa was still known and being handed down at that time.[24] The mural combines several incidents from the story as told in the MhV into one picture. The different episodes share a single space, the Missaka rock.[25] The ornamental decoration at the upper margin joins up the different scenes while separating the realms of *deva*s and men. The distinction of scenes is evident to the observer since King Devānaṁpiyatissa is shown twice in the left half of the picture: once standing with bow and arrow, and once kneeling unarmed. The pictorial space to the right, embedded in the Missaka rock, again shows Mahinda, the king, and his retinue.

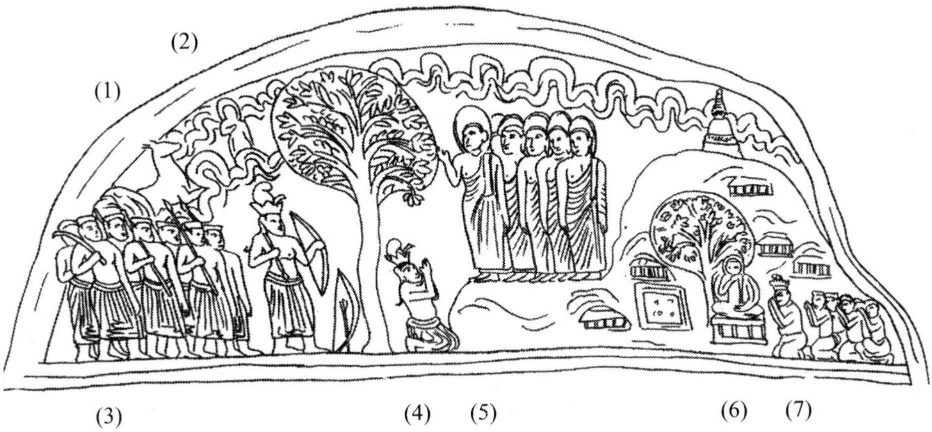

Fig. 1. Rangiri Dambulla Râjamahâvihâra, drawing by Prof. Monika Zin after after BANDARANAYAKE (1986: 169, plate 84).

The different scenes are to be looked at from top left to bottom right. At top left we see the stag (1) which changes back to a *deva* (2). At bottom left the royal guards stand behind the armed king (3). The next scene centres on the tree: to its left is the bow, placed there by the king after Mahinda had earned his trust, to its right the

[24] On the history of the Dambulla caves, stretching over two-thousand years, see BANDARANAYAKE (1986: 153–160).

[25] It is well known that this continuous representation has been widely used for the purpose of visualising narratives in Indian art during different eras. The central character is repeatedly shown in one pictorial space, thus making it possible to distinguish different plots. Thus one finds in the reliefs of Sāñci different scenes from the Vessantarajātaka in one pictorial space, and (to mention a non-Buddhist example) in the Virūpākṣa-Temple at Paṭṭaḍakal the same technique is used to depict the descent of the river Gaṅgā. SCHLINGLOFF (1981: 108–201) has shown that this mode of representation is not limited to Indian and Near-Eastern art but is also found in European art.

king himself (4) is seen kneeling in front of Mahinda and his fellow monks, who have reappeared (5). To the right of Mahinda's companions, framed by the Missaka rock, we see buildings which will later be erected by King Devānaṁpiyatissa (6). In the pictorial space to the bottom right, showing the *thūpa*-shaped rock topped by a *thūpa*, Mahinda is delivering a sermon to the king and his retinue (7).

The narrative unity of the mural does not strictly follow its literary source in the MhV but combines information from various chapters. Most of the scenes shown (the transformation of the stag into the *deva*, the conversation between Mahinda and the king, and Mahinda's sermon) come from chapter 14 of the MhV. However, the erection of *thūpa*s and other buildings has been taken from the subsequent chapters. Moreover, not all incidents from chapter 14 are depicted, only those which take place on the mountain peak of Mihintale. The artist has thus constructed a new narrative unity. In comparison to the MhV we observe a shift of the narrative's main focus; this is caused not only by the selection of certain parts of the plot, but also by a difference of emphasis. While the MhV focuses on the evolution of the *sāsana*, giving Mahinda and the *deva*s a more important role than King Devānaṁpiyatissa, the pictorial depiction of fourteen centuries later makes the Sinhalese king the focal point of the painting by depicting him twice on the left. The artist chose not to include the miraculous journey of Mahinda and his companions through the air and their arrival on the Missaka rock. Instead he showed the king returning from the stag hunt, putting down his bow and paying his respects to the monk. The illustration of the *thūpa* and the other buildings also relates to the king, as it is he who will build them. In comparison to older literary versions of this narrative, it is evident that the focus has shifted away from the spread of Buddhism with monks as key players towards the figure of the Sinhalese king who receives the Buddhist teachings and firmly establishes them in Sri Lanka.

If one compares the 19th-century mural with a wall-painting from the early 20th century [fig. 2],[26] it is evident that in the later work Mahinda's arrival and the king's conversion are no longer depicted as a sequence of several scenes. Instead, the whole narrative is represented by one scene, namely the king's conversation with Mahinda.[27] The *deva*s as well as the king's retinue are left out completely.

---

[26] I have selected a painting from the Ghaṇāndarāmavihāra at Kapumulagoda near Ratgama, the photograph of which was kindly made available to me by Dr. Rolf Heinrich Koch (Munich).

[27] The painted sequence has a caption reading: 'The establishment of the Buddha's *sāsana* in Sri Lanka through Mahathera Mihindu'.

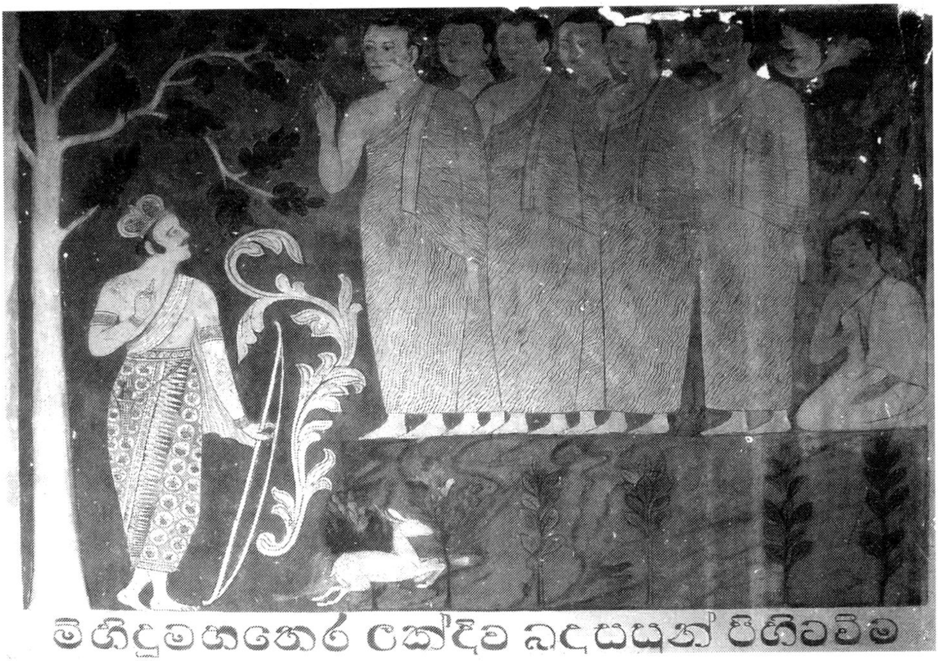

Fig. 2. Kapumulagoda Ghaṅāndarāmavihāra, private collection Dr. Rolf Heinrich Koch, Munich. [For a colour print, see the Appendix]

Compared with fig. 1 this painting focalises the king since he appears unescorted. Moreover, the fact that the king is standing rather than kneeling down places him on a level with the monks, not quite as subordinate to them as in the older painting. The kneeling position is now taken by the layman, who can easily be distinguished from the ordained monks in the more recent painting. This careful distinction between Mahinda and his companions is lacking in the older painting, another significant difference. The posture of the stag in the 20th-century painting resembles that in the older one. However, the animal is not shown next to a *deva* in the upper part of the picture but in the foreground near the lower margin, in a forest opposite the Mihintale rock. In this way the painter neglects the divine circumstances of the king's meeting with Mahinda. The painting may now be understood as if the king, while hunting stags, met the monk Mahinda and his followers simply by chance.

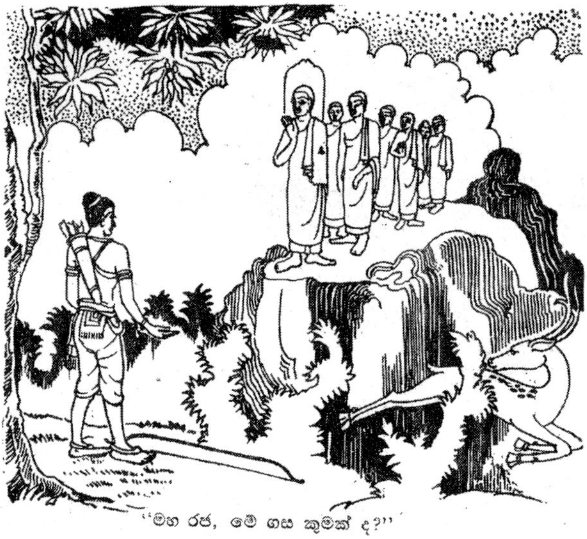

Fig. 3. Illustrator S. P. Charles, after SM 46.

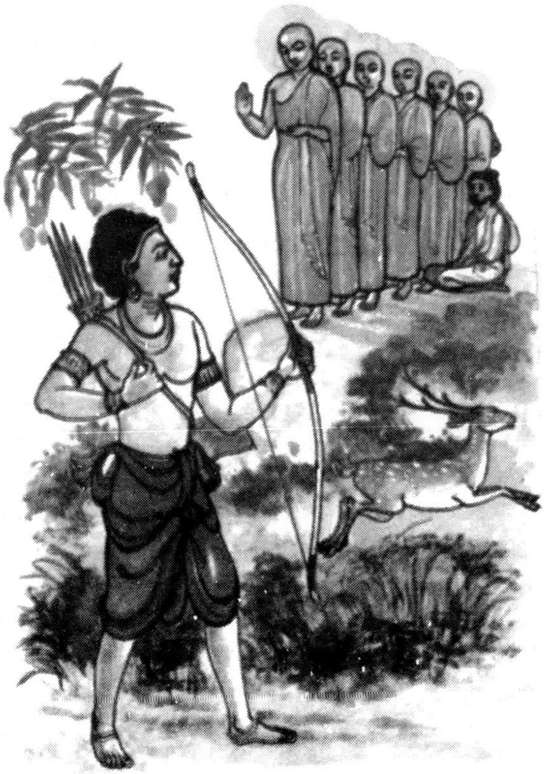

Fig. 4. Illustrator unknown, after BDh 28.

Similar representations are found in *Sadaham Maga* (hereafter SM), the third grade state school textbook on Buddhism dating from 1960 [fig. 3], and in the current textbook on Buddhism, the *Buddha-dharmaya* (hereafter BDh), which was first published in 1993 [fig. 4]. Both books devote separate chapters to the king's meeting with Mahinda.[28] Their illustrations [fig. 3 and 4] seem to closely follow the modern wall-painting [fig. 2], even if the perspective is different. The caption of SM [fig. 3] draws further attention to the king, as he is addressed: 'Great King, what kind of tree is this?'[29] While the mural at Rangiri Dambulla Rājamahāvihāra emphasises the king through his repeated appearances in the painting, the same effect is now achieved by way of a single motif, the conversation between him and Mahinda, in which he appears in the foreground.

Comparing the narrative as found in the SM with the tradition in the MhV, it is evident that the king is depicted in an entirely different way. The account in the SM centres on the courageous King Devānaṁpiyatissa, through whose intelligence Buddhism was established in Sri Lanka.[30] Excluding the *deva*-episode, the SM relates how the king meets the monks while on a stag hunt. The illustration [fig. 3] depicts the stag in a similar way to the early 20th-century painting [fig. 2], namely in the wooded foreground, so implying that the stag is indeed an animal, not a *deva*. The textbook narrative also omits all mention of the king's fear as related in the MhV. According to the SM, the king confronts the strangers with self-confidence, and there is no mention of Mahinda making his companions disappear. The king's courage is underlined in the illustration by the fact that he is not shown with his retinue but on his own. After the description of Mahinda's conversation with the king and his sermon, the book goes on to describe the king's conversion to Buddhism. Here it is pointed out that by accepting Buddhism the king renounced violence and stopped killing animals. It is further reported that the king gives presents to the community of monks and builds *thūpa*s. Like the 19th-century mural, the SM associates his erection of *thūpa*s with his first meeting with Mahinda. The author of the textbook thus borrows the narrative unity of the wall painting [fig. 1], not that of the MhV. The textbook narrative clearly individualises the figure of the king, turning him into a role model. By depicting the Sinhalese as an intelligent people and Buddhism as the

[28] Chapters 14 and 15 in SM 42–49 and chapter 18 in BDh 28.

[29] SM 46.

[30] SM 42–49. The meeting of Devānaṁpiyatissa and Mahinda is described in chapters 14 ('King Devānaṁpiyatissa') and 15 ('The venerable Arhat Mahinda'), the latter section containing additional information on Mahinda. The twofold treatment of this episode shows how much importance is attached to it.

underlying cultural force securing their prosperity, the narrative also displays a religiously biased nationalistic motif.

It is possible to single out two major changes in the depictions mentioned above: the shift in focus towards the figure of the king, a process already visible in the early 19th and even more distinctly in the 20th century; and the omission of the *deva*-motif since the early 20th century.

While the author of the MhV strove to present the history of the *sāsana* as a predestined soteriological process extending beyond time and space, the 19th century saw the Sinhalese king coming to the fore. It is possible that the age-long reality of European colonisation experienced by the Sinhalese is reflected in the desire to give prominence to their own cultural achievements and to the indigenous ruling dynasty.[31] This new viewpoint, with its glamorous depiction of past Sinhalese kings, properly established itself in the 19th century. At the turn of the century, the strengthening of national identity by an appeal to the memory of a glorious Sinhalese past was particularly advocated by Anagārika Dharmapāla and carried on by the independence movement.[32] The stressing of King Devānaṁpiyatissa's role in the spread of Buddhism from India to Sri Lanka may therefore be traced back to specific political conditions. However, the omission of the *deva*-motif points to another influence typical of the time in question, namely the rationalisation of Buddhist teachings brought about by the encounter with Christian missionaries in the 19th century. The Christians had challenged the Buddhists to justify their views and teachings through rational arguments and in line with scientific facts. The Buddhist reactions came in form of debates and publications, and their adoption of the Christian method of reasoning led to a de-mythologisation of Buddhist doctrine.[33] The

[31] The increase, during the 13th and 14th centuries, in the account of Sinhalese narrative literature dealing with historical topics shows that even in these periods of declining Sinhalese rule and fragmentation of power there was a return to the values of a common Sinhalese-Buddhist past. The same strategy was employed in the phase of European colonisation, and is also reflected in works of art.

[32] Anagārika Dharmapāla promoted the reinterpretation of Sinhalese cultural history in order to provide an indigenous counterpoint to the foreign rule of Christians and the European lifestyle, which he despised. In his *Message to the Young Men of Ceylon* of 1912, describing the paradisiacal conditions in terms of economy and morality in Sinhalese-Buddhist society under the rule of the kings, he reminds his fellow countrymen of an ideal conception of civilisation. On his importance and the impact which he had for decades, see e.g. the detailed description by SENEVIRATNE (1999: 28–129 and 189–210).

[33] As early as 1881 OLCOTT devoted a whole chapter to the relationship between Buddhism and science in his *Buddhist Catechism* intended for Sinhalese lay people. This chapter, the fifth section of the book, was meant to demonstrate in 61 questions and answers that Buddhist teachings are consistent with scientific explanations. OLCOTT

representation of King Devānaṁpiyatissa's meeting with the monk Mahinda in the early 20th-century temple painting, the SM from the mid-20th century, and the BDh from the late 20th century bears witness to this rationalisation of doctrine. The omission of the *deva* makes the narrative seen much more realistic and like a historically valid account in words and pictures.[34]

As shown above, it is possible to detect in Sri Lankan painting and literature the influence of intellectual developments, either internal or coming from the West, on the way a well-known narrative has been presented over the centuries. In the 19th century the arrival of Buddhism in Sri Lanka is visualised through the technique of continuous representation, which combines several consecutive incidents from the narrative in the same image. The artists perceive a narrative unity visualised in the context of a sequence of several scenes located in the same landscape. This traditional form of painting not only provides a continuous narration, it also enables the viewer to perceive multilayered actions and to establish relations between events taking place at different times and in different spheres. In the 20th century, this traditional manner of representation is replaced by another technique that represents the whole narrative in a single scene. In the course of this development it is possible to make out a transmission of pictorial representation: the 20th-century resorts to earlier forms of illustration. The limitation to one scene not only results from a change in viewing patterns, it also expresses a new understanding of the historical events. The literary and pictorial depictions focus increasingly on the achievements of a single person, in contrast to the earlier depiction of a multilayered soteriological process. This evidently shows the closely interweaving of intellectual history and artistic forms of expression. The revised interpretation of historical events leads to a modified visual depiction, or—in other words—a changed viewing pattern supports the modern concept of individuality, which developed into a major perceptual pattern from the 19th century onwards.

aims a rational explanation of all those phenomena denounced by Christians as scientifically untenable. Numbers 384 to 386 are a treatment of the *deva*s.

[34] Like OLCOTT before him, the Buddhist monk Nārada, who wrote the SM, tries to give a rational account of Mahinda's flight through the air with his companions. He simply ascribes it to certain mental abilities.

BIBLIOGRAPHY

BANDARANAYAKE 1986 = Bandaranayake, Senake: *The Rock and Wall Paintings of Sri Lanka*. Lake House Bookshop, Colombo 1986.

BDh = *Buddha-dharmaya.* Adhyāpana Prākāśāna Depārtmēntuva (ed.): *Buddha Dharmaya. 1 Vana Vasaya*. Fifth Edition, [no publisher], Colombo 1997 [First Edition: Colombo 1993].

DEGALLE 2006 = Degalle, Mahinda: *Popularizing Buddhism. Preaching as Performance in Sri Lanka.* State University of New York Press, Albany 2006.

EDUSSURIYA 2005 = Edussuriya, Bandu: *A Simplified English Summary of the Mahawamsa*. Sarasavi Publishers, Nagagoda 2005.

JAYAWICKRAMA 1971 = Jayawickrama, N. A.: *The Chronicle of the Thūpa and the Thūpavaṁsa. Being a Translation and Edition of Vācissara's Thūpavaṁsa*. Luzac & Company Ltd., London 1971.

MhV = Mahānāma: *Mahā-vaṁsa.* (1) Geiger, Wilhelm (ed.): *The Mahāvaṁsa.* PTS. Oxford University Press, Amen Corner 1908. (2) Geiger, Wilhelm (transl.): *The Mahāvaṁsa or the Great Chronicle of Ceylon.* PTS. Oxford University Press, Amen Corner 1912.

OLCOTT 1881 = Olcott, Henry Steele: *Buddhist Catechism.* [no publisher], Colombo 1881.

RAJAPAKSE 2003 = Rajapakse, Ruwan: *Concise Mahawamsa. History of Buddhism in Sri Lanka.* Sri Lanka 2003: www.sinhalanet.com/ concisemahavamsaweb.pdf [download 20/07/2008].

SCHLINGLOFF 1981 = Schlingloff, Dieter: 'Erzählung und Bild. Die Darstellung von Handlungsabläufen in der europäischen und indischen Kunst', *Beiträge zur Allgemeinen und Vergleichenden Archäologie*. Bd. 3, München 1981: 87–213.

SENEVIRATNE 1999 = Seneviratne, H. L.: *The Work of Kings. The New Buddhism in Sri Lanka*. University of Chicago Press, Chicago 1999.

SENEVIRATNE 2007 = Seneviratne, Maureen: *Some Women of the Mahawamsa and Chulawamsa*. Wimal Enterprises, Colombo 2007.

SM = *Sadaham Maga.* Nārada, Thera: *Sadaham Maga. Te Väni Peḷa.* Sixth Edition, Lakehouse Investments Co. Ltd, Colombo 1971 [First Edition: Lakehouse Investments Co. Ltd., Colombo 1960].

SThūp = Parākrama: *Siṁhala-thūpa-vaṁsa.* (1) Dhammānanda, Dharmakirtti (ed.): *Siṁhala Thūpavaṁsaya.* [no publisher], Colombo 1950. (2) Berkwitz, Stephen C. (transl.): *The History of the Buddha's Relic Shrine. A Translation of the Sinhala Thūpavaṁsa.* Oxford University Press, Oxford 2007.

WETTAMUNI 2002 = Wettamuni, Siripala: *Sarala Sinhala Mahawamsaya*. Sri Lanka [no publisher and no place] 2002.

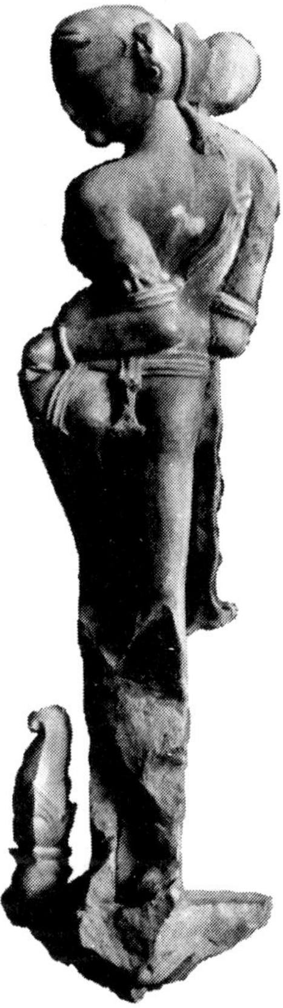

Ritual, Sex and Power

Temple Consecration Rituals in the Hindu Tradition of South and South-East Asia: A Study of the Textual and Archaeological Evidence

ANNA ŚLĄCZKA
(Rijksmuseum, Amsterdam)

1. Introduction

Excavation and restoration works conducted on ancient sites of South-East Asia brought to light numerous miscellaneous objects installed at different locations inside the walls or in the foundations of ancient temples. These objects include precious and semiprecious stones, figures cut out of gold leaf, fragments of metals, inscribed metal sheets, grains and seeds, often enclosed in containers, such as jars or boxes. The number of excavated containers and stray objects is very high. In the course of my research I could trace over one hundred such finds originating from the temples of South-East Asia.[1] But their number is certainly higher as not all finds have been documented.

The excavated objects have been mentioned in a number of publications, mainly in the archaeological reports. Yet, there was, until present, no publication in which all the information about these finds would be gathered and analysed as a group. Consequently, no satisfactory explanation of the function and meaning of these finds could be given. A few scholars—see, for example O'CONNOR (1966) and MITRA (1981)—suggested a connection between one or other specific find and temple construction ceremonies. But no thorough study on this subject was ever conducted. The hints as to how to interpret the excavated objects cannot unfortunately be found in the very regions where the objects were discovered. In Java, Cambodia, Malaysia and Vietnam, where the majority of the objects were found, the indigenous manuals on temple architecture and temple building rituals either did not exist or did

[1] Similar objects are also frequently found in both Hindu and Buddhist sites of Sri Lanka. For a list of excavated objects, see ŚLĄCZKA (2007: Appendix 4).

Art, Myths and Visual Culture of South Asia
Warsaw Indological Studies 4 (2011) 167–181.

not survive. The surviving textual sources—the literary works of Java or Cambodia and the inscriptions—do not mention such objects or their installation within temples.

2. The archaeological finds

Among the objects unearthed from ancient monuments of South-East Asia, at least two types can be distinguished on the basis of shared characteristics. The first type consists of cubical containers divided into a fixed number of regular compartments. Inside these compartments were found numerous small items, such as those listed above, namely semiprecious stones, figures cut out of gold leaf, grains, and so on. The second type consists of four bricks and a number of miscellaneous items. At the moment of discovery, the four bricks formed a square and the small items were lying in the middle of them.

In my paper I would like, first, to present a few examples of each of the two mentioned types of archaeological finds. And next, I would like to argue—on the basis of the correspondences between archaeological and textual data—that these and similar objects are remains of temple consecration ceremonies, which were performed according to the prescriptions given in a particular group of Sanskrit manuals on ritual and architecture, written and employed in ancient India.

2.1. Jolotundo

As an example of the first type, I would like to give the stone box discovered in Jolotundo, a well-known site and a sacred bathing place near the village of Pandaan, south of Surabaya in East Java. On the site there is a terraced structure cut into a slope of a mountain. The terraced structure consists of three so-called ponds. In the middle of the central 'pond' there is a stone structure that resembles a small shrine. The site is Hindu and is dated to a year equivalent to 977 CE on the basis of an inscription.[2]

The stone box was unearthed in 1817 [fig. 1]. It was found buried in the ground, probably a few meters below the small shrine. The box is cubical and rests on a double lotus cushion. It is divided in nine compartments, which are square and arranged in three rows of three. At the moment of discovery, the compartments of the box were filled with several objects, which included a small gold casket, pieces of silver and

---

[2] For the information about Jolotundo and the box discovered there, see: van HOËVELL (1851: 112), GROENEVELDT (1887: 120, 216–217), KROM (1923/2: 38–39), STUTTERHEIM (1937b), BOSCH (1961), BOSCH–HAAN (1965).

several figures cut out of gold leaf, namely a tortoise, two snakes, a crescent and two rectangles. All the gold pieces bore inscriptions in Old Javanese script.

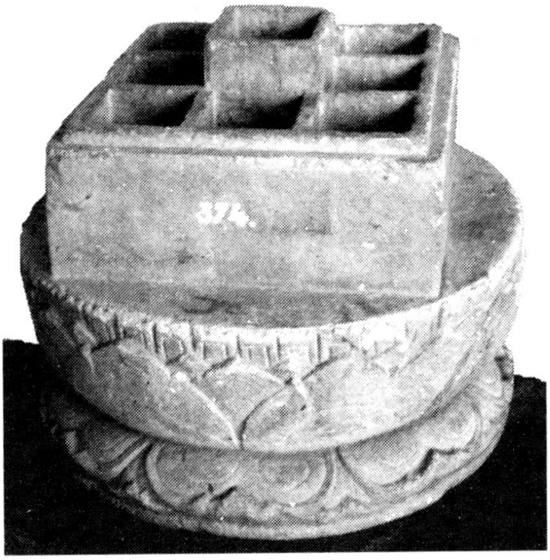

Fig. 1. Stone box found in Jolotundo (East Java). Museum Nasional, Jakarta, inv. no. 374. Photograph: M.J. Klokke. [For a colour print, see the Appendix]

Containers with compartments, such as the JolotundoJolotundo box, are a common appearance among the objects excavated from ancient temples throughout South-East Asia. They were found in Java, Bali, Thailand, Malaysia and Sri Lanka.[3] Unfortunately, in many cases the items that originally occupied the compartments were stolen in antiquity by treasure seekers. Apart from Jolotundo, compartmented boxes still containing a number of items were found in Candi Ngempon on the Dieng Plateau, in the Loro Jonggrang complex on the Prambanan Plain, in Karangrejo in East Java, in Candi Bukit Batu Pahat in Kedah, Malaysia and in several locations in Sri Lanka [figs. 2–4]. In Candi Gebang near Yogyakarta bronze and gold objects were found in the vicinity of a compartmented box.[4] Empty compartmented boxes can be seen on various archaeological sites and in museums. They are especially frequent in Java. In all the cases where the boxes still contained objects, the objects were of the same nature as those discovered in Jolotundo. They included figures cut out of gold leaf, inscribed metal sheets, semiprecious stones, and so on.

[3] In Bali, compartmented boxes were discovered in Gunung Kawi, in Thailand in Sukhothai, Ku Bua and Songkhla and in Malaysia in the so-called Site no. 19 in Kedah. See: DAMSTÉ (1921), WALES (1940) and (1964), and ŚLĄCZKA (2007: Appendix 4).

[4] For these finds, see SOEKMONO (1995: 10) (Candi Ngempon), STUTTERHEIM (1939: 106–107) (Loro Jonggrang), STUTTERHEIM (1939: 121) (Karangrejo), WALES (1940: 18–21) and LAMB (1960a), (1960b) and (1961) (Candi Bukit Batu Pahat) and STUTTERHEIM (1937a: 24) (Candi Gebang).

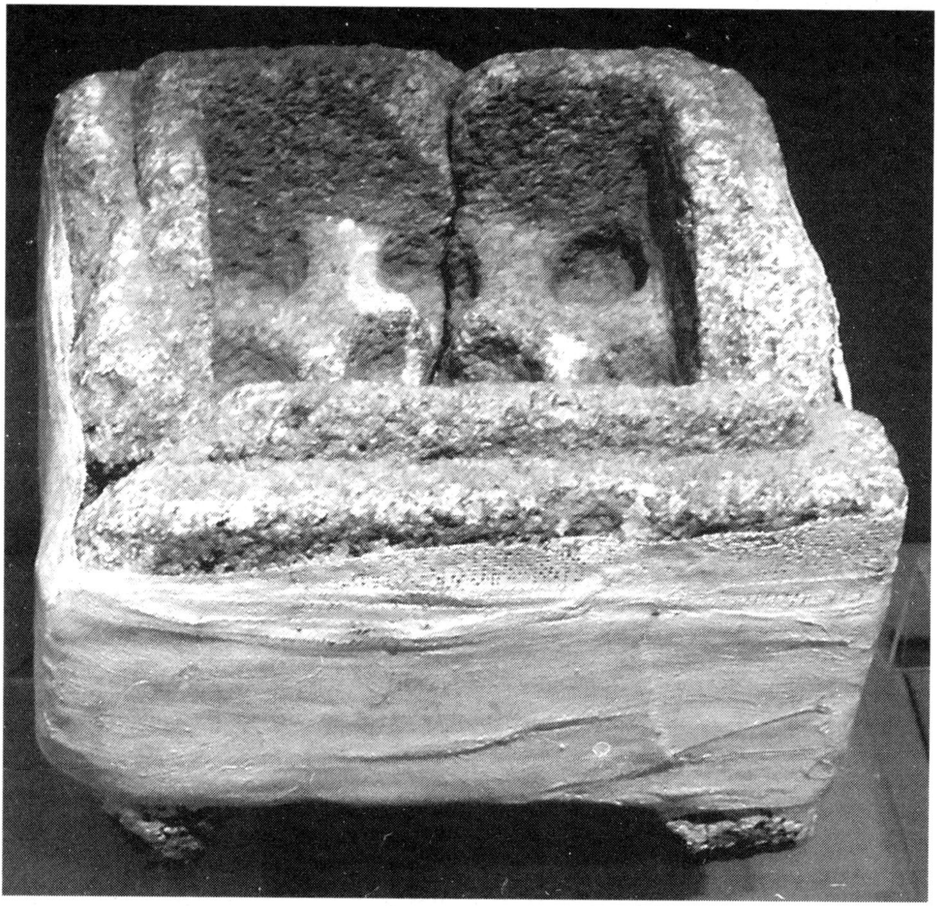

Fig. 2. Stone box found in Candi Bukit Batu Pahat (Malaysia). Bujang Valley Archaeological Museum, Pengkalan Bujang, Merbok, Malaysia. Photograph: A.A. Ślączka. [For a colour print, see the Appendix]

2.2. Po Nagar

As an example of the second type of the archaeological finds originating from South-East Asian temples, I would like to present the objects discovered in Po Nagar in present-day Vietnam. Po Nagar is a group of Śaiva temples in the city of Nha Trang, in the South of the country. All the temples of the Po Nagar group have a deep shaft in the centre of their foundations, formed by the interior sides of four very thick foundation walls. The objects, which probably date to the 8th or early 9th century CE,[5] were discovered on the bottom of the shafts belonging to the so-called northwest tower and the west tower of the temple complex. The shaft of the north-west tower contained, on the bottom, four bricks, which were touching each other at the corners, thus forming a square. In the small cavity between the bricks a number of gold sheets were found, apparently deposited according to a specific order. Four square gold sheets were engraved with the figure of an elephant. The remaining gold sheets were cut out in various forms, namely a crocodile, a tortoise and a trident. In the centre there was a golden lotus. The objects discovered in the foundations of the west tower of the Po Nagar group also included four bricks forming a square and a number of gold objects.

Although bricks forming a square and housing gold objects between them were not as frequently found in the foundations of ancient temples as containers with compartments, still, a few other examples can be named. These were found in Prasat Trapeang Run and Prasat Ak Yom in Angkor, Cambodia (see PARMENTIER (1936: 283–284); TROUVÉ (1933: 1130–1131)).

3. Texts

As mentioned previously, it was suggested that the objects excavated from ancient temples are remains of one or other construction ritual. Yet, partly because of the lack of indigenous textual sources and partly because the tradition of temple building, at least in some of the regions concerned, died out centuries ago, it could not be established exactly which ceremony guided the depositing of the objects in the ancient temples.

Indigenous sources would, of course, form the best basis for the study of the excavated objects. In the lack of indigenous sources, however, it is desirable to search for answers outside South-East Asia. I specifically think here of India—the region that for centuries kept close relations, via trade and diplomatic contacts, with several countries of South-East Asia, and where the first Hindu and Buddhist temples were

[5] The temples of Po Nagar have been rebuilt several times and the present exteriors can be dated to the 11th or 12th centuries CE (GUILLON (2001: 195–196)). However, the construction of the temples begun at the late 8th century CE and some of the towers bear inscriptions from the early 9th century. It can therefore be assumed that the foundations of the towers were not altered and that the objects discovered there should therefore date to the late 8th or early 9th centuries at the latest (William Southworth, personal communication). For the objects discovered at Po Nagar, see: PARMENTIER (1906), (1918: 443).

built. Contrary to South-East Asia, in India, where the tradition of constructing Hindu temples is still very much alive, ancient texts on temple building and temple building rituals survived in great abundance. These texts are written in Sanskrit and date from around the 6th to the 16th century CE. That these sources were thus far not used for the study of the objects excavated from South-East Asian temples is surprising.[6]

The Indian texts that mention construction rituals are either technical manuals on temple building and iconography, the so-called *vāstu-* and *śilpa-śāstra*s, or ritual treatises written by followers of distinct religious schools. Further to this, construction rituals are briefly mentioned in certain *purāṇa*s. For the interpretation of the archaeological finds discussed today, the most important is the fact that one of the rituals described in the ancient Indian texts involves the placing, in a temple under construction, of a cubical box with compartments, and that another ritual mentions the depositing, in the foundation or in the lower strata of a temple, of four bricks forming a square, accompanied by miscellaneous objects.

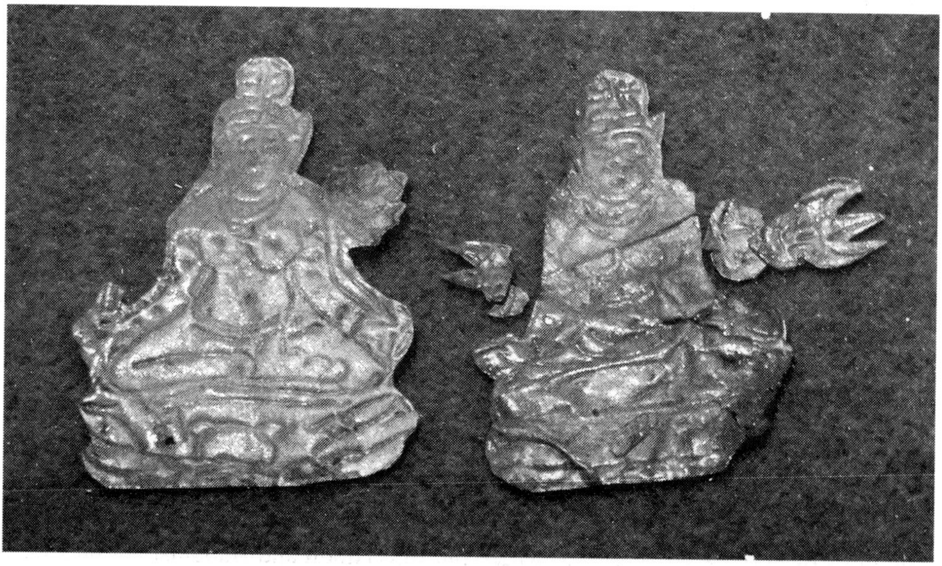

Fig. 3. Images of goddesses found in Candi Bukit Batu Pahat (Malaysia). Bujang Valley Archaeological Museum, Pengkalan Bujang, Merbok, Malaysia. Photograph: A.A. Ślączka. [For a colour print, see the Appendix]

[6] DAGENS (1994: 121, nn. 1 and 3) and MITRA (1981) suggested a link between a few specific objects excavated in South-East Asian temples and Indian textual tradition but these ideas were never fully developed.

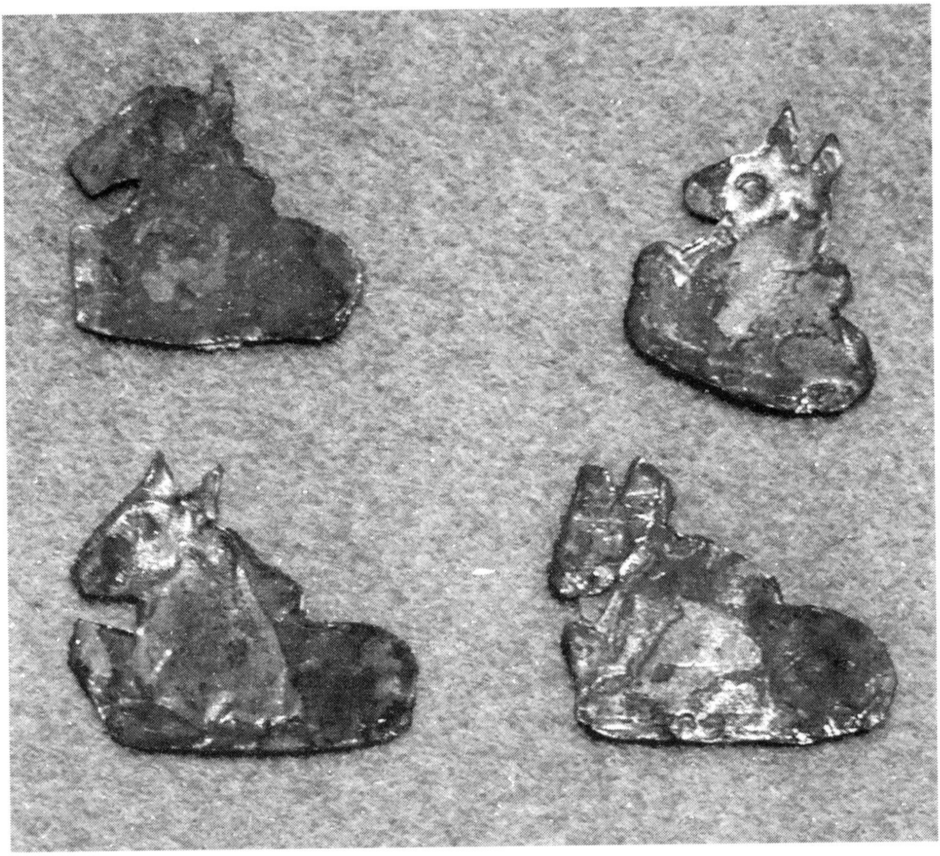

Fig. 4. Images of bulls found in Candi Bukit Batu Pahat (Malaysia). Bujang Valley Archaeological Museum, Pengkalan Bujang, Merbok, Malaysia. Photograph: A.A. Ślączka. [For a colour print, see the Appendix]

3.1. *Garbha-nyāsa*

The ritual that involves placing a compartmented box in a temple under construction is described in a large number of Sanskrit architectural and ritual manuals.[7] The majority of the texts that describe this ritual originated in the South of India. This

[7] I was able to find and read twenty-five of them. For the complete list, see ŚLĄCZKA (2007: Appendix 2).

ritual has in the Sanskrit literature a curious name *garbha-nyāsa* (in a few texts: *garbhâdhāna*), 'the depositing of the embryo', which is the same term as used to refer to one of the Hindu *saṃskāra*s, the one performed to assure a conception of a child. The 'embryo' in the *garbha-nyāsa* ritual is a compartmented box, especially constructed for the occasion. The number of the compartments is usually nine and arranged in three rows of three, or twenty-five, arranged in five rows of five. A few treatises also add that such a box should be in the shape of a lotus (*padma-ākāra*).

During the ritual the box is filled up with objects of symbolic value, which mainly include various 'riches of the earth', such as minerals, grains, metals, precious stones, herbs and earth taken from different locations as well as miniature emblems of the main deity of the temple, in which the box is installed. According to Śaiva texts, the 'embryo-box' also receives, additionally, a series of *bīja*s and *akṣara*s (the 'seed-syllables' and letters of the Sanskrit alphabet). The placing of the objects and the letters is accompanied by the recitation of various *mantra*s. The objects and the *akṣara*s are deposited according to a well-defined scheme: it is of great importance to put the right ingredient in the right compartment. Prior to the ceremony of placing the objects, the box is purified and receives a protective thread (*kautuka* or *prati-sara*), which is tied around it. Further follows the ceremony of placing the jars (*kubha-* or *kalaśa-sthāpana*), during which either the Guardians of the Directions (*loka-pāla*s) or, according to Śaiva texts, various forms of Śiva, are invoked, and the fire oblation. Finally, the purified and filled up box is placed in the base, the plinth, or in the foundation of the temple. The level on which the box is installed depends on the caste of the patron—the higher the caste, the higher the level on which the box will be installed.

The Sanskrit texts that mention the *garbha-nyāsa* are mainly technical manuals and do not contain extensive information about the meaning of the rituals that they describe. Yet, it can be deduced from the few available passages that the principal function of the *garbha-nyāsa* is to bring prosperity and welfare to human beings in general and to those who perform the ritual in particular. Besides, in a few texts the 'embryo-deposit' is called 'life' (*jīva*) or the 'life breath' (*prāṇa*) of the temple to be constructed.[8]

[8] See DĀ 4.1cd–3ab and *Kāśyapa-śilpa*, *Garbha-nyāsa* Chapter, 1cd, in ŚLĄCZKA (2007: 84).

3.2 *Prathamêṣṭakā-nyāsa*

The ritual involving the depositing of four bricks is described in more or less the same Sanskrit texts as the *garbha-nyāsa*. It is referred to as *prathamêṣṭakā-nyāsa*, 'the placing of the first bricks'. This ritual marks the end of the foundation works and the beginning, after the technical and ceremonial preparation of the soil, of the actual construction of the temple. It forms a part of numerous ritual activities whose aim is to 'take possession of the site', to consecrate it and make it fit to serve as a construction ground. In the texts it directly precedes the *garbha-nyāsa*.

During this ritual a number of specially prepared bricks or stones are installed within the lower strata of a temple under construction. According to the majority of the texts, the number of bricks is four and they are placed in such a way as to form a square. Inside the square several small objects are deposited. They are similar to those placed into the compartments of the 'embryo-box'. The installation of the bricks is accompanied by the same activities and ceremonies that take place during the *garbha-nyāsa* ritual. It must be added that the so-called bricks should, in fact, be of the same material as the building in which they are installed, namely one should use genuine bricks for a brick temple, stones for a stone temple, and so on.[9]

4. Correspondences between the textual and the archaeological data

It can easily be noticed that there are significant correspondences between the objects installed in the course of these two rituals described in the Indian texts and the objects excavated from the temples of South-East Asia. The appearance of the deposit boxes excavated in JolotundoJolotundo and many other sites corresponds very well with the prescriptions for the 'embryo-box' as given in the Indian Sanskrit manuals. Not only are the excavated boxes divided in compartments, but the prescription that an 'embryo-box' should have the shape of a lotus brings in mind several Javanese containers that have their compartments in the shape of lotus petals [fig. 5]. Also the objects discovered inside the compartmented containers, such as pieces of metals and figures cut out of gold leaf as found in JolotundoJolotundo, Karangrejo and Candi Bukit Batu Pahat and minerals and semiprecious stones as found in Candi Ngempon, Loro Jonggrang and Candi Bukit Batu Pahat, correspond very well with the prescriptions given in the Indian textual sources. It should be added that depositing images of snakes, two of which were found inside the

[9] See, e.g., KārĀ 4.93, DĀ 2, SĀ 27.3cd-4ab, PSaṁ 5.43cd-44ab, MM 12.103cd.

Jolotundo box, is especially prescribed for structures connected with water—wells and ponds—such as Jolotundo.[10]

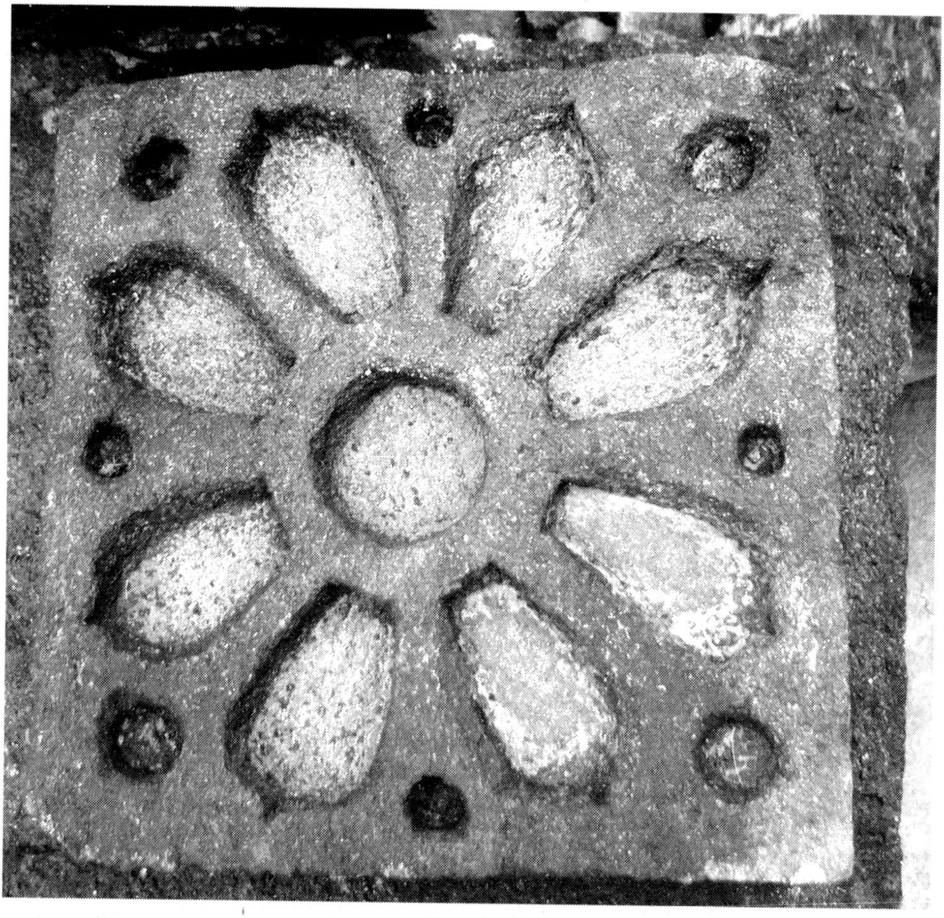

Fig. 5. Stone box in Candi Merak (Central Java). Photograph: M.J. Klokke. For a colour print, see the Appendix]

The inscribed gold plates discovered in Jolotundo provide another link with the Indian texts. Two of the inscribed pieces bore invocations to the Guardians of the Directions, namely to Īśāna and Agni. Although the textual sources do not explicitly state that the names of the Guardians of Directions are written down and placed into

[10] See, for example MM 12.99.

the deposit casket, as stated previously, the *loka-pāla*s are invoked in the jars placed during the *kumbha-sthāpana* ceremony, which is a part of the *garbha-nyāsa* ritual. Subsequently, by pouring water from the jars over the deposit casket, the *loka-pāla*s are transferred into it. This may explain the presence of the invocations to these deities inside the Jolotundo box.

The same as between the *garbha-nyāsa* ritual and the compartmented boxes, there are also significant correspondences between the ritual involving the installation of four bricks described in the Indian texts and the objects discovered in Po Nagar, Prasat Trapeang Run and Prasat Ak Yom. These correspondences are noticed both in the way the bricks were positioned and in the nature of the objects deposited along with the bricks. Also the prescription that the so-called bricks should be made of the same material as the temple in which they are installed seems to have been followed. In the stone temples of Prasat Trapeang Run and Prasat Ak Yom the 'bricks' are in fact large stones while in the brick towers of Po Nagar genuine bricks were deposited.

On the other hand, there are also a few points on which the archaeological finds of South-East Asia do not correspond with the textual passages. The most important of them concern the material of which the 'embryo-box' should be made and the location on which the four bricks should be installed within a temple. According to the texts, the box should be made of metal while the majority of the excavated boxes are made of stone. Stone is mentioned by only one text (KāmĀ 31.13) as a suitable material for a deposit box. There are a few examples of compartmented boxes made of metal but they were found in India and in Sri Lanka, not in South-East Asia. Concerning the location, there is a difference between the texts that originated in south India and those that originated in north India. Four bricks forming a square and housing miscellaneous items between them are prescribed by the south Indian texts only. And, according to these, the bricks should be installed to the right or to the south of the entrance to the *garbha-gṛha* (*sanctum sanctorum*)[11], not at the centre of the building as found in Po Nagar, Prasat Trapeang Run and Prasat Ak Yom. The north Indian texts do prescribe the bricks to be installed in the centre but then the number of the bricks is higher, namely eight or nine. The *Viṣṇu-dharmôttara-purāṇa* Chapter 94 seems to allow the installation of four bricks in the centre of the foundation pit. Yet, it does not mention that any objects should be placed, without a container, in the middle of the bricks.

[11] The expression used is *dvārasya dakṣiṇe* or *dvāra-dakṣiṇe*, which might be translated both as 'to the right' and 'to the south' of the door.

5. Conclusion

Although no hundred-percent correspondence between a particular object excavated in South-East Asia and a description of a ritual in a specific text could be found, several excavated objects do correspond with the descriptions of the texts as far as many important features are concerned. The characteristic shape of the deposit box as employed in Jolotundo and other ancient sites of Java, Bali, Thailand, Malaysia and Sri Lanka—namely a cubical box with square or lotus-shaped compartments—and the practice of installing four bricks forming a square as attested in Vietnam and Cambodia, are consistent with details given in the Sanskrit treatises. The majority of the objects placed in the compartmented boxes and deposited along with the four bricks, such as gold images of tortoises and elephants, metal sheets inscribed with 'seed letters', grains and semiprecious stones as well as the importance apparently attached to the geographical directions and their guardians, the *loka-pāla*s, too, agree with the prescriptions in the Indian texts.

Burying precious objects in the foundations of buildings under construction is, and was, a well-known custom that is spread far beyond the area of Indian cultural influence. Yet, it does not seem likely that certain specific features, like those mentioned above, were invented in each of the regions from India to Indonesia independently. Rather, the fact that numerous Indian texts describe comparable items points to India as a plausible source of inspiration.

Therefore, it can be assumed that the objects—at least those of the type discussed today—excavated from ancient temples of South-East Asia are consecration deposits whose installation was directly or indirectly inspired by the Indian ritual tradition as described in the Sanskrit manuals. In the present state of knowledge, it is impossible to tell how far this inspiration of the Indian texts reached and whether it had any implications for the way these rituals were viewed by the people of South-East Asia. In Java, for example, the presumable modification of the function and meaning of the construction rituals is reflected in the fact that the foundations of temples and even the excavated consecration deposit boxes (not the compartmented boxes though) sometimes contained animal ashes and bones.[12] And animal remains are never prescribed as a part of a consecration deposit in the Indian treatises. The presence of animal remains inside and in the vicinity of consecration deposit containers in Java therefore suggests the influence of the local tradition, which is one of the

---

[12] It is true that many claims concerning animal remains being a part of a consecration deposit proved false (see SOEKMONO (1995)). On the other hand, animal bones were indeed found in some temple shafts, for example in Loro Jonggrang and in the (Buddhist) Candi Plaosan Lor (IJZERMAN (1891: 67–68)).

reasons the consecration deposits discovered in South-East Asia should not, in my opinion, be referred to by the Sanskrit terms used in the Indian texts.

Nevertheless, the fact that the outer appearance of a great number of temple consecration deposits discovered in South-East Asia show such close correspondences with the Indian textual tradition, and in many cases, for example in Jolotundo, especially with the South Indian tradition, is certainly significant and may improve our understanding of the transition and transformation of ritual forms as part of the historic process of cultural interaction between India and South-East Asia.

BIBLIOGRAPHY

BOSCH 1961 = Bosch, Frederik David Kan: 'Review of "Chandi Bukti Batu Pahat: A report on the excavation of an ancient temple in Kedah" and "Candi Bukit Batu Pahat: three additional notes," by Alastair Lamb', *Bijdragen tot de Taal-, Land- en Volkenkunde* 117 (1961) 485–491.

BOSCH–HAAN 1965 = Bosch, Frederik David Kan; de Haan, B.: 'The Oldjavanese bathing place Jalatunda,' *Bijdragen tot de Taal-, Land- en Volkenkunde* 121 (1965) 189–232.

O'CONNOR 1966 = O'Connor, Stanley J.: 'Ritual deposit boxes in Southeast Asian Sanctuaries,' *Artibus Asiae* 28,1 (1966) 53–60.

DAGENS 1994 = See: MM.

DĀ = *Dīptâgama*. (1) *Dīptâgama*. Institut Français de Pondichéry T1018. Paper transcript in Devanāgarī script. (2) Marie-Luce Barazer-Billoret; Bruno Dagens; Vincent Lefèvre; S. Sambandha Sivacarya (eds.): *Dīptāgama*. Tome I: *Chapitres 1 à 21*. Institut Française de Pondichéry, Pondicherry 2004.

DAMSTÉ 1921 = Damsté, Henri Titus: 'Een Boeddhistisch rotsklooster op Bali,' *Oudheidkundig Verslag*, Tweede kwartaal 1921: 60–62.

GROENEVELDT 1887 = Groeneveldt, Willem Pieter: *Catalogus der archeologische verzameling van het Bataviaasch Genootschap van Kunsten en Wetenschappen*. Albrecht and Co., Batavia 1887.

GUILLON 2001 = Guillon, Emmanuel: *Cham art*. Thames and Hudson, London 2001.

HOËVELL 1851 = Hoëvell, Wolter Robert van: *Reis over Java, Madura en Bali, in het midden van 1847, met platen en kaarten*. Vol. 2. P.N. van Kampen, Amsterdam 1851.

IJZERMAN 1891 = Ijzerman, Jan Willem: *Beschrijving der oudheden nabij de grens der residentie's Soerakarta en Kjogdjakarta*. Bataviaasch Genootschap van Kunsten en Wetenschappen, Batavia 1891.

KārĀ = *Kāraṇâgama.* Institut Français de Pondichéry T313a. Paper transcript in Devanāgarī script.

KāmĀ = *Kāmikâgama.* Svāmināthasivācārya (ed.): *Kāmikāgama, Pūrvabhāga*. South India Archaka Association, Madras 1975.

KROM 1923 = Krom, Nicolaas Johannes: *Inleiding tot Hindoe-Javaansche kunst.* 2 vols. Nijhoff, s'Gravenhage 1923.

LAMB 1960a = Lamb, Alastair: *Chandi Bukit Batu Pahat: A report on the excavation of an ancient temple in Kedah.* Eastern Universities Press, Singapore 1960.

LAMB 1960b = Lamb, Alastair: 'Report on the excavation and reconstruction of Chandi Bukit Batu Pahat, Central Kedah,' *Federation Museums Journal* 5 (1960) X-108.

LAMB 1961 = Lamb, Alastair: 'Chandi Bukit Batu Pahat: Some additional notes,' *Federation Museums Journal* 6 (1961) 1–9.

MM = *Maya-mata.* Bruno Dagens (ed.). *Mayamatam. A Treatise of Housing, Architecture and Iconography.* 2 vols. Indira Gandhi National Centre for the Arts, New Delhi 1994.

MITRA 1981 = Mitra, Debala: 'Observations on some carved slabs and deposit boxes in Museum Pusat, Jakarta,' in: Amita Ray; H. Sanyal; S. C. Ray (eds.): *Indian studies: Essays presented in memory of prof. Niharranjan Ray*. Caxton Publications, Delhi [1981].

PSaṁ = *Pādma-saṁhitā.* H. Daniel Smith (ed.): *Pāñcarātraprāsādaprasādhana: chapters 1–10 of the 'kriyāpāda', Pādmasamhitā: a Pañcarātra text on temple-building.* With an introduction in Sanskrit by T.S.M. Varadarājabhaṭṭar. Rathnam Press, Madras 1963.

PARMENTIER 1906 = Parmentier, Henri: 'Nouvelles notes sure le sanctuaire de Po-Nagar Nhatrang,' *Bulletin de l'École française d'Extrême Orient* 6 (1906) 291–300.

PARMENTIER 1918 = Parmentier, Henri: *Inventaire descriptif des monuments Chams de l'Annam.* Vol. 2, *Étude de l'art Cam*. Leroux, Paris 1918.

PARMENTIER 1936 = Parmentier, Henri : 'La construction dans l'architecture khmère Classique,' *Bulletin de l'École française d'Extrême Orient* 35 (1936) 242–311.

ŚLĄCZKA 2007 = Ślączka, Anna A.: *Temple consecration rituals in ancient India: Text and archaeology*. Brill, Leiden 2007.

SOEKMONO 1995 = Soekmono, R.: *The Javanese candi: Function and Meaning*. Brill, Leiden 1995.

STUTTERHEIM 1937a = Stutterheim, Willem Frederik: *Oudheidkundig Verslag* (1937) 24.

STUTTERHEIM 1937b = Stutterheim, Willem Frederik: 'Het zinrijke waterwerk van Djalatoeṇḍa,' *Tijdschrift voor Indische Taal-, Land- en Volkenkunde* 77 (1937) 214–250.

STUTTERHEIM 1939 = Stutterheim, Willen Frederik: 'De archaeologische verzameling. Lijst van aanwinsten,' *Jaarboek van het Koninklijk Bataviaasch Genootschap van Kunsten en Wetenschappen* 6 (1937) 97–122.

SĀ = *Suprabhedâgama.* Institut Français de Pondichéry T360. Paper transcript in Devanāgarī script.

TROUVÉ 1933 = Trouvé, Georges : '[Rapport sur de dégagement du] Prasat Ak Yom,' *Bulletin de l'École française d'Extrême Orient* 33 (1933) 1129–1130.

VDhP = *Viṣṇu-dharmôttara-purāṇa.* Priyabala Shah (ed.): *Viṣṇudharmottara-Purāṇa: Third Khaṇḍa (A Study on a Sanskrit Text on Ancient Indian Arts).* Oriental Institute, Baroda 1958–1961.

WALES 1940 = Wales, Quaritch H.G.: 'Archaeological research on ancient Indian colonization in Malaya,' *Journal of the Malayan Branch of the Royal Asiatic Society* 18/1 (1940) 1–85.

WALES 1964 = Wales, Quaritch H.G.: 'A stone casket from Satinpra,' *Journal of the Siam Society* 52/2 (1964) 217–221.

Facial Expression in the Erotic Art of Khajurāho. A Preliminary Investigation

DAVID SMITH
(Lancaster University)

Although much progress has been made in understanding the architecture of the Hindu temple, it would, I believe, be fair to say that the appreciation of the temple sculpture has lagged behind. Many art historians of South Asia have deep knowledge of sculptural forms and styles, but do not set out in detail the basis for their judgements. Then again, although erotic sculpture as a field from the point of view of art history in general is unquestionably dominated by Indian models, the achievements of Indian sculpture here have certainly not been subjected to sustained analysis. This paper is an attempt to discuss the erotic sculpture of Khajurāho in terms that are somewhat parallel to the type of study which is the norm in Western art history. Of course the scholarship of Western art history builds on a long and multifarious tradition with many toilers in the field, whereas in the context of South Asian studies the material is extensive and scholars relatively few. But the situation in India has not been helped by the primacy accorded to the written text. The texts to which architects and sculptors may have referred are of great importance, when we know what those texts were. However, there are grounds for saying that the search for textual support has distracted attention from the study of the art itself. The now forgotten art historian Charles FABRI (1974: xxiv) boldly declared that he knew 'of no artist of ancient Orissa who ever followed the *Śilpa-śāstras*.' S. K. Ramachandra RAO (1976: 3), in his review of FABRI's *History of the Art of Orissa*, remarked that FABRI's 'reputation as an art critic was never on firm grounds', and doubted whether 'he really understood or appreciated the spirit of Indian art.' It may be fairly said that there is a strong intellectualist tendency in Indian interpretation of the arts, in the case of Sanskrit poetry as well as the visual arts; and one might go on to say that interpretators are more at their ease with listing the rules and prescriptions of self-proclaimed authorities than with actually examining the practice of

Art, Myths and Visual Culture of South Asia
Warsaw Indological Studies 4 (2011) 183–201.

creative artists. FABRI (1974: xxiv) choose to stress the 'individualism and originality' of artists, and I believe that to be a fruitful attitude.

FABRI's choice chimes in with Susan SONTAG's famous essay 'Against Interpretation', which called for concentration on the art object in itself without being distracted by unnecessary interpretation. (Although FABRI's *History of the Art Orissa* was published in 1974, his preface is dated 1965, a year later than the first publication of SONTAG's essay.) SONTAG (1967: 3, 10) put it thus:

> 'I don't mean interpretation in the broadest sense, the sense in which Nietzsche [rightly] says, "There are no facts, only interpretations." By interpretation, I mean here a conscious act of the mind which illustrates a certain code, certain "rules" of interpretation. Directed to art, interpretation means plucking a set of elements [the X, the Y, the Z, and so forth] from the whole work. The task of interpretation is virtually one of translation. The interpreter says, Look, don't you see that X is really—or, really means—A? That Y is really B? That Z is really C?
>
> Like the fumes of the automobile and of heavy industry which befoul the urban atmosphere, the effusion of interpretations of art today poisons our sensibilities. In a culture whose already classical dilemma is the hypertrophy of the intellect at the expense of energy and sensual capability, interpretation is the revenge of the intellect upon art.
>
> The aim of all commentary on art now should be to make works of art—and, by analogy, our own experience—more, rather than less, real to us. The function of criticism should be to show *how it is what it is,* even *that it is what it is,* rather than to show *what it means.*
>
> In place of a hermeneutics we need an erotics of art.'

It might be argued that SONTAG's use of erotics here is part and parcel of a modern tendency to misuse such terms as grammar, syntax, poetics and so, in speaking of the grammar or what not of a topic that has nothing to do language, when all that is really meant is a detailed study of general details; a tendency arising from the departure in the west from systematic philological study of texts. But SONTAG's erotics comes close to the root meaning of philology, sharing and promoting the love.

A striking instance of the 'erotics of art', or at least of attitudes relevant to SONTAG's prescription, might be the photographer Raymond Burnier. Burnier took highly distinctive photographs of Khajurāho in the 1940s, photos that summed up Khajurāho in the 50s and 60s; and which provided the illustrations for Kramrisch's study, *The Hindu Temple.* Alain DANIÉLOU (1987:174) has given a description of Burnier's procedure.

> 'The work was very difficult. We had to clean the sculptures, remove wasp nests, and carefully scrape off the remains of lime that coated the temples. Then we had to build scaffoldings, wait under the burning sun for the perfect light, and adjust the mirrors to enhance it. ... Raymond worked with passion, striving to reanimate the stone gods that had been abandoned for centuries in secluded forests. ... Some of the statues became so real to him that he would fall passionately in love with them. He wrote [in a letter to a friend, Benares, 17 November, 1946]: "These thousand-year-old statues have finally been released from their stone bodies and found another form, more volatile, more subtle, more alive. They will find their way to you. They will travel around the world".'

A good instance of the interpretation that SONTAG opposes is DESAI's rereading of the famous panels between the hall and *sanctum* (*antarāla*) panels of the Lakṣmaṇa, Viśvanātha, and Kandariyā Mahādeva temples, in her attempt to defuse their eroticism by means of a spiritual reading: 'Don't you see that X is really A?' DESAI has spent many years backtracking from the findings of her brilliant study of erotic sculpture of 1975. In so doing she has made many valuable contributions to the understanding of the general iconography of Khajurāho, but her application of the *Śilpa-prakāśa* (ŚiPr) to the *antarāla* panels can be seen as a denial of her initial pathbreaking work. She invites us to look beyond the sculpture to a secret underlying *yantra*, a mystic diagram. Here in a particularly condensed and striking form is the problem of Indian sculpture in a nutshell. Never mind the actual composition in stone, let's look for the text: only the text can tell us what's really there.

A celebrated art historian and painter who comes close to what SONTAG was getting at might be Ratan PARIMOO (1994) and (2000), who, though he does pay more than lip-service to the importance of authoritative texts, certainly is deeply concerned with the form and practice of sculpture. In his paper, 'Khajuraho: the Chandella sculptor's paradise. Is there a Chandella style of Medieval Indian sculpture? Its sources and characteristics', first published in *Perspectives on Khajuraho*, and then revised in his *Studies in Indian Sculpture*, PARIMOO (2000: 252) stresses his concern with sculptural values, with the rendering of the undulation of the spine, 'of the sensuality ... of the soft feminine flesh'. And he declares that the achievement of the Indian sculptor is 'not "to be put under the carpet"'; 'preference' should not be given 'to the very weighty philosophising on the particular groups of coitus sculptures.' Here he no doubt refers to readings such as those of Desai, Rabe, and White, who all refer to the *Śilpa-prakāśa*, a text 'discovered' by Pandit Rath Sharma, forger of several other texts.

PARIMOO (2000: 348), I believe, is exemplifying what SONTAG was calling for when he says Khajurāho 'is a paradise conjured up by the sculptor; it is his paradise, it is also the paradise for the aesthetic participant.' His passionate concern to describe the effects of the sculptor's chisel is, I suggest, an instance of the 'erotics of art.' PARIMOO (2000: 348) said, 'Never has a sculptural tradition handled the human body with such obsessiveness and complexity as the sculptors of Khajurāho' and 'The Chandella sculptors were truly the worshippers of the female body, as if they too were made intoxicated by the arrows of the Kāmadeva.' Here PARIMOO illustrates his meaning with a photograph of an *apsaras* on the Viśvanātha temple, twisting her back in the movement PARIMOO finds so important to the art, and twisting also her hair, wringing the moisture out of it, though there is no goose to drink the water [fig. 1]. I was at first surprised by his choice of *apsaras*, though in one sense any *apsaras* would have done, surprised because this nymph has the tubular leg he finds typical of the Kandariyā temple, and because the *apsaras*'s face seems distorted, malformed. However, this partly due to the angle the photograph is taken at. Her absorption in herself, her body contorted as she contorts her hair, her whole being contorted by the sculptor at his pleasure, all go to make her a good choice for PARIMOO's point; even if here the body seems paramount over the face.

Particularly significant for the purposes of this paper is a remark of PARIMOO (2000: 355) distinguishing between the sculpture of the Lakṣmaṇa and that of the Kandariyā: 'The warm smile and sparkling eyes of the faces from Lakṣmaṇa temple [are] replaced by a blank expression in the faces of the Kandariya Mahadeva.' In the human face the mouth and the eyes are especially expressive. As Dante says in the *Convivio* (3.8), 'the soul operates very largely in two places … that is to say in the eyes and mouth, which it adorns most fully and directs its whole attention there to beautify them as far as possible' (KEMP (2006: 260)). The mouths of Indian sculptured faces tend to be more expressive than the eyes, though the situation might have been more equal in the case of sculptures originally finely plastered and painted. Often in the sculpture as we have it now, the irises are not marked, and the direction of the gaze has to be inferred or imagined. The mouth is nearly always, if not invariably, the governing factor: the emotion apparent in the mouth is imagined to be present in the eyes. There is perhaps an unavoidable tendency in the viewer of the sculpture to read into the stone eyes the kind of expression the viewer expects to see, given everything else the sculpture expresses.

PARIMOO illustrates his remark about the 'warm smile and sparkling eyes' of the Lakṣmaṇa sculptures with two illustrations [fig. 2], captioned as belonging to the Lakṣmaṇa. Arguably, other instances such the two females from the Lakṣmaṇa in

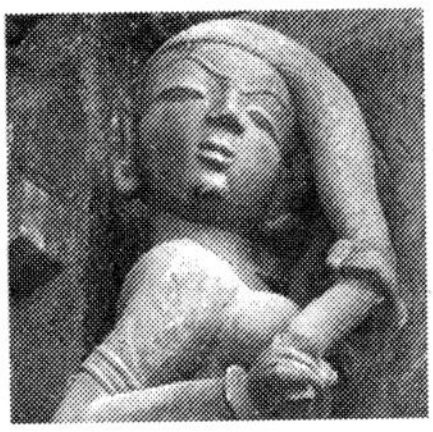

Fig.1

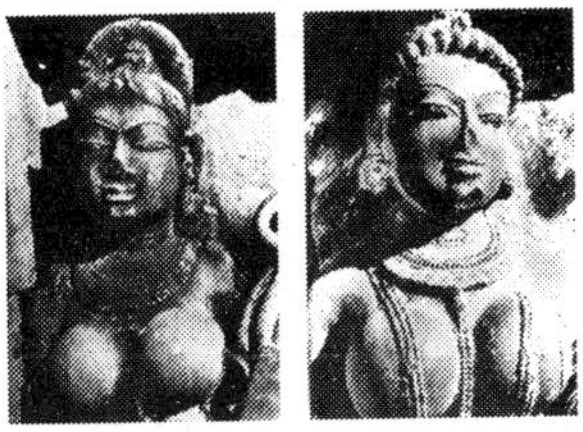

Fig.2

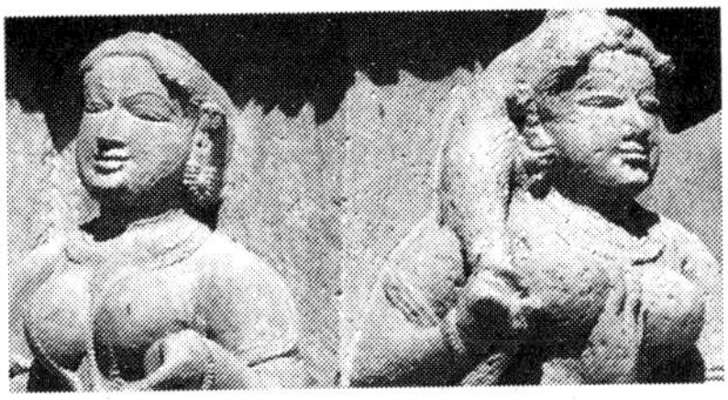

Fig. 3

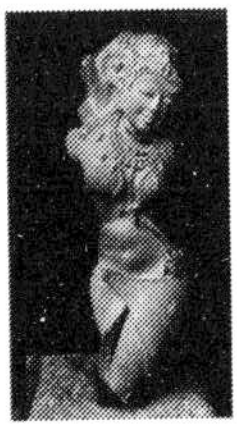

Fig.4

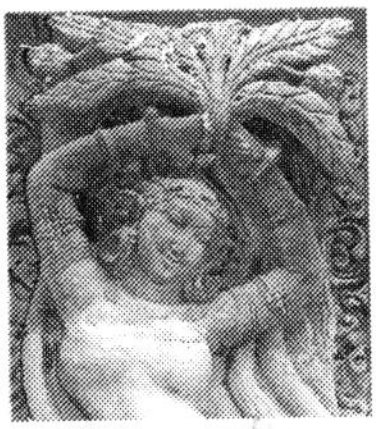

Fig.5

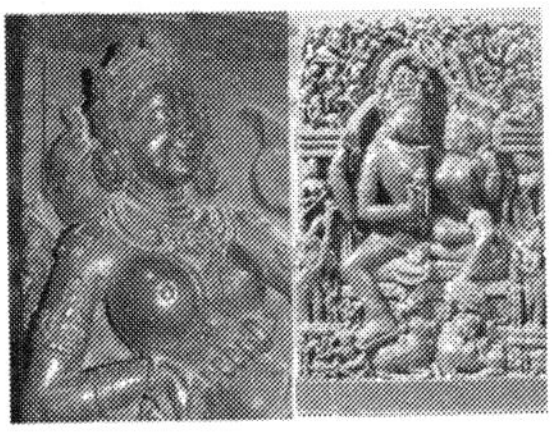

Fig.6

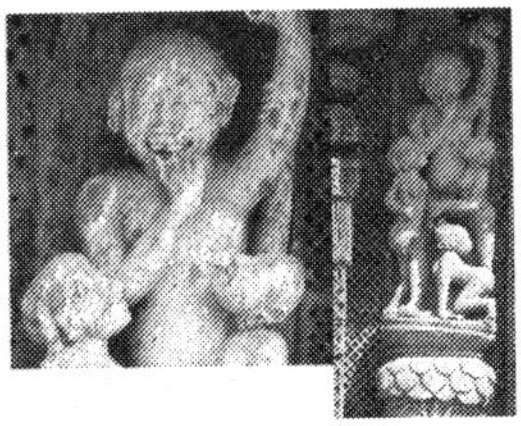

Fig.7

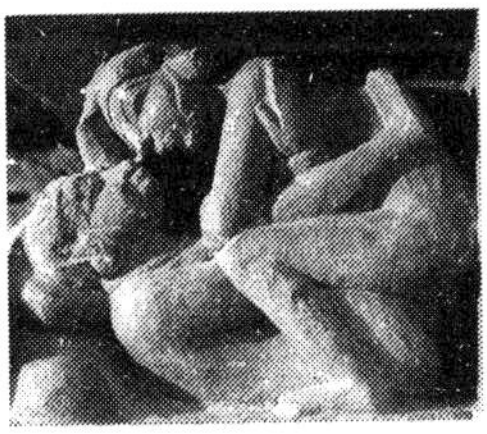

Fig.8

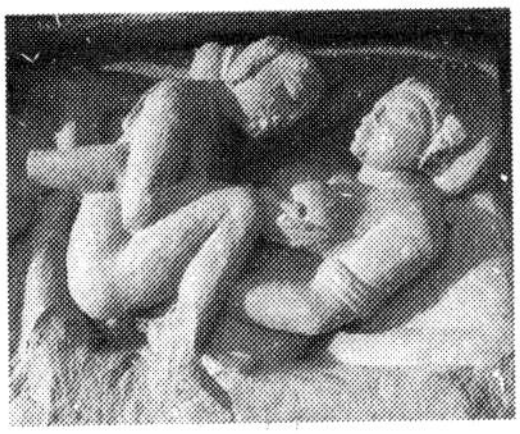

Fig. 9

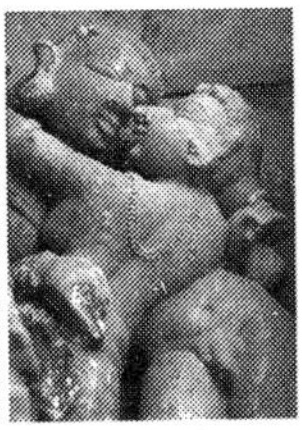

Fig.10

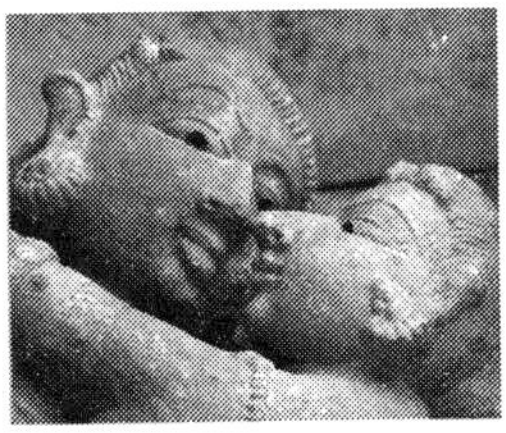

Fig.11

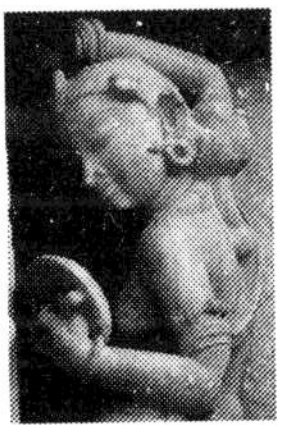

Fig.12

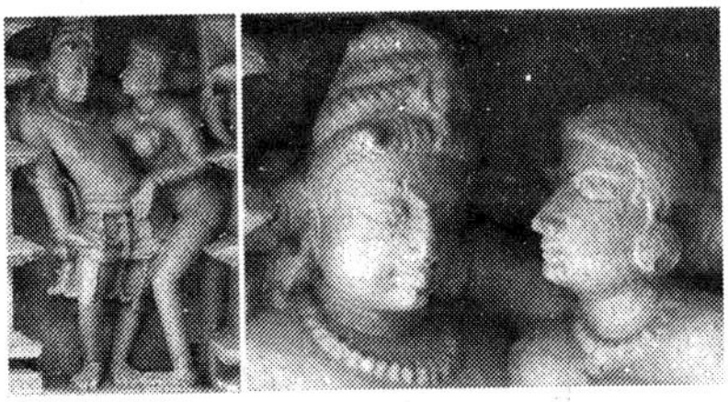

Fig.13

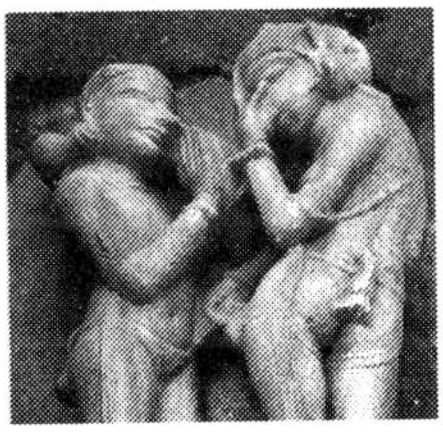

Fig.14

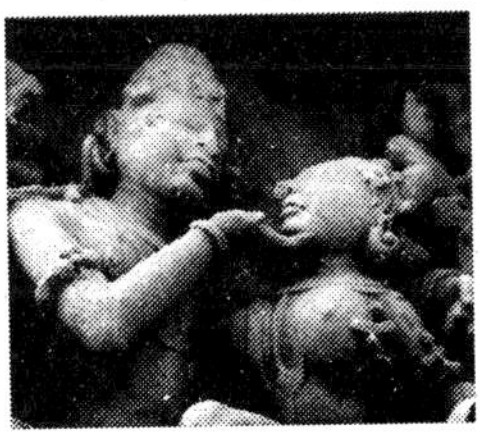

Fig.15

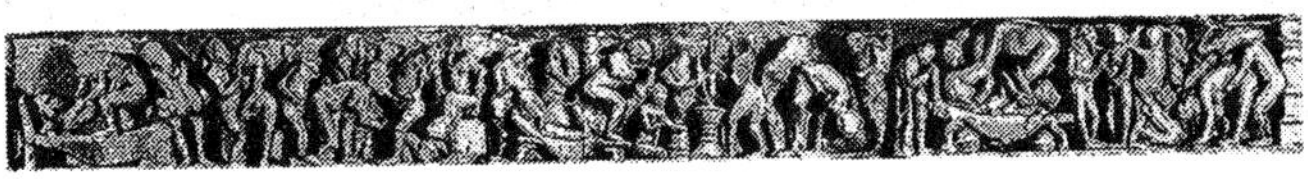

Fig.16

fig. 3 better exemplify PARIMOO's argument. Note that irises seem to be marked in both faces. These latter two to my mind really are smiling. But in looking the sculptures on the wall generally, I find it hard to see the difference alleged by PARIMOO. The Khajurāho face in general is aloof and superior, self-conscious but withdrawn when alone, as for the most part they all are. The case could well be made that Khajurāho is not that good at smiles.

The famous *vṛkṣikā* of the Mālādevī temple in Gyāraspur, which PARIMOO refers to elsewhere in his paper, as an instance of 'archetypal beauty', but without mentioning her smile [fig. 4], is an instance of a smiling face from Madhya Pradesh where we do have warmth of smile, along with 'sparkling eyes'; but it is in Orissa that smiling faces are in abundance. Thus at the Rājārānī in Bhubaneshwar [fig. 5], and the wonderful Śiva and Pārvatī in the British Museum (accession no. 1872,0701.70, from Orissa, and perhaps from Koṇārk (Konarak); first collected by 'Hindu' Stuart). Indeed, the latter sculpture is a supreme instance of the sculpture of the smile. The smile of the god and goddess are only faintly suggested, but all forty so faces on the stele are smiling.

Most splendidly saucy is the chowrie bearer beside Śiva, shown enlarged [fig. 6]. Below Pārvatī, to the side, stands the wife of the donor making an offering, her daughter beneath her does the same; and husband and son the same over on the other side. A remarkable feature of this masterly composition is the way the faces of those on Śiva's side, particularly the donor and the female chowrie-bearer above him, have a bold and open look, while his wife and the female chowrie-bearer above her have demure and averted gazes, while not at all lacking self-confidence. There is a similar distinction between Śiva's bull and Pārvatī's lion at the divine couple's feet. Śiva's jolly bull smiles happily at Pārvatī's lion, who, though his whiskers form a magnificent moustache, simpers, and scratches his back with his right rear paw in a highly submissive manner. Above the celestial world throngs to honour the divine couple, every face distinct and expressing loving awe. Each of the forty or so faces expresses an individual character and emotion.

Lastly, from Orissa, from Koṇārk, the grin of gross self-congratulation on the part of an ascetic about to be pleasured by three women [fig. 7]. His grin is toothy, and his eyes looking at the women are narrowed in the expression of his happiness. One hand pours water on himself from his *loṭā*, and he has three fingers in his mouth, expressing perhaps his uncertainty as to how best employ the services of the three women.

I now propose to look at the erotic sculpture of Khajurāho in the manner that SONTAG calls for. In the attempt to win back from the textualists a degree of priority for the artist, one is on particularly firm ground in the case of erotic art, since no one has yet found a rulebook for it. Not only does the investigation of the facial expression of the erotic sculpture form a narrowly focussed set among the many hundreds of sculptured anthropomorphic forms at Khajurāho, it is preeminently in erotic sculpture that people are shown interacting. The Khajurāho sculptures look outwards, over and above the worshipper; the great majority are individual figures, isolated in their own space, however close to their neighbours. This massed isolation is one of the most remarkable features of the Khajurāho temples, especially in the way that the gods for the most part are not framed in shrines, but rub shoulders, so to speak, with *apsaras*es and *vyāla*s. The *vyāla*s set off the beauty of the *apsaras*es. It is also the case, I think, that the gods set off the power of the *apsaras*es. The *apsaras*es are on an equal footing with the gods, on a one to one basis, and furthermore, because they occupy equal space and the gods have crowns, the *apsaras*es are actually taller in themselves than the gods.

There are group scenes in the many friezes, most of them armies on the march, where the massed faces are not interacting; and also scenes, noteworthy on the Lakṣmaṇa plinth frieze, where there are several instances of what has generally been taken to be gurus and their pupils, but plausibly interpreted by Alok TRIPATHI (2008) as kings and their courts. At all events, I restrict my inquiry to the erotic scenes, where we clearly have people interacting in an intense and by and large clearly defined manner; and in the scenes we shall consider, several people in each case.

When Khajurāho first became known in the modern world, through the photographs of Raymond Burnier, Dolly Saher and others, the famous erotic sculptures seemed to represent simply the intense union of the human couple, a union easily transposed to the universal and the individual self. But that was because the accomplices and onlookers integral to the sculpture were omitted, left out of the photograph. In this paper, I will examine aspects of the principal instances of erotic art at Khajurāho, that is to say, in the erotic scenes on the frieze around the base plinth of the Lakṣmaṇa temple, and on the erotic *antarāla* panels of the Lakṣmaṇa, Viśvanātha, and Kandariyā. In the case of the Lakṣmaṇa frieze, I consider every face on the erotic panels; in the case of the *antarāla* panels, for reasons of space, I shall be selective.

Burnier's photographs are immediately recognisable by their lack of shadow, since he used mirrors to direct sunlight on the sculpture; and by their lack of plaster, since he scraped all the plaster off before photographing. Now nearly all the plaster—lime wash—has gone. But originally the plaster would presumably have been painted—some painted portions remain; and this would have had great importance for the expression of emotion. Some sculptures have the irises shown in the stone, and that serves to show how necessary that detail is for the onlooker: all eyes, surely, would have had irises marked out, and the direction of the gaze would have

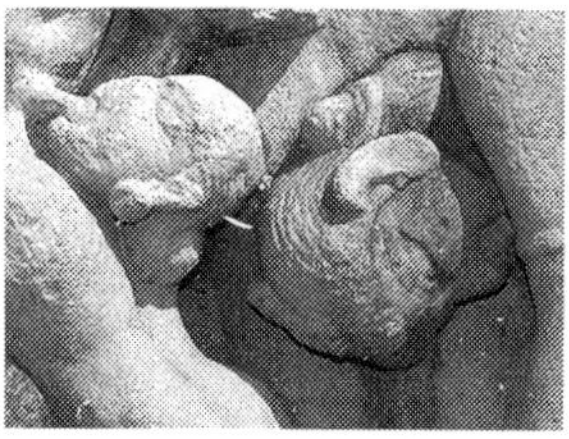
Fig.17

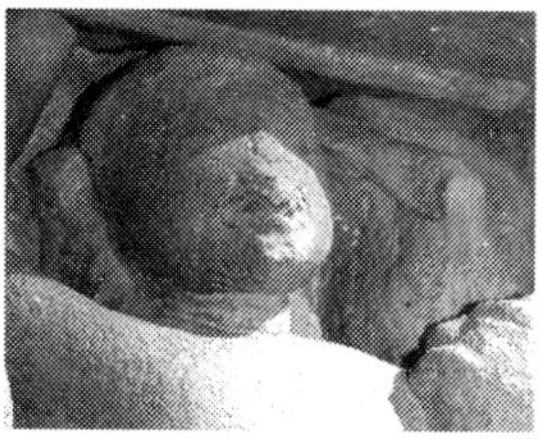
Fig.18

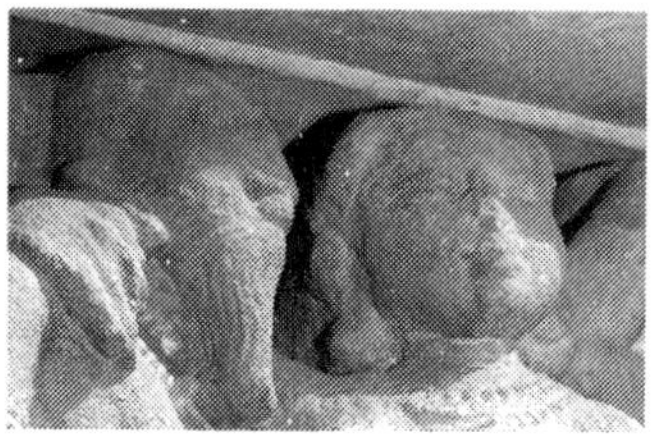
Fig.19

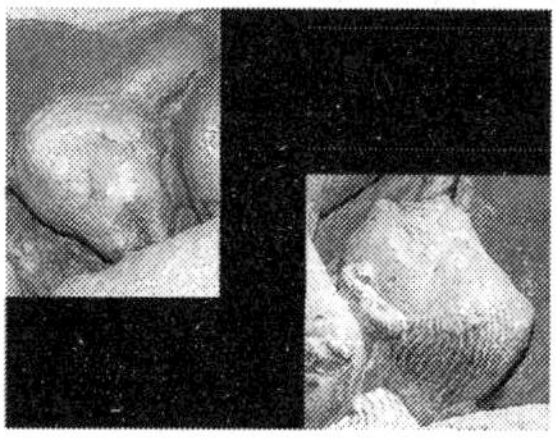
Fig.20

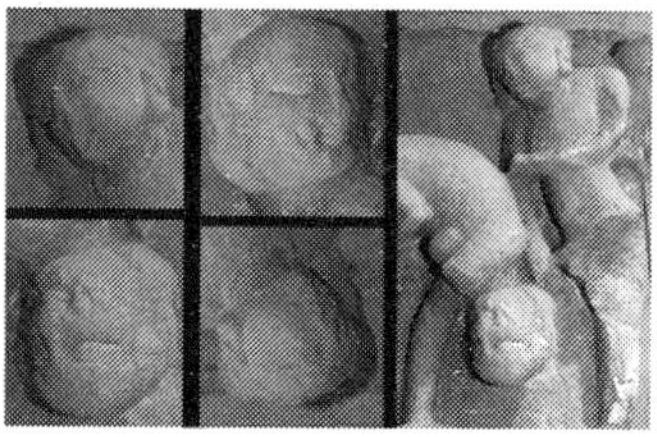
Fig.21

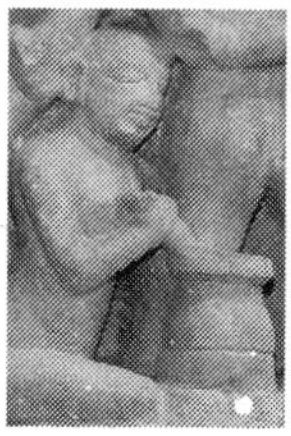
Fig.22

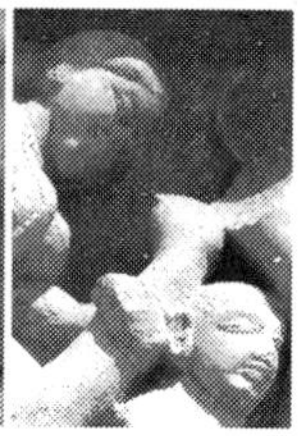
Fig.23

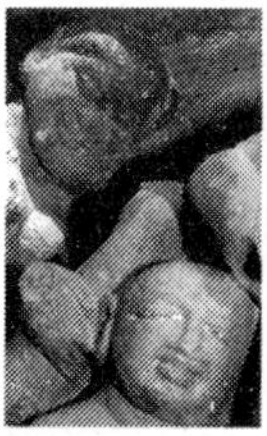
Fig.24

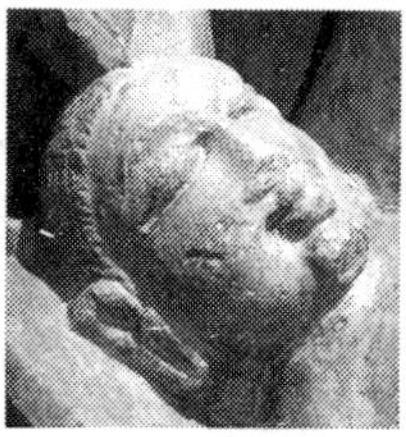
Fig.25

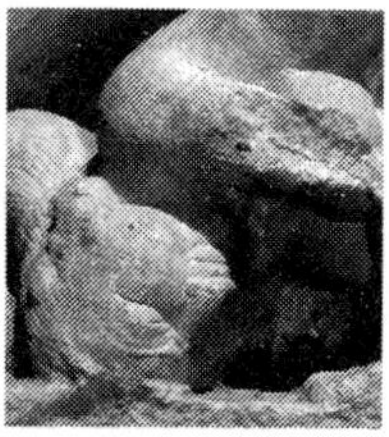
Fig.26

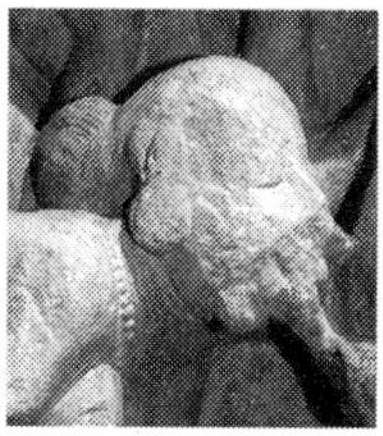
Fig.27

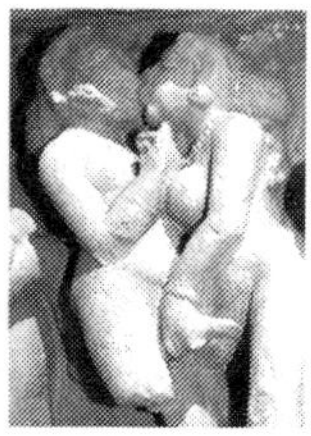
Fig.28

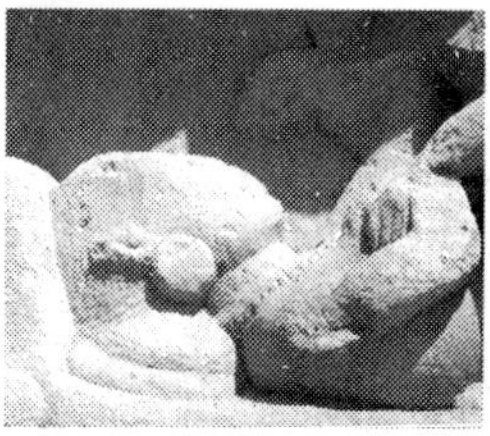
Fig.29

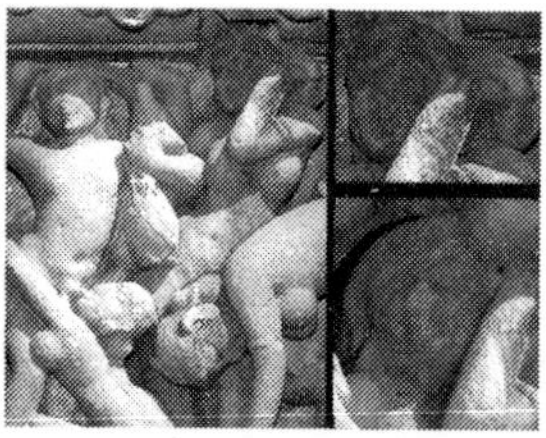
Fig.30

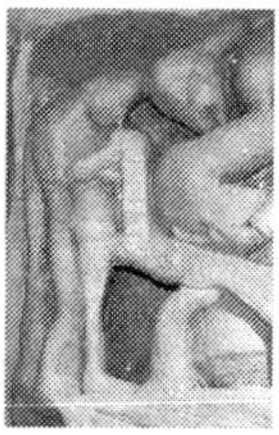
Fig.31

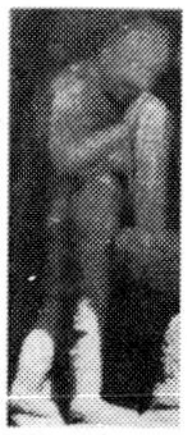
Fig.32

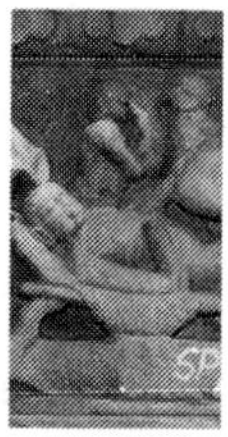
Fig.33

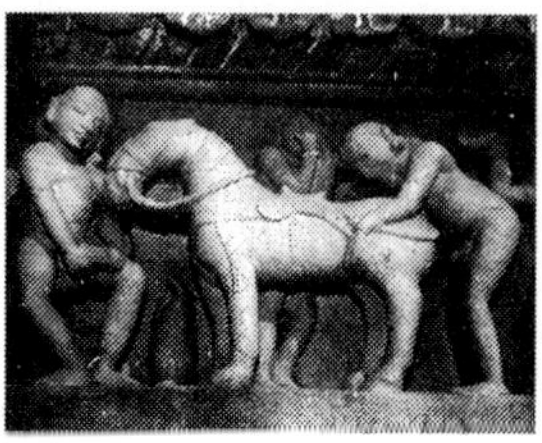
Fig.34

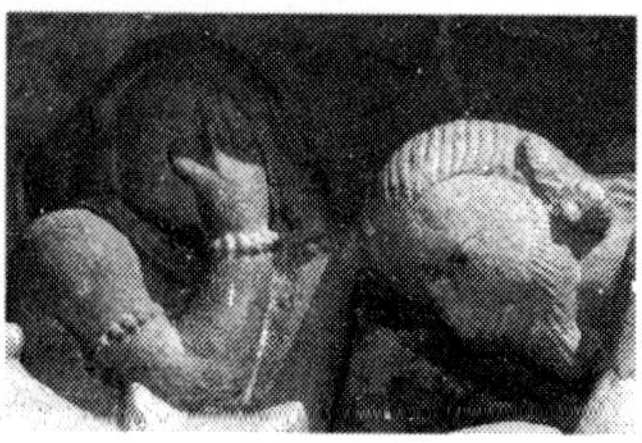
Fig.35

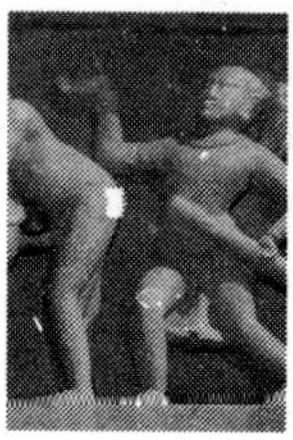
Fig.36

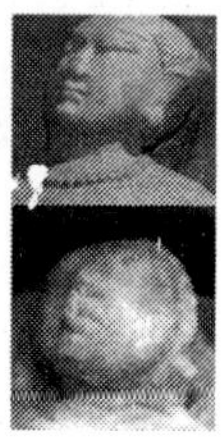
Fig.37

been more apparent. And again facial expression of emotion would have been more apparent, with lips in particular more expressive when coloured. The mouth is more easily shown in sculpture, but above all it is the eye the human needs to read in fellow humans. Sometimes the viewer is led to imagine that a mark or flaw in the stone is an iris, when in fact it is not. The eye of the viewer of the sculpture, the eye of a human being, is pre-programmed to find an iris, a directed gaze on the part of the beheld eye.

The sculpture of Khajurāho is most famous for its representation of the gaze of lovers, of the longing looks of lovers. We find this even in small-scale lovers, in unemphatic parts of the temples [fig. 8]; though not invariably [fig. 9]—close together on the upper frieze on the *jaṅgha* of the Viśvanātha. What is often noticeable is that in couples the woman looks at the man, but the man looks away from the woman. Sometimes this isn't clear [fig. 10 Viśvanātha], and the viewer has to decide for themselves [fig. 11]. When an *apsaras* gazes into her mirror, admiring her own beauty or checking whether it needs cosmetic improvement, the direction of her eye is crystal clear [fig. 12 Viśvanātha]. Presumably the elegant males on the *antarāla* panels, and in the courts, also used mirrors to check their own elaborate coiffeur, but they are never portrayed as so doing. In *Kumāra-saṁbhava* 7.36, Kālidāsa describes Śiva in his wedding finery looking at himself in the reflection of a swordblade; and it may well be that it was considered effeminate for a man to look at himself in a mirror in public. But it is not only at herself that the woman is considered to look more intently. Her gaze is more urgent than the man's, and indeed it can be commanding—sharp and alert, while the man is bashful and vague [fig. 13]. Or, with the aid of fingers, expressive of extreme disappointment, in one woman's response to an inadequately endowed, or at the very least totally unresponsive man [fig. 14 Citragupta].

I end these introductory instance of gaze with a more conventional masterpiece from the Viśvanātha, where a supremely commanding Śiva chucks Pārvatī under the chin, and summons her loving look [fig. 15]. Here her iris, if the photograph renders the eye correctly, seems to be looking away, not yet moving to its final goal, meeting Śiva's eye. There is a high serious and deep mystery in the relationship of the parents of the universe, but the scene leaves no doubt that smiles will follow.

We turn now to the erotic sculpture in the best known instances at Khajurāho, explicit and of humans rather than gods and *apsaras*es. We begin with an examination of the active participants in the orgy on the Lakṣmaṇa plinth. This famous sequence on the plinth frieze takes up two metres of the eastern edge on the south side of the plinth, the frieze thereafter consisting of armies on the march, interspersed with occasional gurus and their pupils, or, more probably, monarchs and their courts. The whole frieze is published in SIVARAMAMURTI

(1977: 402–408). It should be noted that this south side of the plinth which adjoins the Mātaṅgeśvara temple forms a narrow passage which was at some point in time filled in with masonry and revealed only in the early 1960s (MISHRA (2001: 87)). In the sketch of fig. 16, it can be observed that the orgy, covering three blocks of stone, is punctuated by three beds, each occupied by a couple. There might be a single scene of one large space with three beds, or it might be three successive scenes, each punctuated on the left by the bed. On balance, I would suggest that it is a single space with three beds, and the central area occupied by the *kṣapaṇaka* figure whose face is the most emphasised in the whole orgy section of the frieze. It is also the case that the face of the woman who is riding him, even though at angle, is very clearly defined, as is the man to her left engaged in some action with the container. It is perhaps no accident that these three central faces are the clearest and best defined.

The first figure in the frieze, proceeding from right to left, from east to west, lacks a head. It would be useful to have a detailed knowledge of the condition of the temples prior to restoration, and to be able assess whether damaged figures owed their condition to accidents in the course of time, or everywhere bore the marks of disapprobation. The erotic scenes one might think would have been more liable to attack than others. On the other hand, they are indeed only a small part of the overall sculptural programs, and could easily have been overlooked by attackers. As noted above, the southern stretch of the plinth was until recently hidden by infill.

Although the first figure in the frieze lacks a head, his buttocks protrude beyond the vertical frame of the frieze. To my mind, this shows the artistic skill of the sculptor: the erotic part of the frieze is intended to extremely realistic, to jump out at the viewer. The ends of the frieze at the other corners of the plinth do not so obtrude beyond their frame.

In figure 17 we see two heads of women, the one on the right bending over, being made love to by the man who has lost his head. As we commence consideration of these sexual scenes, with regard to vocabulary, I follow John CLARKE (1998: 14) in his study of Roman sexuality in using the deliberately bland term—'the most neutral term'—'lovemaking' for copulation. More generally, I should explain that I am aware that emotion is expressed by the whole body, not just the face; even more so in the case of sculpture, than say painting. Thus in a sculpture such as Auguste Rodin's *Kiss*, by no means irrelevant in the consideration of Khajurāho sculpture, the two faces are in fact only rudimentarily sculpted, and are of minor significance within the piece as whole. There is indeed a major distinction between the frieze and the large *antarāla* panels, in that in the limited confines of the frieze, the bodies and their actions are no doubt supremely important, and the faces are relatively unimportant. Nevertheless, the faces are the concern of this paper; and these faces on the frieze provide context and perspective for understanding the *antarāla* panels. The close proximity of the two heads, one facing up and the other facing down, is an instance of the sculptor's skilful use of space. The crowded scene of the orgy is cleverly organised. Fig. 18 is the face of the man receiving fellatio from the woman on the left in fig. 17. This man holds over his head a peacock feather brush, which shows him to be a naked Jain monk, a *kṣapaṇaka*. This identification is confirmed by the caption on the central figure of this orgy; and there are many other instances of *kṣapaṇaka*s performing in the erotic sculpture of Khajurāho, most notably in some of the *antarāla* panels, as we shall see in due course (TRIPATHI 1959–60). The broad features, here almost a square, are typical of the majority of the *kṣapaṇaka*s at Khajurāho. This man also holds a container within a netted bag, which he seems to be lifting up, to display and emphasise it; or perhaps only to keep it from getting in the way of his partner. Most of the *kṣapaṇaka* figures at Khajurāho carry just such a flask, though not usually so large. Here the man is receiving fellatio, and his narrowed eyes, set rather crookedly in his smoothed over face, along with his tensed mouth, express the intensity of his pleasure.

Fig. 19 is the faces of a standing couple who are in the centre of what may be the first of three sections of the orgy, or anyway within the subsidiary space framed on the left by the first bed. This couple is very distinctive, man and woman standing side by side, their only contact the woman's right hand on the man's shoulder. They seem rather remote from the proceedings. What is very unusual is that the woman is looking away from the man, despite what is surely an originally visible but now destroyed erection on his part. She might be somewhat annoyed because he is slow to start. Perhaps his face shows only mild desire. Are they an elderly couple, lacking in energy? At all events, their standing pose, their relatively impassive features are a striking contrast from the busy scene around them.

Little comment is necessary for the two counterbalanced heads in fig. 20, yet, though rudimentarily sculpted, they express intensity of sensation.

In fig. 21, more than the two heads is seen. The rudimentarily presented man, masturbating over the woman's inverted face, expresses perhaps a kind of excluded yearning. His face moves forward, following the direction of his eyes. His inadequate, spindly arms, lacking the definition of hands, make his whole figure appear rather like some modern work of sculpture, wherein the inadequacy of the human body and human experience is what is aimed at.

His face strongly contrasts with the inverted face of the woman, who is smiling with satisfaction. The man who is making love to her from behind has had his face removed, as have the two figures to the left, who are busy pounding something in a tall vessel, into which their pensises are directed.

We are now virtually at the very centre of the orgy scene in fig. 22, where a *kṣapaṇaka* is stirring the pot. His face is seen again in fig. 23, along with a woman who is holding onto the end of the middle bed. She is riding the chief figure of the whole scene. We see her face again with the stirrer of the pot, in fig. 24, her broad face, made rather more ugly because she is here seen not at the angle intended by the sculptor, is smiling with warm and beneficent contentedness. Fig. 25 is the *kṣapaṇaka* who is surely the master of ceremonies, from his central position in the scene, the emphatic largeness of his face, and his look of supreme and perhaps enlightened satisfaction.

Fig. 26 is the inverted face of a woman, who is being made love to a man who holds her in the wheelbarrow position. His head has been destroyed. Her beautifully shaped eyes perhaps express intensity of pleasure, or possibly simply the disorientation arising from her position.

Fig. 27, the head of a woman fellating; has her face been damaged by attack, or the clumsiness of a sculptor?

Fig. 28, the only kiss, and the only mutual gaze in the whole orgy scene. He chucks her under the chin, but his face seems perhaps to retreat in the face of her eagerness. Their eyes are vividly drawn, his at sloping angles that make them somewhat anxious. How utterly different from fig. 15, Śiva chucking Pārvatī under the chin.

Next in the sequence, a standing man makes love to a woman he lifts up; her back curves beautifully to her buttocks, but they are not illustrated here for her head has been broken off, and the man's face is obscured.

The final face of a participant in the orgy is rudimentary, though the woman's eye and mouth are discernible [fig. 29]. The head of the man making love to her has been broken off. Above the woman's head, to the side, is a clenched fist with the thumb tightly held over the forefinger and middle finger that at first sight might be taken as the woman's left hand, but on reflection has in fact to be the man's right hand. It must suffice here to observe that gestures and body language generally are highly expressive in this sculpture, scarcely less than the faces.

This concludes the review of the faces of the participants in the orgy. However, other faces remain to be discussed, for there are also non-participant observers, observers some of whom express disapproval. From the right, the first of these [fig. 30] is well drawn, and dramatically positioned, but I find her ambiguous. This may well be the intention of the sculptor. On the one hand, she is naked and in the thick of it, her uplifted arm could be on its way to reveal her armpit, and anyway could signify interest and a wish to participate. On the other hand, she could be shielding her eyes from the scene to her left. The lower of the two photos of her head alone, a direct view of her turned face, if by a modern artist would be acclaimed for its raw power. Further faces will amplify what I mean by the ambiguity of this figure, but the next figure, moving left, at the end of the first third of the orgy, is quite different [fig. 31]. Indeterminate of sex, the figure holds the end of the bed and gazes at the cunnilingus scene, so closely that the figure's head touches the head of the male participant. That a curved back is shown suggests the figure is a woman; the head, from the hairstyle, is perhaps male. The half turned figure of the watcher expresses a diffident curiosity, and so too the face, even though almost all features have been smoothed away. Fig. 32 is an earlier photograph where still remaining plaster gives the figure a stronger and masculine look.

Altogether clear cut are the two figures standing behind the chief *kṣapaṇaka* [fig. 33]. Themselves *kṣapaṇaka*s, the hands that cover their faces are even more expressive than the hidden faces. So, they are horrified, they disapprove. At the same time, the one on the left is clearly peeping: his right eye is visible. Likewise, without doubt, in the sculptor's intention, the other, though his eye is not discernible. This kind of observer is found elsewhere in the erotic sculpture of Khajurāho, and also at other sites of erotic sculpture. Figures such as these are extremely valuable for the interpretation of this kind of art; they are a commentary on the scene by the artist himself. The scene is shocking and yet deeply interesting; the shocked person cannot refrain from looking.

A similar watcher occurs in figs. 34 and 35, though he is not a *kṣapaṇaka*. We have now moved on several yards, and are in the midst of the progressing army that takes up most of the frieze. The onlooker confronts a scene of bestiality. On the left, viewed by the watcher's right eye, an arrogant and poised man displays his large penis to a small mare. To the watcher's left, our right, a more roughly sculpted man, and perhaps a rougher man, makes love to the mare, his gaze upon the mare's back clearly shown, his mouth in a determined smile.

But there is more. We have not only a watcher who disapproves but peeps; we have also an onlooker who protests [fig. 36]. To read this figure, we really do have to take account of all his body language, his slightly twisted body the more emphatic, and above all his upraised arm, with palm flat, expressing outrage. His right hand holds some sort of large pole? Is he going to attack the performer of bestiality with it? Perhaps that is deliberately left ambiguous. And then there is, lastly, the face [fig. 37, upper]. The tilted back head shows a recoiling from the scene, and a looking upwards towards higher levels of behaviour that are absent at ground level. Clearly shown irises would aid understanding here. Does the right eye show extreme indignation?

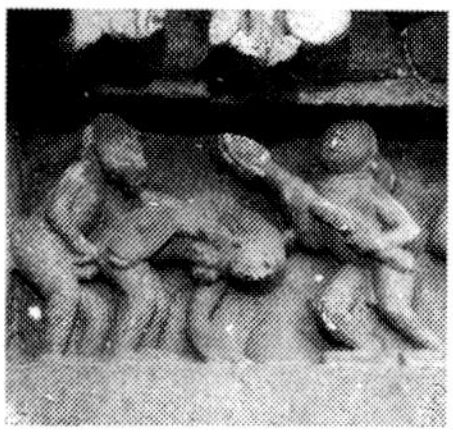

Fig.38

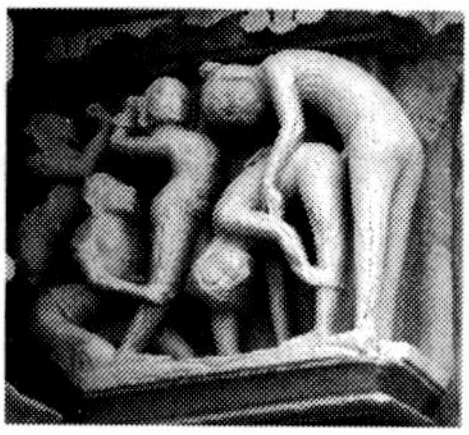

Fig.39

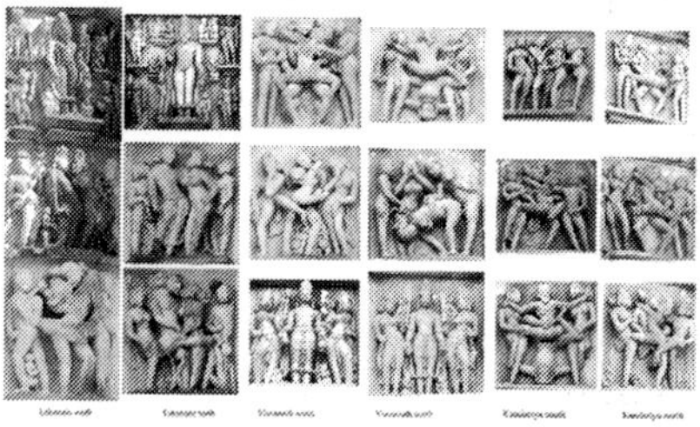

Fig.40

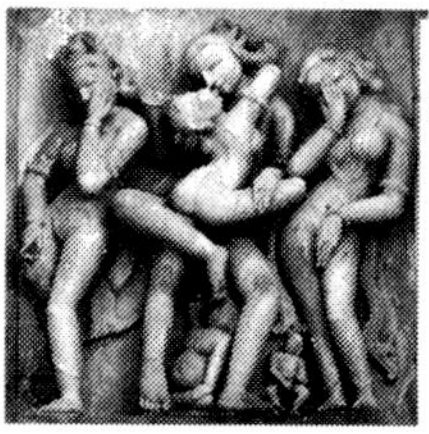

Fig.41

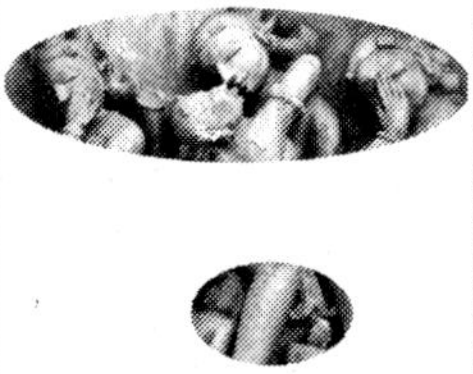

Fig.42

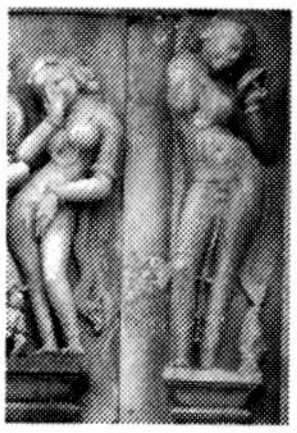

Fig.43

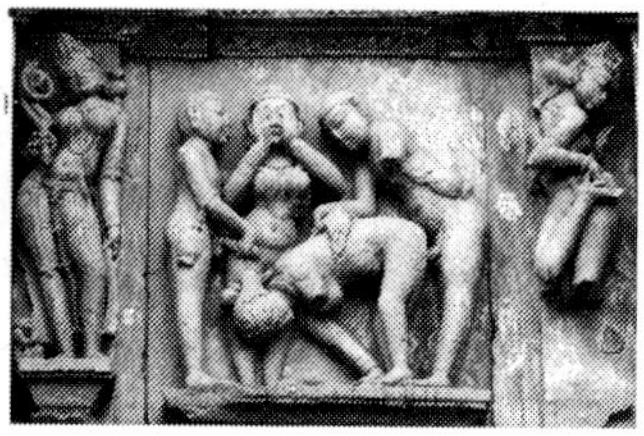

Fig.44

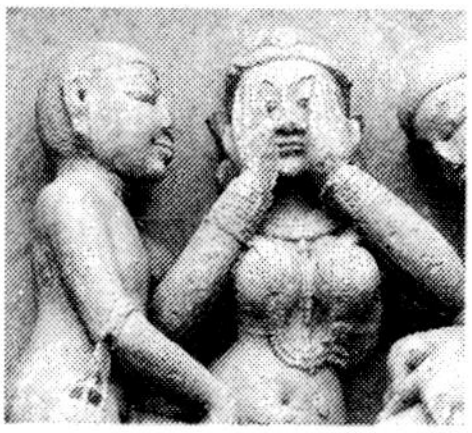

Fig.45

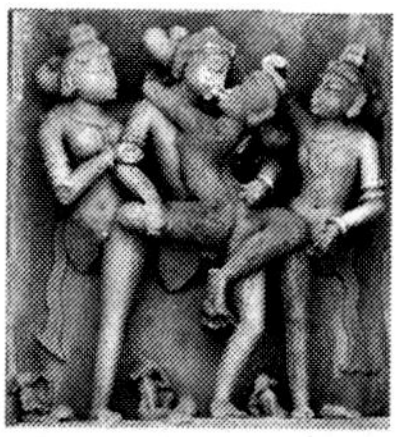

Fig.46

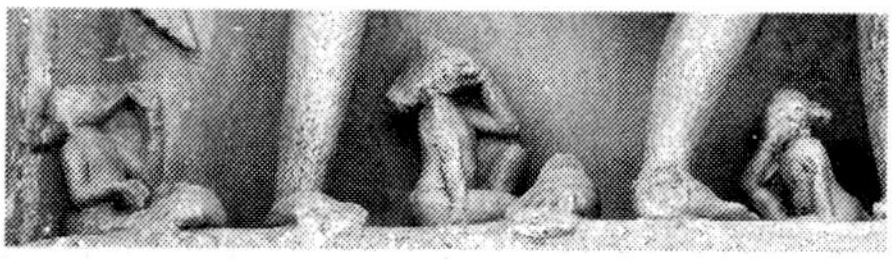

Fig.47

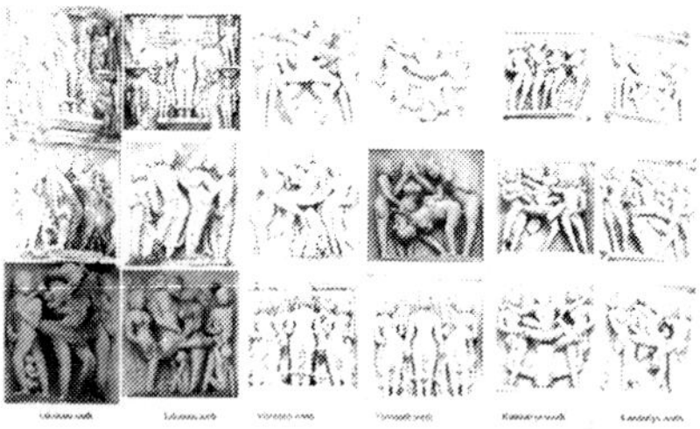

Fig.48

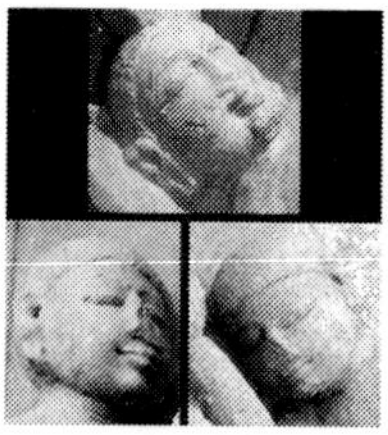

Fig.49

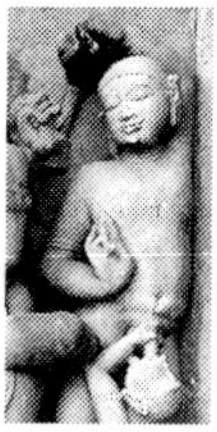

Fig.50

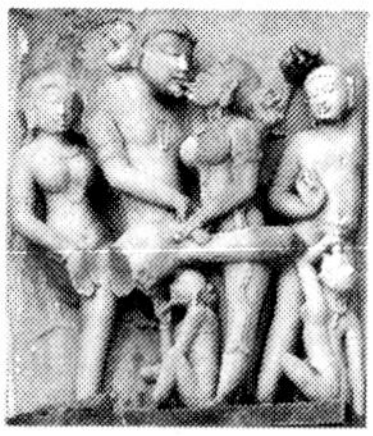

Fig.51

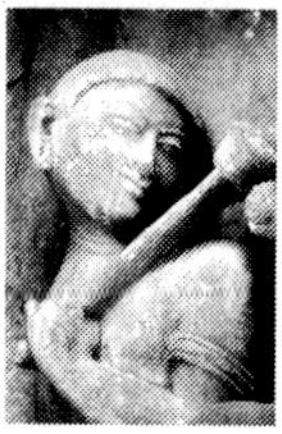

Fig.52

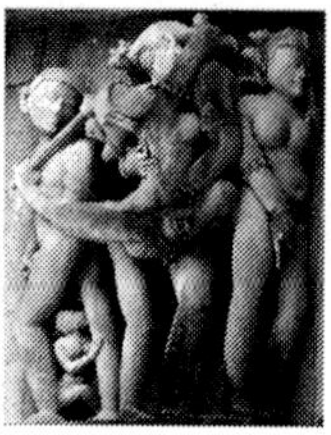

Fig.53

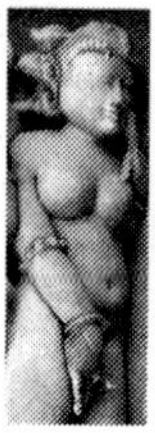

Eig.54

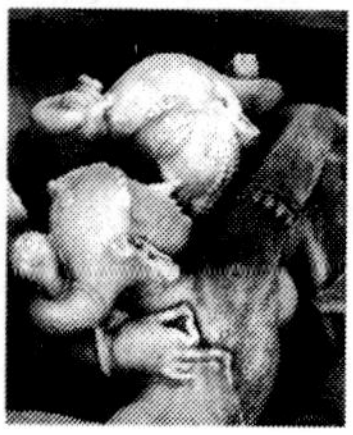

Fig.55

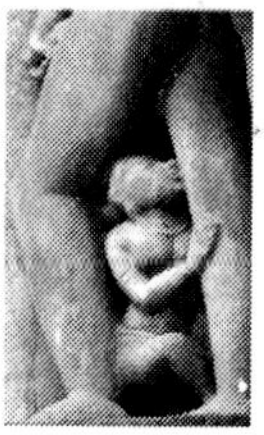

Fig.56

A helpful parallel to this figure is found in a brief and incidental scene on a frieze on the north wall of the Viśvanātha temple [fig. 37 lower, and fig. 38]. Here a man with a gigantic and altogether phallic spear confronts a couple making love, and what is particularly significant here, has his face upraised in a similar way to the admonisher previously noted [fig. 36], though the latter seems a more powerful personality. A more complex scene of remonstration, directed against a *kṣapaṇaka* is to be found on the Citragupta temple [fig. 39]. Two of the remonstrators have upturned faces, though there is doubt as to whether the kneeling figure is actually a remonstrator since he is restraining the man with an upraised fist who is looking downwards on to the monk. Nevertheless, the face of the kneeling figure strongly parallels that of the remonstrator behind him. All the figures are beautifully articulated, and the weathering of the stone detracts almost nothing from the sculptor's art.

We are now ready to study the much more carefully carved faces of the *antarāla* panels, which are presented all together in fig. 40. I continue with the topic of viewing and peeping, though all the human size figures present in the erotic panels are also participants to some degree. In the centre of the overview, are the two middle panels of the Viśvanātha *antarāla*s. Peepers are prominent, but differ greatly between the two panels.

In fig. 41, two lovely women, with elaborate coiffeurs, go through the motions of pretending to cover their eyes, but wholeheartedly participate in the scene, all four bodies swaying in unison, and their two heads at the same angle as the man's. At the principal couple's feet a plump man, perhaps a eunuch, leans back. It is not clear whether or not he is looking upwards. Certainly looking upwards is the small boyish figure who is masturbating. Can he be a *kṣapaṇaka*? Fig. 42 highlights the faces in the panel.

Exceptionally, it is here worth straying outside the panel. The *apsaras* to our right of the panel is noteworthy in that her face, counterbalancing the inclination of three of the heads on the panel, looks into her mirror which is showing the scene beside her, as well as her own face [fig. 43]. And she has a lovely smile. But all the panels under discussion are flanked by standing figures who look outward, and are each self-contained and isolated. This isolation of individuals is present everywhere at Khajurāho except in the erotic scenes; and excepting also of course divine couples. It should be added that dwarf figures are sometimes present at the principal figure's feet; and also there are the small warriors with the *vyāla* monsters, one on the *vyāla*'s back, one beneath its rearing form.

Utterly different from the lovely women of fig. 41 is the one face directed outwards on the middle panel on the other side of the temple [fig. 44]. The mouth droops, there is a high degree of disapproval expressed. But also interest, and on further inspection, we realise that the *kṣapaṇaka* who is masturbating over the bending woman, also has his hand under the breast of the woman who seems to be shocked [fig. 45].

One instance of peeping remains to be discussed. We move to the bottom panel of Kandariyā north [fig. 46] and to ground level in that panel. To the left, a man strokes his beard as he looks upward avidly, but the other two figures, indistinct, perhaps women, are clearly covering their eyes, the one on the left looking up at the same time, while the right hand one probably is not looking upwards. Small figures appear at the bottom of several erotic panels, as well as at the feet of many sculptures at Khajurāho, as elsewhere are an intriguing problem. Their small size, the emphatic disjunction in size from the main figure or figures, points up their unimportance. Yet there they are, on the wall of the temple.

As we have seen there are two *kṣapaṇaka*s in the middle panel on the northern *antarāla* of the Viśvanātha temple. The two bottom panels of the Lakṣmaṇa temple's *antarāla*s are the only two others in which *kṣapaṇaka*s appear, and I shall now consider all their faces. The faces of the two *kṣapaṇaka*s in the middle panel of Viśvanātha north benefit from being considered in isolation [fig. 49, lower two]. Both have the distinctive shape of a rounded square, both are alert, have the ends of their mouths upturned, and if I may so express it, by no means seem bereft of an inner spirituality. The face of the central figure of the Lakṣmaṇa orgy frieze can fruitfully be referred to here [fig. 49, upper]. The similarity is strong, though the latter figure by comparison is arguably somewhat bloated.

The last two *kṣapaṇaka*s are from the bottom panels of the Lakṣmaṇa, and they are both outstanding pieces of sculpture. The monk on the northern panel, who is received fellatio, has surely the most beautiful male mouth, indeed the most beautiful mouth at Khajurāho [fig. 51]. His face has the characteristic shape of his type, but is exceptional in its beauty. No less extraordinary is the face of the young monk, who looks back over his shoulder at the united couple in the centre of the panel [fig. 52]. He masturbates, his body facing away from the couple. He smiles at the couple, participating privately in their pleasure. The sculptor does not set out to demean this young man; the smile of this companion to the couple is almost a blessing. We should note that the physiognomy of his face differs from the other *kṣapaṇaka*s we have looked, for the lower part of his face is markedly triangular, rather than a round square.

On the other edge of the group is a very beautiful woman, who provides a kind of unity by facing like the monk to our right—though her gaze thus looks away from the couple—and like the monk she masturbates, or is about to do so [fig. 54]. Her lovely face, her cheek touched by the fingers of her left hand, has an inner delight, reflecting sweet memories, or so we might be intended by the sculptor to imagine.

In the centre of this panel we have the embracing and conjoined couple, gazing the famous Khajurāho gaze [fig. 55]. The woman pulls the man's face to her by his hair; her face is dominates his, and her eye takes in all his face, while he does not meet her eye, but looks downward to her lips. If we again stand back to take in the scene as a whole, and take cognisance of the combination of faces and expressions, the depth and complexity of the situation enthrals. On the ground a small woman, perhaps a servant, sensuously touches the monk's leg as she watches, head uplifted, not as a remonstrator, but an onlooker wishing to imagine in the couple's bliss [fig. 56]. It might be that her eyes are shut.

The status of the onlookers is particularly important is the process of trying to understand what was in the minds of the creators of these temples and these sculptures. Not only the gods and *apsaras*es have at times small figures at their feet; so too do the manifestly human figures erotically engaged. A natural presumption, though not necessarily correct, is that the onlookers in the sculptured scenes are intended to have reference also to the people looking at the main actors portrayed in the sculptures. We, the spectators, are intended to acknowledge our diminutive status in respect of the erotic performers no less than in respect of the divine and semi-divine figures.

BIBLIOGRAPHY

CLARKE 1998 = Clarke, John R: *Looking at Lovemaking: Constructions of Sexuality in Roman Art 100 B.C.–A.D. 250.* University of California Press, Berkeley 1998.

DANIÉLOU 1987 = Daniélou, Alain: *The Way to the Labyrinth.* New Directions, New York 1987.

DESAI 1975 = Desai, Devangana: *Erotic Sculpture of India: A socio-cultural study.* Tata McGraw-Hill, New Delhi 1975. [Second edition: Munshiram Manoharlal, New Delhi 1985].

FABRI 1974 = Fabri, Charles Louis: *History of the Art of Orissa.* Orient Longman, Bombay 1974.

KEMP 2006 = Kemp, Martin: *Leonardo da Vinci: The Marvellous Works of Nature and Man.* Oxford University Press, Oxford 2006.

MISHRA 2001 = Mishra, P.K.: *Khajuraho—With Latest Discoveries.* Sundeep Prakashan, New Delhi 2001.

PARIMOO 1994 = Parimoo, Ratan: 'Khajurāho the Chandella Sculptors' Paradise: Is there a Chandella style of Medieval Indian Sculpture? Its sources and characteristics', in: K.K. Chakravarty, M.N. Tiwari, K. Giri (eds.): *Khajuraho in Perspective.* Commissioner Archaeology and Museums Madhya Pradesh, Bhopal 1994: 113–119.

PARIMOO 2000 = Parimoo, Ratan: 'Khajurāho the Chandella Sculptors' Paradise: Is there a Chandella style of medieval indian sculpture? Its sources and characteristics', in Ratan Parimoo (ed.): *Studies in Indian Sculpture (Regional Genres and Interpretations*). 2 Vols., Books & Books, New Delhi 2000 in two vols: 344–370.

RAO 1976 = Rao, S. K. Ramachandra: 'Review of Fabri's History of the Art of Orissa', Deccan Herald Weekly Sunday, July 11, 1976.

ŚiPr = [Claimed to be by Rāmacandra Kaulācāra:] *Śilpa-prakāśa.* Alice Boner; Sadāśiva Rath Śarmā (transl.): *Śilpa-prakāśa: Medieval Orissan Sanskrit Text on Temple Architecture.* Translated and annotated by … ; illustrations from the original palmleaf manuscript, text-drawings by Sadāśiva Rath Śarmā. E. J. Brill, Leiden 1966 [Second revised edition: Bettina Bäumer, Rajendra Prasad Das, Sadananda Das. Indira Gandhi National Centre for the Arts, Delhi 2005].

SIVARAMAMURTI 1977 = Sivaramamurti, C.: *The Art of India.* H.N. Abrams, New York 1977.

SONTAG 1967 = Sontag, Susan, *Against interpretation; And Other Essays.* Eyre & Spottiswoode, London 1967 [Originally published: Farrar, Straus & Giroux, New York 1966. The essay 'Against Interpretation' was first published in *Evergreen Review*, December 1964].

TRIPATHI 1959–60 = Tripathi, L.K.: 'The Erotic Scenes of Khajuraho and Their Probable Explanation', *Bharat* 3 (1959–60) 82–104.

TRIPATHI 2008 = Tripathi, Alok: 'Historic Scenes in Khajuraho', in: B.R. Mani; Alok Tripathi (eds.): *Expressions in Indian Art: Essays in Memory of Shri M.C. Joshi*. Agam Kala Prashan, Delhi 2008: 179–186.

Building Visual Order in Kashmir. Analysis of Architectural Structures as Described in the *Viṣṇu-dharmôttara-purāṇa*

VALDAS JASKŪNAS
(Vilnius University)

1. Introduction

The geographical location of Kashmir until the beginning of the 7th century made this region a part of various political and religious formations. Within the trade map of the pre-Mediaeval South Asia Kashmir has been an important stopover on the silk route. With the spread of Buddhism that used trade routes for its expansion, Kashmir linked Buddhist centres in ancient Gandhāra, Swat and mountainous borderland areas in north Pakistan with the silk route oases of the southern Tarim Basin. This merger of cultures contributed to the fact that no predominating religious power could be established in Kashmir for a longer period, though clear traces of intermittent predominance of Buddhism or Brahmanical orthodox power as well as remnants of Nāga worship are traceable. The conditions necessary for establishing the framework of orthodox Hindu rituals to take root here and for this region to be regarded by the Hindus as a centre of traditional Hindu culture, or the Great Tradition, could be fulfilled no earlier than the 7th century CE. In the history of Kashmir this coincides with the period during which the Hindu Kārkoṭa dynasty was established and flourished.

First attempts to link the traditions of the Little Tradition of Kashmir to the authority of the traditions of the Great Tradition of the Hindus and to integrate the two are seen in composition of the *Nīlamata-purāṇa* compiled between the 7th to 8th centuries in Kashmir (IKARI (1993: 187)). The other *purāṇa* set to be compiled in Kashmir soon—the *Viṣṇu-dharmôttara-purāṇa* (henceforth VDhP)—certainly embodied a fundamental shift in ritual system by introducing the Pāñcarātra Vaiṣṇavism as imperially patronised ritual practice (INDEN (2000)). This change was fol-

Art, Myths and Visual Culture of South Asia
Warsaw Indological Studies 4 (2011) 203–227.

lowed by an extensive program of temple building that explored a distinctive architectural style of Kashmir merging features of Buddhist structures and north Indian *latina* temples.

So far the attempts to trace the history of Kashmiri architecture have been predominantly dependent on the framework of art historical and stylistic development and influences (KAK (1933); GOETZ (1969); FRANZ (1980); etc), which undoubtedly yielded over the years the thorough material about buildings, both those ruined and almost beyond retrieve as well as those still remaining. Least studied, however, remain the textual sources from this region, such as the *Nīlamata-purāṇa* and VDhP, with regard to both social history of the Kashmirian architecture of the period between 7th and 8th centuries and, more generally, the appropriation of a certain architectural structures for settling the newly introduced Hindu ritual practices. What we hope to achieve with the study of textual sources from this region is, mostly, critical assessment of the legitimacy of art historical reconstructions within the broader enterprise of visual culture. Given the scarcity of architectural remains to trace the period of transformation in building practices, it is the text of VDhP and wider visual narratives rather than stylistic interactions that are attested in this article as a primary legitimising device of visual interactions in the north-western India over the period of Kashmir's imperial expansion. By combining art historical and archaeological data with descriptions of architectural constructions described in VDhP, it can be argued that Buddhist buildings were appropriated to design the basal part of the Kashmirian temple most probably as a result of sharing the expertise of the architects that previously mastered building *stūpa*s and other Buddhist structures.

The attempt in this essay is made to reconstruct the change of 'visual order' in architecture was the effect of the introduction of Pāñcarātra ritual practices in Kashmir. Ronald INDEN (2000: 34) has clearly demonstrated that 'the VDhP was produced by and for a complex agent consisting of Pāñcarātra adepts and an imperial king and his court.' To articulate the strategies of textualisation of architectural practices in VDhP, the model of 'imperial formation' by INDEN is taken as a point of departure and theoretical base for assessment of art historical and archaeological material. The focal interest in the essay lays in structural development of temples of Kashmir, especially in its basal part—the platform—with an attempt to argue for possible Buddhist influences on the formation of a distinctively Kashmirian style of Hindu temple.

This study posits the object of critical analysis of architectural development primarily as something pertaining to visual culture studies rather than to art history. Mieke BAL (2003: 22) has aptly described this object as being 'the master narratives that are presented as natural, universal, true and inevitable' that are dislodged so that 'alternative narratives can become visible.' Methodologically this essay follows the principle of the historical-analytical examination of visual culture order that is associated here with the emerging master narrative of the Pāñcarātra Vaiṣṇavism as embodied by temple building as imperial practice in Kashmir from the 7th century onward. Therefore as its primary object the article sets to explore the visual program of the Pāñcarātra Vaiṣṇavism in Kashmir which is supposed to issue from the pursuit of identity of Lalitāditya's empire that was a result of successful military campaigns in north India.

To provide a clue for historical development of architecture, the introduction of a sustainable visual order in Kashmir was stimulated by the development of a unifying Buddhist architectural style during the 7th to 8th centuries in the greater Kashmir and parallel foreign influences. As for the emergence of a distinct Kashmirian type of temple, it might have been seriously affected by the experimentation with *nāgara* architecture in north Pakistan from the 6th to 11th centuries.

1. Architecture in the *Viṣṇu-dharmôttara-purāṇa*

The references to architecture are found in the Chapters 86 to 88 of the third *khaṇḍa* of VDhP. Chapter 86, of particular interest for the present article, provides typological description of the shapes of a hundred temples while the next Chapter 87 supplies lengthy description of a certain shape of temple called *sarvato-bhadra*. The last of these chapters treats of the proportions of the general type (*sāmānya-prāsāda*) of the temple common for all the one hundred and one forms of the temple.

The distinctive feature of the *sāmānya* type of the temple (particularly derived from the 64-grid plan) is the triple division of the total height of the temple into the platform (*jagatī*), ground floor or the walls of the temple (*bhitti*, *jaṅghā*, or *kaṭī*) and the superstructure (*mañjarī*, *kūṭa*). Apart form VDhP, *sāmānya* type of temple is found described in the *Bṛhat-saṁhitā* (BSaṁ 56.10–16) and the *Bhaviṣya-purāṇa* (BhP 1.130.17–23ab), which word-by-word follows the treatment of the subject of temple architecture in the Vārahamihira's treatise. Taking into account the passing reference to the three-fold vertical division, the platform being mentioned as the lowest part of it in the *Bṛhat-saṁhitā* and the *Bhaviṣya-purāṇa*, one immediately notices the importance of the platform that features in the classification of the shapes of temples in VDhP. As it will be demonstrated further on, I am tempted to think that the *jagatī*, or platform, on which the main temple rests, is a distinctive element of the temple structure, and this architectural practice is reflected in VDhP.

It was Stella KRAMRISCH (1996: 412) who noticed that amongst extant buildings few seemed to conform to the three-fold division of the height while the temples of Kashmir from the 7th to 9th centuries were relatively closest to this model. Yet, apparently nowhere KRAMRISCH has elaborated this conjectural relation between the

Kashmir temples and the description of 101 temples in VDhP despite the three-fold division of the temple structure in the latter. Although scholars shared opinion about the Kashmiri provenance of this *purāṇa*, only recently Ronald INDEN (2000) has persuasively suggested that VDhP was an imperial *purāṇa* compiled in Kashmir between the late 7th and early 8th centuries. The reconstruction of the historical footing of the *purāṇa* by INDEN also involves the historiography of the third *khaṇḍa*, the architectural material it contains in particular.

INDEN is tempted to think that the complex author of VDhP completed Part Two of the text before Candrāpīḍa's (c. 712/13–720/1) death, at the moment when the Kashmiri court was itself preparing for a protracted military campaign. Part Three, the largest of the three, and the one concerned with enumerating temple types and describing the construction of a *sarvato-bhadra* temple for the image of Vāsudeva Kṛṣṇa, in conjunction with the 'conquest of the quarters' by which Lalitāditya made India into his imperial formation (INDEN (2000: 82, 84)).

The ideological project of Lalitāditya primarily concerned the promotion of the Pāñcarātra order and elaboration of the means of the worship of Viṣṇu. Temple worship was considered essential for this purpose, therefore the interest in temple construction and its classification in VDhP seems to be a logical consequence of the overall project. Further, if we admit the idiosyncratic character of the *purāṇa*, some architectural innovations supporting the newly-shaped identity of the Kashmiri Pāñcarātrins could be expected to be seen in temple buildings, too. It is mainly these expectations that led me to take the task to reconsider the material on temple architecture in the chapters 86 to 88. What follows is a tentative identification of a few problems that arise from an attempt to explain the internal logic of the textualisation of architectural practice which conditioned the classification of 100 temples in Chapter 86 of VDhP.

If one hypothesises the relation between Kashmir at the turn of the 8th century and architectural practice of VDhP it is most likely that this relation might be reconstructed on the basis of the extant temple in the region and its neighbourhood. Without getting into details, it is known that in Kashmir the construction of the first Hindu temples coincided with the foundation of the Kārkoṭa dynasty by Durlabhavardhana (r. 626/7–662/3), who was the follower of the Vaiṣṇava order and displaced[1] Śaivism as pre-eminent form of theism in the region and acculturated forms of Nāga worship. On the basis of the *Xiyouji*, an account of the Chinese Buddhist scholar and pilgrim Xuanzang (Hsüan Tsang), who visited Kashmir from 631 to 633, historians have come to a conclusion that Durlabhavardhana had been forced to

[1] Śaivism is likely to have been the pre-eminent for of theism before Durlabhavardhana. The latter replaced Śaivism with Vaiṣṇavism.

cede the eastern Gandhāra, Takṣaśilā and other provinces. He is reported to have built a temple dedicated to Viṣṇu in Śrīnagara, presumably to mark his victory in establishing an imperial polity (INDEN (2000: 75)).

Although this temple has not survived in any form till now and two of the earliest Brahmanical temples in Kashmir, the Śaṅkarācārya on the Takht-i-Suleiman hill at Śrīnagar (c. 675–700) and the larger shrine at Lāduv (c. 700–725) are dated on stylistic grounds to the last quarter of the 7th century and the first quarter of the 8th century respectively, we know that the eclectic but nevertheless unique architectural style of Kashmir was strongly influenced by Gandhāran structures—either Buddhist, that prevailed from the 1st century BCE to the fifth century CE, or Hindu—that evolved into a distinctive school of Gandhāra-Nāgara architecture (MEISTER (1996), (2000), (2010)).

Relying on the contacts with Gandhāra during the rule of Durlabhavardhana, we may presume that to build his temples he had employed the architects from Gandhāra or other areas who were obliged to experiment to match the requirements of Vaiṣṇava worship. The *purāṇa* of Kashmir which supposedly was completed at his court—the *Nīlamata-purāṇa*—is generally silent on architecture which probably means that temple construction has not been considered central to Vaiṣṇava idiosyncrasy. Consequently the material of VDhP on temple construction is very informative and suggests us to consider temple architecture already not in terms of stylistic influences or adaptation of constructions but rather in terms of particular discursive practice centred on Pāñcarātra Vaiṣṇava worship. As Ronald INDEN (2000: 62) says, 'The story of the VDhP … is about the progressive manifestation of the Pāñcarātra godhead and concomitantly of those knowledges, previously withheld or misunderstood, that prove the validity of claims for divine truth.'

Given the historical, although rather conjectural, explanation of the establishment of Brahmanical structures in Kashmir, the question raised previously remains: Is it reasonable to treat the material on temple architecture in VDhP as pertaining to the actual architectural practice of the 7th to 8th century Kashmir? If so, is the established Pāñcarātra discourse traceable in the architectural knowledge of this *purāṇa*?

2. Interpretation of the Three-Tiered Platform in the *Viṣṇu-dharmôttara-purāṇa*

It was already in the 1930s that Indian scholar Ram Chandra KAK (1933: 61–62) paid attention to the fact that Brahmanical temples of Kashmir appropriated various Buddhist forms, particularly the form of the Buddhist monastery, a quadrangle with monks' cells along the sides facing the courtyard. Within the Śaiva and Vaiṣṇava temples it turned into a rectangular courtyard surrounded by the peristyle with cells reduced to small niches to suit their primarily decorative and subordinate function.

Strangely, VDhP nowhere, as far as I know, mentions this element characteristic to the temples of Kashmir.

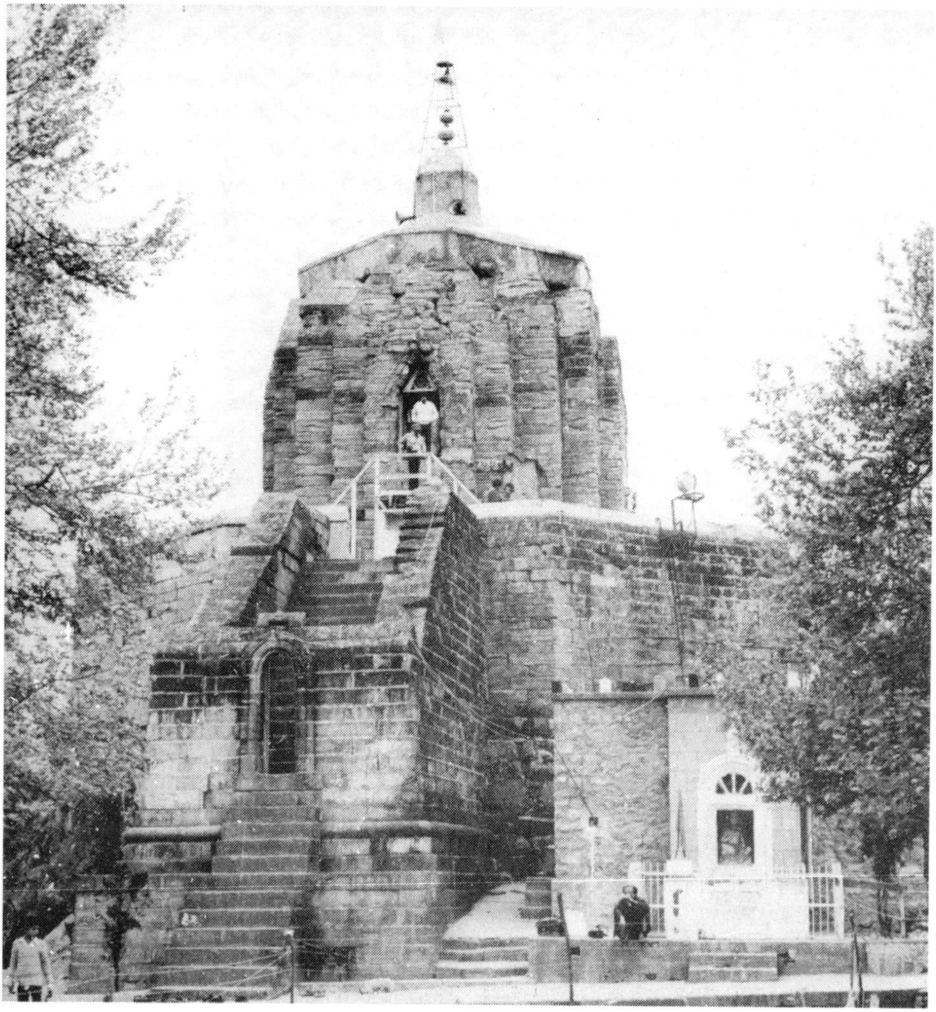

Fig. 1. Śrīnagar. Śaṅkarācārya temple, c. 675–700 C.E. Source: EITA, pl. 704. Courtesy: American Institute of Indian Studies

Despite the extent and depth of the influence of the Buddhist art of Gandhāra on that of Kashmir, as argued by KAK (1933: 15), that 'it would be more correct to say that ... the two are practically identical', so far this influence has been only indirectly accepted on the base of VDhP. This fact is to be explained by the lack of obvious similarities of structure between the extant Kashmirian temples and types of temples described mainly in the chapters 86 and 87 of VDhP. However, the latter provides at least one structural element that is hardly found in any known temple in Kashmir with the exception of the Śaṅkaracārya temple at Śrīnagar (fig. 1) and Gop temple in Saurāṣṭra (dated to the last quarter of the 6th century) (fig. 2), belonging to a different architectural tradition though.

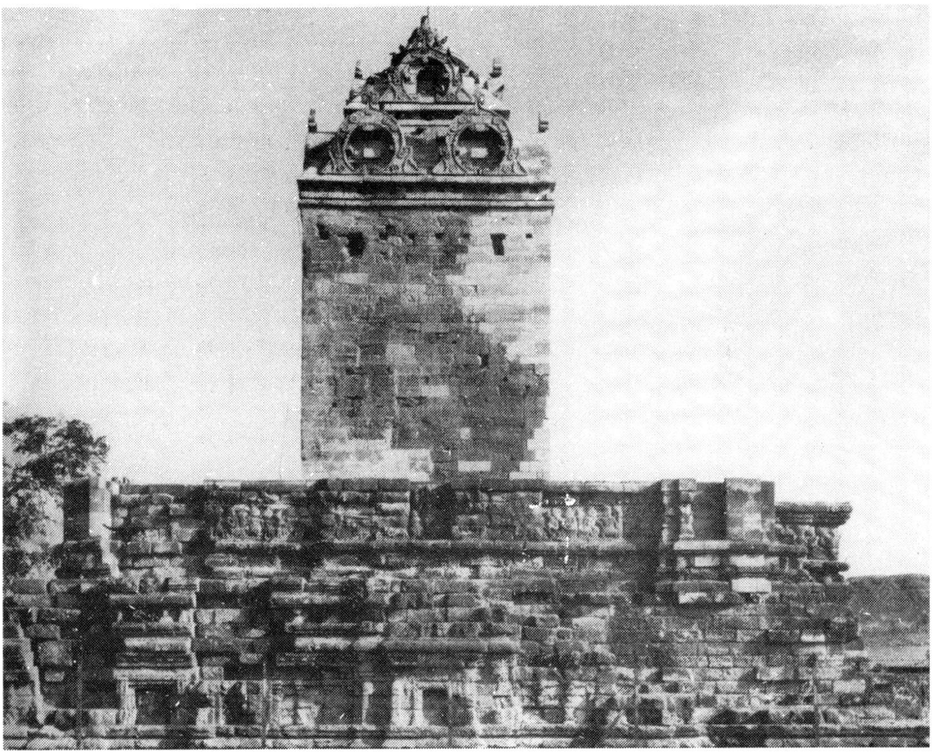

Fig. 2. Gop. Old temple, c. late 6th century C.E. Source: EITA, pl. 328. Courtesy: American Institute of Indian Studies

The structural element under discussion is a tiered platform (*jagatī*) on which the main temple is constructed. Specifically in VDhP 3.86.4–5, *jagatī* is prescribed to be three-tiered and constructed as a stepped structure with three zones (*gati*, further in the text—*mekhala*) suitable for working around:

> '[4] The height of the temple should be equal to [the height of] the platform. The platform should consist of the three tiers (*bhūmikā*) of equal height. [5] The width of each [stepped] tier should be half of its height. The shape of each tier is that of the pedestal of an image (*bhadra-pīṭha*).'

As already noted, the three-tiered *jagatī* described in VDhP is found in a single temple, and although maintained as a fundamental feature of Kashmiri temple, is reduced to two-tiered in later Brahmanical constructions such as Mārtaṇḍa temple of Maṭṭan (dated 725–750), Viṣṇu temple of Ṭāpar (750–760), Avantisvāmī temple of Avantīpur (850–860), etc.

The German scholar Heinrich Gerhard FRANZ (1980: 39) extensively explored the Indian terraced temples and came to the conclusion that their terraces are genetically common with those of the *stūpa*s. Mainly under the rulership of the Kuṣāṇa dynasty in the 2nd to 4th centuries CE in the Gandhāran regions the Indian *stūpa* was erected upon a square pedestal and so was transformed into the shape of the terrace-*stūpa*. One of the new features that *stūpa* acquired in Central Asia before the last quarter of the fifth century is high tower and a multi-storeyed terrace (see especially *stūpa*s of Khocho (Xočo, pinyin: Gāochāng) in the oasis of Turfān; see FRANZ (1980: 41–43)) (fig. 3). Therefore, since Gandhāra was the common source for the temples in Kashmir and for Gop temple in Saurāṣṭra, one can assume that also the multi-storeyed terrace common to both regional styles comes from the Buddhist architecture. Moreover, taking into consideration the close contacts with Gandhāra and Central Asia during the rule of the Kārkoṭa dynasty as well as the historical prevalence of Buddhism in Kashmir, it is tempting to think that the three-tiered platform, as described in VDhP, is perhaps an actual Kashmirian appropriation of the *stūpa*-basement from Central Asia.

In Chapter 86 of VDhP the one-hundred temples are classified in eight groups (as grouped by KRAMRISCH (1996: 412 ff.)), of which the temples belonging to the first group are considered variations of the *himavat* type. This type of the temple is described more extensively than the remaining ninety-nine types in that chapter, and most scholars, even though hesitatingly, read the temple called 'Himavān' as an elaboration of the stone temples extant in Kashmir. The three-tiered platform is prescribed to this very group of temples, however what is of equal importance for the reconstruction of the structural origins of terraced temples found in the list of VDhP is that the number of tiers of the platform (the number of the stepped walking zones, to be precise) is a unique discriminative criterion among the temples of the second group, too.

The hypothesis of a common provenance of different groups of temples which have the so-called walking zones within the platform could be easily dismissed on the basis of the difference of terms (*gati* or *mekhala*) used in the same chapter to designate them. Yet, my argument rests simply on the irregularity of architectural terminology met in the *purāṇas* as well as functional identity of the elements designated by these terms. The tentative comparison of the usage of the terms *gati* and *mekhala* in other purāṇic texts shows that *mekhala* (lit. 'girdle') is found more frequently, therefore, since the description of the types of temples in Chapter 86 (with exception of the *himavat* type) is supposedly a compilation from other sources, I am inclined to think that the incongruity of terminology appeared due to compilative reasons.

To sum up the discussion about the distinguishing feature of *jagatī* as described in VDhP, it is very likely that a three-tiered terrace as it appears in the text was appropriated from the Buddhist structures starting with the early establishment of Hindu architecture in the region, yet its rare application in the extant structures may lead us to the conclusion that the practice was soon abandoned. Apparently with the introduction of a new Pāñcarātra visual order in Kashmir by Lalitāditya the three-tiered platform was abandoned in favour of a simplified structure that developed in the Gupta milieu in north India and was associated with the fire-shrined (*pañca-yātana*) *sarvato-bhadra* type, the description of which, as it will be suggested later, is most probably styled in VDhP after the Viṣṇu temple from Deogaṛh (Uttar Pradesh). The tendency to assimilate earlier Buddhist structures is apparent from the inclusion of the elements of the *himavat* type of temple into the fabric of the *sarvato-bhadra* temple (VDhP 3.87.7). Without getting into details, it could be argued that the remaining six groups of temples from the VDhP list also reflect various regional styles of architecture that could have been acknowledged during the successful military campaigns of the famous king Muktāpīḍa Lalitāditya (c. 733–735) to the Middle Region of India in the pursuit of a tremendous ideological program outlined already in the *Nīlamata-purāṇa*—i.e. to make Kashmir the centre of Bharatavarṣa.

3. The *Aiḍūka* Structure in the *Viṣṇu-dharmôttara-purāṇa*

Given the historical changes that resulted in the introduction of a new visual order to Kashmir with the aim to support the preferred Pāñcarātra ritual practices, an attempt to reconstruct the architectural practices that existed at the beginning of emergence of Brahmanical temple architecture is should be undertaken.

Despite the description of one-hundred types of temples in Chapter 86 and a particular shape of the temple called *sarvato-bhadra* in the following chapter, one more architectural structure drew the attention of the compiler of VDhP—a nominally Śaivite structure called *aiḍūka* found in VDhP 84.1–15. The *aiḍūka* structure is described as built of three receding square platforms (*bhadra-pīṭha*), with steps on the four sides. On the third platform a *liṅga* (*liṅga-rūpa*) is erected, but one which is not decorated with lines (*rekhā*). In the middle of the *liṅga* an immovable square column (*yaṣṭi*) is fixed. There are thirteen *bhūmikā*s ('stages in steps') attached to it, on the top of which there is an *āmala-sāraka* ('cog-wheel stone') capped in its turn with a round *yaṣṭi* column. This column is decorated with a medallion (*candraka*). The thirteen stages in steps (*bhūmikā*) and the cog-wheel stone (*āmala-sāraka*) are said to represent the fourteen *bhuvana*s ('worlds'). The *liṅga* represents Maheśvara, the round column Pitāmaha and the square column Janārdana. The three platforms represent the three *guṇa*s ('qualities of human being'). In between the stages in steps (*bhūmikā*) and the *liṅga* the four *loka-pāla*s are situated, Virūḍha, Dhṛtarāṣṭra, Virūpākṣa, and Kubera, with lances (*śūla*) in their hands, wearing armour and ornaments. Virūḍha is Śakra, Dhṛtarāṣṭra is Yama, Virūpākṣa is Varuṇa, and Kubera is Rājarāja. This *aiḍūka* is called '*prajāhita*' ('serving the welfare of the people'); the people who worship it obtain happiness and heaven after death.

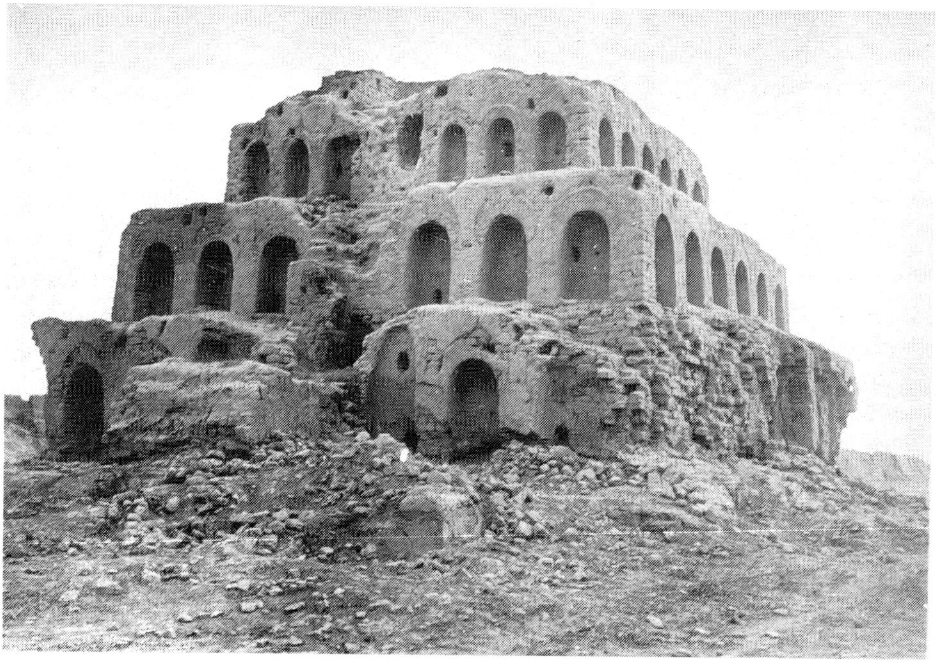

Fig. 3. Khocho near Turfan (Turpan, East Turkestan, now Xinjiang, China). Ruins of a terrace-temple. Source: FRANZ (1965: pl. 286).

It has been attempted to deduce from the text that the *aiḍūka* structure with Maheśa as a basic deity and the guarding *loka-pāla*s labelled after the names of the Buddhist *yakṣa*s carry Buddhist associations (see SHAH (1961: 170, 175)). Regarding the architectural influences scholars differ in opinion. AGRAWALA (1947–48), ALLCHIN (1957), SHAH (1961), PAL (1971–72), GOSWAMY (1980), ROTH (1980), and recently BAKKER (2007) discussed the *aiḍūka* described in Chapter 84 of the third *khaṇḍa* of VDhP. The attempts to find the traces of an *aiḍūka* structure among the extant architectural remains led the scholars to contradictory conclusions. Pratapaditya PAL (1971–72) has attempted to demonstrate 'with visual evidence that the *aiḍūka*, in fact, is basically a Buddhist *stūpa*', whereas AGRAWALA (1947–48) and SHAH (1961) suggested that the *aiḍūka* must have been basically a Śaivite structure. All of them considered the *aiḍūka* as a cult structure, be it Buddhist or Śaivite. With regard to the function of the *aiḍūka* both GOSWAMY (1980) and BAKKER (2007) held the view that this structure is a Hindu funerary shrine although architecturally it certainly follows the *stūpa*.

Most frequently the argument for Buddhist provenance of the *aiḍūka* was a consequence of the rejection by most scholars that the veneration of the human remains had ever been practised in Hindu rites. That is most probably the reason also for INDEN (2000: 89), who largely follows PAL's lead, to read in VDhP the denigratory meaning of the Buddhist *eḍūka* as if it represented the attitude of the Pāñcarātra Vaiṣṇavas. However it was already GOSWAMY (1980: 6) who drew the attention to the fact of 'how widely the holy man is revered and how frequent are monuments raised over his remains, becoming objects of widespread veneration' in Hindu religious practices. To elaborate on the GOSWAMI's argument, Hans T. BAKKER carried out a lengthy research on the monuments devoted to the dead in North India that led to the conclusion that *aiḍūka*, as one of the types of funerary monuments—in contrast to the predominantly Buddhist *eḍūka* (mortuary repository)—does not contain the actual mortuary remains. Consequently both, GOSWAMY and BAKKER, divested the *aiḍūka* of its Buddhist association to support the non-Hindu provenance of buildings memorials to the dead generally assumed (the often quoted passage in the *Mahā-bhārata* (MBh 3.188.64–66) notably refers to the *eḍūka* as mortuary repository rather than the *aiḍūka* although the meaning of the latter is undisputedly a derivative from the former one).

The word form *aiḍūka*, which means 'derived from / related to / of the nature of *eḍūka*', explains the difference of *aiḍūka* form the original Buddhist ossuary (*eḍūka*) (BAKKER (2007: 13)). Since Gustav ROTH (1980), we may take it for certain that the author of VDhP modelled his Hindu *aiḍūka* on a Buddhist example of the *stūpa* structure. According to ROTH, a comparison of the description of *aiḍūka* in VDhP with Buddhist sources reveals that the VDhP passage (84.1–15) follows an older Buddhist tradition of erecting funerary monuments, most frequently referred to as *stūpa*s and intended to dispose of the relics of the members of the *saṅgha*—an innovation documented by the later non-Pāli traditions. Architectural descriptions of those monuments (*aiḍūka*s and *stūpa*s) are found in the chapters of the Tibetan version of the lost Sanskrit original *Caitya-vibhāga-vinayôdbhāva-sūtra* (ca. 1st century CE), the Nepalese Sanskrit treatise *Stūpa-lakṣaṇa-kārikā-vivecana* (ca. 2nd century CE), and the *Kriyā-saṁgraha* by Kuladatta (ca. 8th century CE) (see ROTH (1980: 200)). A Mention of the structure of the *stūpa* which follows that of the above mentioned texts is also found in the *Divyâvadāna* (ca. 3rd century CE). With respect to the *aiḍūka* in particular, Hans T. BAKKER (2007) adds the *Mahā-vastu* and the *Amara-kośa* to this list. With regard to both textual references and archaeological material BAKKER (2007: 14–15) rightly concludes, *pace* B.N. GOSWAMY (1980), that 'the erection of funerary monuments was not strictly limited to the heterodox tradition.' Therefore, we can agree with BAKKER's (2007: 40) opinion that the authors of VDhP, while referring to the *aiḍūka*, 'elaborated on what must have been a monumental tradition that was common to all Indian religions, most pronounced within Buddhism, less in Jainism and inconspicuous in the Hindu mainstream.' However, as rightly states BAKKER (2007: 43),

> 'the general Hindu reluctance to connect it (*aiḍūka*-like structure—V.J.) with actual remains of the dead rendered it futile: being neither temple nor relic sanctuary there were not enough incentives to construct, worship and maintain it; the Hindu funerary monument or *aiḍūka* never really came off the ground. ... The *aiḍūka* of the *Viṣṇudharmottara-purāṇa* is a hybrid product of śāstric imagination, calqued on a Buddhist example.'

The function of the *aiḍūka* as a funerary monument can perhaps explain why the compilers of VDhP placed the description of it in a separate chapter, apart from the variety of temples discussed later, even though structurally both types of buildings bear close similarities.

Thus, even though structural parallels and textual affinities between the Buddhist *eḍūka* and the description of the *aiḍūka* in VDhP are discernable, what complicates a more comprehensive view of the Hindu *aiḍūka* is, as BAKKER (2007: 29) has rightly noticed, that 'so-far there have not been discovered in the Hindu sphere structures that conform, more than superficially, to the description of the *aiḍūka* in VDhP.' So the hypothesis suggested by SHAH (1961: 174) that *aiḍūka*s became as popular sacred objects of worship that almost replaced gods and temples—an argument based on mostly linguistic and descriptive speculations—is subject to serious revision and requires additional supporting archaeological material.

On the other hand, while confining ourselves to architectural elements of the structure, we can, trace both in the texts and actual buildings of Buddhist funerary monuments and the *aiḍūka* of VDhP, the continuity of the structure of the *stūpa* in the *aiḍūka* as found in VDhP and appropriation of their structural elements in the temple structures of Kashmir. Moreover, acknowledging striking parallels in the description discussed by ROTH, it is tempting to think that Buddhist sources, apparently through the mediation of practicing architects of Buddhist buildings, were known also at the court of Kashmir and thus took their shape in VDhP.

4. Foreign Influences in the Temples of Kashmir

There are a few structural elements that prompt any association between the funerary monument—be it *eḍūka* or *stūpa*—described in the Buddhist texts and the *aiḍūka* of VDhP. Apart from the three-tiered platform, which is common to both constructions, thirteen *bhūmikā*s that are erected on the square column (*yaṣṭi*) in VDhP 3.84.5 find their parallel in the Tibetan version of the *Vinaya Kṣudraka-vastu* of the Mūlasarvāstivādins, as noted by ROTH. There the umbrella canopy is said to consist of one or two, or three, or four up to thirteen (superimposed) umbrella canopies (*gdugs*, *chatra*). Similarly in the passage called *Caitya-lakṣaṇa-vidhi* included at the end of *Vajrā-cārya-kriyā-samuccaya* we read about one, three, five, seven, nine, or thirteen umbrella canopies. Striking similarity with the VDhP vocabulary comes out as these umbrella canopies, or wheels, are named *bhūmi*s in the *stūpa* passage found in the eighth chapter of Kuladatta's *Kriyā-saṁgraha*, a Sanskrit text which belongs to the category of Buddhist *Kriyā-tantra*s (ROTH (1980: 184–198)).

The description of the cog-wheel stone (*amala-sāraka*) topped with another pole (*yaṣṭi*) above the thirteen *bhūmikā*s, and the crowning of the whole structure in the form of the sun and moon, as found to in VDhP, also follows the structure of a *stūpa* mentioned in the DivA 244.7 ff. and the KSaṁ (edited in ROTH (1980: § 12)), a version, later modified, of the passage entitled *Prakīrṇaka-caitya-lakṣaṇa* included in the Nepalese Sanskrit treatise *Stūpa-lakṣaṇa-kārikā-vivecana* (ROTH (1980: 200–202)).

The other structural similarity shared by the *aiḍūka* of VDhP and by the *stūpa* structures described in the Buddhist sources, is the four flights of steps at each of the four cardinal points that lead up to terraced platforms (ROTH (1980: 200)). It is known that the *stūpa* with the four flights of steps, the so called cruciform *stūpa*, was a characteristic structural type of the Gandhāran Buddhist architecture from the mid 5th to 8th century. Cruciform *stūpa*s are found in a few sites that still had active patronage in the Peshawar basin and Taxila (Takṣaśilā) after a relative decline of Buddhism in that region after the mid 5th century; the examples are Shāh-jī-kī-ḍherī, the Taxila site of Bhamāla, Sahrī-Bahlôl Site G. The cruciform *stūpa* can be compared to the cruciform *stūpa*s of the 7th to 8th centuries found in Kashmir (for example, Caṅkuṇa and Uṣkar *stūpa*s, both from the mid-eighth century; see EITA 366–

367), in Afghanistan and in other parts of Central Asia (KUWAYAMA (1997), BEHRENDT (2004: 206)). That important Buddhist monuments of this shape must have existed is confirmed by the terracotta memorial plagues and small clay-models of *stūpa*s for the pilgrims and devotees (FRANZ (1980: 40)). Historically, the decline of Buddhist centres in Greater Gandhāra as a consequence of the waning of patronage was first felt in the Peshawar basin and Taxila in late 5th and 6th centuries, while centres in Swat and Afghanistan probably prospered till the 7th to 8th centuries CE. It is highly possible, therefore, that the architects from the thriving Buddhist centres moved to Kashmir and there continued their practices, this time under the patronage of Hindu rulers, and responded to new ritual expectations.

Further, non-Indian elements in mediaeval Kashmirian art also reveal alternative sources, one of them, as Hermann GOETZ 1969: (56–57) has persuasively argued, being the 7th-century Byzantine Syria. Expert architects, masons, sculptors and other artists might have been brought from the Tarim Basin Tarim Basin and from China where Syrians as followers of the Nestorian church had congregations and with which Kashmir was linked by the minister of Lalitāditya, Caṅkuṇa, and later on by Lalitāditya's own conquests. Lalitāditya must have imported a small colony of late Gupta sculptors from Kanauj and Gauḍa as a result of his military expansion, which explains the finds at the Mārtāṇḍa temple of 'friezes and reliefs in the purest and best late Gupta style' (GOETZ (1969: 60)).

The cruciform plan of the *stūpa* was apparently appropriated for the terraced temples in Kashmir along with other structural elements of Buddhist buildings, namely, the peristyle of the Buddhist monasteries surrounding the rectangular courtyard of temple(-complexes), trefoil niche within large pediments at the cardinal entries of the shrine, and pilastered mouldings of the wall. Below I will elaborate on the last two elements which because constituent features of the Hindu shrine.

The reluctance on the part of some scholars, e.g. WILLIAMS (1982) and RAVEN (2008), to consent to the opinion, expressed by AGRAWALA (1981), FRANTZ (1975) and EITA 22, which derives the brick terraced temples, the earliest of which date back to the early Gupta period, from the multi-tiered *stūpa*-shrines of the Buddhists, is primarily motivated by the hypothesis which assumes a rather independent origin of the brick terraced structure as a stone-slab worship platform (*pūja-śilā* or *śilā-paṭa*) that developed into a terraced temple at least in the Gupta period, although the Nāga provenance of this structural type is also likely (WILLIAMS (1982: 18–20)). However, despite the divergence of opinions, it is highly probable, as complex appearance of Buddhist structural elements listed above indicate, that the building practice of the *stūpa*s in Kashmir were adopted in the course of actual cultural and religious influences.

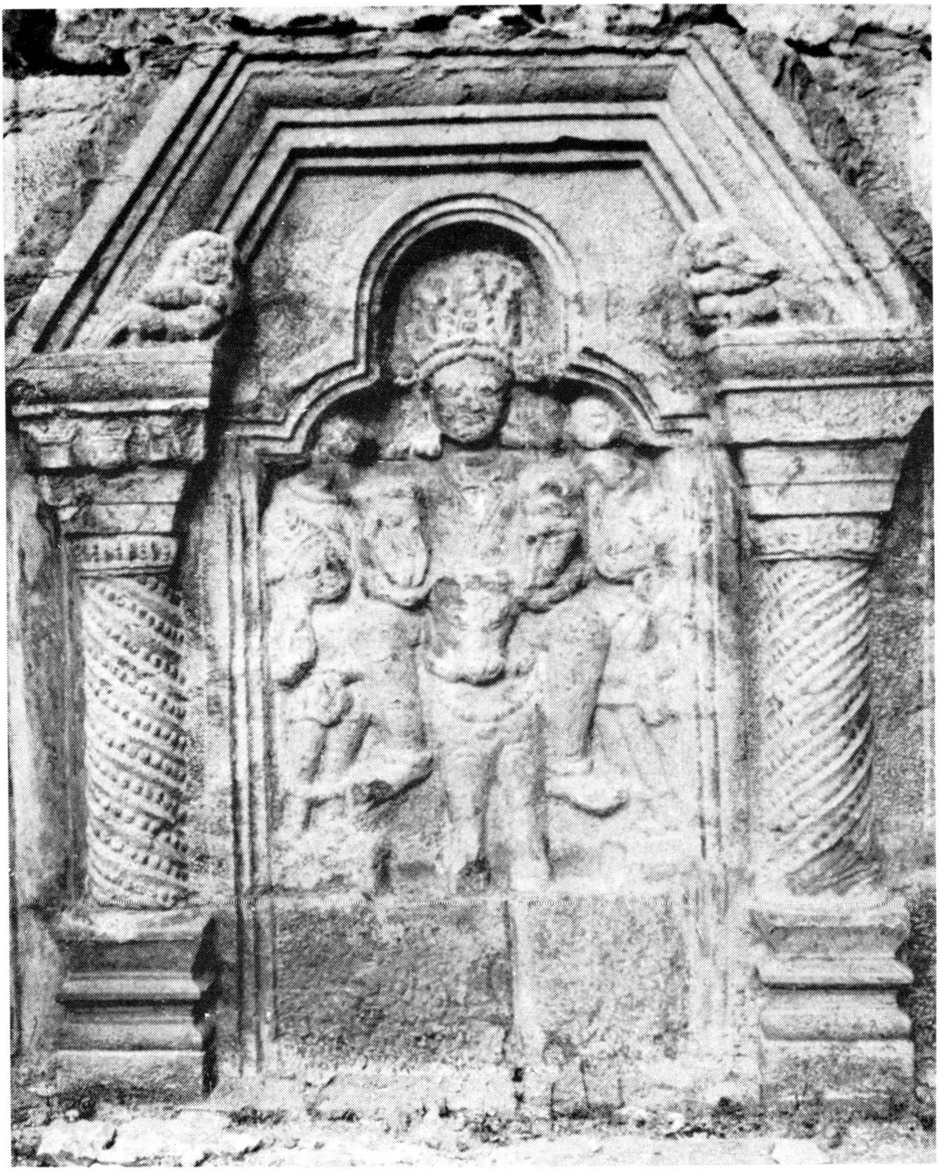

Fig. 4. Maṭṭan. Mārtaṇḍa temple, trefoil niche of the upper *jagatī*, c. 725–750 C.E. Source: EITA, pl. 715. Courtesy: American Institute of Indian Studies

Another conspicuous borrowing of the Buddhist Gandhāra architecture in the temples of Kashmir is the trefoil niche (GOETZ (1969), EITA 357). Jorinde EBERT (1994: 287) argues that the trefoil niche mode started around the mid-6th century in India, reached its full-blown phase in Bāmiyān around the 6th to 7th century CE, and went out of fashion in India itself around the end of the 8th century. Her exploration of the petroglyphs with *stūpa* depictions found at the Upper Indus Valley made her assume the Gandhāran provenance of the decorative mode of trefoil *stūpa* niche that was introduced, possibly via Kashmir, into the petroglyph *stūpa* depiction, which, at the same time, 'still retain the "Gandhāran" fondness for the rhythmic articulation of *stūpa* bases with columns and pilasters not seen in India proper' (EBERT (1994: 285)).

It is known from the recently discovered Mahāyāna Sanskrit *vāstu* text, the *Mañjuśrī-vāstu-vidyā-śāstra*, dating to the 5th–7th centuries, that over this period the niches were provided with clear-cut symbolism. This text (MVVŚ 3.59 f.), which supposedly reflects the *stūpa* architecture in the Indian and Central Asian areas, describes the niches along the drum or dome on the outside of the *caitya* that correspond to the second chamber inside the dome.[2]

What, however, indicates the influences of Gandhāran *stūpa*s in typical Kashmirian temples assigned to Lalitāditya's reign is the trefoil niche that is flanked by pilasters supporting a pediment truncated at the top (fig. 4). The motive of rhythmic articulation of wall surfaces by pilastered arches that is seen in Kashmiri temples is decidedly of Hellenistic origins and reached India through the *stūpa* decorations in Afghanistan in the first centuries CE.

The pilastered wall in general is one of the features of the temples built in Kashmir from the 7th century onwards that show foreign influences. In India, as George MICHELL (1980: 60) persuasively demonstrated, the idea of structural masonry architecture with the pilastered wall was unknown. He argues that the pilastered wall of the Indian temple is a foreign architectural feature, inherited through the contacts with the Hellenistic world. In the Hellenistic architecture it functioned not as a load-bearing structural element, but its purpose was rhythmic articulation of the wall surface. In *nāgara* temple architecture of north India, on the contrary, two traditions, both using load-bearing constructions, can be traceable: a pillared, primarily wooden, tradition and a masonic tradition, with stone enclosing an inner cell.

---

[2] The critical edition of the text is based on the Singhalese copy and its editor E.W. MARASINGHE (1989) attempted to demonstrate the closeness of the description of the Buddhist *caitya* to the *stupa*s of Sri Lanka. However, Giovanni VERARDI (1992) in his final report on the excavations at Harigaon remarked, that the text is much better suited to a context in the Indian and Central Asian areas; see EBERT (1994: 274).

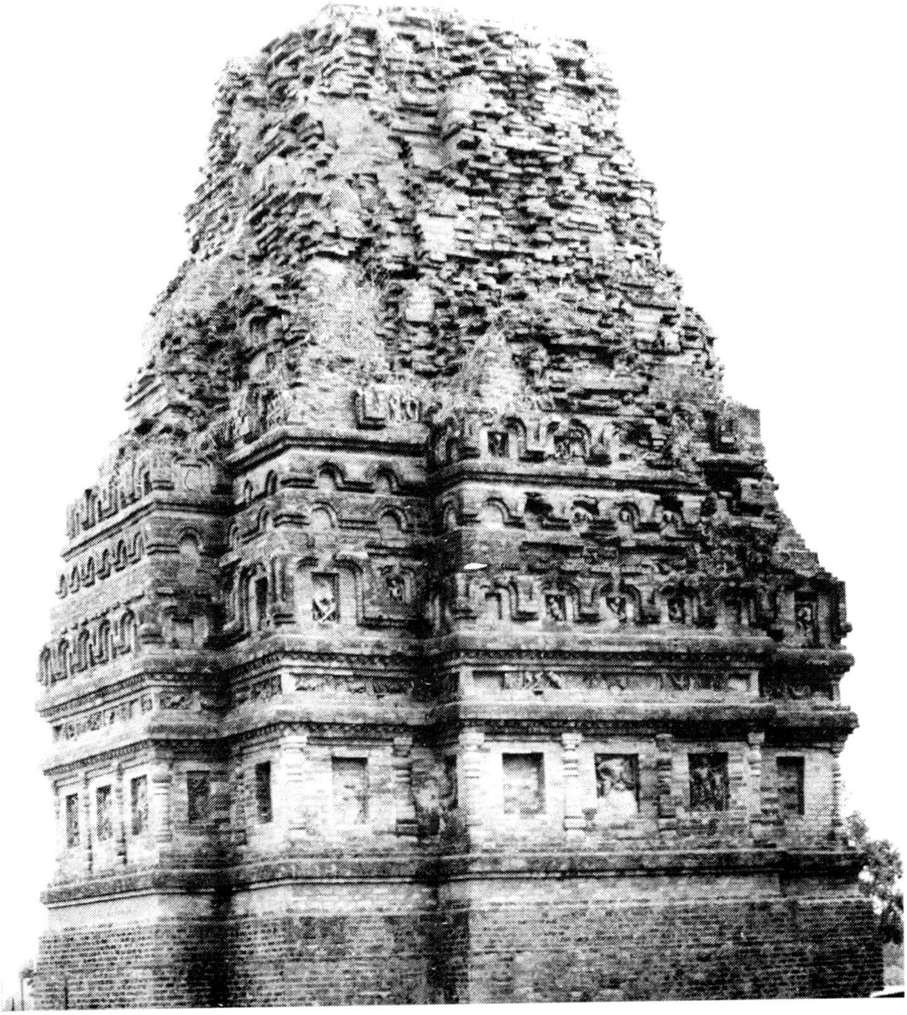

Fig. 5. Nālandā, site no. 3. Corner towers, c. 575–600 C.E. Source: EITA, pl. 228. Courtesy: American Institute of Indian Studies

The absence of the pilastered wall in the earliest examples of Indian masonic architecture, coinciding with the Gupta period, continues north of the Deccan. However, from the 8th century the application of the pilaster pattern to an essentially masonry fabric is traceable through many temples of central India and reaches its aesthetic culmination in the 9th century in Gyāraspur and other sites. According to Michael W. MICHELL (1985), this mixture of masonry with applied pilasters was introduced into the central India in the 8th century through the contacts with Malwa and eastern Rajasthan. It suggests that the origins of this structural device should be sought in the milieu different from the masonic Hindu temple architecture.

Early medieval experiments in masonic structures were apparently an outcome of the introduction of the pilastered wall structures in the temples of north India that took place a few centuries earlier in Gandhāra and later spread to central India through the contacts via Rajasthan and Malwa. Importantly, it is in the milieu of intensive correlation between Buddhist and Hindu brick architecture in the 5th and 6th centuries that the usage of the pilastered wall can be clearly visible (cf. corner towers at the site no. 3 at Nālandā (fig. 5) and the temple at Bhitargaon (Bhītargāṁv) (fig. 6)). As MICHELL (1980: 64) notes, such a correspondence of details does not exist in the stone building tradition that was developing at the same time in central India.

That architectural experiments in the north-west region were fundamental for the overall development of temple architecture of north India is also corroborated by the fact that the multi-storeyed masonry elevation—the unique feature of this style of temple architecture—was probably an innovation that began in north India around this time. All these innovations are seen in the brick temples from Katās, Kāfirkot, Bilot, Māri, etc. in the Salt Range, Pakistan, dating from the 6th century (MEISTER (2000)), and they all display the same features of the pilastered wall, applied to the buildings with more developed superstructure of north India style. Due to structural attributes they are seen as having grown out of previous local Gandhāran conventions, especially earlier Buddhist architecture (MEISTER (1996), (2000) and (2010), MASIH (2002)). As in some of the temples from Kashmir of the 8th to 10th centuries, the niches of the central wall offset are flanked by the pilasters with pseudo-Corinthian capitals closely resembling those found on the so-called 'Shrine of the Double-Headed Eagle' at Taxila (1st century BCE) and other pilastered *stūpa* basements from Gandhāran and the adjacent areas (INGHOLD (1957), MEISTER (2000)).

Variety of structural appropriations referred to above enables us to draw hypothesis that architectural practices of present north Pakistan survived an experiment that consisted primarily of merging the elements of Buddhist and northern Hindu temple traditions and which resulted in new structural solutions. The period of architectural experimentation most evidently traced in the temples of the Indus or Gandhāran style of *nāgara* architecture investigated by Michael W. MEISTER with the assistance of Abdur Rehman and Farid Khan. It disclosed a local tradition of temple architecture cultivated between the 6th and early 11th centuries CE along the Indus river that differed from the Kashmirian style (even though it was long misclassified as a variant or the latter) but due to structural attributes is seen as growing out of previous local Gandhāran conventions, especially of earlier Buddhist architecture (MASIH (2002), MEISTER (2000), (1996) and (2010)). The temple architecture of the Indus

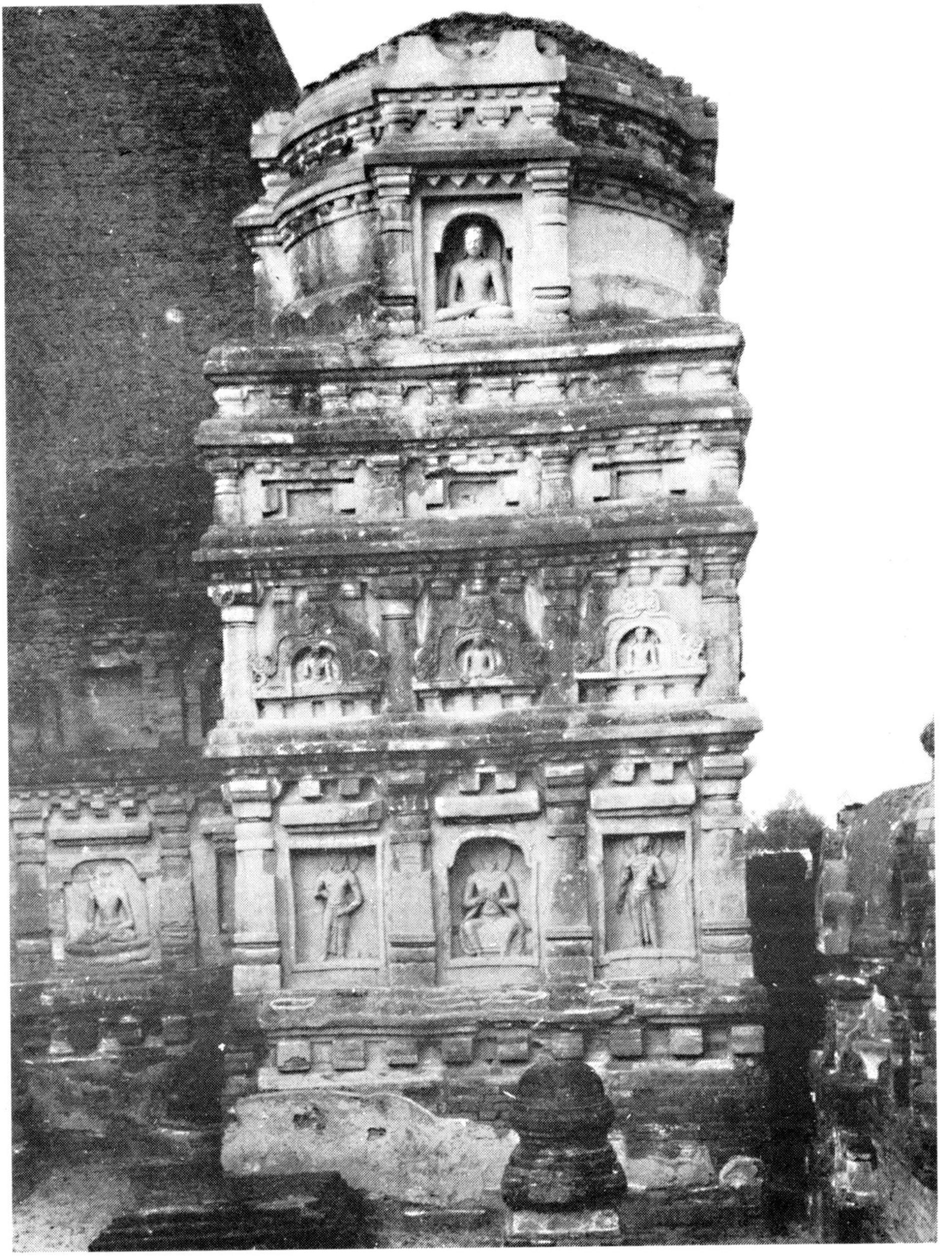

Fig. 6. Bhitargaon (Bhītargām̐v). Gupta temple, c. 425–450 C.E. Source: EITA, pl. 45. Courtesy: American Institute of Indian Studies

reveals long-term experimentation with the *nāgara* style of north India, although it maintained its unique features, different from other regional schools developed within the *nāgara* style. More visual evidences of the process of merging the architectural styles of the Indus region and Kashmir are found in the temples built after late 9th century by the Hindu Śāhi kings after the marriage alliances between the two political units was formed (MEISTER (2000: 1329–1334)).

To situate the Kashmiri architectural style in the broader canvas of cultural flows that took place in the regions adjacent to Kashmir after 7th century, it is necessary to assume close interaction between mountainous regions of northern Pakistan and northwest India, on the one hand, and eastern Afghanistan, on the other. The historical importance of the art of Kashmir derives from its relations to the Turki Ṣāhi art of Afghanistan and Pakistan and the continuity of this artistic tradition in northwest India and the western Himalayas till 11th century. It is known, for example, that Paṭola Ṣāhi rulers from North Pakistan were arduous patrons of Buddhist art, discovered mostly in Gilgit, from the late 6th century to the downfall of this dynasty in the middle of the 8th century. The influence of this tradition on the art of Kashmir can be explained by the expansion of the Kārkoṭa dynasty of Kashmir after 602 CE, which gradually became the dominant power in an area henceforth referred to as greater Kashmir, which stretched from eastern Afghanistan to Ladakh, and south to Taxila. According to Kalhaṇa's *Rāja-taraṅgiṇī*, by the end of the 7th century, the Turki Ṣāhis in Pakistan were incorporated into the Kārkoṭa Empire (RT Book IV, pp. 133–134). Kalhaṇa also provides numerous examples of Lalitāditya's interactions with Turks in the early 8th century and their conquest and consequent incorporation of their nobility into his administrative system. The same elite patronised Buddhist establishments from the eastern Afghanistan to Kashmir. In the 6th through 8th centuries in the Hindu Kush and adjacent centres Buddhism became a state religion or at least there was close relationship between Buddhist and princely institutions in Bāmiyān (KLIMBURG-SALTER (1989: 121 ff.)). On the other hand, some rulers around Kapiśa and Kabul in Afghanistan also patronised Hinduism. Hindu temples were found at Tepe Iskandar, Kapiśa, and at Chegha Serai in the Kunar Valley. Therefore it is probable that Kashmiri style emerged from the practice of Turki Ṣāhi experimentations in northern Pakistan from the 6th century and influenced the regions east of Kashmir. Consequently, KLIMBURG-SALTER (1989: 31–38) supports the view that these were Kashmiri artists who transmitted the elements of Ṣāhi art to neighbouring areas.

5. A Note on the Classification of Temples in the *Viṣṇu-dharmôttara-purāṇa*

I would conclude my arguments with the problem which, taken for granted 'the inclination of the Indians to classification', is usually ignored in the discussions on temple architecture in VDhP. What was the reason to list one-hundred types of temples in Chapter 86 of VDhP and why was it followed with the one-hundred first, the *sarvato-bhadra* type, to which the entire Chapter 87 is devoted? Notably the list of one-hundred types of temple is unique to VDhP; in other texts on architecture the numbers range from 20 in the *Bṛhat-saṁhitā* 56.17–30, the *Matsya-purāṇa* 269.28–45, or the *Viśvakarma-prakāśa* 6.82cd–106ab to 45 in the *Agni-purāṇa* 104.15–30, the *Garuḍa-purāṇa* 1.47. In comparison with the texts mentioned above, VDhP might be treated as being as comprehensive as possible but nevertheless the number one hundred is strikingly unmotivated, particularly because of the lack of any internal logic to enumerate 100 types which completely differ from those found in the lists of 20 and 45 types, in both of which the temples are classified according to basic structures.

Presumably we may think of number 100 as being symbolically related with divine manifestation as the very temple is considered the body of the god. I even guess that the list of 100 types of temples has substantial affinity with the symbolism of the *aiḍūka* discussed earlier (*vide supra*, p. 211). The fact that the *aiḍūka* structure as the *liṅga* symbolises the entire universe calls for the identification of number 100 with multiple manifestations of the universal god, who in the case of VDhP is Viṣṇu. This presupposition is rather conjectural, nevertheless I am inclined to think that chapters 86 and 87, the former describing 100 temples and the latter elaborating on a unique *sarvato-bhadra* type with full Vaiṣṇava iconography displayed in it, are fully complementary in the sense that Chapter 86 supplies a universal image of Viṣṇu in the form of an infinite number (termed *śata*, 'hundred-[fold]', or *sahasra*, 'thousand-[fold]') of its bodily manifestations as temples, while Chapter 87 provides a description of a unique temple structure that encompasses an infinite form of the god within a single temple displayed merely by iconography. The respective sculptural Vaiṣṇava symbol is the Viśvarūpa described in the preceding Chapter 83 of VDhP and known in Kashmir (MAXWELL (1988: 237)).

It is not the aim of this article to undertake an enquiry into the provenance of the multiform Viṣṇu image in Kashmir. One could merely assume that the idea to manifest Viṣṇu in multiple images or constructions was perhaps brought to Kashmir after Muktāpīḍa Lalitāditya's defeat of vast territories in the north and east India. He must have got acquainted with the *sarvato-bhadra* temple through reports about them on or even by himself paying a visit to the Viṣṇu temple at Deogaṛh, which later served as a model of the Pāñcarātra temple in VDhP. The iconographical programme of the Viṣṇu temple at Deogaṛh seems to agree with the scheme of the *sarvato-*

bhadra temple (LUBOTSKY (1996)). The traces of the Kashmiris in Deogaṛh are identified on stylistic grounds in the case of the Viśvarūpa temple that was excavated in the vicinity of the Viṣṇu temple and shows smothered trace of a Kashmiri iconography (MAXWELL (1988: 237)). As for the accommodation of various regional temple structures amounting to 100 types in VDhP, all of them must have been known throughout north India, the sacred area of the Middle Region (*bharata-varṣa*), during the military campaign of Muktāpīḍa Lalitāditya, and it might have been a logical decision from the point of view of the hegemony of Pāñcarātra Vaiṣṇavas ideology to include them into the 'imperial *purāṇa*', as VDhP is called by INDEN (2000: 86).

The temples described in VDhP can be seen as closely related, symbolically and architecturally, to the Śaivite *aiḍūka* structure, which might have been actually known to the compilers of the text of VDhP on the basis of the prevalence of Śaivism in the pre-Kārkoṭa period. The incorporation of Buddhist structures in VDhP through the likely Śaivite practices can be interpreted as architecturally expressing a hegemonic attitude of the Pāñcarātra Vaiṣṇavas established through the old structures but by the obliteration of old meanings.

6. Conclusion

Acknowledging VDhP as a great narrative of the Pāñcarātra ritual order introduced in Kashmir with the advent of the Kārkoṭa dynasty from the early 7th century, it is reasonable to treat the architectural material found in this *purāṇa* as a conscious attempt to establish a new visual order that might have resulted in the adoption of the *sarvato-bhadra* type of temple and the iconographical program of Pāñcarātra Vaiṣṇavism. This shift of the visual order was preconditioned by long-term experimentation with the north Indian type of the temple in the region where Buddhist structures prevailed; the process entailed the adaptation of Buddhist structural elements to Hindu temple. However, with the advent of the Pāñcarātra ritualism and its imperial promotion by Muktāpīḍa Lalitāditya, the *sarvato-bhadra* type, supposedly modelled on the example of the Deogaṛh Viṣṇu temple, was introduced chiefly for the purpose of displaying the iconographical programme of the Pāñcarātra.

On a structural plane, with the advent of the Pāñcarātra visual programme the cross-plan and the three-tiered base were adopted, though not necessarily directly, from Buddhist structures, since by the time of Lalitāditya's imperial expansion the architectural practice, only few examples of which remain, had developed as a result of architectural experimentation in north Pakistan where Buddhist and north Indian *latina* temple structures merged. IT is this practice that is preserved in VDhP in the form of *aiḍūka* structure.

BIBLIOGRAPHY

AGRAWALA 1947–1948 = Agrawala, Vasudeva S.: 'Terracotta Figurines of Ahichchhatrā, District Bareilly, U.P.', *Ancient India* 4 (1947–1948) 104–179.

AGRAWALA 1981 = Agrawala, P.K.: *Gupta Temple Architecture*. Second revised edition, Prithivi Prakashan, Varanasi 1981 (first edition: 1968).

ALLCHIN 1957 = Allchin, Fran Raymond: 'Sanskrit *Eḍūka*—Pāli *Eluka*', *Bulletin of the School of Oriental and African Studies* 20 (1957) 1–4.

BAKKER 2007 = Bakker, Hans T.: 'Monuments to the Dead in Ancient North India', *Indo-Iranian Journal* 50 (2007) 11–47.

BAL 2003 = Bal, Mieke: 'Visual Essentialism and the Object of Visual Studies', *Journal of Visual Culture* 2, 1 (2003) 5–32.

BhP = *Bhaviṣya-purāṇa. Śrī-bhaviṣya-mahā-purāṇam*. Vol. 1: *Brāhma-parvan*. Nag Publishers, Delhi 1984.

BSaṁ = *Bṛhat-saṁhitā*. M. Bhat (.ed.): *Varāhamihira's Bṛhat-saṁhitā*. Part 1, Motilal Banarsidass, Delhi 1995.

DALLAPICCOLA–ZINGEL-AVÉ LALLEMANT 1980 = Dallapiccola, Anna Libera; Zingel-Avé Lallemant, Stephanie (eds.): *The Stūpa: Its Religious, Historical and Architectural Significance*. Beiträge zur Südasienforschung 55, Franz Steiner Verlag, Wiesbaden 1980.

DivA = *Divyâvadāna*. Andy Rotman (transl.): *Divine Stories: Divyāvadāna*. Wisdom Publications, Boston 2008.

EBERT 1994 = Ebert, Jorinde: 'Niches, Columns, and Figures in Some Petroglyphic Stūpa Depictions of the Karakorum Highway', *Artibus Asiae* 54, 3–4 (1994) 268–295.

EITA = Meister, Michael W.; Dhaky, M.A.; Deva, Krishna (eds.): *Encyclopaedia of Indian Temple Architecture*. Vol. 2: *North India. Foundations of North Indian Style*, Pt. 1: *Text*. Oxford University Press, American Institute of Indian Studies, Delhi 1988.

FRANZ 1975 = Franz, Heinrich Gerhard: 'Der indische Terrassentempel', in: Pramod Chandra (ed.): *Studies in Indian Temple Architecture*. American Institute of Indian Studies, New Delhi 1975: 166–178.

FRANZ 1980 = Franz, Heinrich Gerhard: 'Stūpa and Stūpa-Temple in the Gandhāran Regions and in Central Asia', in: DALLAPICCOLA–ZINGEL-AVÉ LALLEMANT (1980: 39–58).

GOETZ 1969 = Goetz, Hermann: *Studies in the History and Art of Kashmir and the Indian Himalaya*. Otto Harrassowitz, Wiesbaden 1969.

GOSWAMY 1980 = Goswamy, Brijinder Nath: 'Introductory Speech: The Stūpa—Some Uninformed Questions About Terminological Equivalents', in: DALLAPICCOLA–ZINGEL-AVÉ LALLEMANT (1980: 1–11).

IKARI 1993 = Ikari, Yasuke: 'Aspects of the Evolution and Cultural Integration of Hinduism: The Case of a Purāṇa from Kashmir', in: Yasuhiko Nagano; Yasuke Ikari (eds.): *From Vedic Altar to Village Shrine. Towards the Interface between Indology and Anthropology*. Senri Ethnological Studies 36, National Museum of Ethnology, Osaka 1993: 185–195.

INDEN 2000 = Inden, Ronald: 'Imperial Purāṇas: Kashmir as Vaiṣṇava Center of the World', in: Ronald Inden, Jonathan Walter, Daud Ali (eds.): *Quering the Medieval. Texts and the History of Practices in South Asia*. Oxford University Press, New York 2000: 29–98.

INGHOLT 1957 = Ingholt, Harald: *Gandhāran Art in Pakistan. Introduction and Descriptive Catalogue*. Pantheon Books, New York 1957.

KAK 1933 = Kak, Ram Chandra: *Ancient Monuments of Kashmir*. India Society, London 1933.

KLIMBURG-SALTER 1989 = Klimburg-Salter, Deborah: *The Kingdom of Bāmiyān. Buddhist Art and Culture of the Hindu Kush*. Istituto Universitario Orientale, Istituto Italiano per il Medio ed Estremo Oriente, Naples, Rome 1989.

KRAMRISCH 1996 = Kramrisch, Stella: *The Hindu Temple*. 2 Vols., Motilal Banarsidass, Delhi 1996 [first edition: University of Calcutta, Calcutta 1946].

KSaṁ = *Kriyā-saṁgraha*. See: ROTH (1980).

KUWAYAMA 1997 = Kuwayama, Shoshin: *The Main Stupa at Shāh-jī-kī-ḍherī: A Chronological Outlook*. Kyoto University, Institute for Research in Humanities, Kyoto 1997.

LUBOTSKY 1992 = Lubotsky, Alexander: 'The "Sarvatobhadra" Temple of the Viṣṇudharmottarapurāṇa and the Viṣṇu Temple at Deogarh', in: A.W. Van Den Hoek; D.H.A. Kolff; M.S. Oort (eds.): *Ritual, State and History in South Asia. Essays in Honour of J.C. Heesterman*. Memoirs of the Kern Institute 5, E.J. Brill, Leiden 1992: 199–221.

LUBOTSKY 1996 = Lubotsky, Alexander: 'The Iconography of the Viṣṇu Temple at Deogarh and the Viṣṇudharmottarapurāṇa', *Ars Orientalis* 26 (1996) 65–80.

MARASINGHE 1989 = Marasinghe, E.W. (ed., trans.): *The Vāstuvidya Śāstra ascribed to Mañjuśrī*. Sri Satguru Publications, Delhi 1989.

MASIH 2002 = Masih, Farzand: 'Style of the Salt Range and Kafir Kot temple in Pakistan: A critical analysis', *Pakistan Vision* 3,1–2 (2002) 105–140.

MAXWELL 1988 = Maxwell, Thomas S.: *Viśvarūpa*. Oxford University Press, Delhi–New York 1988.

MBh = *Mahā-bhārata*. Kisari Mohan Ganguli (transl.): *Mahabharata of Krishna Dwaipayana Vyasa: Translated Into English Prose From The Original*. 4 Vols. Munshiram Manoharlal, New Delhi 1993.

MEISTER 1985 = Meister, Michael W.: 'Symbol and Surface: Masonic and Pillared Wall-Structures in North India', *Artibus Asiae* 46,1–2 (1985) 129–148.

MEISTER 1996 = Meister, Michael W.: 'Temples Along the Indus', *Expedition* 38,3 (1996) 41–54.

MEISTER 2000 = Meister, Michael W.: 'Chronology of Temples in the Salt Range, Pakistan', in: Maurizio Taddei; Giuseppe De Marco (eds.): *South Asian Archaeology 1997*. Istituto Italiano per l'Africa e l'Oriente, Rome 2000: 1321–1339.

MEISTER 2010 = Meister, Michael W.: *Temples of the Indus. Studies in the Hindu Architecture of Ancient Pakistan*. Brill's Indological Library 35, Brill, Leiden–Boston 2010.

MICHELL 1980 = Michell, George: 'Pilastered Walls on Indian Stūpas and Temples', in: DALLAPICCOLA–ZINGEL-AVÉ LALLEMANT (1980: 59–71).

MVVŚ = *Mañjuśrī-vāstu-vidyā-śāstra*. See: MARASINGHE (1989).

NMP = *Nīlamata-purāṇa*. Ved Kumari, J. & K. (ed.): *The Nīlamata-purāṇa*. Vol. 2: *A Critical Edition and English Translation*. Academy of Art, Culture and Languages, Srinagar 1973.

PAL 1971–1972 = Pal, Pratapaditya: 'The *Aiḍūka* of the *Viṣṇudharmottarapurāṇa* and certain aspects of Stūpa Symbolism', *Journal of the Indian Society of Oriental Art*, New Series, 4,1 (1971–72) 49–62.

RAVEN 2008 = Raven, Ellen M.: 'Brick Terraces at Ahicchatra and Mansar. A Comparison', in: Hans Bakker (ed.): *Mansar. The Discovery of Pravareśvara and Pravarapura Temple and Residence of the Vākāṭaka King Pravarasena II. Proceedings of a Symposium at the British Museum, London, 30 June–1 July* (on-line). Library of the University of Groningen, Groningen 2008. Available from: http://mansar.eldoc.ub.rug.nl/FILES/root4/Mansar.pdf [accessed 2 November 2009].

ROTH 1980 = Roth, Gustav: 'Symbolism of the Buddhist Stūpa', in: DALLAPICCOLA–ZINGEL-AVÉ LALLEMANT (1980: 183–209).

RT = *Rāja-taraṅgiṇī*. M.A. Sten (transl.): *Kalhaṇa's Rājataraṅgiṇī: A Chronicle of the Kings of Kaśmīr*. Translated with an Introduction, Commentary and Appendices. 3 Vols., Motilal Banarsidass, Delhi 1979–1988.

SHAH 1961 = Shah, Priyabala: *Viṣṇudharmottara-purāṇa. Third khaṇḍa*. Vol. 2: *A study on a Sanskrit text of Ancient Indian Arts*. Gaekwad's Oriental Series 137, Oriental Institute, Baroda 1961.

WILLIAMS 1982 = Williams, Joanna Gottfried: *The Art of Gupta India*. Princeton University Press, Princeton 1982.

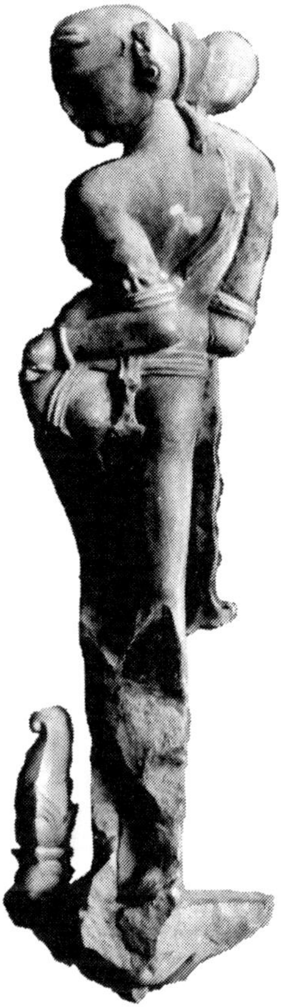

Cultural Heritage

Terracotta Art in the Gangetic Valley under the Guptas*

SAMIR KUMAR MUKHERJEE
(University of Calcutta)

1. Introduction

The rule of the Guptas during the 4th and 6th century forms an important chapter in the whole range of Indian history. There was an all-out progress and development in all spheres during the Gupta rule in India and as such this period is known as the 'Golden Age' in Indian history. In the field of artistic activities, terracotta received an equal attention like its counterparts in stone. The art expressions through the medium of terracotta are available mainly at various archaeological sites in the Gangetic valley.

The Gangetic plains form one of the major homogeneous regions of India having a unique monotony of relief. The entire region with its rich fertile land, having inexhaustible mineral resources, elaborate network of perennial rivers providing excellent irrigational as well as navigational facilities attracted the attention of early settlers from a remote past. This fertile land forming a pivotal region of India passed through vicissitudes of Indian history. On the basis of prevailing climate, drainage system, soil character, crop pattern and other related geographical features, the entire stretch of the plains is sub-divisible into three sub-regions like Upper, Middle and Lower Ganga Plains.

The Upper Ganga Plain lies approximately between Hardwar (Haridvār) in the West to Prayag (Prayāga; confluence of Gaṅgā with Yamunā at Allahabad (Ilāhābād, Uttar Pradesh) on the east. Some of the major rivers flowing over this region include

---

* The author gratefully acknowledges the receipt of some photographs from the American Institute of Indian Studies, Varanasi (Uttar Pradesh) and from the Indian Museum, Kolkata. The map (fig. l) was drawn by the author's late father Anil Chandra Mukhopadhyay (Mukherjee), a renowned Cartographer in 1970.

Art, Myths and Visual Culture of South Asia
Warsaw Indological Studies 4 (2011) 231–250.

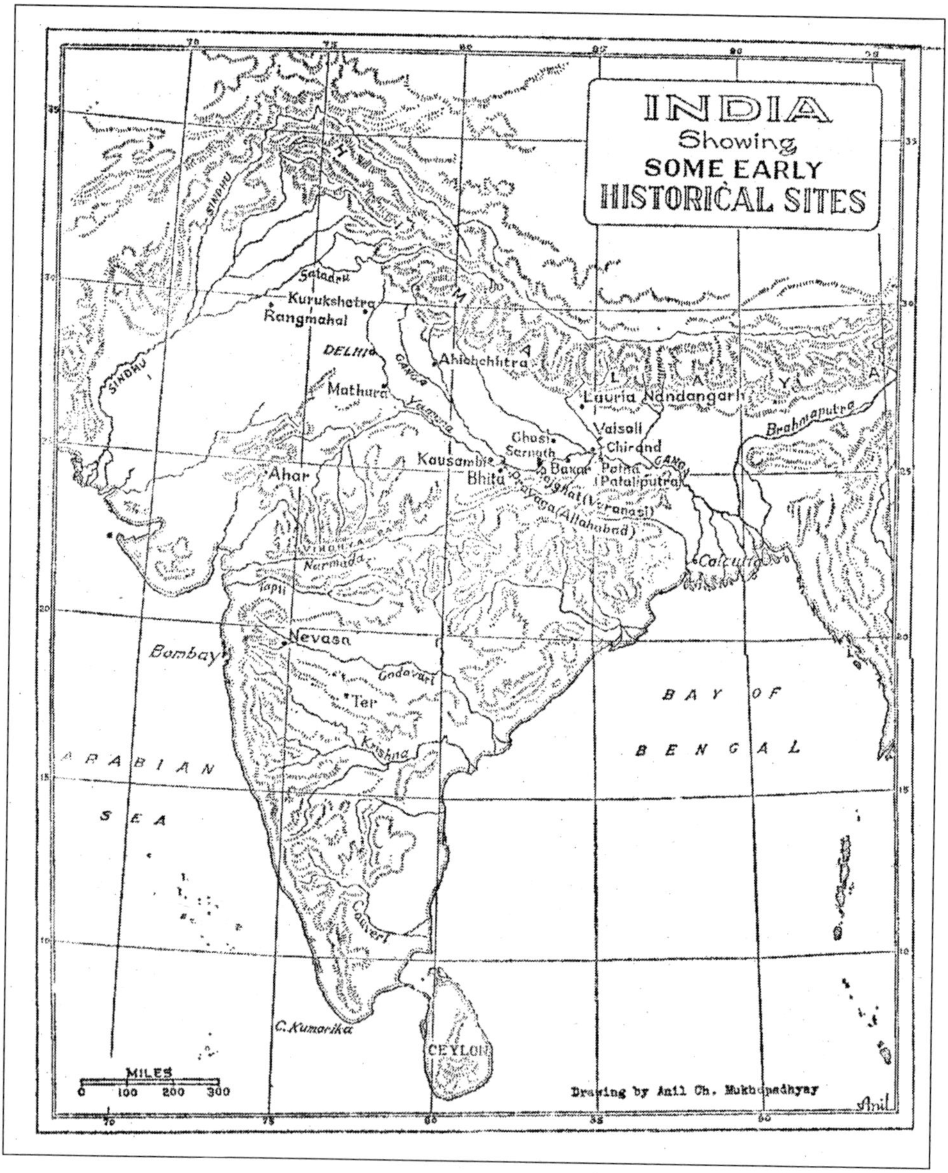

Map 1. Map of India showing the early historical sites

include the Yamunā, the Ramganga (Rāmagaṁga) and the Ghaghra (Ghāghrā). This region witnessed the growth of some prosperous urban centres like Hastināpura,

Kannauj, Ahichchhatra (Ahicchatra), Sravasti (Śrāvastī), Mathura (Mathurā), Alamgirpur (Ālamgīrpūr), Sringaverpura (Śriṅgaverpūra), Kaushambi (Kauśaṁbī), Bhita (Bhīta, Uttar Pradesh), Jhusi (Jhūsī), etc. The Middle Ganga Plain is basically an intermediary zone covering an extensive flat land from Allahabad in the west to Bengal-Bihar boundary on the east. This region is more riverine in character and the mainstream of Gaṅgā is joined by a few important tributary rivers like the Gandak (Gaṇḍak), the Kosi (Kośī), the Son and the Ghaghra. Availability of mineral resources like copper, tin, zinc, lead and above all iron in addition to abundance of timber near at hand led to the growth of material prosperity of the people here in the early historical period. Further, the principal rivers flowing over the plains serving as arteries of trade and commerce hastened the rapid growth of cities in this area. All these favourable situations helped towards the flourishing of some *mahā-janapadas* (major states) in the 6th century BCE such as Aṅga, Magadha, Kasi (Kāśī), Kosala (Kośala) etc. The leading urban centres in the historic period consist of Pataliputra (Pāṭaliputra; modern Patna (Paṭnā), Buxar (Baksar), Rajgir (Rājgīr), Champa (Campā), Rajghat (Rājghāṭ), Ayodhya (Ayodhyā), Masaon, Sonepur (Sonāpūr), Chirand (Cirand), Vaisali (Vaiśalī), Balirajgarh (Balirājgaṛh) and others.

In comparison with the Upper and Middle Ganga Plains, the Lower Ganga Plain forms relatively smaller region. The two major rivers, viz. the Gaṅgā and the Brahmaputra along with their innumerable tributaries drain the entire area. Urbanization in this part of the country began rather later. The leading urban centres that flourished here include Mahasthangarh (Mahāsthāngaṛh), Bangarh (Baṅgaṛh), Karnasuvarna (Karṇasuvarṇa), Mangolkot (Maṅgolkoṭ), Tamluk (Tamlūk), Chandraketugarh (Candraketūgaṛh) etc.

The entire plain was under the domination of the Guptas at their heyday. Abundant terracotta figurines and objects ascribable to this period enable us to study the form and character of the Gupta art idiom through the medium of clay. Due to easy availability of suitable clay in the riverine plains in abundance, terracotta appears to be the most common and cheap medium of art expression here. There exists unmistakable uniformity between the terracotta figurines from all sites due to their inheritance of a common artistic tradition. Another notable feature is their prominent urbane sophistication in appearance.

This period also ushered a new phase of activities in the domain of religious structures made both in stone and in bricks in various parts of their Kingdom. The building activities of temples, monasteries are generally patronised either by the newly emerging feudal aristocrats or by the ruling classes and these reflect the growing popularity of the *smārta-pauraṇic* ideology and beliefs. During this period, the Doab region in particular witnessed several brick built temples which were embellished with exquisite terracotta panel highlighting primarily Brahmanical gods, goddesses, composite figures and mythological scenes from the epics and the *Purāṇa*s. The theme of representation did not confine to religious scenes only. We often find plentiful variety of decorated bricks used for orating temples. The theme

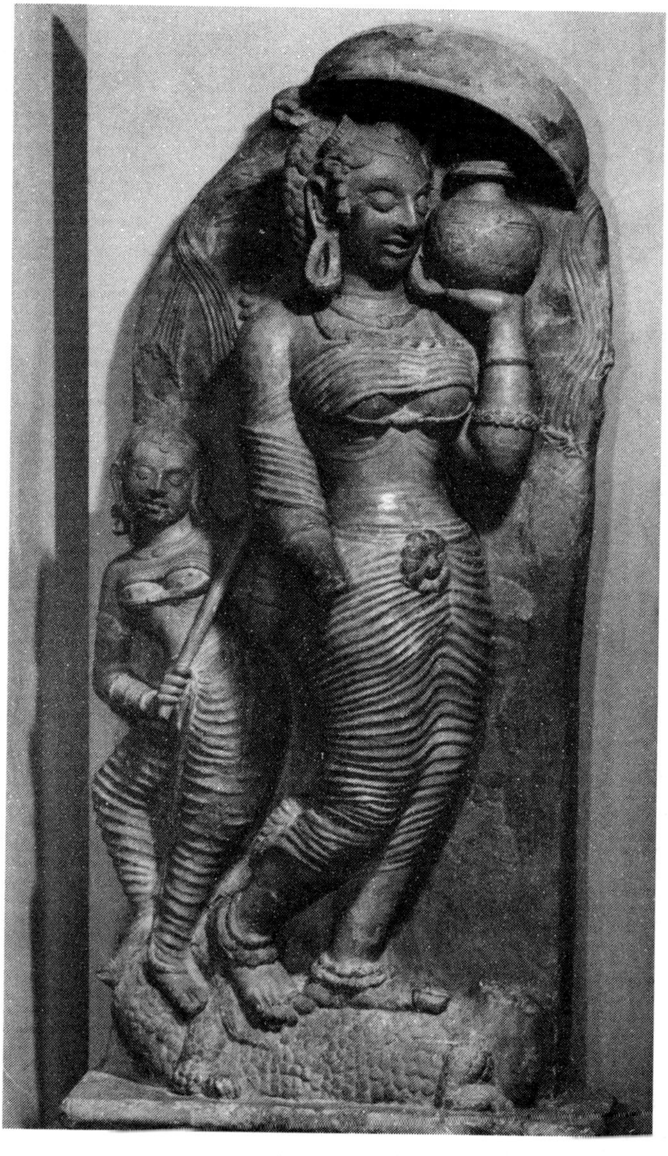

Fig. 1. Gaṅgā riding on Makara (crocodile) with parasol-bearer, Ahicchatra, U.P.

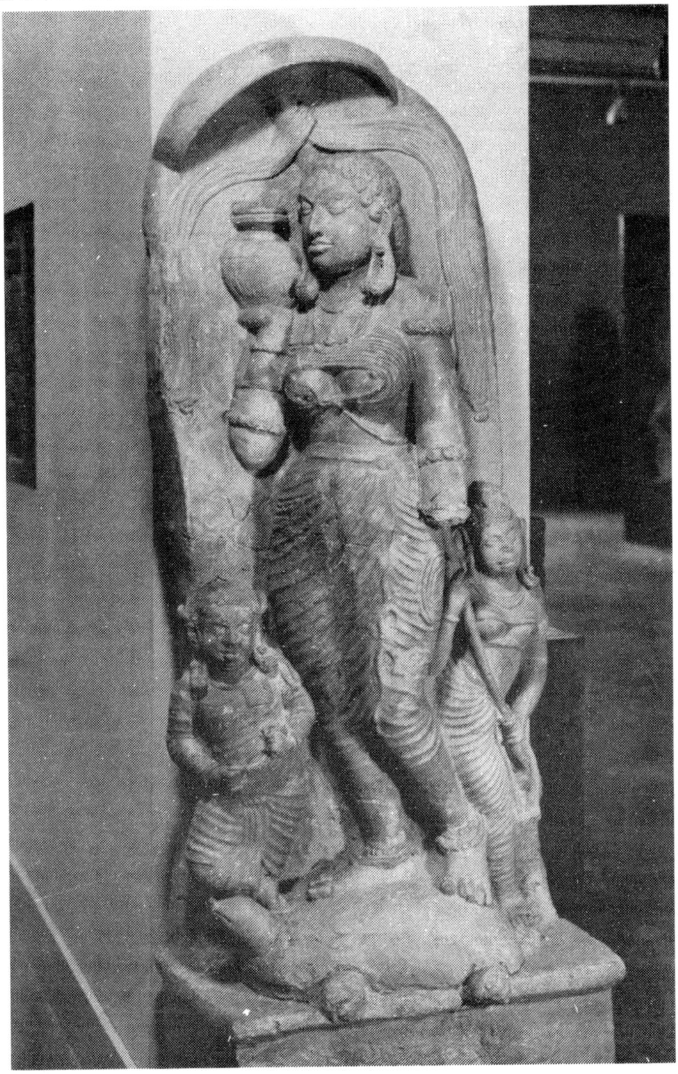

Fig. 2. Yamunā riding on Kurma (tortoise) with parasol-hearer and Gaṇa figure, Ahicchatra, U.P.

of depiction centres round human, animal, floral motifs and designs. The best surviving examples come from Bhitargaon (Bhītargâṁv), Śrāvastī, Ahicchatra, in the Doab region. A hoard of decorated plaques and bricks are noticed in various museums and private collections in India and abroad. All these betray unmistakable Doab character. It is quite likely that many more temples might have existed once in this pivotal region of

India where suitable clay for production of terracotta was available in plenty and served as alternate to stone, latter being both expensive and rare in the plains. Temples and monasteries ornamented with decorated bricks and plaques have been found outside the orbit of the Doab region. The finer examples survived at Mirpur Khas (Mīrpūr Khāṣ), Brahmanabad (Brāhmaṇābād; Sindh, Pakistan), Bodopal (Bodopāl), Rangmahal (Raṅgmahāl), Nagri (Nagrī; Rajasthan), Devnimori (Gujrat). There exists many stylistic parallelisms between the terracotta productions and stone sculptures of the time.

2. Technique of Manufacture

The technique of terracotta manufacture in this period did not differ fundamentally much from the present day method prevalent till recently in India specially in remote rural areas. In India, one can easily study the continuity of many traditional arts and crafts, although the necessity of using figures and objects in clay has diminished due to fragile character as well as high cost involved in production and change of taste. Still on account of observance of religious rites and social customs objects made out of clay are in need even today. Till now as playthings of children, toys made out of clay applied with variety of synthetic colours are in use in rural India and these are generally available on the occasion of village fairs and festivals. Due to easy availability of toys made out of synthetic medium comparatively at cheap rate, terracotta toys are no more in demand. Same is the fate of painted animal wooden toys of Benares (Vārāṇasī; Uttar Pradesh). Till recently these attractive colourful toys were available in Beneras but hardly available now.

The terracottas in this period are primarily produced out of moulds. Both single and double moulds were in use. These were applied with pigments to make them attractive to children. Generally red ochre (hematite clay containing iron oxide) was applied. Other common colours being white and black, for obtaining white pigment, calcium carbonate known as *khadi* or *khariya* was used. A kind of pyrolusite (manganese dioxide) produced black pigment or sometimes lamp black or soot (*kājal*) was used. The Gupta artists gave emphasis on the selection of clay. Unlike the Kūṣāṇa artists they used well levigated clay for producing terracottas. These were well fired and as such when found in excavation these remain intact.

3. Broad Classification of the Types

The whole range of terracotta art of the period under review can be classified into two distinct categories on the basis of their functional roles, sizes and mode of manufacture. The first category comprises of images, either in relief or in the round, installed in the niches of temples or on bodies of temples, monasteries, *stūpa*s. To this

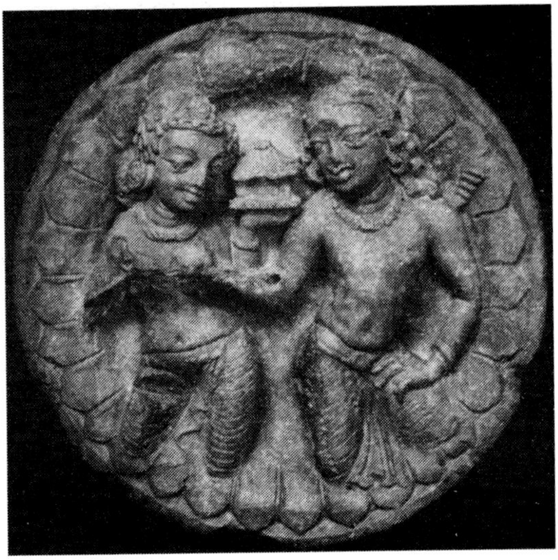

Fig. 3. Amorous couple, Mahāsthān-gaṛh, Bangladesh.

variety belongs the figures of Gaṅgā and Yamunā from Ahicchatra (Uttar Pradesh). This category also includes the moulded ornamented bricks, tiles and panels used as part of architectural decorations, depicting divine, semi-divine human figures, narrative scenes from the epics and the *Purāṇa*s, composite animals, vegetal motifs etc. All these are produced out of single mould. We have examples of this category from some sites in the Uttar Pradesh like Bhitargaon (Bhītargâm̐v), Sahet Mahet, Mahasthangarh (Mahāstāngaṛ), Saralpur, Palasbadi (Bangladesh). Parallel examples are available from Bodopal, Raṅgmāhal (Rajasthan), Devnimori (Gujarat), Mirpur Khas (Mīrpūr K͟hāṣ), Brāhmaṇābād (Sindh, Pakistan), Akhnur (Akhnūr; Jammū) etc. It is interesting to note that in the Gangetic plains we come across the identity-tag written near the figures in characteristic Gupta script thereby making the identity beyond any doubt. This kind of identity tag has not been found in the terracottas of the preceding Kūṣāṇa period.

The second category of terracottas of this period consists of small figurines and plaques. Most of these plaques represent isolated male and female heads, busts, standing male and female figures in various poses and postures with elaborate hair styles and motifs, mother and child variety, riders on horse and elephant, Gaṇa figures, *Dampati* (couple). Here both religious and secular themes are represented, latter outnumbering the former. These are produced almost mechanically from single mould but plaques made out of double moulds are not wanting. Terracottas of this category hail from many renowned Gupta centres in the Doab like Ahicchatra, Bhīta, Kauśam̐bī, Jhūsī, Rājghāṭ (Uttar Pradesh), Kumrahar (Bihar), Tamluk, Deulpota (West Bengal) and many others. We should remember that in Gupta art human figures played the pivotal role. The artists paid particular attention in representing human figures with

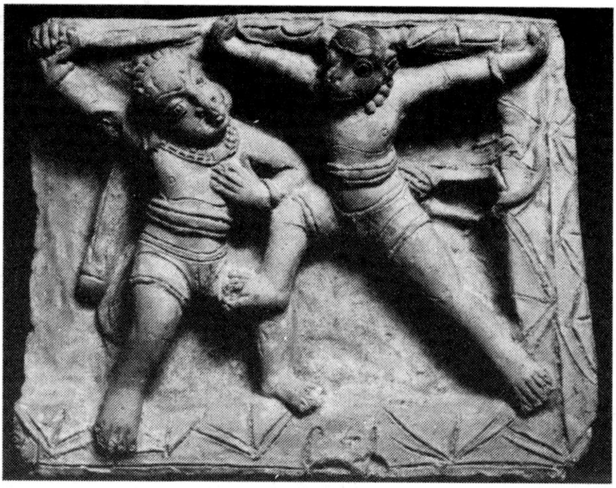

Fig. 4. Hanuman fighting a devil, Bhītargâṁv, U.P.

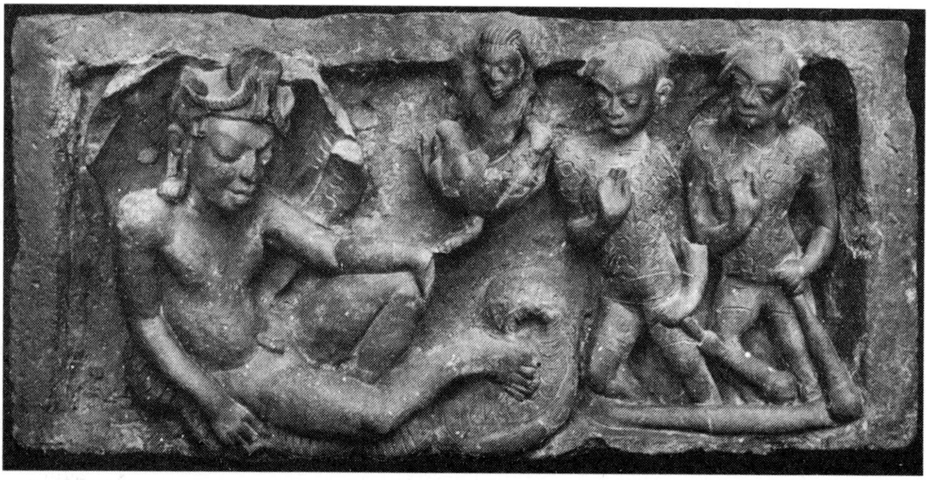

Fig. 5. *Viṣṇv-ananta-śayin*, Vishnu lying on snake Ananta, Bhītargâṁv, U.P.

varieties of hair fashions. No other period paid so much attention to the prevailing style. This is a distinct feature in Gupta period terracottas. The most common prevailing hairstyle in female coiffure consists of trefoil hairstyle with hair arranged in two prominent side masses and a central topknot. The man's fashion during the time under review consists of twisted curly hair arranged in parallel tiers and superimposed one above the other extending either to the shoulder or to the ears. The following male and female hair doing are noticeable among the Gupta terracotta figures in the valley.

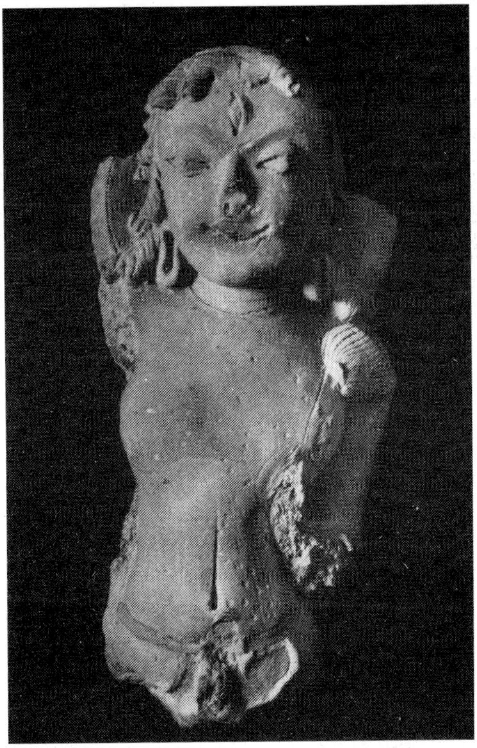

Fig. 6. Śiva, Faizabad, U.P.

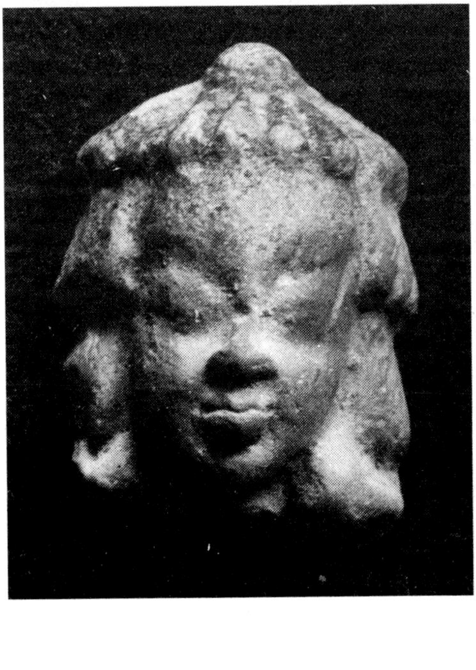

Fig. 7. Male head, Jhūsī, U.P.

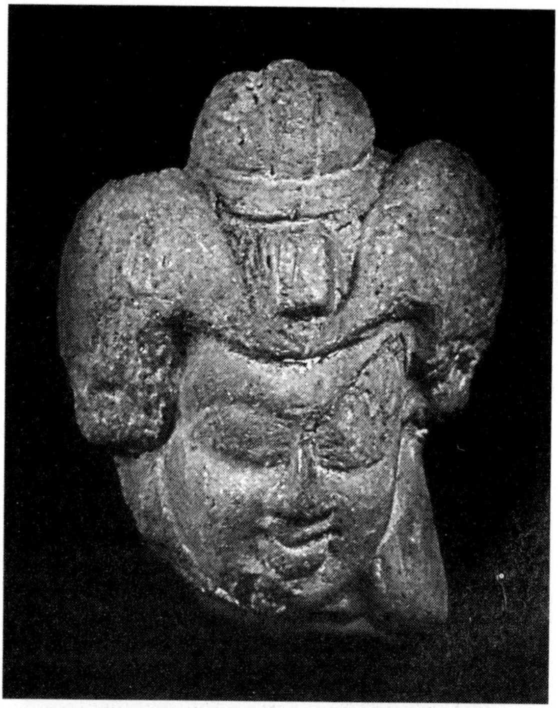

Fig. 8. Female head with trefoil hair style and crest-jewel, Bhīta, U.P.

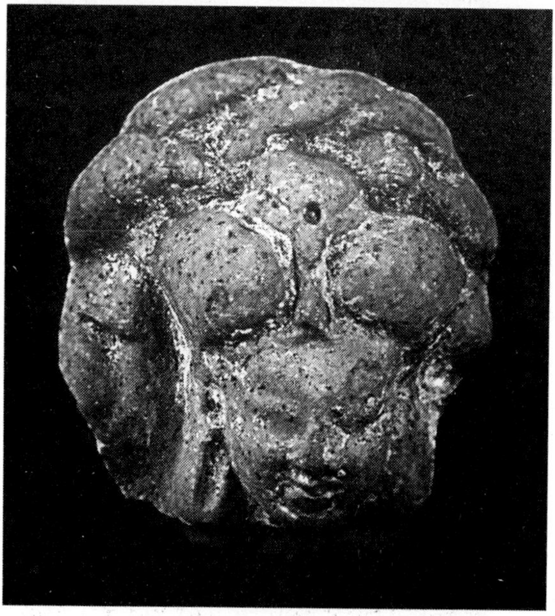

Fig. 9. Female head with crest-jewel, Bhīta, U.P.

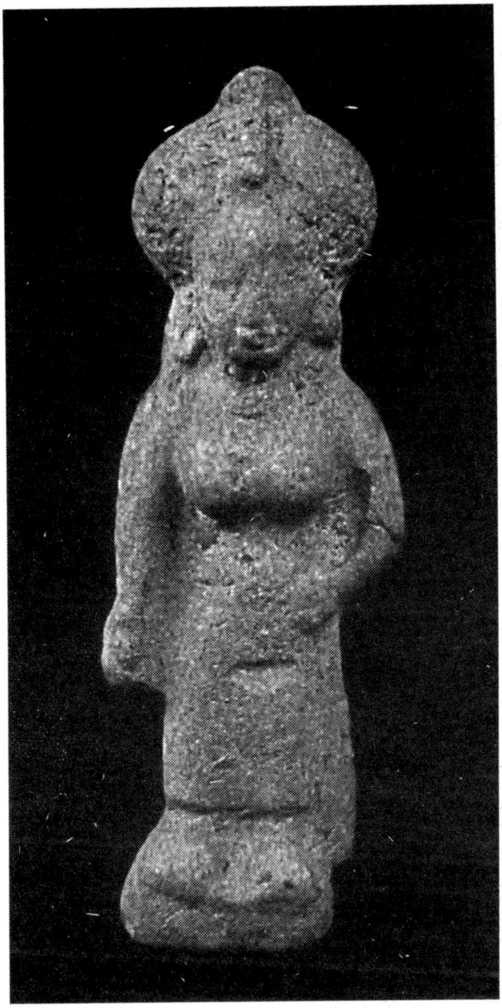

Fig. 10. Female figure, Kauśaṁbī, U.P.

4. Types Available

4.1. Male and Female Heads and Busts

A large number of terracotta figurines represent men and women conforming to a standard and style. These are all cast from single moulds. Most of these appear to be pigmented, as traces of pigments can still be seen in many heads and busts. A great variety of hair doing is noticeable in both male and female heads, pointing out the prevailing hair fashions in this period. That kind of hairstyle was widespread over

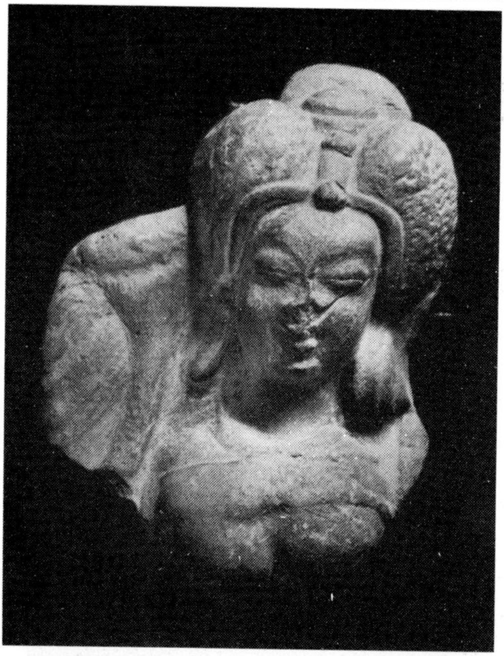

Fig. 11. Female bust, Bhīta, U.P.

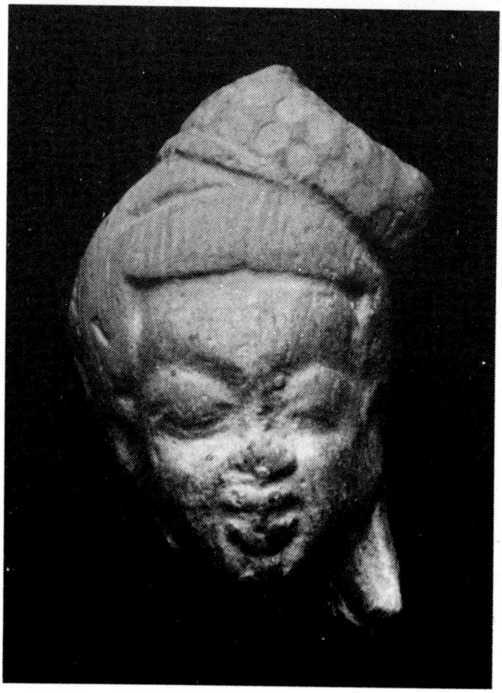

Fig. 12. Female head with coiffure, Jhūsī, U.P.

an extensive region from Begram (Bagrām, Afghanistan) in the west to Deulpota (West Bengal) in the east.

The following fashions of hair doing are noticeable among the men's heads:

1) The hair covers the head resembling a semi-circular parasol (*chattrâkara*) with hair locks set like ribs close to each other all radiating from a topknot. On the two sides, the gorgeous wig-like hair (*alakâvatī*) comes down in three or even more, gradually receding tiers either to the ears or on to the shoulder (fig. 7).
2) In others, same style is noticeable but with a central parting. The latter in mentioned in the literature as *sīmanta* or *keśa-vīthī.*

This type of wig like hair extending up to the shoulder was a fashion in Europe in the late 18th and in the 19th centuries.

A variety of hair fashions has been observed in the female heads of the Gupta period. The common prevailing fashion consists of the trefoil style comprising two prominent side masses with a crest jewel placed in the centre.

a) Trefoil hairstyle with a single or double crest-jewel adorning the central parting (*sīmanta*). This kind of fashion may be designated as *catula-tilaka-maṇi* or *śikhaṇḍa-khaṇḍikā*. Sometimes the crest-jewel rests on a flat band in the middle. Further, the shape of the jewel differs, sometimes being round or elongated and sometimes with dots on either end (figs. 8, 9, 10 and 11).
b) In honey-comb fashion the lateral masses are shown like a honey-comb of cellular structure. The style is extremely beautiful and appears to be widely popular at many places like Ahicchatra, Bhīta, Kauśaṁbī, Rājghāṭ and Mathurā.
c) The hair is tied in a single prominent bun and found tilting to the left or to the right. Sometimes, a jewel string, possibly of pearls is tied on the coiffure, thereby adding more beauty to the hair (fig. 12).

4.2. Mother and Child Group (fig. 13)

This group is widely prevalent in the Gaṅgā-Yamunā Valley in the early historical period. This was well known in the Kūṣāṇa period. Generally these are produced in shallow mould. Two varieties, viz. *kṣīra-dhātrī* (mother with a sucking baby) and *arika-dhātrī* (mother with a baby in arms) are known. In some Sanskrit Buddhist texts, particularly in the *Divyâvadana*, we come across references to female nurses who were employed to attend on the royal princes and scions of the nobility.

Many of these specimens have been found in stratigraphic contexts from excavations at Ahicchatra, Rājghāṭ and Kumaher, which confirms their chronology.

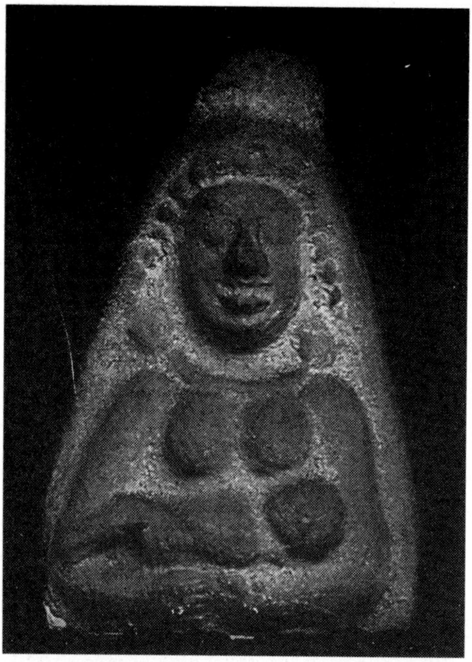

Fig. 13. Mother and child, Bhīta, U.P.

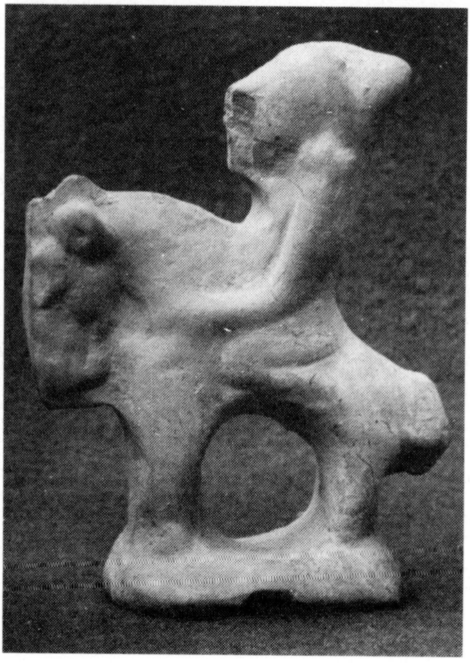

Fig. 14. Horse rider, Kannauj, U.P.

4.3. Horse and Elephant Riders Type

A large number of horse and elephant riders variety have been found in all the Gupta sites in the Doab region. Sometimes the above two animals are noticed with or without riders. A close study of the two varieties reveals that both survived side by side in the period under review. The figures are invariably produced out of double moulds, either solid or hollow inside. The horses are generally beautifully modelled. The details of the horse's trappings are present in some specimens, which consist of beautiful saddle, reins and stirrup. A few well-preserved horse and elephant-riders wear conical skullcap tilting backwards (fig. 14).

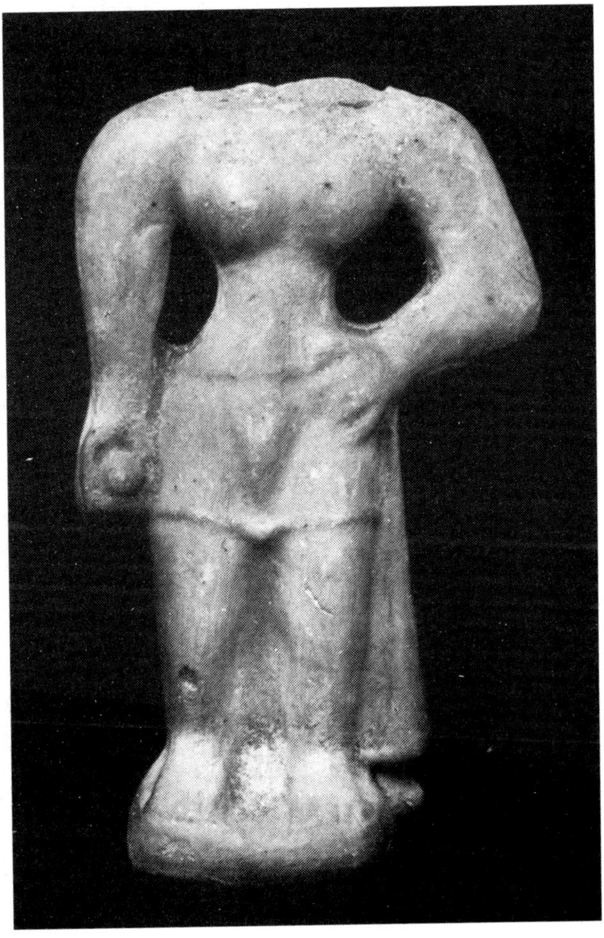

Fig. 15. Worshipper variety, Bhīta, U.P.

4.4. Worshipper Variety (fig. 15)

This group is mainly confined to male figures, characterised by a distinct position of the two arms, the left resting on the waist (*kaṭi-vinyasta-vāma-pāṇi*) and the right hanging by the side (*laṭa-hasta*), holding a round shaped object which may be identified as the citron fruit (*bīja-pūraka*, *citrus medica*). We come to know from the Sanskrit text *Mālavikâgnimitra* by renowned poet Kālidāsa that the prevailing custom of the time was that the visitors waiting on persons of high position did not go empty-handed but with some gift. The revered lady, *parivrājikā* directs her attendant to get a citron fruit from the royal pleasure grove with which, as a mark of respect, she should visit the queen.

The worshipper variety was a popular theme of the time as attested by plentiful finds from Ahicchatra (Uttar Pradesh), where these are found in Stratum IIIa, dated CD 650–750. At the site of Kumrahar (Patna, Bihar), this group is ascribed to periods IV and V (CD 300–600).

Similar finds are found at Bhīta (Uttar Pradesh) in plenty. This group is distinguished by prominent masculine form with broad shoulders. The finest variety of the worshipper group is found at Bhīta. The figures are found standing in the *dvi-bhaṅga* posture, wearing embroidered cloth down to the knees and a twisted upper garment (*uttarīya*) wound round the waist obliquely, the flowing ends of which are held by the left hand, while the right hand holds the fruit. The figures are characterised by soft, pliant body, having a supple gracefulness. Their distinct plastic modelling with luminosity betrays unquestionable Gupta character (fig. 16).

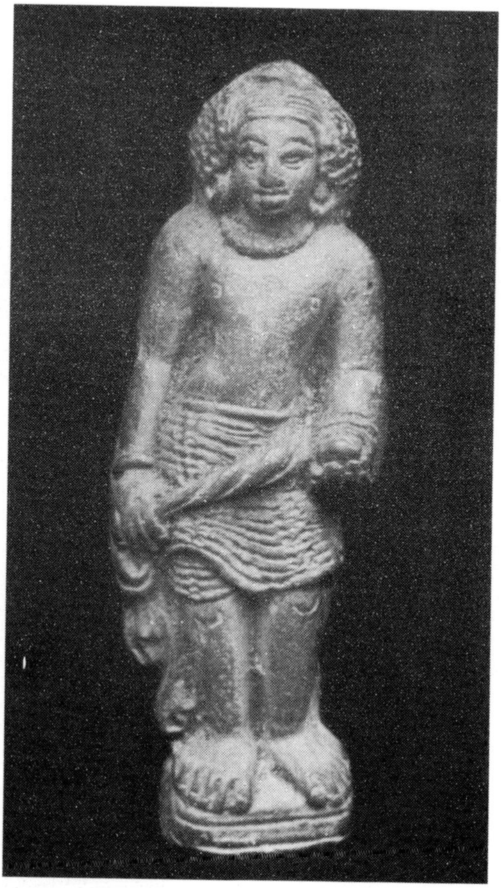

Fig. 16: Worshipper variety, Bhīta,U.P.

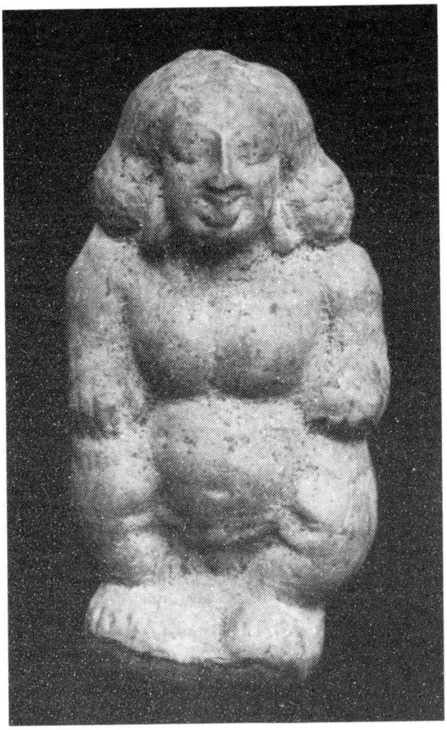

Fig. 17. Gaṇa figurine, Bhīta, U.P.

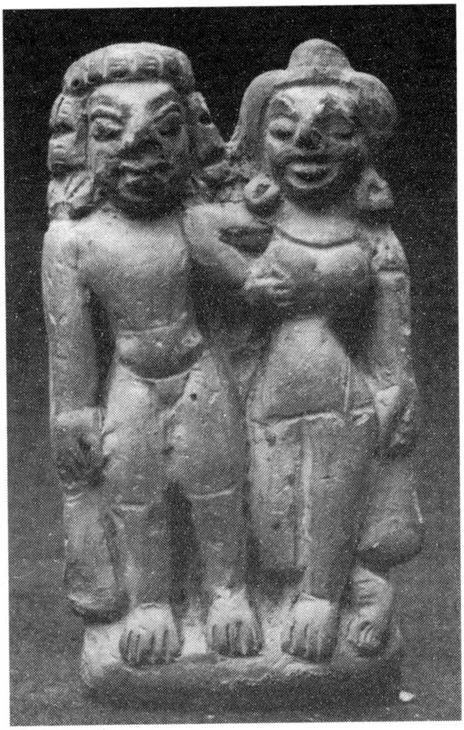

Fig. 18. *Dampati* (Couple), Kannauj, U.P.

4.5. Gaṇa Figures (fig.17)

Gaṇa figures were popular theme in this period. These are characterised by short bodies, beautiful curly hair extending up to the shoulders with a *sīmanta* (central parting) and a top-knot in the middle. The figures also hold a round-shaped object, possibly a fruit (*bīja-pūraka*) in the right hand while the left in akimbo. These grotesque figures are described in Sanskrit literatures under various names, like *vamana*, *vikaṭa*, *kubjaka*, *gaṇa*, *kumbhâṇḍa* etc. They are regarded as the tutelary attendants of Śiva, Gaṇapati (Ganeśa) Kārttikeya and Kuvera.

4.6. *Dampati* or Couple (fig. 18)

Dampati, or couple standing side by side, seems to be a popular theme in the Gupta terracotta art. This variety has been found almost in all the Gangetic valley sites in this period. The sites include Ahicchatra, Bhīta, Jhūsī, Kauśaṁbī, Rājghāṭ, Kumrahar.

4.7. Female Heads with Haloes (fig. 19)

A few female figures, mostly incomplete are characterised by haloes behind their heads. The very presence of haloes associated these with some divinities. Due to absence of any other details, nothing definite can be said about them.

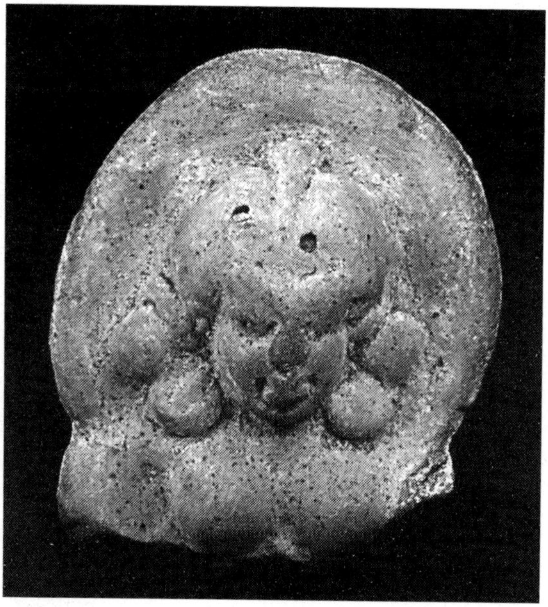

Fig. 19. Female head with haloe, Bhīta, U.P.

The artists paid equal attention to toys for children. Generally, two types of game objects were popular, one consisting of rattles and the other toy-carts on wheels. The animals represented include pig, bull, tortoise and bird. Ram having prominent curved horns seems to be a favourite theme for the toy-carts. These are either pushed by a stick inserted through a hole at the back made for the purpose, or drawn by a cord. In the preceding Śuṅga and the Kūṣāṇa periods, we come across plentiful of toys for children. The same tradition continued in the Gupta period also. The workmanship appears to be finer than the preceding periods.

BIBLIOGRAPHY

AGARWALLA 1947–1948 = Agarwalla, Vasudeva, Sharana: 'Terracotta figurines of Ahichchhatra, District Barielly, U.P' *Ancient India* 4 (1947–1948) 104–179.

ALTAKER–MISHRA 1959 = Altaker, Anant Sadashiv; Mishra, V.K.: 'Report on Kumrahar Excavations 1951–55' Patna 1959.

ASIAR 1911–1912 = *Archaeological Survey of India-Annual Report*, 1911–1912.

BASU 2005 = Basu, Durga: *The N.B.P. Culture of Eastern India*. 2 Vols, Kolkata 2005.

BAUTZE 1995 = Bautze, Joachim Karl: *Early Indian Terracottas*. E.J. Brill, Leiden 1995.

BHATTACHARYA 2002 = Bhattacharya, Ashok. K.: 'Terracotta of Bengal: Sunga and Kushana', [in:] Pratapaditya Pal (ed.): *Indian Terracotta Sculpture: the Early Period*. Marg Publication, Mumbai: 58–73.

CHANDRA 1977 = Chandra, Promode: *From River Banks and Sacred Places: Ancient Indian Terracottas: An Exhibition to Commemorate the One-hundredth Anniversary of the Birth of Ananda K. Coomaraswamy*. Museum of Fine Arts, Boston 1977.

DAS GUPTA 1961 = Das Gupta, Charu Chandra: *Origin and Evolution of Indian Clay Sculpture*. Calcutta 1961.

DESAI 1978 = Desai, Devangana: 'Social Background of Ancient Indian Terracottas in History and Society (circa 600 B.C. – A.D. 600', [in:] Chattopadhyaya (ed.): *Essays in Honour of Professor Niharranjan Ray*. Calcutta 1975: 143–168.

DEVA–MISHRA 1961 = Deva, Krishna; Mishra, Vijaya Kanta: *Vaiśālī Excavations 1950*. Vaiśālī Saṅgh, Vaiśālī (Bihar) 1961.

GUPTA 1972 = Gupta, P.L.: *Gangetic Valley Terracotta Art*. Varanasi 1972.

HARLE 1974 = Harle, J.C.: *Gupta Sculpture: Indian Sculpture of the 4th to the 6th Centuries*. Oxford 1974.

JOSHI–MARGABANDHU 1976–77 = Joshi, M.C.; Margabandhu, C.: Some Terracottas from Excavations at Mathura—A Study', *Journal of the Indian Society of Oriental Art* 8 (1976–77) 16–32.

KALA 1980 = Kala, Satish Chandra: *Terracottas in the Allahabad Museum*. Allahabad Municipal Museum, New Delhi 1980.

MUKHERJEE 1971 = Mukherjee, Samir Kumar: 'Some Interesting Gupta Terracotta Figurines from Lower Bengal', *Journal of the Asiatic Society* 13 (1971) 1–4 [Calcutta].

MUKHERJEE 1972 = Mukherjee, Samir Kumar: 'Terracotta from Bhita', *Artibus Asiae* 23 (1972) 71–94.

MUKHERJEE 1987 = Mukherjee, Samir Kumar: 'Terracotta Art in Bengal and Its Aftermath', *Ancient Indian History Philosophy and Culture (Essays in memory of Prof. Radhagovinda Basak Vidyāvācaspati.* Calcutta 1987: 180–185.

MUKHERJEE 1987 = Mukherjee, Samir Kumar: 'Terracotta Art in the Gangetic Valley under the Kushans', [in:] Pratapaditya Pal (ed.): *Indian Clay Sculptures Early Period.* Mumbai 2002: 74–85.

MUKHERJEE 1991 = Mukherjee, Samir Kumar: 'Early Terracotta Figurines from West Bengal—A Study Based on Stratigraphic Evidence from Excavations', [in:] Asok Datta (ed.): *Studies in Archaeology: Papers presented in Memory of P.C. Dasgupta.* New Delhi 1991: 217–230.

PAL 1978 = Pal, Pratapaditya: *The Ideal Images: The Gupta Sculptural Tradition and Its Influence.* Asia Society, Asia House Gallery, New York 1978.

Poster 1986 = Poster, Amy G.: *From Indian Earth 4000 years of Terracotta Art,* The Brooklyn Museum, New York 1986.

ROY 1983 = Roy, T.N.: *The Ganges Civilization.* New Delhi 1983.

SANKALIA–DHOVLIKAR 1969 = Sankalia, H.D.; Dhovlikar, M.K.: 'The Terracotta Art of India', *Marg Publications* 23,1 (1969) 32–54.

SENGUPTA–CHOWDHURY–CHAKRABORY 2007 = Sengupta, Gautam; Chowdhury, Sima Roy; Chakrabory, Sharmi: *Eloquent Earth. Early Terracottas in the State Archaeological Museum, West Bengal.* Directorate of Archaeology and Museum, Kolkata 2007.

SHARMA 1960 = Sharma, G.R.: *The Excavations at Kaushambi (1957–59).* Dept. of Ancient History, Culture and Archaeology, Allahabad University, Allahabad 1960.

SHARMA 1969 = Sharma, G.R.: *The Excavations at Kaushambi (1949–50).* Memories of the Archaeological Survey of India 74, Calcutta, 1969.

VOGEL 1907–1908 = Vogel, J.(P.): *Excavations at Saheth-Maheth.* Archaeological Survey of India-Annual Report, Delhi 1907–1908: 81–131.

VOGEL 1908–1909 = Vogel, J.(P.): *Temple at Bhitargaon.* Archaeological Survey of India Annual Report, Delhi 1908–09: 5–16.

Chemical Conservation Of Hīnayāna Paintings 2nd BCE, Cave No. 10 Ajanta*

M. SINGH, R.S. TRAMBAKE, D.A. GUPTA
(Archaeological Survey of India, Science Branch, Ajanta Caves)

Abstract

The conservation problems of cave paintings of Ajanta (Eds. Ajantā / Ajaṁtā) are highly complex and vary from cave No. 1 to cave No. 26 situated adjacent to each other. A few square meters of Hīnayāna mural paintings (2nd century BCE) still surviving in caves no. 9 and 10 in Ajanta, poses greatest problem of conservation on account of application of many layers of varnishes in the past after its discovery in 1819. Various kinds of varnish layers intermixed with soot and dirt have made the original paintings totally invisible and the surface is marked with pattern of cracks and loss of pigment layers. Extensive damage on account of visitor's graffiti can also be noticed on these panels. For the first time a two-component chemical system were used for removal of accretions and to expose of painted surface in cave no. 10, Ajanta. The scientifically treated area is closely being monitored since last ten years. This paper outlines the measures adopted for the scientific conservation work of highly complex Hīnayāna paintings along with the results obtained.

Introduction

The increasing interest of the conservators and art historians in the caves of Ajanta as part of world heritage site is more than justified. Ajanta is a sole monumental record of classical Buddhist culture, which has influenced the culture of Asian countries[1]. The painted Buddhist legends proclaim ethics wherein help to distress is valued

---

* We are thankful to Shri K. S. Rana, Director (Science), Archaeological Survey of India, Dehradun, for his support and encouragement.

[1] ZIN (1998: 435–448).

Art, Myths and Visual Culture of South Asia
Warsaw Indological Studies 4 (2011) 251–259.

higher than one's own life[2]. Ajanta painters were guided by a highly developed sense of blending of colours with a view to produce total impression with three-dimensional effect giving true perspective to lines and planes. Ajanta masters use woman as incarnation of all the beauty of the world with extensive use of ornamentation.

Two of the six pre-Christian Ajanta caves, the cave no. 9 and cave no. 10 are decorated with paintings on their walls, ceilings and pillars. These most ancient cave paintings of 9 and 10 caves dates back to 2nd century BCE .At some point during the second phase of building activity in Ajanta around 5th century CE, artist redecorated the caves of earlier period by introducing intrusive paintings. However, some of the original paintings were left untouched and survived to this day. The oldest mural of cave no. 10 presents Jātaka stories in a number of different scenes.

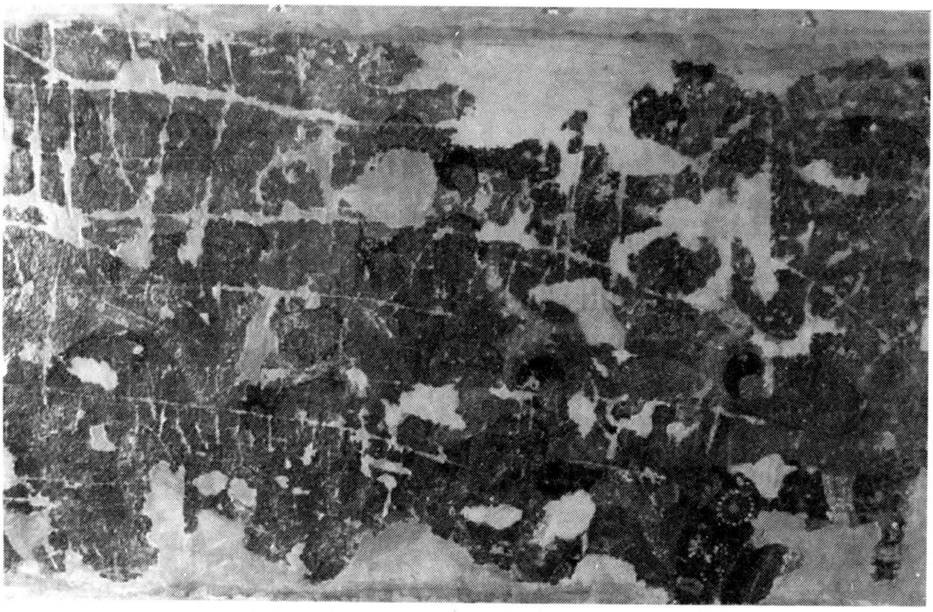

Photo 1. Visitors graffiti on painted plaster of cave no. 10, Ajanta.
[For a colour print, see the Appendix]

Most of early wall paintings in cave no. 10 were copied in the 19th century when they were in much better state of preservation than today. On the basis of these copies a number of Jātaka stories were identified in the cave no. 10, the important being the *Saddanta*- and *Śyāma-jātaka*s. All the painted plaster has been perma-

[2] SCHLINGLOFF (1998).

nently lost upto 4–5 feet from the floor level and, at the time of discovery of the caves, painted pillars were found damaged at different height. Some of the painted pillars were permanently lost due to accumulation of filth and mud in the cave during its long history.

As the caves remained undiscovered for about 1500 years, many painting has been fallen of the wall with the layers of lime plaster and have been irretrievably lost[3]. Parts that are intact are worn off, darkened by soot from lamps or washed out by bat's excreta. Apart from the aforesaid damages, the paintings of cave no. 10 have probably been lost badly by scratches of visitor's graffiti (Photo 1), which is observed upto 8–9 feet from the floor level. To save the painting of cave no. 10 from graffiti, the whole panel was kept under glass protection in 1965 and now popularly known as glass panel paintings both on the right- and left-hand sides of the *caitya* hall.

In contrast to other caves of Ajanta, the whole painted plaster of cave no. 10 has been executed on thin lime plaster on a basaltic rock carrier of Deccan trap having smooth surface. Of the many causes of deterioration of the painting been noticed at Ajanta, probably the most dangerous are humidity and insect activity along with water seepages in the caves. Variation in temperature and humidity in the painted caves of 1, 2, 16 and 17 are being monitored on a long terms basis to study its impact on the painted surfaces. While the caves are almost thermally stable (temperature variation between 27°–30° C), wide fluctuation in the humidity has been observed. From the measurement of humidity inside the cave no. 1 (fig. 1), it has been observed that humidity (inside) reaches upto max. of 65 to 72.5% in the month of September and to the low of 28 to 35% in the month of March. This variation in the humidity causes the pigment to flake from the ground and at other point causes ridges, brusting of paint layers or the whole of painted plaster fallen from its stone carrier. This adds to the already existing problem of the flow of visitors within the caves during the tourist season of September to January every year. For this purpose the number of visitors inside the caves were counted by manual counting at every 15–minute interval from 9 am to 5:30 p.m. when the caves are open. Electronic Thermo hygrograph ISUZU model 3126 was placed in the central hall of the cave no. 2 with one-day chart to measure humidity. As the cave remains closed to visitors on Monday, the humidity was recorded when there is no visitor at all. The result of our observations is shown in fig. 2. The humidity remains static on Mondays at around 36% to 37 % level. However, as soon as visitors entered the caves at 9 a.m. the humidity due to exhale of visitors started to increase. Though the entry of more than 40 visitors at one time is restricted in the caves, due to tourist rush at some point of time there were approximately 100 visitors and at an average more than 60

[3] SPINK (1991).

visitors were always present inside the caves. The resultant impact is 7 to 8% increase in R.H. on account of visitor's inflow, which takes 1–2 hours to come to normal value after 5:30 p.m.

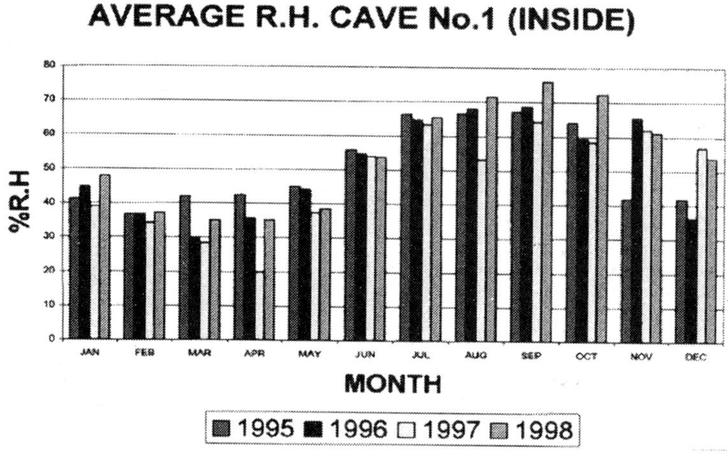

Fig. 1. Graph showing average R.H. inside the cave no.1 in Ajanta

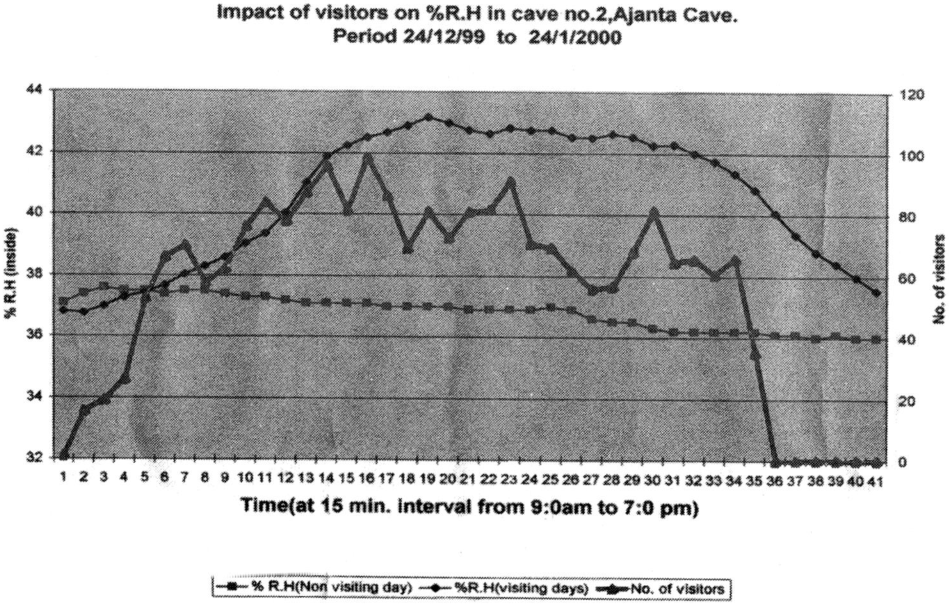

Fig. 2. Graph showing impact of visitors on %R.H cave no. 2 in Ajanta

To undo the cause and distribute the tourist equally to the entire cave, the Archaeological Survey of India has recently undertaken the following measures:

1) Two causeways in front of Waghur River have been constructed to avoid rush to the painted caves no. 1 and 2. This will also reduce the visitors' perspiration on account of their climbing up the hill.
2) All the caves have now been properly illuminated so the visitors can see every point of the caves carefully. The painted caves no. 1, 2, 16, 17 and 19 have been illuminated with newly introduced fiber optic system which gives very cool light with intensity below 20 LUX without any heat.
3) On the basis of geotechnical studies carried out by the Geological Survey of India, some conservation measures have also been taken to strengthen the existing drainage system on the top of the caves to stop seepage of water.

Chemical Conservation and Preservation

The glass panel paintings of cave no. 10 were taken up for carrying out chemical cleaning work in the years 1999–2000 after an in-house long deliberation with the conservators of Archaeological Survey of India. The glass of the panel was carefully taken out and external dust, dirt etc. on the painted plaster were slowly removed with very soft sable hair brushes. On close observation the paintings were found completely masked under thick accretion of varnishes, soot, dust, and on top were visitors' graffiti. So thick were the accretionary deposits on this panel that the entire painted figures were totally obscure and hardly visible. On tracing the reasons for such thick accretions not present in any other cave at Ajanta, it was understood that for each coping of the painting, varnishes such as copal etc., were applied on the surface to brighten the colours under the light of oil lamp. The subsequent copier never removed the varnishes and soot deposited by earlier copier, before applying his/her own varnishes. Finally in 1920 an Italian restorer applied a thick coat of unbleached shellac varnish to the already varnished surface without removing the old layers[4], which resulted in a thick coat of varnishes admixed with soot, dust/dirt and accretion from outside. Meanwhile, the thick shellac also changed colour to reddish brown due to oxidation in Indian climate and on contraction created a pattern of cracks in the body of the original paintings. Meanwhile, a tragedy occurred and most of the copies of the paintings carried out in 19th century were lost in crystal palace fire in London in 1866 and Victoria and Albert Museum fire in London in 1885. So fascinated were Buddhist scholars from Japan to see these paintings that in

[4] PARAMASIVAN (1936–37: 25–30).

1918 a Japanese copiest Mr. Sentaro Sawamura, a professor of Oriental art at Kyoto University and a painter Kampo Arai made copies of the paintings using sheets of thin Japanese art paper which they dampened witt some varnish and then pressed against the walls and took hundred of copies. However, an earthquake destroyed the entire collection some years later.

The paintings were so fragile that there was a great fear even to touch them with hand. At some places the pigment was found completely detached from the ground plaster and at a number of points voids were observed between the plaster and stone surface. The insect holes such as silver fishes etc. were noticed all around the body of the paintings. The gray colour filleting materials used in 1920 by Italian restores were also found detached at some places. Some of the pigments such as green, red etc. were found particularly lost from the surface owing to its lesser adherence. Intrusive fifth century CE paintings were also noticed in the panel, which is of different artistic signification. All the above reasons made the work of conservation of these paintings highly sophisticated and challenging one.

The whole of the panel were thoroughly photographed including microphotography at some of the places where condition of the painting was very alarming. The conservation work of the panel was initiated after filling the gaps and fixing the detached layer of the paintings by lime that is very close to the composition of original lime used in ground surface. Particular care and precautions were taken not to alter even a grain of pigments during the course of fixing and filleting work. The panel was left to dry for about two months after the fixing work for proper adherence at the surfaces.

After complete drying of the surface actual chemical cleaning work was initiated under a magnifying lens. As the accretion and varnishes applied at different times were quite different in nature from one another, it was not possible to devise a solution, which was applicable universally. Hence, a different class of organic solutions in proper proportion was prepared as per experience and demand of the work for removal of each type of accretions.

The hard soot along with a thick coating of shellac varnishes encountered in the first stage was chemically removed with the help of mixture of morpholene, N-butyl amine, butyl lactate, butanol, ethanol, dimethyl formamide, approximately in the ratio of 1 : ¼ : ½ : 2 : ½ respectively with the help of sable hairbrushes. The painted surface was kept dampened with this mixture for about 3–4 minutes depending on the thickness of shellac layer (time may vary and depends on thickness of shellac). Subsequently the accretion of varnish was removed with the help of this mixture by gently rubbing with the sable hairbrushes followed by removal of accretions with wet cotton swab dipped in the mixture.

After removing the first shellac accretions with the help of cotton swabs as above, another mixture of solvents was applied on the painted surface in order to remove sooty accretion including grime. For this purpose a pinch of EDTA was dissolved in the minimum quantity of distilled water. A few drops of ammonia were added to this with stirring. Methanol (AR grade) 17–18 ml was added in the mixture followed by 2–3 drops of triethanolamine for 25 ml solution. This solution is kept for about 15–20 minutes as a standby solution for complete mixing of solvents.

This mixture of solvent was very carefully used for the removal of accretion with the help of sable hair brushes with a pressure, which exclusively depends on the dexterity of the conservator. Particular precautions had to be taken while using this solvent so as to restrict its action only on the sooty accretion by the use of the minimum quantity of this mixture. After the removal of accretion the painted surface was dried with the help of turpentine and alcohol mixture and left for 5–6 months for complete evaporation of any left-over solution. No attempts were made to remove the last trace of accretions and as a precautionary measure 20–25% accretions have been left on the painted surface. The work was very meticulously executed with utmost precautions and 3.5 square meter painted panel of cave no. 10 was cleaned by six conservators belonging to different disciplines in one year.

The conditions before the treatment and after chemical conservation and preservation work in Cave no. 10, Ajanta, are shown in photographs 2a and 2b as well as 3a and 3b as an example.

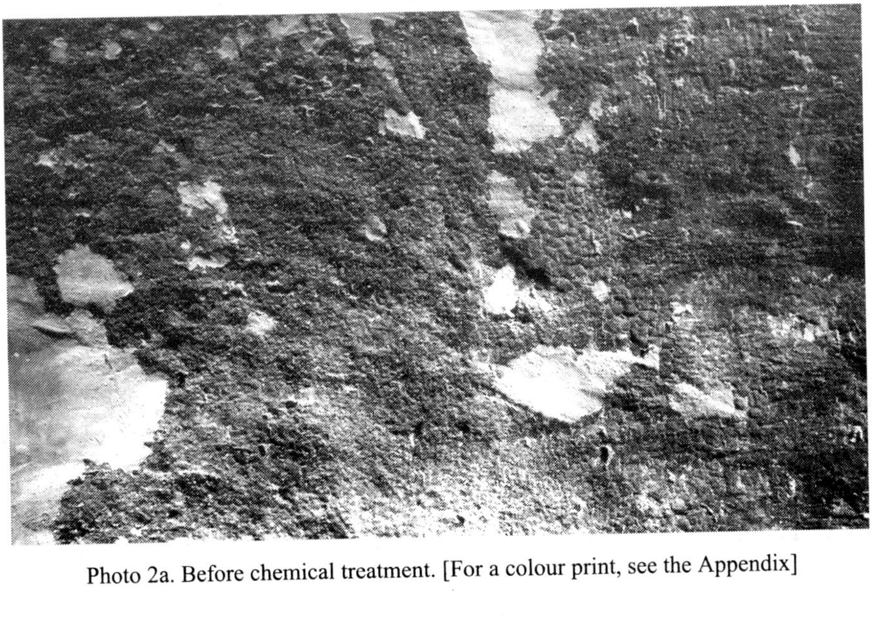

Photo 2a. Before chemical treatment. [For a colour print, see the Appendix]

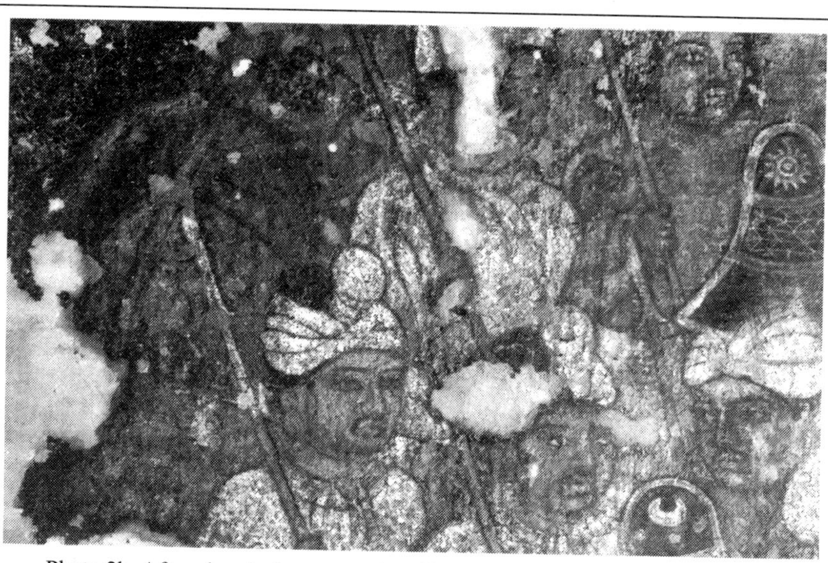

Photo 2b. After chemical conservation. [For a colour print, see the Appendix]

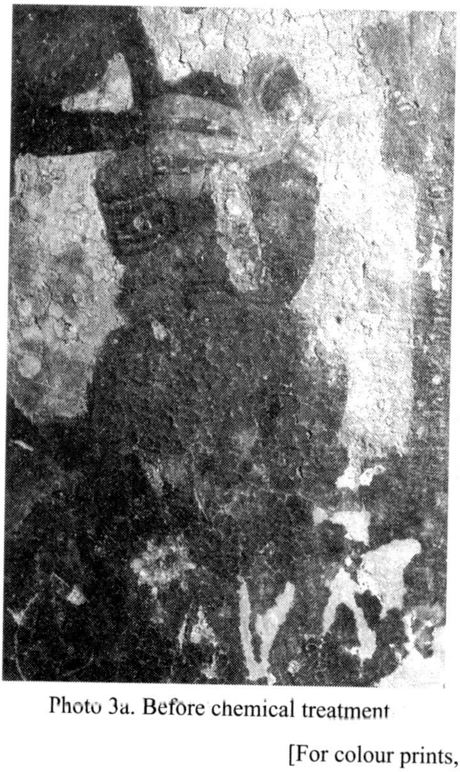

Photo 3a. Before chemical treatment

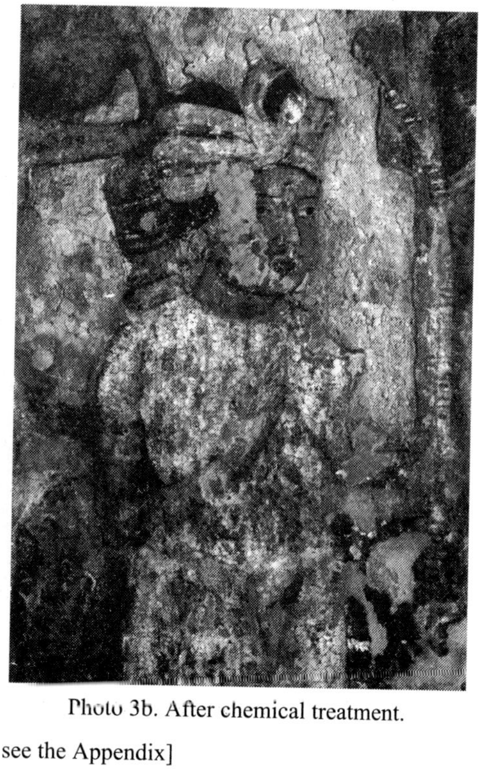

Photo 3b. After chemical treatment.

[For colour prints, see the Appendix]

Conclusion

On complete chemical conservation the following points were noticed which will be very important to carry conservation work of remaining part of the panel.

1) The surface of the outer layer of lime plaster ground is very thick.
2) The background of the colour is very simple and undecorative.
3) Maximum cracks and crevices are noticed wherever white colour has been applied in the painting.
4) Lower lips of some of the human figures are in red colour, which is very sensitive as compared to other colours.
5) Most of the human figures are painted in yellow colours.
6) All the figures' outlines have been drawn in black colours of equal thickness.
7) Green pigments are always found less adhering than any other pigments.
8) From our experimental work it was observed that the removal of accretion from white coloured surface is easier to any other colour.
9) Black outline is very thin and in contrast to cave no. 17 painting very less sensitive to cleaning solvent mixture.

The panel painting is being observed after this experimental treatment and the work will be extended to other part of the panel after strict monitoring and discussion.

BIBLIOGRAPHY

PARAMASIVAN 1936–37 = Paramasivan, S.: 'Technique of the Painting Process in the Cave Temples', *Annual Report of the Archeological Department of his Exalted Highness the Nizam's Dominions 1936–37*. Hyderabad 1939: 25–30.

SCHLINGLOFF 1998 = Dieter, Schlingloff: *Studies in the Ajanta Paintings. Identifications and Interpretations*. South Asia Books, New Delhi 1998.

SPINK 1991 = Spink, Walter M.: 'The Archaeology of Ajanta', *Ars Orientalis* 21 (1991) 67–94.

ZIN 1998 = Zin, Monika: 'The Oldest Paintings of the Udayana Legend', *Berliner Indologische Studien* 11–12 (1998) 435–448.

Reading Images and Interpreting the Context: Differentiating Between Iconography and Iconology According to Erwin Panofsky's Three Phase Analysis

ASOKA DE ZOYSA
(University of Kelaniya)

Images are seen, observed and read. This may happen consciously or unconsciously, intentionally or unintentionally. Hence observing and comprehending an image is a psychological process, and the interpretation of images is very much embedded in the culture it belongs to. To illustrate this, I select some images from Buddhist temples of the Kandyan Era.[1]

I would begin with a simple exercise in reading images at the Sūriyagoda Tämpiṭa Vihāraya, which I will refer to as 'Suriyagoda Temple'.

On entering the Suriyagoda Temple, the 'naïve visitor' who has no knowledge of rituals and arts of Buddhist culture, will take into account that the doorway is flaked by two male figures bearing swords [fig. 1]. He or she will see white objects flanked by three pairs of seated figures on the horizontal panel above the doorway. The three shapes above the doorway may appear as bell shaped buildings to our 'naïve' observer. Because the three pairs of figures are seen worshipping the object, it would seem that the edifices are being regarded with high esteem. As the images are not observed isolated, but in the context of a Buddhist Temple, our 'naïve visitor' would then identify the bell shaped buildings as *stūpa*s or *dāgäb,* which can actually be seen in the temple premises.

The naïve visitor may inquire why *stūpa*s are shown above the doorways. The Buddhist devotee on the other hand, on entering the temple, does not 'read' or process the images in the above mentioned manner, but may casually take into account

---

[1] BANDARANAYAKE (1986:17) introduces the paintings of this era as 'The Kandyan Paintings of the central highlands and contiguous north central plains, i.e. the area constituting the territory of the Kandyan Kingdom in the 18th and early 19th centuries.'

Art, Myths and Visual Culture of South Asia
Warsaw Indological Studies 4 (2011) 260–291.

that there was a 'typical doorway' marking the entrance to the image house (*vihāraya*). Because of his previous experiences in entering Buddhist temples, he may not question the given picture program around the door way. If asked, he might say that the sword-bearing figures are '*doratu-pālayo*', whose function would be guarding the doorway.

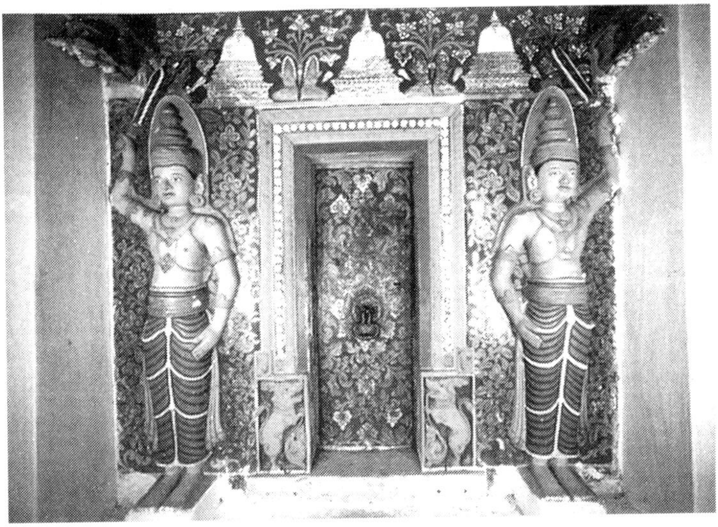

Fig. 1. Suriyagoda Temple Entrance

Many visitors may very much ignore the two small animal figures at the bottom of the door jamb. As the animal has undergone much 'stylisation', only deeper knowledge of the 'Kandyan Art' would help to identify these small figures as lions or (*siṁha*). Why the pair of lions appear in upright position, flanking the entrance of most of the Kandyan temples would be a question from a more curious visitor or an art historian. As such, visiting a few more temples from the Kandyan Period would familiarise the visitor with certain 'essentials' which can be seen when entering the sacred space.

Reading and understanding images especially in a religious concept has been a subject worthy of discussion among theoreticians in the 20th century. Many tools for a formal analysis of images have been tried out. In the process, the word 'Iconography' has been introduced.

In his thesis *Studies in Iconology*, first published in 1939, the German art historian Erwin PANOFSKY suggested a three-stepped analysis of interpreting images, which enables the observer to read and contextualise images more deeply.[2]

---

[2] Erwin Panofsky (1892–1968) was professor in Art History at the University of Hamburg till his emigration from Nazi Germany in 1933. From 1935 to 1962 he was

PANOFSKY (1939: 5–7 introduces his model for interpreting images in three strata.

1. Primary or natural subject matter: This is the most basic level of understanding images. At this stratum one perceives the work in its most pure form. It could begin by describing the image in terms of shape, form and colour which will be useful for an everyday experience. This very naïve description will lay the foundation for further reading of the image. As in the example cited above, the naïve visitor perceived some *stūpa*s above the doorway at this stratum, but did not analyse them.
2. Secondary or conventional subject matter (Iconography): This stratum goes a step further and supplements our analysis with cultural and iconographic knowledge. Interpretation of the subject matter takes place at this level. Textual knowledge or earlier visual experiences are necessary for this. For example memory of passages from the Bible would help us to understand the 'The Last Supper' or narrations from the Buddha's life to identify scenes like the 'The Birth of Prince Siddhārtha'. In its absence, a reference to similar images with 'known' identification will be required. Hereby a specific 'Iconography' will be established which will lead to decoding of the symbols attached to the images.
3. Intrinsic meaning or content (Iconology): This stratum takes into account personal and technical information as well as cultural history and incorporates this in the understanding of a work. At this level the viewer looks at the work of art not isolated, but as the product of a historical process. Essentially this last stratum is a synthesis. Here the art historian may ask 'What does it all mean?' or 'Why is it shown here?'. In this kind of contextualisation of the image, the observer uses the 'seen image' as a starting point to look out for the cultural and historical knowledge that would give deeper insight to the context in which the image is to be understood.

The act of interpretation of images begins just as a reading process: first, by 'feeling out' the image. This careful movement of the eye is to first locate a beginning of the 'grasping', which PANOFSKY calls in German 'erfassen' of a picture. The eye moves over the surface in specific manner. It may begin at a point, say, a focal point somewhere, which attracts the eye at first glance, whereupon the eye works out the visible structure to discover and identify familiar colours, shapes and textures. If there is a series of images separated from one another, then the eye would move from left to right or from right to left, from top to bottom, diagonally or, sel-

lecturer at the Institute for Advanced Study in Princeton. Panofsky's influence on Art History of the 20th century cannot be underestimated. He has been the father of the discipline termed 'Iconolology', which has become one of the most often cited methods of interpreting works of art in a more holistic sense.

dom, from bottom to top. In this process the picture is comprehended in its entirety and viewed with reference to other images of the group. At the doorway of the Suriyagoda Temple, the observer's eye, after identifying the bell-shaped building as a '*stūpa*', recognises repetition. The viewer stops the identifying process, because the Stūpa with two worshipers is repeated three times above the door with no variation. Parallel to this process of reading the image, the 'grasping' and 'identifying' of images takes place. The process is carried out with the help of images stored in the 'visual memory', which are called up, and immediately a 'decoding' follows. The operation of ruling out other possibilities of naming the image and of correcting the identification would continue. Here the conscious interpretation of the image is completed. If we need the image to be located in the cultural history, and find out its development, then we must necessarily look for repetitions of the image and their variations.

To illustrate the above process, I would use the first two strata or levels of PANOSFSKY's model.

For this purpose I have selected a series of more complex images from the Mädawala Tämpiṭa Vihāraya[3], which will be referred to as 'Mädavala Vihāraya' (CHUTIWONGS–PREMATILLEKE–SILVA (1990a)).

Let me begin with the upper register of the northern wall [figs. 2 and 4]. Seen on the wall are a series of *stūpa*s, which any person with some knowledge of Buddhist architecture would be able to identify. He may correct his assumption by noticing that the edifice is actually present in the premises and is worshiped by the devotees visiting the temple.

If we stopped at the 'first stratum', as defined by PANOFSKY, such a picture could only be perceived as a two-dimensional rendering of a *stūpa* against the red background, with floral designs in-between. This first level reveals the most basic understanding of a work without any added cultural knowledge.

[3] The name of the Vihāraya is derived from the location, as the temple is situated in the village of Mädawala, 290 meters beyond the Mädawala Bazaar about 9 km from Kandy. It can be approached from Kandy along the Katugastota-Ranavana Road. The murals of the Mädawala Vihāraya have been subjected to much scholarly research. In 1964 the Art Series of the Archaeological Department of Sri Lanka dedicated its third volume to the temple. The importance of the murals was evident, and the Archaeological Survey of Sri Lanka in its series *Paintings of Sri Lanka* identified the content of the murals and statues in 1990 [figs. 2 and 3]. Charles GODAKUMBURA (1964), Senake BANDARANAYAKE (1986), CHUTIWONGS–PREMATILLEKE–SILVA (1990a), Marie GATELLIER's (1991) and Gamini JAYASINGHE (2006) have discussed the murals in the context of late medieval murals in Buddhist temples. This very valuable research has laid a solid foundation for further research by identifying the images and statues.

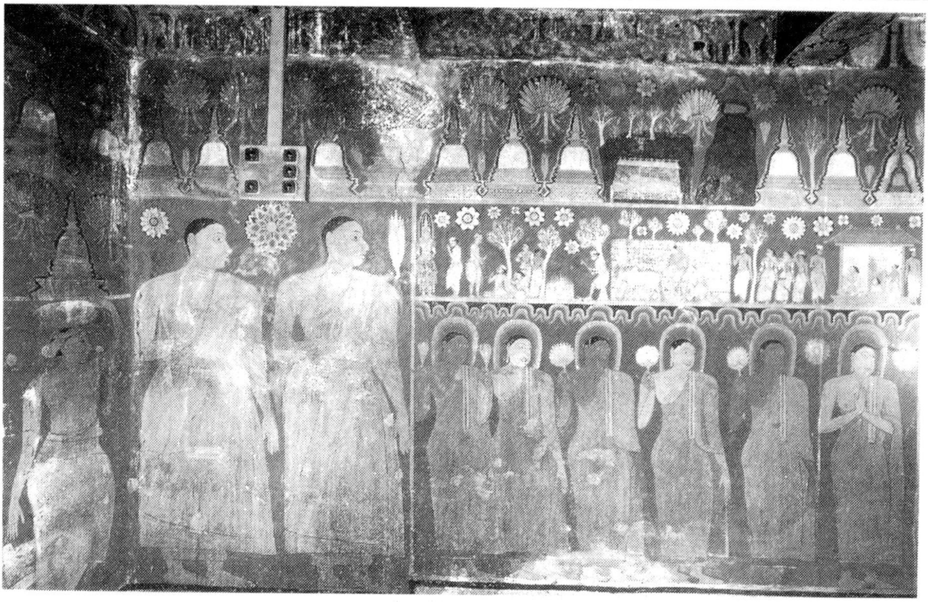

Fig. 2. Mädawala Vihāraya—Sanctum. Northern (left) wall

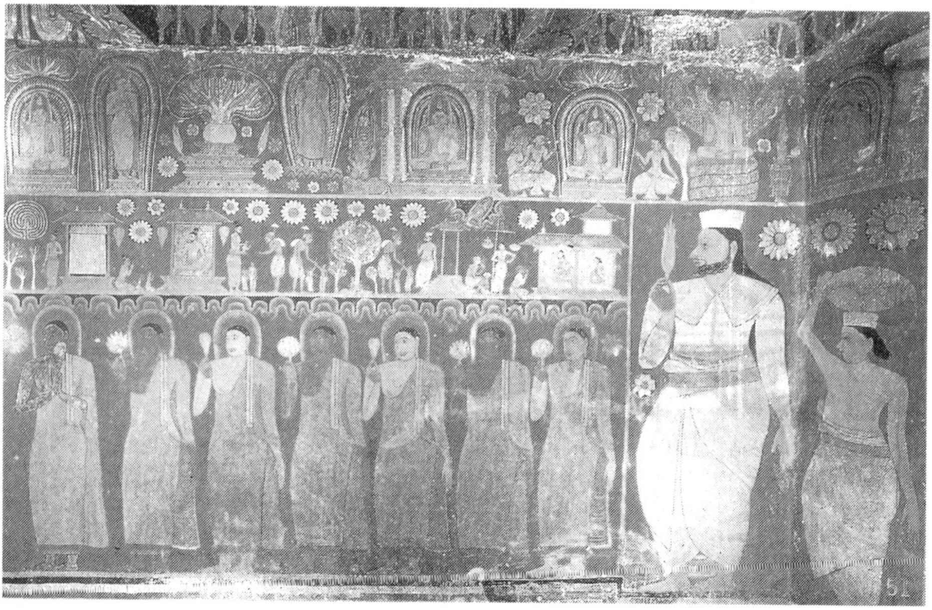

Fig. 3. Mädawala Vihāraya—Sanctum. Southern (right) wall

Moving left on the same register, one may notice that the line of *stūpa*s is broken by what may seem a rock and a cave, shown very much in a manner that even the naïve visitor will be able to recognise [figs. 4, 5 and 6]. The rock and the cave are fairly naturalistic in their representations [fig. 5]. Such series of *stūpa*s interrupted by a rock and cave and a stylised single tree later on, are seen in murals of many Kandyan Temples following the pattern in Mädawala. In the cave as seen in Mädawala, the Buddha appears to be sleeping under 'a mosquito net'. To identify the figure of the Buddha, some prior basic knowledge of how the Buddha is shown in the Sri Lankan context should be expected. A large corpus of Buddhist canonical texts from the *Tri-piṭakaya* and non-canonical texts, such as commentaries to the *Tri-piṭakaya* and later works like *Pujâvaliya*, have contributed to establishing a distinct Iconography of the Buddha. After identifying the figure in the cave as the Buddha, the naïve observer will then enquire, why the Buddha lies in a cave, and what the 'mosquito net' signifies. Proceeding with his observation of further images to the left, he or she would see a series of *stūpa*s ending up over the entrance of the image house [figs. 2 and 8].

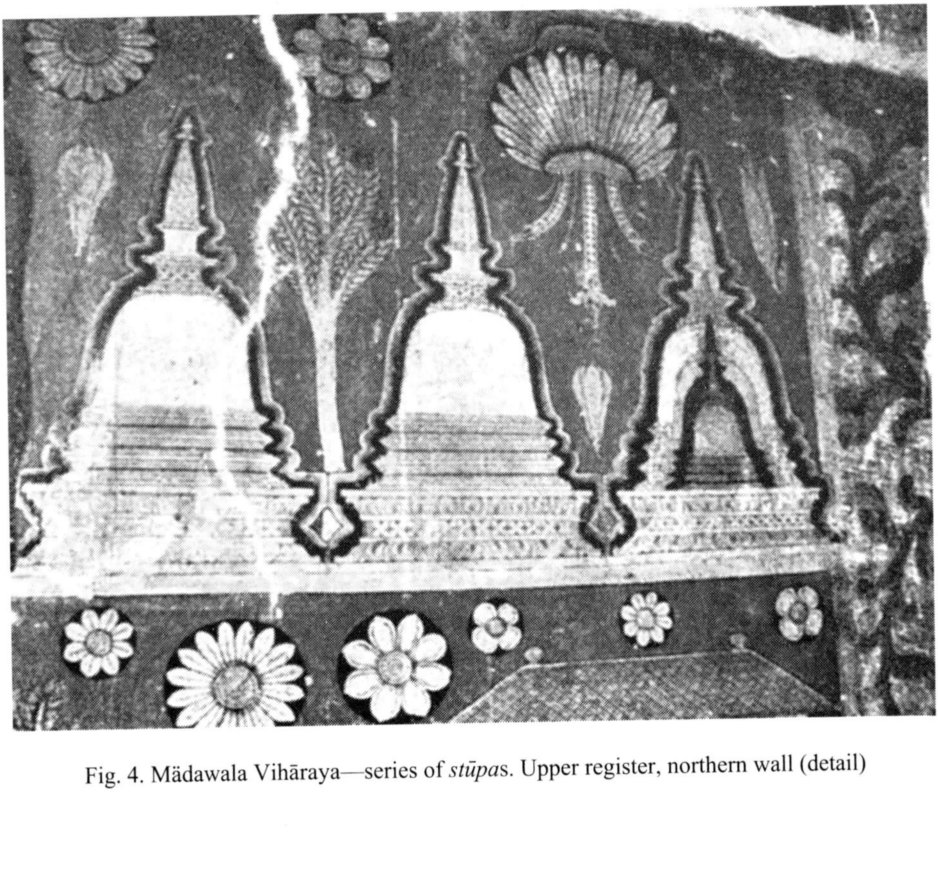

Fig. 4. Mädawala Vihāraya—series of *stūpa*s. Upper register, northern wall (detail)

In all, thirteen *stūpa*s can be seen in this series. Gamini JAYASINGHE's (2006: 51) photograph shows a switch board covering the 8th *stūpa*, which is yellow in colour. Between the 6th and the 7th *stūpa* a tree-like image can be seen on a pedestal. On closer observation, one may notice that the first *stūpa* has a peculiar design of '*stūpa*s within *stūpa*s' [fig. 4]. A set of similar images can be found in the image houses in Degaldôruwa and Gaṅgārāmaya too, which belong to the same phase of Kandyan Art (JAYASINGHE (2006: 28), CHUTIWONGS–PREMATILLEKE–SILVA (1990c: 82–89)).

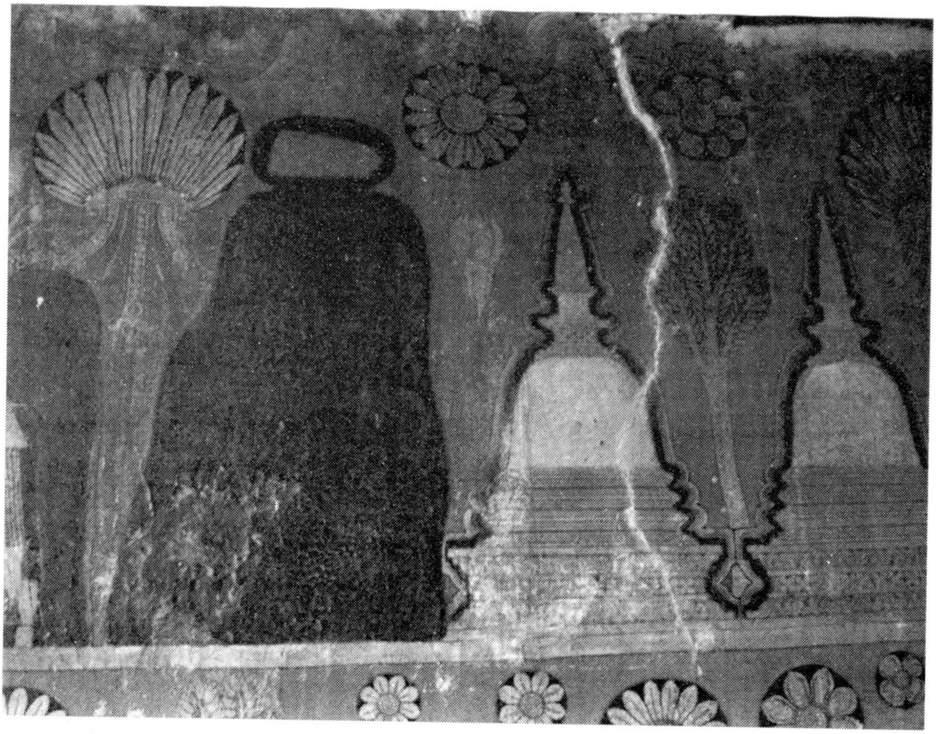

Fig. 5. Mädawala Vihāraya—*stūpa*s and mountain. Upper register, northern wall (detail)

In the Degaldôruwa temple, a set of images are seen in the inner shrine. The above-mentioned design of '*stūpa*s within the *stūpa*' begins a series on the left hand side. The fourth image is a mountain, the fifth shows the Buddha in a cave with no 'mosquito net'.

The *stūpa*s above the doorway in Suriyagoda did not show any variations. One may assume that is was a decoration, where as the images in Mädawala, Degaldôruwa and Gaṅgarāmaya show a similar succession. Before identifying the series of images, I would like to list out the order of the sixteen images.

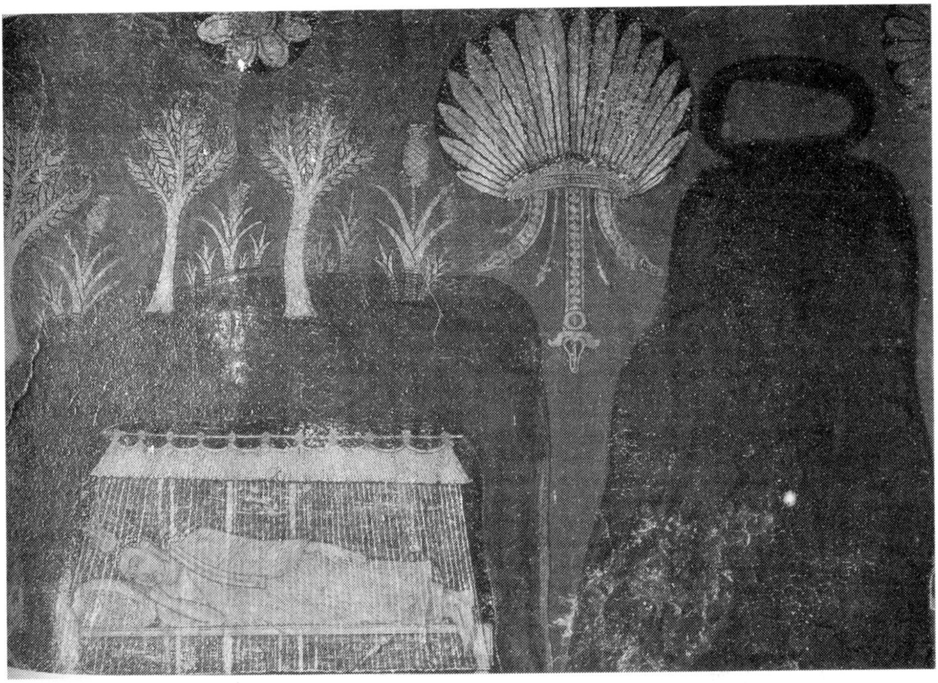

Fig. 6. Mädawala Vihāraya—mountain and cave. Upper register, northern wall (detail). [For a colour print, see the Appendix]

While reading the set of images in Mädawala from the right to left, one could identify [fig. 8]:

1. A *stūpa* with three *stūpa* designs within *stūpa* no. 1 of the '*stūpa*s within a *stūpa*', i.e. a *stūpa* with outlines of smaller *stūpa*s within (*stūpa* no. 1);
2. A *stūpa* with a tree standing next to it (*stūpa* no. 2);
3. A *stūpa* (*stūpa* no. 3);
4. A mountain with the 'footprint design' on the summit;
5. A cave in which the Buddha seems to be resting;
6. A *stūpa* (*stūpa* no. 4);
7. A *stūpa* (*stūpa* no. 5);
8. A *stūpa* (*stūpa* no. 6);
9. A tree (not very clearly visible in Mädawala);
10. A *stūpa* (*stūpa* no. 7);
11. A *stūpa* in yellow (*stūpa* no. 8);
12. Five *stūpa*s (*stūpa*s no. 9–13; *stūpa* no. 13 is on a lower register of the wall facing the main image).

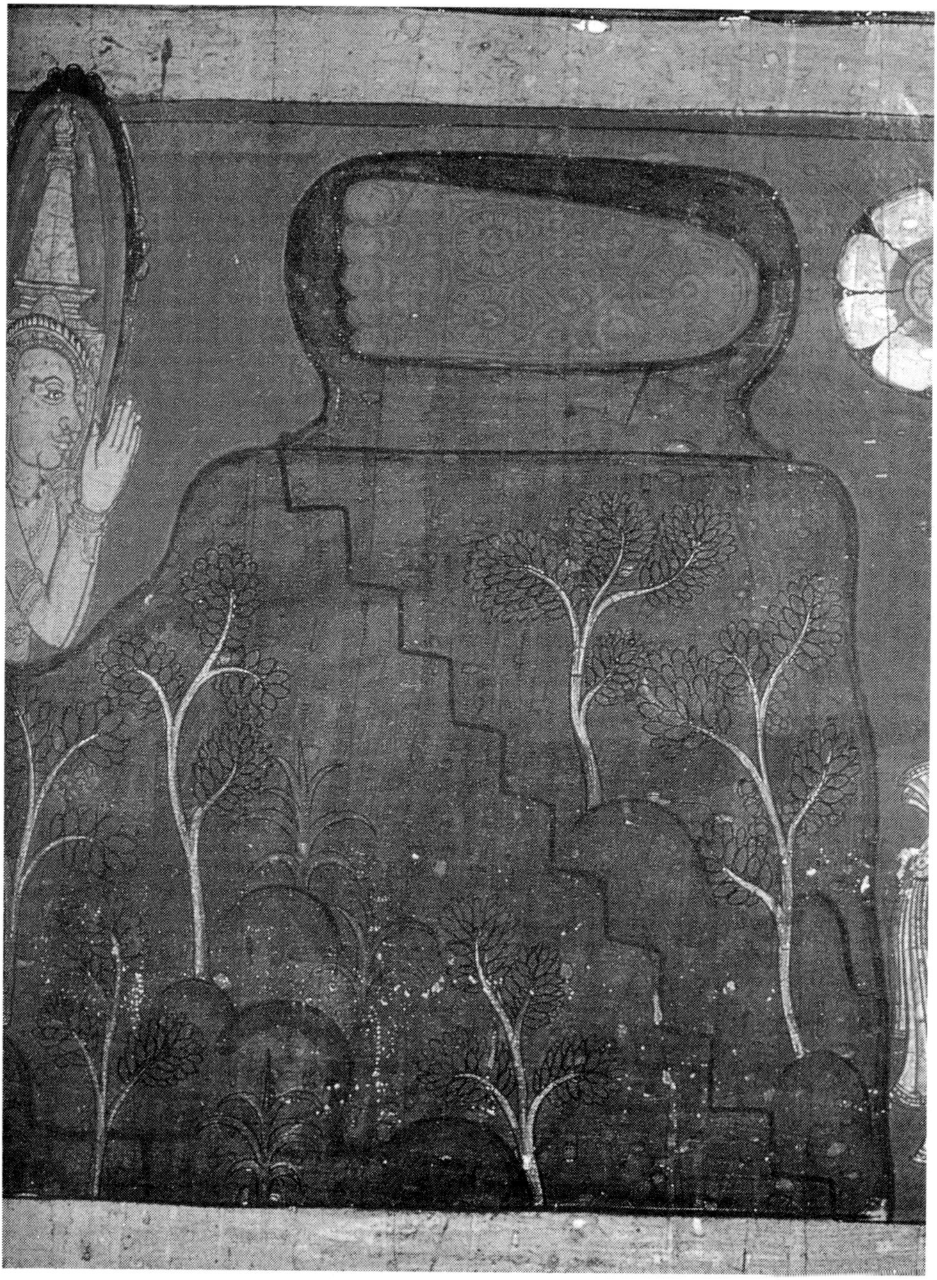

Fig. 7. Ridī Vihāraya—deity worshiping Foot Print. Upper image house, left wall (detail)

A similar series of sixteen images, can be seen in Ridī Vihāraya, in the 'Uda Vihāraya' ('Upper image house'), albeit with some interesting variations. Here the 'footprint design' with its floral symbols is placed at the top of the mountain, which has steps leading up to the top [fig. 7]. Referring to similar 'footprint designs' that are worshiped in Buddhist temples in Sri Lanka, the naïve visitor would be informed that they denote Śrī Pāda (Sirī-pāda), the footprint of the Buddha. The mountainous landscapes showing vegetation are common to both series. This mountain then would be representations of Śrī Pāda, known as 'Adam's Peak' in colonial times. In Ridī Vihāraya the foot print of the Buddha (Śrī Pāda) is worshiped by a deity. If the observer is aware of the practice of the pilgrimage to Śrī Pāda in Sri Lanka and of the narrations connected with it, then the cave next to it points to the Divā-guhāva, where—according to narratives connected with Śrī Pāda—the Buddha took a noontime rest. In the Ridī Vihāraya there is no 'mosquito net' but a simple curtain. One could then assume that also in Mädawala, the Buddha is lying behind a curtain.

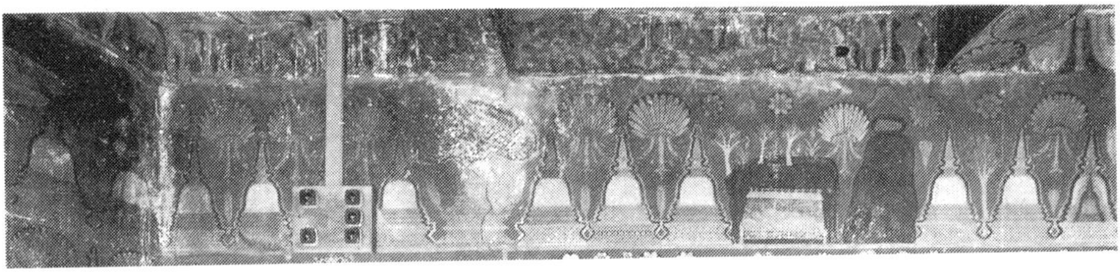

Fig. 8. Mädawala Vihāraya— northern wall. Upper register far left end (detail)

In the Ridī Vihāraya only a single deity worships the footprint. With the help of the *Vaṁsa-kathā* narratives, which first recorded the visits of the Buddha, this god could then be identified as Saman, who today is venerated as the 'Guardian of Śrī Pāda'[4].

PANOFSKY (1939: 6) in his second stratum mentions that not the 'optical appearance', which he calls 'form' but the content, 'subject', should be the object of analysis here: 'This would be manifested in Images, Anecdotes and Allegories'. The anecdote that connects the image of the 'footprint on the mountain' is the visit of the Buddha to Sri Lanka. The halo (*bhā-maṇḍala*) around the head of the deity known as Saman shows him as a personage of a higher rank, but no special 'Iconography' is additionally attributed to him. His identification here was possible because he was

[4] The Buddha's three visits to the island were first recorded in the *Dīpa-vaṁsa* (4th century CE) and the *Mahā-vaṁsa* (5th century CE). There seems to be no controversy regarding the dating of these most ancient *Vaṁsa-kathā* narratives of Sri Lanka; see GURUGE (1993: 13).

shown as worshipping the Śrī Pāda. The *Vaṁsa-kathā* narratives help us to identify the cave next to the mountain as Divā-guhāva, where the Buddha took a noon time rest (see fig. 6) and the 'mosquito net' turns out to be a curtain providing privacy to the resting Buddha. Such identification is possible by a comparison of a similar set of images and by using 'iconographic information' to identify the design as the Buddha's Foot print. At the second level, to identify the images the following 'external information' was required:

Image	Evidence in ritual and worship	Text providing iconographic or historical information
1. 'Footprint design'	'Footprint images' worshiped in temples	*Magul-lakunu* ('Auspicious symbols') of the Foot Print in post-canonical texts
2. 'Śrī Pāda'	Pilgrimage to Adam's Peak (Śrī-pāda)	Anecdotes of the Buddha's visit to Lanka in the *Vaṁsa-kathā* narratives

If the devotee viewing the images inside the temple is aware of the Buddha's three visits to Sri Lanka and believes that he visited 'Adam's Peak' and set his foot there, he does not require any additional 'Iconographic Information' from the *Vaṁsa-kaṭhā* narratives: He or she simply recalls the 'Oral Memory' preserved in the anecdote.

After identifying the images at the Mädawala Vihāraya as places visited by the Buddha, one could also consult the earliest narrative of the *Vaṁsa-kathā*. The *Dīpa-vaṁsa* narrates the visits of the Buddha Siddhārtha Gautama in the first chapter. It is commonly accepted as a work earlier than the *Mahā-vaṁsa* and would be the oldest narration available for research. Western and Sri Lankan scholars both firmly believe that this narration was less influenced by the politics of the most powerful monks of the Mahāvihāraya Monastery in Anurādhapura. As such, the *Dīpa-vaṁsa* contains a collection of older and unbiased narratives, more ancient than the 5th century CE.

The locations indicated in the *Dīpa-vaṁsa* as visited by the Buddha are as follows:

The first visit: 1. Māhiya Pokkha (DīpV 1.52);
The second visit: 2. a place 'between the islands of the Nāgas' (DīpV 1.39);
The third visit: 3. a place 'at the mouth of the Kaḷyāṇi river' (DīpV 2.42), 4. 'the place of Dīgha-vāpi-caitya' (DīpV 2.60), and 5. 'Mahā-megha-vana' / 'Mahā-megha-vanârama, where the Bodhi tree stands' (DīpV 2.61).

It is conspicuous that the *Dīpa-vaṁsa* does not mention any visit to the Śrī Pāda Kūṭa (Adam's Peak), where the Buddha set his foot and thereby impressed his footprint. The veneration of the mountain had, according to this narration, not entered the cannon of places to be worshiped and, consequently, the *Dīpa-vaṁsa* cannot be taken as a source to identify the places visited by the Buddha. Many art historians claim that the evidence for the Buddha's three visits to Sri Lanka is found in the 'Great Narration' of the *Mahā-vaṁsa*. Consulting the very first chapter of this narrative, one comes across nine or ten sites only.

The locations indicated in the *Mahā-vaṁsa* as visited by the Buddha are as follows:

The first visit:	1. Mahā-nāga-vana, or the Mahānāga Garden (MhVG 1.21–22),
The second visit:	2. Nāga-dīpa, or the Island of the Nāgas (MhVG 1.46–47);
The third visit:	3. Kaḷyāṇi-desa, or Kaḷyāṇi country (MhVG 1.74), 4. Sumana-kūṭa, or the Mountain top called Sumana (MhVG 1.77), 5. Dīgha-vāpi, or the long tank (MhVG 1.78), 6. The Bodhi tree (MhVG 1.81), 7. Mahā-thūpa or Ruvanväliseya (MhVG 1.81), 8. Thūpârāma (MhVG 1.82), 9. Silā-caitya (MhVG 1.82). (Locations 6–8 are places in the Mahāvihārā Monastery in Anurādhapura).

The fourth place Mädawala, the mountain with the footprint, is mentioned as Sumana-kūṭa. In the Mädawala series the next location is a cave, which is today commonly known as Divā-guhāva in Sinhala. This cave (*guhāva*) of the noon time rest (*divā*) does not appear in the *Mahā-vaṁsa*. However, the narrative gives the following information:

> 'And after he has spent the day as it pleased him at the foot of this mountain, with his brotherhood, he set forth for Dīghavāpi. At the foot of this mountain, where the Buddha takes a noontime rest (*divā-vihāra*)'.[5]

Although according to the *Mahā-vaṁsa* the mountain Sumana-kūṭa was visited by the Buddha, it is not given any prominence required for a future *stūpa* or *caitya*. It may be due the fact that the Buddha did not perform any miracle or preach or rest in 'the *samādhi* state' on the two sites connected with the Śrī Pāda / Sumana-kūṭa. As already mentioned, these two sites are not recalled by the narrator of the *Dīpa-vaṁsa*.

The next three sites visited by the Buddha are to be places within the future city of Anurādhapura, which at the time the *Mahā-vaṁsa* was composed in the 5th century was the seat of the government. The Mahā-vihāra Monastic Complex was also located here, serving as the centre of Buddhist studies. According to the narrator of the *Mahā-vaṁsa,* these sites were chosen by the Buddha as fit to be visited. This statement seals

[5] GEIGER (1912: 8). The original text of MhVG 1.78 reads:

tasmiṁ pabbata-pādamhi saha-saṁgho yathā-sukhaṁ /
divā-vihāraṁ katvāna dīgha-vāpim upāgami //

the possibility of any other locations outside the Mahā-vihāra claiming the status of a 'fit place' worthy of the Buddha's visit. One may also not forget that the monks of the Mahā-vihāra were responsible for writing these lines. In the verses 81 and 82 of the first chapter of the *Mahā-vaṁsa* the place of Bodhi tree, Thūpârāma, Mahā-thūpa (Ruvanväliseya) and Silā-caitya (modern name: Sela-caitya) are very briefly mentioned, all locations are within the monastic complex of the Mahā-vihāra. The mention of the places visited by the Buddha is routinely devoid of any details:

> 'After he had seated himself with his disciples at the place, where the sacred Bodhi-tree came afterwards to be, the Master gave himself up to mediation; and likewise there where the Great Thūpa stood (in later days) and there also where (afterwards) the thūpa in the Thūpārāma stood. They when he rose up from meditation he went to the place of the (later) Silācetiya…'.[6]

As the 4th century *Dīpa-vaṁsa* did not mention them, one may assume that these sites were added later on. Nevertheless the *Mahā-vaṁsa* brings out two points.

First, the verses 33 to 43 of the opening chapter narrate how the Buddha offered 'a handful of hairs' to God Mahā-sumana, who requested from the Buddha 'something worthy of worshipping'. The God enshrines the hair relics in a *stūpa* of sapphire. At the death of the Buddha a monk named Sarabhu procures the 'collar bone' from the funeral pyre and enshrines the relics on the same spot covering the original sapphire *stūpa* with a *stūpa* 'twelve cubits height'. A line of later kings build a *stūpa* over the existing *stūpa*: King Uddha-cūḷābaya, brother of the king Devānamiyatissa, covers the original *stūpa* and makes it 'thirty cubits' high. Finally King Duṭṭagāmiṇī builds a mantle over it making it 'eighty cubits' high (GEIGER (1912: 5)). Accordingly, the very first *stūpa* seen in the Mädawala series shows these four *Kañcuka-stūpa*s, or 'Jacket *Stūpa*s'. The '*stūpa* within a *stūpa*' design appearing in the first *stūpa* can be explained in this manner [fig. 4].

Secondly, art historians describing the Mädawala murals overlook the importance of the tree stranding between the second and the third *stūpa*. The verses MhVG 1.52–57 narrate of the 'Rājâyatana Tree' brought by the God named Samiddhisumana from the Jetavana monastery, where the Buddha was residing at this time. The tree is held like a parasol over the Buddha's head on his second visit to the island. On his departure from

---

[6] Translation: GEIGER (1912 :9). The original text of MhVG 1.81–82 reads:

mahā-bodhi-ṭhita-ṭṭhāne nisīditvā sasāvako /
samadhiṁ appayī nātho mahā-thūpa-ṭṭhite tathā // 81 //
thūpâramamhi thūpassa ṭhitaṭṭhāne tatheva ca /
samadhito' tha vuṭṭhāya silācetiya-ṭhāna-go // 82 //

Nāgadīpa, the tree is planted there and as such becomes the first *Pāribhogika-cetiya* ('Relic of Utility') to be installed in Sri Lanka, predating the Srī Mahabodhi Tree. In the Mädawala series, one can see the Rājāyatana Tree exactly between the second and the third *stūpa*s, which would denote the spot of Nāgadīpa and Kaḷyāṇi [fig. 5].

Further, among the images at the Mädawala Vihāraya, one discovers ten *stūpa*s on the upper register of the southern wall and final three *stūpa*s on the wall by the entrance. The line of *stūpa*s is then interrupted by a further tree, which would correspond to the depiction of the Śrī Mahābodhi in Anurādhapura. This is the ninth image of the series, which is somewhat deteriorated. According to the *Mahā-vaṁsa* the Srī Mahabodhi is the sixth place visited by the Buddha. If the 'Cave of Noon Time Rest' (*divā-guhā*) is to be taken into consideration, it would be the seventh site. In Mädawala the total number of sites is sixteen. As such, the first chapter of the *Mahā-vaṁsa* narrating the three visits of the Buddha to the island could not have been the source for the Kandyan artist who painted the murals for the Mädawala Vihāraya[7].

At this point only the 'Oral Memory' of the Sri Lankan devotee would come in useful. He or she would immediately recite the following verse when confronted with the question of finding textual evidence for worshipping the Soḷosmasthānaya, the Sixteen Great Places:

> 'Mahiyaṅgaṇa, Nāgadīpa, Kaḷyaṇi, Padalāñcana (Footprint of the Buddha), Divāguhāva (Cave of Noon-Time Rest), Dīghavāpi, the Stūpa of Mutiyaṅgana, Tissamahāviharaya and Śrī Mahābodhi, Maricavaṭṭiya (Mirisaväti Stūpa), the great Stūpa Soṇṇamāli (Ruwanväliseya), Thūpārāmaya, Bhayāgiriya (Abhayagiriya), Jetavanārāmaya Selacaitya, Kāccarayāma (Katharagama)—I worship [all of them]'.[8]

---

[7] Scholars in recent times have begun to claim that textual evidence to the Buddha's visit to sixteen sites around Sri Lanka (*Soḷosmasthānaya*) is derived from the *Mahā-vaṁsa* HOLT (1996:57) and TAMMITA-DELGODA (2006:87). Reading the *Mahā-vaṁsa.* shows that this hypothesis is not true. In the same manner, it seems that HOLT had not consulted the *Pūjâvaliya* and *Buthsaraṇa* in his research, which he claims to have consulted.

[8] BA 135:

> *mahiyaṅgaṇaṁ nāgadīpaṁ kaḷyāṇaṁ padalāñcanaṁ /*
> *divā-guhaṁ dīgha-vāpi cetiyaṁ mutiyaṅganaṁ //*
> *tissa-mahā-vihārañ ca bodhiṁ maricavaṭṭiyaṁ /*
> *soṇṇamāli-mahā-cetiyaṁ thūpārāma bhayā-giriṁ //*
> *jetavanaṁ selacetiyaṁ tathā kācaragāmakaṁ /*
> *soḷasethāni ṭhānāni ahaṁ vandāmi muddhanā //*

This *gāthā* recalling the most venerated sixteen sites of worship on the island of Sri Lanka is recited during almost every *Buddha-pūja* at numerous Buddhist temples and at Sinhala *budhu-geya*, or shrine room of private houses. The sixteen locations have come to be venerated as places believed to have been visited by Siddhārtha Gautama Buddha in his life time. Here the Buddhist devotee, who is familiar with the above *gāthā,* will have no problem in identifying each location.

In recent times the above cited *gāthā* worshipping the Soḷosmasthānaya has been popularised through the *Buddha Ädahilla* compiled by Rev. Kiriälle Gñānawimala, which was a conscious effort to integrate the worship of the sixteen sites in a new Buddhist Litany. It was first printed in 1955. Since then, this *gāthā* has been firmly integrated into the daily practices of worship (*vandanā-gāthā*) of Sri Lankan Buddhists.

The *Mahā-vaṁsa*, as we have already seen, stands testimony to only ten sites, although the above-quoted *gāthā* from *Buddha Ädahilla* describes sixteen such locations: (1) Mahiyaṅgana, (2) Nāgadīpa, (3) Kalyāṇa, (4) Padalāñcana, (5) Divāguhā, (6) Dīghavāpi Cetiya, (7) Mutiyangana, (8) Tissamahā Vihāra, (9) Bodhi Tree, (10) Mariccavaṭṭiya, (11) Soṇṇamāli Mahācetiya, (12)Thūpârāma (13) Bhayāgiri, (14) Jetavana, (15) Selacetiya, (16) Kācaragāmaka.

In order to find a narration that would provide some evidence of all the sixteen sites I have consulted the following Pāli and Sinhala texts:[9]

Pāli Texts: *Dīpa-vaṁsa*, *Mahā-vaṁsa*, *Vaṁsatthappakāsinī* of the 8th[th] or 9th century (a Pāli commentary on *Mahā-vaṁsa*; VaṁsP (1935: 59–80)), *Dāṭa-vaṁsa*, narrating the story of the Tooth relic (12th or 13th century; DhāV (2000: 59–73)), and *Samanta-kūṭa-vaṇṇanā*, written in the 13th century to elaborate the visit of the Buddha to Samantakūṭa (Adam's Peak) (SV (2001: 64–141);

Sinhala Texts: *Daḷadā-sirita*, written during the reign of Parākramabāhu IV of Kurunegala (1244–1325) (DS (2000: 44–46)), *Pūjâvaḷiya,* written during the reign of Parākramabāhu II (ca. 1266–75 CE) (PU (1997: 746–756), *Sad-dharma-ratnâkaraya*, written in the Kotte period (ca. 1410–1597) (SR (1967: 244–310)).

For the sake of clarity, let me map the places visited by the Buddha according to the sources. The results have been given in Table 1 (p. 287 f.).

The embarrassing absence is the *stūpa* Mirisavätiya (or Maricavaṭṭiya as mentioned in the *Mahā-vaṁsa*), to which the *Mahā-vaṁsa* devotes Chapter 26, describing its construction and the enshrinement of relics within it. GEIGER (1973: 233–

[9] Thc detailed analysis of the *Vaṁsa-kathā* narrations in Pāli has been published in: DE ZOYSA (2009: 391–431).

256) has already pointed that chapters 12–33 are later additions to the *Mahā-vaṁsa*, which may have come from a 'Volksepos', a national epic narrated around the heroic deeds of Duṭṭagāmiṇi. Tissamahārāma, Mutiyaṅgana, Katharagama (Kācaragāma in the *Vandanā-gāthā*), Abhayagiri (Bhayāgiri) and Jetavanārāma too do not appear in any list of places believed to have been visited by the Buddha. According to later Sinhala texts, namely the *Sad-dharma-ratnâkaraya* and *Pūjâvaḷiya*, the concentration of places visited by the Buddha is more on the sites in Anurādhapura. Mihintale, which today enjoys the status of a place where Buddhism was first preached in Sri Lanka, is added as a site visited by the Buddha.

The list of places visited by the Buddha seems to vary increasingly in number through the centuries. However, the *Pūjâvaḷiya*, written in the 13th century, and the *Sad-dharma-ratnâkaraya*, written in the 15th century, reveal the same sites.

Chapter 32 of the *Pūjâvaḷiya* contains a list which includes the following locations, making up a total of 14 sites[10].

In the course of time, the centre of power moved to Kandy, and the there seems to be a unity in the tradition as to what was regarded as the 'Sixteen Great Places of veneration'. These sites are identical with the temples which were actually visited by the pilgrims of the 17th and 18th centuries. Similar types of the *Vandanā-gāthā*, i.e. veneration verses composed in Pāli and printed in the 20s and 30s of the 20th century can be found in collection of pamphlets of the National Archives. The structure and the sequence of worship as described in the *gāthā* of the *Buddha Ädahilla*, published in 1955 and reprinted in 1956 which established modern religious practice, seems to be of relatively recent origin. In an attempt to trace the origins of the *gāthā,* I have searched the Palm Leaf Manuscripts at the Library of the

---

[10] The Sinhalese names are as follows: (1) *Mahā-vāluka-gaṅgāva-samīpayehi mahā-nāga-vana-udyānayehi*—in the vicinity of Mahāvāluka River in the Park named Mahānāgavana, (2) *Maṇi-nāga-divayina*—to the Island of Nāga called Maṇi, (3) *Käḷani-mahā-säya-pihita-täna*—the place of the great *stūpa* of Käḷaniya, (4) *Samanta-kūṭa-parvataya*—The rock of Samantakūṭa, (5) *Bhagavat-leṇa*—the cave called Bhagavat, (6) *Dakuṇu-mahāseya-pihitana-sthānaye*—the plce where the Great Stūpa will be built at the southern gate, (7) *Mahā-meunā-uyan-mäda*—in the middle of the Mahameunā park, (8) *Śrī-mahā-bodhi-pihitana-shānaya*—the location where the Śrī Mahābodhi will be planted, (9) *Lovamahā-pāya-pihitana-shānaya*—the location where the 'Brazen Palace' will be built, (10) *Piritlāgeya-pihitana-shānaya*—the location where the house for 'Chanting Pirith' will be built, (11) *Dantâdara-pokuna-pihitana-shānaya*—the location where the bathing pond 'Dantādara' will be built, (12) *Ruvanväli-mahā-seya-pihiti-täna*—the location where the Ruvanväliseya will be built, (13) *Mihintalehi-mahā-sala-säya-pihitana-täna*—the location where the 'Mahāseya' will be built in Mihintale, (14) *Ruhuṇu-digānaka-pihitana-täna*—the location where the 'Digānaka' Stūpa will be built (PU (2007: 753–756)); see also SR (1967: 297–308).

Colombo National Museum. Despite the fact that most catalogues that give the name *Soḷosmasthāna-vandanā-gāthā* ('Verses worshipping the Sixteen Places'), do not list the same sixteen sites as given in the *gāthā* of the *Buddha Ädahilla*, I have discovered one palm leaf manuscript which gives the same *gāthā*[11].

This may be a copy of similar manuscripts containing Pāli verses used for worship, and one may assume that the *Soḷosmasthāna-vandanā-gāthāva* goes back to earlier times. But as the bulk of palm leaf manuscripts in Sri Lanka do not go beyond the late 18th century, and the colophons giving the date are rare, the quest to find the original source may be futile. However, the compiler of the *Buddha Ädahilla*, Rev. Kiriälle Gñānawimaḷa mentions that the original text dated back to the times of the Kandyan King Kīrthi Śrī Rājasiṁha (1747–1782). If we rely on this statement, we may assume that the *Soḷosmasthāna-vandanā-gāthāva* dates back at least to the time of King Kīrthi Śrī Rājasiṁha. The hiatus left in the quest of textual evidence now is reduced from the 16th century *Sad-dharma-rathnâkaraya*, written in the Kotte period (ca. 1410 to 1597), to the 18th century, i.e. the rule of King Kīrthi Śrī Rājasiṁha.

The Sixteen Great Places as worshiped in the *Soḷosmasthāna-vadana-gāthāva* seem to appear in Mädawala Vihāraya

for the first time, which is one of the earliest image houses of the Kandyan Period. The Copper plate grant of King Kīrthi Srī Rājasiṁha, of the year 1677 of the Saka Era, made it possible to date the Mädawala Murals to 1755 CE. The question would be why the Soḷosmathānaya suddenly emerged in the period coinciding with the temples of late 18th century[12]?

Returning to Ervin PANOFSKY's third level (Intrinsic Meaning or Content), one would have to seek for an answer of the 'Iconology' of the set of the sixteen sites visited by the Buddha and depicted in a such a prominent place as the Mädawala Vihāraya. It should not just to be ignored in any way as a decorative frieze. Due to

[11] Catalogue Number: 22/ A 1 in the the catalogue compiled by W. A DE SILVA (1938).

[12] The series of the Sixteen Great Places appears along with the Sūvisi-vivaraṇaya (the twenty-four meetings with former Buddhas) and *Sat-satiya* (the seven weeks before the Enlightenment) in Mädavala, Degaldôruwa, Ridī Viharaya, Talava Rajamahāvihāraya, Telvatta, Dove and Kelaniya Rajamahāvihāraya. It becomes almost a compulsory cycle of the sixteen images shown in prominent places within the inner *sanctum* of the image house. In the early twentieth century, scenes or vignettes painted after monochrome black and white photographs depicting *Soḷosmasthānaya* published in the many editions of the *Buddha Ädahilla* have become a compulsory decoration on temple ceilings.

the lack of space, the artist placed the 16th *stūpa* in a lower register of another wall, making sure that all the sixteen places are clearly visible[13] [fig. 2].

The *stūpa*s and the Bodhi Tree point to objects of worship established long after the demise of the Buddha. They are in fact a series of symbols which can be decoded with the help of the Pāli verse known only among the Buddhists of Sri Lanka. One may refer to the iconology of the symbols and ask: Why did the artist choose the sixteen visits here, giving the set of images such prominence in Mädawala? Why did the set of images depicting the series of the sixteen places gain so much popularity in the late Kandyan times? Why was the series reproduced on wooden covers of palm leaf manuscripts later?

The constant need to document what happened in the past and to rework them into new narratives brought about a vast number of textual evidences for the places believed to have been visited by the Buddha. The list had never reached sixteen before the 16th century. In the times of King Kīrthi Srī (mid-18th century) the sixteen places, however, became a compulsory cycle of images. Since then the devotee sees the images he or she is actually worshipping in the image house reciting the verse. The same applies to the seven images which narrate the seven weeks after the enlightenment (*sat-satiya*).[14]

In order to contextualise the images, some historical facts will have to be taken into consideration.

---

[13] In the context of other cycles of images it is on par with the *Sat-satiya* ('seven weeks') on the other side of the wall showing the Six Weeks the Buddha spent after the enlightenment. Together with the Soḷosmasthānaya, the *Sat-satiya* emerges in Mädawala on the same levels on the left and right walls. In all the image houses built subsequently both these cycles emerge, occupying similar space on walls in the *Vandanā-gāthā*s as read in the palm leaf manuscripts too. The worshipping of the sixteen places is immediately followed by the *Gāthā* worshipping the seven weeks.

[14] In his monograph HOLT (1996: 57) calls the *Soḷosmasthānaya* 'the Kandyan Visual Liturgy', and comments: 'The upper tier of the south wall contains he most novel constituent portion of what becomes the Kandyan visual liturgy: the *Soḷosmasthāna* or sixteen sacred places of Sri Lanka. Here at Mädavala, we find the oldest extant version of their portrayal. What they represent are the destinations of ritual pilgrimage associated with either the mythic visits of the Buddha to the island or the monumental efforts—usually massive *stūpa* constructions—by past great Sri Lankan kings to enshrine the Buddhas relics. The inspiration for the sixteen places is drawn from the *Mahāvaṁsa* and other important textual sources such as the *Buthsaraṇa* and the *Pūjāvaḷīya*.' The question why this liturgy becomes an essential part of Kandyan murals is not answered by him.

The following timeline will show that the construction of the Mädawala Vihāraya falls into a time, when the rival movements to oust the King Kīrthi Śrī Rājasiṁha were at their peak[15].

1747: Kīrthi Śrī Rājasaṁha ascends the throne at the age of sixteen. Hailing from the Nayakkar Dynasty of South India, he is at the time of his assent to the throne a Hindu. The king nevertheless identifies himself as the custodian of Buddhism and takes steps to revive Buddhist practices and rituals.

1749: Nārenappa Nayak, the father of the King summons Ähalepola, the first Adigār (minister) to his house and threatens him with sword in hand and insults him. Antagonism with the Kandyan chiefs of the Radala-Families (Kandyan nobility) begins.

1749: During the New Year Festival, adigār Ähalepola conspires against the king with other chiefs. A year of much instability and intrigues to dethrone the king follows.

1753: On the invitation of the king, Ven. Upāli Thera from Siam with a group of monks and ambassadors of the King of Siam Boromkot (1732–58) arrive to Kandy to conduct the great 'Ceremony of Higher Ordination' (*upasampadā*). This year marks the last revival of Thera-vāda Buddhism under royal patronage. The king appoints Ven. Välivita Sarana kara as the 'King of the monk-community' (*saṅgha-rāja*) and Ven. Tibboṭovāve Srī Siddhārtha Buddharakkhita as the Mahā-Nāyaka (chief priest) of the newly founded Malvatta Chapter of Buddhist monks. 'Upasampadā' ceremony is held in order to initiate novices (*sāmanera*) and accept them into the 'Higher Ordination' whereby they become full fledged Buddhist Monks.

1755: Another group of Siamese monks arrives, headed by two Great Elders, namely Visuddhācārya and Varagñāna, with whose assistance the practice of meditation on the mindfulness (*vipassanā-bhavanā*) is established. This practice seems to have deteriorated in the Sri Lanka prior to this period. King Kīrthi Śrī Rājasiṁha establishes the forest hermitages in Santāna and Udawatte in Kandy.

1755: Grant to the Mädawala Vihāraya by Kīrthi Śrī Rājasiṁha.

1756: In order to reestablish Thera-*vā*da Buddhist scholarship, the Siamese King Boromkot (1732–58) sends a further group of monks, who bring rare books to Sri Lanka.

1757–60: Insurrection in the Dutch Territory which challenges the rule of the Dutch in maritime areas. Worst affected is the area of 'Mātara Disāvaniya' (a Dutch

[15] See DEVARAJA (1981), MIRANDO (1989) and ROBERTS (2004).

name for Sinhala Disāva), which is the most important area generating revenue. Cinnamon peelers protest against local chiefs appointed by the Dutch governor. The noblemen in Mātara, who were Dutch subjects, such as Leander de Sarem or the Mahā Mudaliya of the Dutch Governor's Gate, are banished to the Dutch colony in the Cape of Good Hope for supporting the rebellions (JAYAWARDENA (2010: 58)).

1760: Conspiracy to kill the King Kīrthi Śrī Rājasiṁha planned by Samanakkoḍi Disāwe (the second Adigār) and Ven. Tibboṭuvāve Srī Siddhārtha Buddharakkhita (high priest of the Malvatta Chapter) and to replace him with a Siamese prince during a religious ceremony. The plot is discovered and Samanakkoḍi Disāwe is punished with death, but the high priest is pardoned later by the king.

1761: Land grant made to Mulgirigala Vihāraya, the most important of the monasteries in the south, situated in the heart of the 'Mātara Disāvaniya'. The King sends artists to paint murals in the renovated temple. The Kälani Vihāraya situated a few kilometers east of Colombo, also very much under Dutch control, is renovated by the king.

1762: Donations by the king to Mädawala Vihāraya and Ridī Viharaya (belonging to the territory of the Dutch in the vicinity of the former capital city of Kununägala) in order demonstrate the royal patronage paid to these sites. Both temples show the Soḷosmathānaya on the murals.

1760–67: The animosity between the Dutch and the king of Kandy culminates in a series of territorial wars. 'People of the maritime areas are urged to join the war of independence renouncing the Dutch rule and showing allegiance to the king of Kandy' (JAYAWARDENA (2010: 62)).

1766: Treaty between Dutch Governor Van Eyk and King Kīrthi Śrī Rājasiṁha brings the king of Kandy within their grip. Kandy loses all claims to the harbors and main roads.

The grant made by the king to the Mädawala Vihāraya coincides with a period when the need for the king to establish his authority and acceptance by the Kandyan Chiefs was at stake. As DEVARAJA (1981: 118) points out, 'The religious revival tended to draw together the people of the Kandyan and coastal areas through the bond of a common faith. This gave strength and dignity to the Nāyakkār ruler, for like the Sinhalese kings of Kandy, he too came to be regarded as the defender of faith and could therefore command the loyalty of the Sinhalese whether they lived in the Dutch territory or his own. The sentimental attachment to the king and religion cut across political barriers and became manifest at this time. The king tried to make political capital out of this and embarrass the Dutch whenever possible.' In spite of the king re-establishing the Higher Ordination of Buddhist monks and making donations to important temples, the conspiracy of 1760 was planed by the same monks whom the King established as the *saṁgha-rāja* ('the king of the Buddhist monks'). At the request of Kīrthi Śrī Rājasiṁha the final section of the *Mahā-vaṁsa* called *Cūla-vaṁsa* (CūV) was written by Tibboṭuvāve Śrī Siddhārtha Buddharakkhita, the *mahā-nāyaka* of the Malvatta Chapter. In the closing chapters (ninety-nineth and one hundredth) the author attempts to write a eulogy of Kīrthi Śrī Rājasiṁha, parallel to the descriptions of other great kings, such as Duṭṭagāmiṇi, Vaṭṭagāmiṇi and Parākramabāhu, found in the narrations in the narrations of the *Mahā-vaṁsa*, thereby highlighting the meritorious deeds of the Kandyan king. One may keep in mind that this very same monk was imprisoned by the King as a suspect in the abortive coup to assassinate the king in 1760.

Lorna DEVARAJA (1981: 126) comments: 'There is no evidence to say when exactly the traitors were pardoned, but certainly by 1768 Saranaṁkara was functioning as the Saṅgha-rāja once again and in his reign the King invited Thibboṭuvāve to bring the *Cūla-vaṁsa* up-to-date.' Hence in much troubled times the *Cūla-vaṁsa*, which stopped its narration with Paṇḍita Parākramabāhu II (1236–1270), received its continuation from the hand of a narrator most eager to be reinstalled in the favour of the king.

In verses 125–129 of the hundredth chapter of the *Cūla-vaṁsa* (CūV, pp. 284–285) the King claims: 'Since the royal envoys (from Siam) wished to do reverence to the Mahiyaṅgana-cetiya and other cetiya places, the king sent them in the company of Lanka officials, to the various places, let them as they desired perform their devotions and sent them home after showing them the utmost befitting favours ... He enabled the *bhikkhu* community with Upāli at the head to visit the sixteen sacred places in Lanka, Mahiyaṅgana and so fourth as well as the *cetiya*s in Sirivarḍḍhana and other towns' (CūV, p. 284–285). This is the earliest written record of the 'Sixteen Great Places' (*Soḷosmasthāna*) and comes from a period about 1768, which is approximately the same period when the *Soḷosmasthāna* appeared in the murals of the early Kandyan Period.

I reproduce two historical maps published in *Lankāve aitihāsika bhūmi situvam* by Ven. Kuḍāvälle Dhīrānanda Kaḷyanavaṁśa in Sinhala LABS (1967: 16, 40). Map 1 of Sri Lanka, which depicts the settlements of the early Anurādhapura Period (3 BCE to 5 CE), shows some of the sixteen places scattered around the island[16]. Map 2, illustrating the occupation of Portuguese and Dutch in the 16th and 17th

[16] As seen in the maps no. 27 and 60 of the historical atlas compiled by Rev. Kudavälle Dhīrananda Kalyānavaṁsa published in 1967, here reproduced as map 1 (p. 282) and map 2 (p. 283) respectively, the sixteen sites are scattered around the island. The place of the second visit Nāgadīpa is today identified as an island far north.

centuries, shows the limited area ruled by Kīrthi Śrī Rājasiṁha centred around the 'Mahā-vāsala' in Kandy. The vertical lined areas in the far north show the parts of the island that were under the Portuguese rule, and later annexed by the Dutch. New acquisitions by the Dutch, in coastal areas of the east, west and south, are dotted.

The exact boundaries of the Kandyan Kingdom kept shifting and are seldom seen in maps. The boundaries of Tri Siṁhale (The Three Sinhala Regions) as claimed by historical documents *Kadaim* are not clear. Not all the sites of the Soḷosmasthānaya, especially Nāgadīpa, identified as an island in the Jaffna District in the far north, are within the Kandyan Kingdom. In the recently published maps (CADEIC) Nāgadīpa

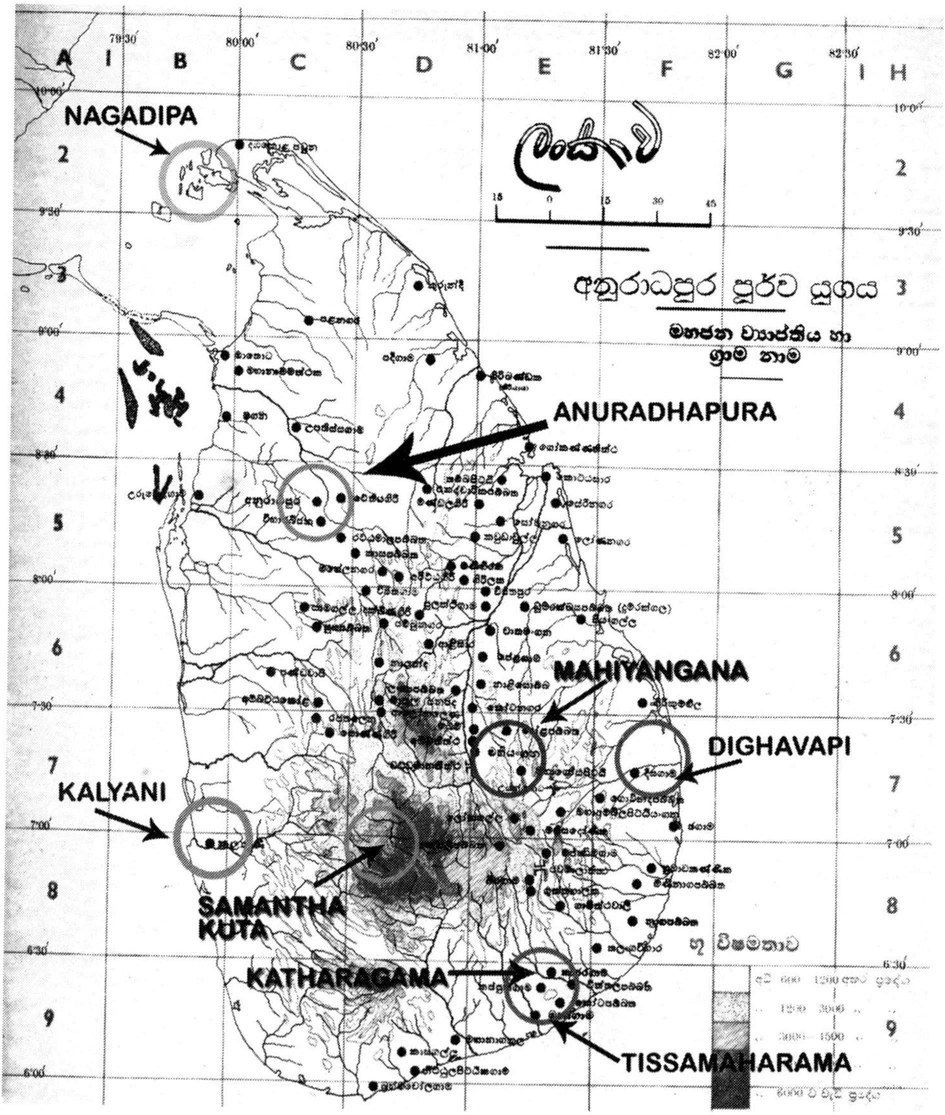

Map 1. Map of Sri Lanka—Sites of the early Anurādhapura Period.
Source: LABS (1967: 16)

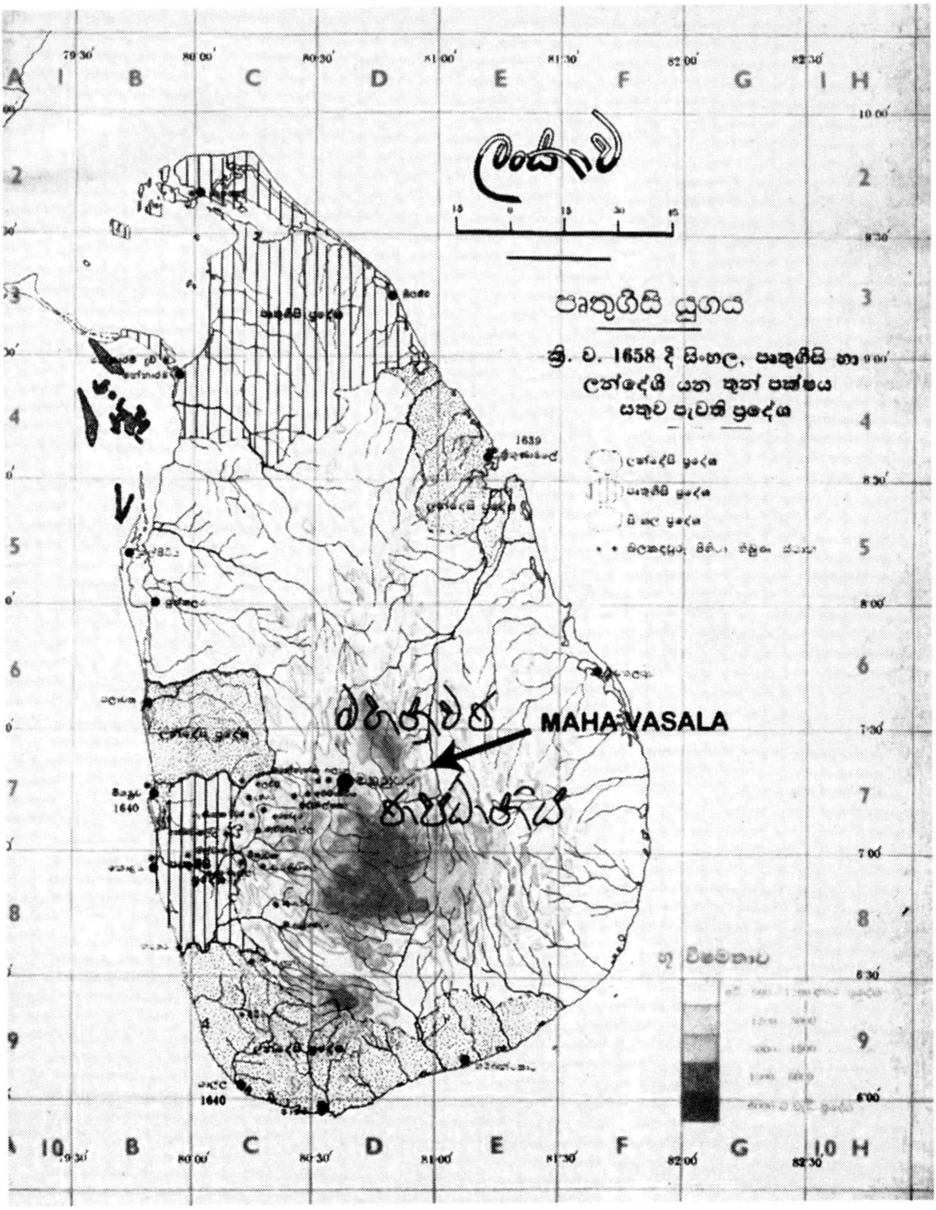

Map 2. Map of Sri Lanka—Occupation by the Portuguese and Dutch.
Source: LABS (1967: 40)

is denoted as 'Nayentivoe of Haarlem', and that was the time when the island was very much under the Dutch control[17].

This map, dated 1766, and other maps of this period do not point to any temple on the island Nāgadīpa. One faces the same disappointment while trying to locate Dīghavāpi in the east coast. Taking into consideration the map illustrating 'Trisimhale Kadaim-Poth' and reproduced by Michael ROBERTS (2004) there seems to be no location that may point to Nāgadīpa or Dīghavāpi. Two independent sources attest to the fact that a 'Pilgrimage to the Sixteen Places', claimed by the King in final chapter of the *Cūla-vaṁsa*, was not possible, if we assume that the locations in the far north and the east correspond to the historical Nāgadīpa and Dīghavāpi, rediscovered in the early 20th century and visited by the pilgrim today. In addition, the *Cūla-vaṁsa* mentions other pilgrimages to the Mahiyaṅgana-cetiya and the Nakhā Vehera, to the Rajarata Vihāra (identified as the Ridī Vihāra, in the former capital city of Kununägala) and a festival in honour of the 'Lotus-hued God' (probably in Devinuvara in the southernmost tip of the island, also in the 'Mātara Disāvaniya'). These pilgrimages would have only been possible if the Dutch had granted access through their territories. As such the claims of the *Cūlavaṁsa*, which reflect that the king had free access to these sites, is questionable.

In the same chapter of the *Cūla-vaṁsa* we read further how the king adorned a triumphal arch: 'Also he (the king) had pictures portrayed in coloured painting of the sixteen holy places, Mahiyaṅgana and the others, further of the famous foot-print on the Saccabaddha mountain of the Ten Pāramīs, of the three forms of (right) action, as well as of many Pāramīs, of the three forms of (right) action, as well as of many *Jātakas* in which subjects like the five great renunciations are treated of' (CūV, p. 295). For the second time, the 'Sixteen Great Places' appear here in a passage which refers to them as images. The hierarchy given to the pictorial cycles described by the narrator Ven. Tiboṭuvāve is interesting. The Soḷosmasthānaya lead all other picture cycles enumerated in the passage which also gives a list of the types of murals which were probably in vogue at the time of Kīrthi Śrī Rājasiṁha. We do not know, when the *Cūla-vaṁsa* was actually written. But it seems that the king was very much interested in projecting a topography of sixteen temples scattered around the island.

Interpreting the emergence of the 'Sixteen Great Places' in Mädawala, HOLT (1996: 57) explains: 'Indeed the *Soḷosmasthāna* may be taken as short hand for the intended function of the *Mahā-vaṁsa*: to show that Sri Lanka is the island abode of

[17] The map was attached to the peace treaty of 1766 between the Dutch United East India Company and Kandy; See map 'The Island of Ceylon in Sinhalese called Lankadiep' (CADEIC, p. 46–47).

the pure and true Dhamma predetermined by the Buddha himself and that the kings have defended and supported that identity through their righteous effort throughout history.' HOLT totally ignores the fact that the King was not in control of the sixteen places scattered throughout the island. The political implications of pilgrimages sent under state sponsorship to far-away places such as Nāgadīpa in the far north or Dīghavāpi in the east are not taken into consideration in his observation. The pilgrimages of Buddhist monks and Siamese emissaries may have had to penetrate areas under strict rule of the Dutch.

Michael ROBERTS (2004: 67), who goes further than Holt, and takes the oral tradition of the Kandyan Era into account, pinpoints the hidden political agenda of the king: 'In highlighting the sacred topography of the island in these striking acts, this king was informed by the ideas embedded in the *Vaṁsa* traditions, in particular the *Dhammadīpa,* and *Sīhaladīpa* (Simhaladvīpa). He was thus affirming the unity of Lanka under his parasol.'

Defending the unity of the island has been the paramount duty of the all the rulers of the island. Weather they were able to exercise power over the whole island and demand the due respect given to a ruler is a question that cannot be answered from the records available.

Conclusion

With the help of Erwin PANOFSKY's three-step model of interpreting images through a systematic analysis of 'icons', a decoding of the series of images in the Mädawala Temple was attempted in this study. After observing visual characteristics of the series of symbols seen on the upper register of the left wall, the images were identified as visual symbols of the 'Sixteen Great Places' (Soḷosmathānaya), which appears in Mädawala for the first time. Similar symbolic representations of the 'Sixteen Great Sites' from other temples of the same period proved helpful in the process of identification. The second 'Iconographic Level', to establish the iconography specific to each place visited by the Buddha, used the *Vaṁasa-kathā* narratives of the period from the 4th to 16th century.

What is crucial is the question when the concept of the 'Sixteen Great Places' began to evolve. The places visited by the Buddha had never reached sixteen before the 16th century. After about the 14th century many new sites seem to have been had been added, and they appear to have actually been venerated by the pilgrims at that time. The texts *Pūjâvaḷiya* (13th century) and *Sad-dharma-ratnâkaraya* (16th century) describe the same sites. The new sites which had been added are the *Lovāmahapāya* (a mansion built for monks) and the *Janṭhā-ghāraya* (bath-house) are situated in Anurādhapura. The *Vandanā-kavi* in the unpublished palm leaf manuscripts in the library of the Colombo National Museum shows that the sites had actually been visited by pilgrims.

The *Soḷosmasthāna-vandanā-gāthā* used even today to worship the Soḷosmasthānaya provided the textual evidence of Sixteen Great Places being worshipped in Buddhist Ritual (*buddha-pūjā*). The origin of that particular *Gāthā* was traced back to the times of the same Kandyan ruler Kīrthi Śrī Rājasiṁha. As such, the King seems to have revived the practice of worshipping the places visited by the Buddha as a ritual known as the *Buddha-pūjā* and had the cycle of the Soḷosmasthānaya painted as a set of symbols in the temples that were built in the vibrant years of the Buddhist revival spearheaded by him. Most of these temples have a portrait of the king showing him as the protector of the shrine. The large image on the southern wall in Mädawala may represent the king [fig. 3].

PANOFSKY's 'Iconological Level' posed the question why an 'Iconic Representation' of the Soḷosmasthānaya was regarded with such high esteem so that it became a compulsory set of symbols on temple walls of that time. For Kīrthi Śrī Rājasiṁha it was important to show his authority over the entire island, although the historical records demonstrate that the boarders of the Kandyan Kingdom were often challenged. Linking the Buddha's visits to the island, maintaining the custodianship of these sites through state sponsored pilgrimages and restoring *stūpa*s at these locations reflect the ambition of the King of alien decent and faith to be respected with similar esteem as the three great kings Duṭṭagāmiṇi, Vaṭṭagāmiṇi and Parākramabāhu. They are the paramount role models as recorded and remembered in the *Vaṁsa-kathā* narrations.

It was expected that the author of the final section of the *Cūla-vaṁsa* the Ven. Tibboṭuvāve Srī Siddhārtha Buddharakkhita, who had planed the unsuccessful coup to assassinate of the King, now basking in royal patronage, would faithfully elevate the king to the highest rank of illustrious rulers of the island. With the final 99th and 100th chapters of the *Cūla-vaṁsa* he thus updated the 'Grand History' of the righteous kings by writing a final chapter to the extended *Mahā-vaṁsa*, the 'Great Narrative'. The emergence of the Soḷosmasthānaya as a cycle of images and its repetition in the most important temples that received royal patronage in the Kandyan Era reveal more than just 'a visual liturgy' or 'sacred topography': The extension of sixteen places to cover sites all over the island may have been important to the Kandyan King Kīrthi Śrī Rājasiṁha to constantly remind the Buddhist World of his supreme power over the island and tradition that was continued by the last few kings of Sri Lanka.

Table 1

The vertical column on the left, gives the names of the Soḷosmasthānaya as known today. The names used in the narratives are given under each text. The vacant horizontal lines show that Mutiyanganaya, Tissamahāvihāraya, Mirisavätiya and Kataragama Kirivehera are not mentioned in any of the narratives up to the 16th century. The *Pūjâvaḷiya* of the 13th century and *Sad-dharma-rathnâkaraya* written about 16th century seem to have added some sites in Anurādhapura. The *Pūjâvaḷiya* locates four ne wsites within the former Mahāvihāraya in: *Lovamahā-paya-pihitana-shānaye, Piritlāgeya-pihitana-shānaye, Dantâdara-pokuna-pihitana-shānaye, Dakuṇu-mahā-seya-pihitana-shānaye*. In Kälaniaya too, the Buddha is supposed to have left a footprint.

Text / **Location**	*Dīpa-vaṁsa* 4th c.	*Mahā-vaṁsa* 5th c.	*Dāṭa-vaṁsaya* 12th or 13th c.	*Samantha-kūṭa vaṇṇanā* 13th c.	*Daḷadā-siritha* 1244–1325	*Pūjâvaḷiya* 1266–75 and *Sad-dharma-rathnâkaraya* 1410–1597
Mahiyaṅga-naya	On the banks of Māhiya Pokkha (site of Subhāṇgana-stūpa)	In the middle of Lanka, in Mahānāga-vanaudyāna (site of Mahiyaṅga-naya)	Mahiyaṅgana Vanauyane, Mahānāga garden	Urunāgavana, by the Vālukā River	On the banks of Mahaveli, Mahānāga Urunāgavana	On the banks of the Mahā-vāḷukā-gaṅgā, Nāgavanodyā naya and Mahiyaṅgana -caityasana
Nāgadīpaya	In the middle of the Nāgadīpa	Nāgadīpa	Nāgadīpa	Nāgadipa	Maṇi-nāga-divayina	Maṇināga Divayina
Kälaniya	At the mouth of the Kaḷyāṇi River, Site of Mahāthūpa	Kaḷyāṇi-desa, site of Kaḷyāṇi Cetiya	Site of Kaḷyāṇi Cetiya	At a lovely spot by the river Kaḷyāṇi	Kelanipura	Kälani-mahā-säya-pihita-täna
Śrīpādaya		Sumaṇa-kūṭa	Sumaṇa-kūṭa	Samanta-kūṭa	Sumangiri	Samanta-kūṭa-parvataya
Dīvā-guhāva		'At the foot of this mountain'	'At the foot of this mountain'	Bhaghavā-guhā (Cave)	Bhagavā-ḷena (Cave)	Bhagavat-leṇa (Cave)

Dīgha-vāpiya	At the site of Dīghavāpi Caitya	At the site of the Dīghavāpi Cetiya	Dīghavāpi	Rohana, site of Dīgavāpi Stupa	Digāmaha-seyatana	Ruhuṇu-digānaka pihiti tana
Mutiyaṁga-naya						
Tissamahā-vihāraya						
Śrīmahā-bodhiya	At the Mahāmegha-vanâramaya (site of Bodhi Tree)	At the site Mahamegha-vanârāmaya (site of the Mahābodhi)	Site of the Mahābodhi	Anurādha (site of the Bodhi Tree)	Anurapura, Mahabosa-mundu pihiti täna	Mahāmegha-vanodya-nayehi
Mirisavätiya						
Ruvana-väliseya		Site of Mahā-thūpa	Site of Mahā-thūpa	Site of Mahā-maṇgala-cetiya. Site in Seruvila?	Ruvamäli-mahā-seya	Ratna-māliciatya pihitana shānaye
Thūpārāmaya		Site of Thūpārāma	Site of Thūpārāma	Site of Mahā-maṅgala-cetiya. Site in Seruvila?	Site of Thumbarupa-seya	
Abhayagiriya						
Jetavanāra-maya						
Seḷacaitya		Site of Silācetiya	Site of Silācetiya		Mihintale?	Mihintalehi Mahā-salasä-pihititäna?
Kataragama Kirivehera						

BIBLIOGRAPHY

BA = *Buddha Ädahilla* [Sinhala Text]. Rev. Kiriälle Gñānawimala: *Buddhädahilla*. M. D. Gunasena saha samāgama, Kolaṁba 1955 [reprinted: 2007].

BANDARANAYAKE 1986 = Bandaranayake, Senake: *The Rock and Wall Paintings of Sri Lanka*. Lake House Book Shop, Colombo 1986.

CADEIC = van Diessen, Rob; Nenemans, Bert (eds.) *Comprehensive Atlas of the Dutch United East India Company (Dutch and English text)*. Volume IV: *Ceylon*. Utrecht University, Atlas Isaak de Graaf / Atlas Amsterdam, The Hague / Voorburg 2008.

CHUTIWONGS–PREMATILLEKE–SILVA 1990a = Chutiwongs, Nandana; Prematilleke, Leelanda; Silva, Roland: *Paintings of Sri Lanka. Madawala*. Archaeological Survey of Sri Lanka, Colombo 1900.

CHUTIWONGS–PREMATILLEKE–SILVA 1990b = Chutiwongs, Nandana; Prematilleke, Leelanda; Silva, Roland: *Paintings of Sri Lanka. Ridīvihāraya*. Archaeological Survey of Sri Lanka, Colombo 1900.

CHUTIWONGS–PREMATILLEKE–SILVA 1990c = Chutiwongs, Nandana; Prematilleke, Leelanda; Silva, Roland: *Paintings of Sri Lanka. Gaṅgārāma*. Archaeological Survey of Sri Lanka, Colombo 1900.

CūV = *Cūla-vaṁsa*. Wilhelm Geiger (transl.): *Cūlavaṁsa. Being the more recent part of the Mahāvaṁsa*. Vol. 2. English Translation. Henly and Boston, London 1927 [reprinted: Asian Educational Series, New Delhi 1992].

DE SILVA 1938 = De Silva, W.A.: *Catalogue of Palm Leaf Manuscripts in the Library of the Colombo Museum*. Colombo Museum, Library, Colombo 1938

DE ZOYSA 2009 = De Zoysa, Asoka: 'Soḷosmasthānavandanā Revisited,' in: Mahācārya Kulatileke Kumārasinha, Mahācārya Jinadāsa Danansūriya, Mahācārya Hurson Dias, Mahācārya Upul Ranjith Hewāwitārana-gamage (eds.): *Saṁsthuti. Mahācārya Candrasiri Palliyaguru Upahāra Kalāpaya 2009*. S Godage saha saha sahodarayo, Kolaṁba 2009: 391–431.

DEVARAJA 1981 = Devaraja, Lorna Srimathi: *Kandyan Kingdom of Sri Lanka 1707–1787*. Lake House Investments Ltd., Colombo 1981.

DhāV = *Dhātu-vaṁsa*. Panditha Ranjith Vanarathna (ed.): *Dhātu-vaṁsa: Vanarathana Vyakya. Pela, sannaya ha visthara sahitayi*. [Pāli and Sinhala Text]. Samayavardhana Pothhala. Koḷamba 2000.

DīpV = *Dīpa-vaṁsa*. Hermann Oldenberg (transl.): *The Dīpavaṁsa: Ancient Buddhist Historical Record*. Pāli Text Society, London 1879 [reprinted: Asian Educational Services, New Delhi–Madras 2001].

DS = *Daḷadā-sirita* [Sinhala text]. V.D.S. Guṇavardhana (ed.): *Daḷadā-sirita*. Samayavardhana Printers. Koḷamba 2000.

GATELLIER 1991 = Gatellier, Marie: *Peintures Murales du Sri Lanka. École kandyenne, XVIIIe-XIXe siècles*. Vol. I. *Texte*. Vol. 2. *Planches*. École française d'Extrême-Orient, Paris 1991.

GEIGER 1912 = Geiger, Wilhelm: *The Mahāvaṁsa, the Great Chronicle of Ceylon*. English Translation. Pali Text Society, London 1912 [reprinted: Government Information Department, Colombo 1960].

GEIGER 1973 = Geiger, Wilhelm: *Kleine Schriften zur Indollogie und Buddhismus-kunde*. Ed. Heinz Bechert, Franz Steiner Verlag, Stuttgart 1973.

GODAKUMBURA 1964 = Godakumbura, Charles E.: *Mädawala Vihara Frescoes*. Art Series No. 3. Archaeological Department of Sri Lanka, Colombo 1964.

GURUGE 1993 = Guruge, Ananda W.P.: 'Purvikāva' (Introduction) to the *Mahā-vaṁsa Gitaya*. Vol. 1. Rajaye Mudrana Nītigatha Saṁsthāva, Koḷamba 1993.

HOLT 1996 = Holt, John Clifford: *The Religious World of Kirti Sri: Buddhism, Art, and Politics of Late Medieval Sri Lanka*. Oxford University Press, New York 1996.

JAYASINGHE 2006 = Jayasinghe, Gamini: *Sri Lankan Buddhist Art. Post-Clasical Revival*. Sarvodaya Vishva Lekha, Colombo 2006.

JAYAWARDENA 2010 = Jayawardena, Kumari: *Perpetual Ferment. Popular Revolts in Sri Lanka in the 18th and 19th Centuries*. Karunaratne and Sons (Pvt.), Homagama 2010.

LABS 1967 = Kuḍāvälle Dhīrānanda Kaḷyanavaṁśa Himi: *Lankāve aitihāsika bhūmi situvam* [Sinhala text]. Sīmāsahita M. D. Goonasena saha samāgama. Koḷamba 1967.

MIRANDO 1989 = Mirando, A.H.: *Buddhism in Sri Lanka in the 17th and 18th Centuries*. Tissara Prakashakayo, Dehiwala 1989.

MhVG = *Mahā-vaṁsa Gītaya. Pāli-gāthā-samaga* [Pāli and Sinhala Text]. Kalāsūri V. V. Abhayaguṇavardhana, Kalāsūri Ariyasen Ahubudu, Kalāvidu A. D. Chandrasekara (eds.): *Mahāvaṁsa Gitaya. Pāli Gāthā Samaga. Paḷamu veluma*. Gī racaka Kalāmanya Heḷa-basmiṇi Mahānāma Disānāyaka. Rajaye Mudrana Nītigatha Saṁ-sthāva, Koḷamba 1993.

PANOFSKY 1939 = Panofsky, Erwin: *Studies in Iconology: Humanistic Themes in the Art of the Renaissance*. Oxford University Press. New York 1939

PU = *Pūjâvaḷiya* [Sinhala Text]. *Pūjâvaḷiya. Mayurapāda piriveṇādhi-pati Buddhaputra Sthavirayānan vahanse*. Bauddha Sanskritika Madhyashānaya, Dehiwala 1997 [reprinted: 2007].

ROBERTS 2004 = Roberts, Michael: *Sinhala Consciousness in the Kandyan Period 1590 to 1815*. Vijitha Yapa Publications, Colombo 2004.

SR	= *Sitiyam sahita Sad-dharma-ratnâkaraya* [Sinhala Text]. V.D.S. Gunavardhana (ed.): *Sitiyam sahita Saddharmaratnâkaraya.* Sasmayavardhana Pothhala, Kolaṁba 1967.
SV	= *Samanthakūṭa-vaṇṇanā* [Pāli and Sinhala Text]. Deniyaye Pagnaloka Himi (ed.): *Samanthakuṭavaṇṇana. Prathama Laṅkā-gamanaye sita avasānaya dakvā.* Samayavardhana, Koḷamba 2001.
TAMMITA-DELGODA 2006	= Tammita-Delgoda, Sinha Raja: *Ridi Vihare. The Flowering of Kandyan Art.* Stamford-Lake, Colombo 2006.
VK	= *Vandanā-kavi* [Sinhala Text]. Jayanetti, Dayapala (ed.): *Vandanā-kavi. Jayanetti, Dayapala.* Samayawardana Pothhala, Kolaṁba 2005.
VaṁsP	= *Vaṁsatthâppakāsinī* [Sinhala Text]. Akuratiye Amaravaṁsa Nāhimi. Hemachandra Disanayaka (eds.): *Vaṁsattha-ppakāsinī. Mahā-vaṁsa-ṭīkava. Sinhala Anuvādaya.* S Godage. Koḷamba 1994 [reprinted: 2001].

GENERAL INDEX

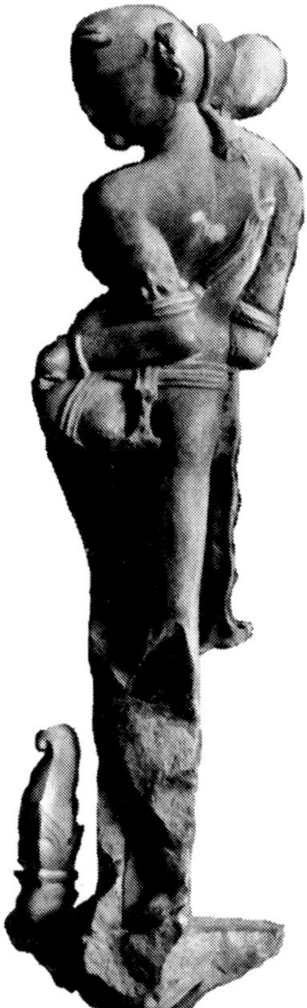

Appendix

List of illustrations

Monika Zin: The Parable of 'The Man in the Well'. Its Travels and its Pictorial Traditions from Amaravati to Today, pp. 33–93:

Fig. 16. *Die Inkunabeln des Directorium vitae humanae*, Ulm 1483.

Fig. 17. Heidelberg, University Library, Cod. Pal. germ. 466, Buch der Beispiele; a colour print in the Appendix. © Universitätsbibliothek Heidelberg

Fig. 18. Woodcut from the *Barlaam und Josaphat* by Günther Zainer, Augsburg ca. 1476.

Fig. 19. The unicorn standing above the pit with the man; Jannina, Epirus, Schola Zosimala Library.

Fig. 20. The unicorn standing above the pit with the man; Rome, Vatican Library.

Fig. 21. Hugo von Trimberg, *Der Renner*, Munich, Bayerische Staatsbibliothek; a colour print in the Appendix. © Bayerische Staatsbibliothek.

Fig. 22. Tree of Life with a man and the unicorn, Barlaam depicted on the side. Kraków, Czartoryskis' Library; a colour print in the Appendix. © Fundacja Czartoryskich.

Fig. 23. Parma, portal on the Soutehern Facade of the baptistery, 1196–1220.

Fig. 24. Ferrara, Cathedral Museum, 14th century.

Fig. 25. Boetius Bolsvert (1580–1633), copper engraving.

Fig. 26. Quanzhou, Twin Pagodas, Kaiyun Temple, 1238.

Fig. 27. Painting roll, Kamakura Period, 14th century.

Fig. 28. Sheet print, China, 19th century.

Fig. 29. Sakaki-Eiju from Nara, Mujo-no-Tora, 20th century.

Fig. 30. Amarāvatī, British Museum, 11.

Fig. 31. Amarāvatī, British Museum, 87.

Fig. 32. Amarāvatī. Drawing by an assistant of Colonel Mackenzie, 1817. The British Library.

Fig. 33. Amarāvatī. Drawing by an assistant of Colonel Mackenzie, The British Library.

Fig. 34. Amarāvatī. Drawing by an assistant of Colonel Mackenzie, The British Library.

Piotr Balcerowicz: The Body and the Cosmos in Jaina Mythology and Art, pp. 95–151:

Fig. 1. Jaina world (*loka*) and its dimensions (drawing). © Piotr Balcerowicz.

Fig. 2. Jaina world (*loka*) in three main parts. CAILLAT–KUMAR (1981: 51).

Fig. 3. Jaina world (*loka*) and its dimensions. JSK, III: 439 (*Tīn Lok*).

Fig. 4. Modern symbol of Jainism, adopted in 1975, with the shape of the Jaina world (*loka*).

Fig. 5. A traditional Jaina representation of the cosmic man (*loka-puruṣa*).

Fig. 6. General view of the universe; KIRFEL (1920: Taf. 5).

Fig. 7. The cosmic man (*loka-puruṣa*) in the form of a woman; GLASENAPP (1925: Tafel 15).

Fig. 8: The spatial arrangement of the eight black fields; a drawing. © Piotr Balcerowicz

Fig. 9. Mout Meru (*meru-parvata*); SŪRĪŚVAR (2008: 32).

Silke K. Yasmin Fischer: The Spread of Buddhism from India to Sri Lanka: Its Visual Representation, pp. 153–164:

Fig. 1. Rangiri Dambulla Rājamahāvihāra, drawing by Prof. Monika Zin after after BANDARANAYAKE (1986: 169, plate 84).

Fig. 2. Kapumulagoda Ghanāndarāmavihāra, private collection Dr. Rolf Heinrich Koch, Munich; a colour print in the Appendix.

Fig. 3. King Devānaṁpiyatissa's meeting with Mahinda. A representation from *Sadaham Maga* (SM), published 1960. Illustrator S. P. Charles.

Fig. 4. King Devānaṁpiyatissa's meeting with Mahinda. A representation from the *Buddha-dharmaya* (BDh), published 1993. Illustrator unknown.

Anna Ślączka: Temple Consecration Rituals in the Hindu Tradition of South and South-East Asia: A Study of the Textual and Archaeological Evidence, pp. 167–181:

Fig. 1. Stone box found in Jolotundo (East Java). Museum Nasional, Jakarta, inv. no. 374. Photograph: M.J. Klokke; a colour print in the Appendix.

Fig. 2. Stone box found in Candi Bukit Batu Pahat (Malaysia). Bujang Valley Archaeological Museum, Pengkalan Bujang, Merbok, Malaysia. Photograph: A.A. Ślączka; A colour print in the Appendix.

Fig. 3. Images of goddesses found in Candi Bukit Batu Pahat (Malaysia). Bujang Valley Archaeological Museum, Pengkalan Bujang, Merbok, Malaysia. Photograph: A.A. Ślączka; a colour print in the Appendix.

Fig. 4. Images of bulls found in Candi Bukit Batu Pahat (Malaysia). Bujang Valley Archaeological Museum, Pengkalan Bujang, Merbok, Malaysia. Photograph: A.A. Ślączka; a colour print in the Appendix.

Fig. 5. Stone box in Candi Merak (Central Java). Photograph: M.J. Klokke; a colour print in the Appendix.

David Smith: Facial Expression in the Erotic Art of Khajurāho. A Preliminary Investigation, pp. 183–201:

Figs. 1 and 3–56: Details of sculptures; Khajurāho temples. Photographs of the author.

Fig. 2: Details of a sculpture; Lakṣmaṇa temple, Khajurāho. Source: of PARIMOO (2000: plates 682 and 684 combined).

Valdas Jaskūnas: Building Visual Order in Kashmir. Analysis of Architectural Structures as Described in the *Viṣṇu-dharmôttara-purāṇa*, pp. 203–227:

Fig. 1. Śrīnagar. Śaṅkarācārya temple, c. 675–700 C.E. Source: EITA, pl. 704. Courtesy: American Institute of Indian Studies.

Fig. 2. Gop. Old temple, c. late 6th century C.E. Source: EITA, pl. 328. Courtesy: American Institute of Indian Studies.

Fig. 3. Khocho near Turfan (Turpan, East Turkestan). Ruins of a terrace-temple. Source: FRANZ (1965: pl. 286).

Fig. 4. Maṭṭan. Mārtaṇḍa temple, trefoil niche of the upper *jagatī*, c. 725–750 C.E. Source: EITA, pl. 715. Courtesy: American Institute of Indian Studies.

Fig. 5. Nālandā, site no. 3. Corner towers, c. 575–600 C.E. Source: EITA, pl. 228. Courtesy: American Institute of Indian Studies.

Fig. 6. Bhitargaon (Bhītargâm̐v). Gupta temple, c. 425–450 C.E. Source: EITA, pl. 45. Courtesy: American Institute of Indian Studies.

Samir Kumar Mukherjee: Terracotta Art in the Gangetic Valley under the Guptas, pp. 231–250:

Map 1. Map of India showing the early historical sites. Drawing by Anil Ch. Mukhopadhyay.

Fig. 1. Gaṅgā riding on Makara (crocodile) with parasol-bearer, Ahicchatra, U.P.

Fig. 2. Yamunā riding on Kurma (tortoise) with parasol-hearer and Gaṇa figure, Ahicchatra, U.P.

Fig. 3. Amorous couple, Mahāsthāngaṛh, Bangladesh.

Fig. 4. Hanuman fighting a devil, Bhītargâm̊v, U.P.

Fig. 5. *Viṣṇv-ananta-śayin*, Vishnu lying on snake Ananta, Bhītargâm̊v, U.P.

Fig. 6. Śiva, Faizabad, U.P.

Fig. 7. Male head, Jhūsī, U.P.

Fig. 8. Female head with trefoil hair style and crest-jewel, Bhīta, U.P.

Fig. 9. Female head with crest-jewel, Bhīta, U.P.

Fig. 10. Female figure, Kauśaṁbī, U.P.

Fig. 11. Female bust, Bhīta, U.P.

Fig. 12. Female head with coiffure, Jhūsī, U.P.

Fig. 13. Mother and child, Bhīta, U.P.

Fig. 14. Horse rider, Kannauj, U.P.

Fig. 15. Worshipper variety, Bhīta, U.P.

Fig. 16: Worshipper variety, Bhīta,U.P.

Fig. 17. Gaṇa figurine, Bhīta, U.P.

Fig. 18. *Dampati* (Couple), Kannauj, U.P.

Fig. 19. Female head with haloe, Bhīta, U.P.

M. Singh, R.S. Trambake, D.A. Gupta: Chemical Conservation of Hīnayāna Paintings of the 2nd BCE, Cave No. 10, Ajanta, pp. 251–259:

Photo 1. Visitors graffiti on painted plaster of cave no. 10, Ajanta; a colour print in the Appendix.

Fig. 1. Graph showing average R.H. inside the cave no.1 in Ajanta.

Fig. 2. Graph showing impact of visitors on %R.H cave no. 2 in Ajanta

Photo 2a. Before chemical treatment; a colour print in the Appendix.

Photo 2b. After chemical conservation; a colour print in the Appendix.

Photo 3a. Before chemical treatment; a colour print in the Appendix.

Photo 3b. After chemical treatment; a colour print in the Appendix.

Asoka de Zoysa: Reading Images and Interpreting the Context: Differentiating Between Iconography and Iconology According to Erwin Panofsky's Three Phase Analysis, pp. 260–291:

Monika Zin: The Parable of 'The Man in the Well'. Its Travels and its Pictorial Traditions from Amaravati to Today, pp. 33–93:

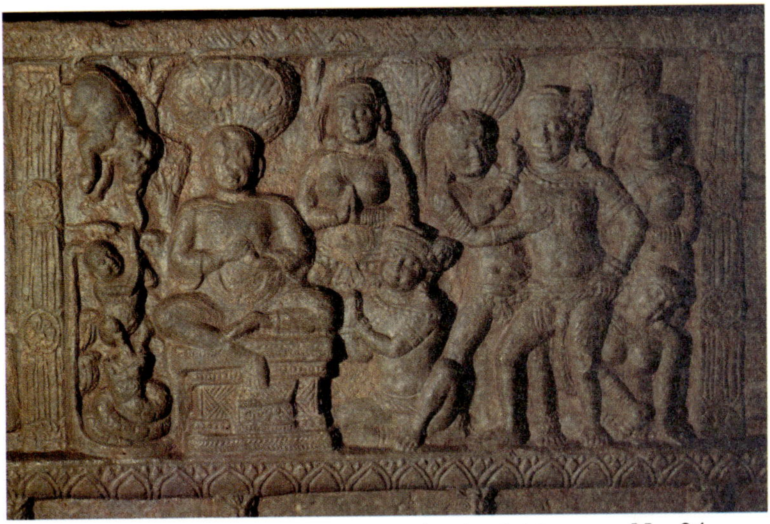

Fig. 1. Nāgārjunakoṇḍā, Site 9, Nagarjunakonda Museum, , No. 24

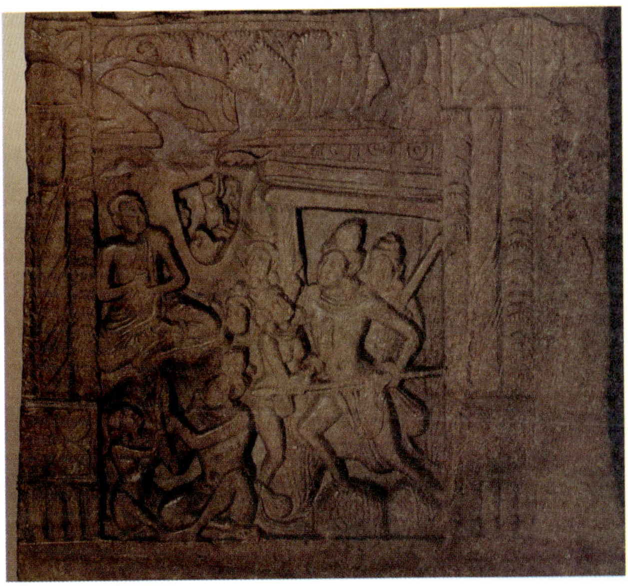

Fig. 3. Nāgārjunakoṇḍā, Site 2, Nagarjunakonda Museum, No. 18

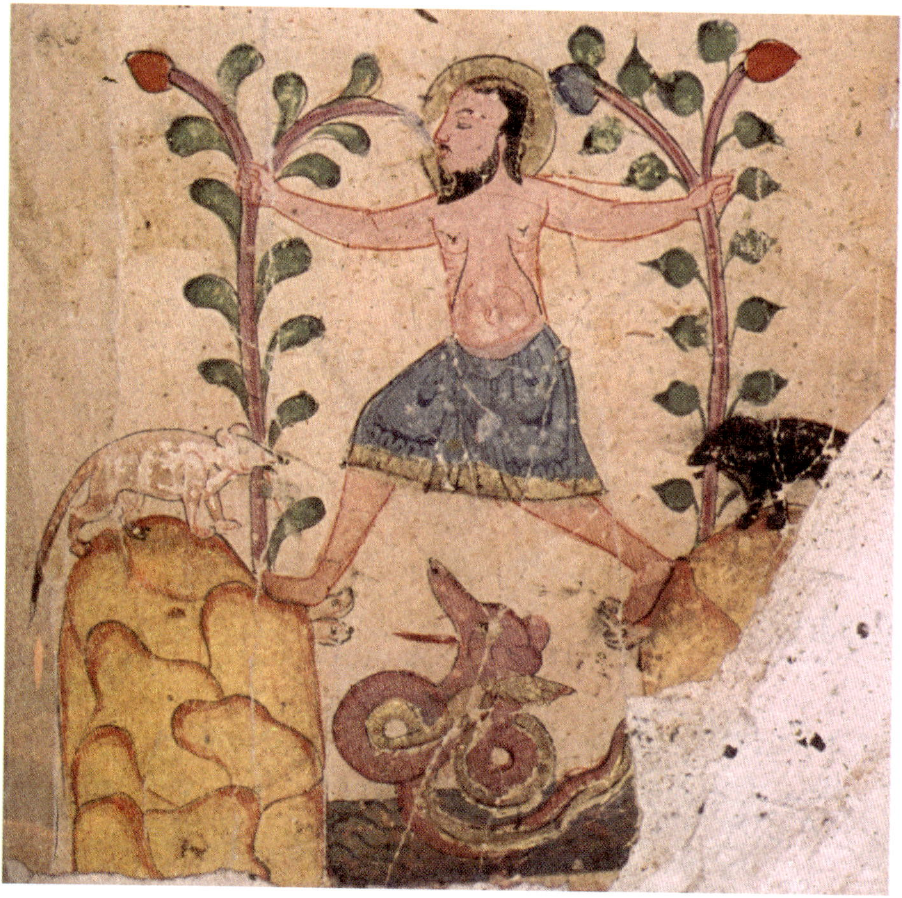

Fig. 11. Egypt or Syria, ca. 1340–1350, Munich,
Bayerische Staatsbibliothek. © Bayerische Staatsbibliothek

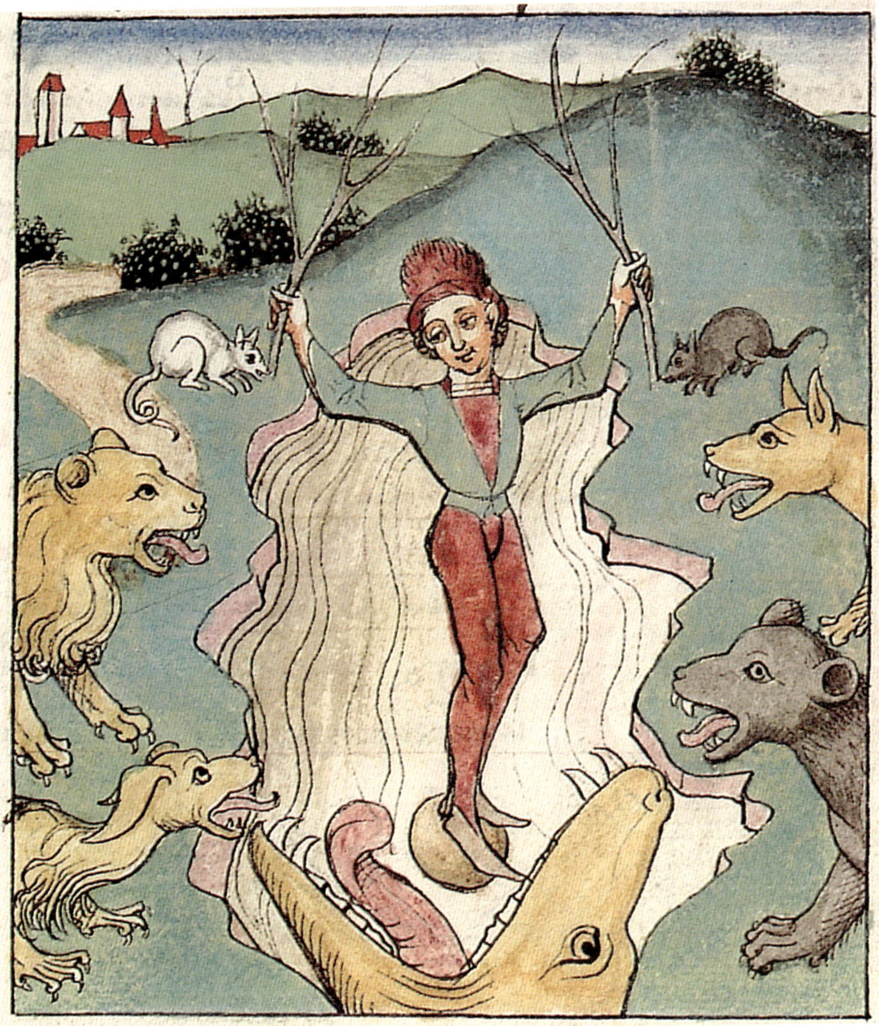

Fig. 17. Heidelberg, University Library, Cod. Pal. germ. 466, Buch der Beispiele. © Universitätsbibliothek Heidelberg

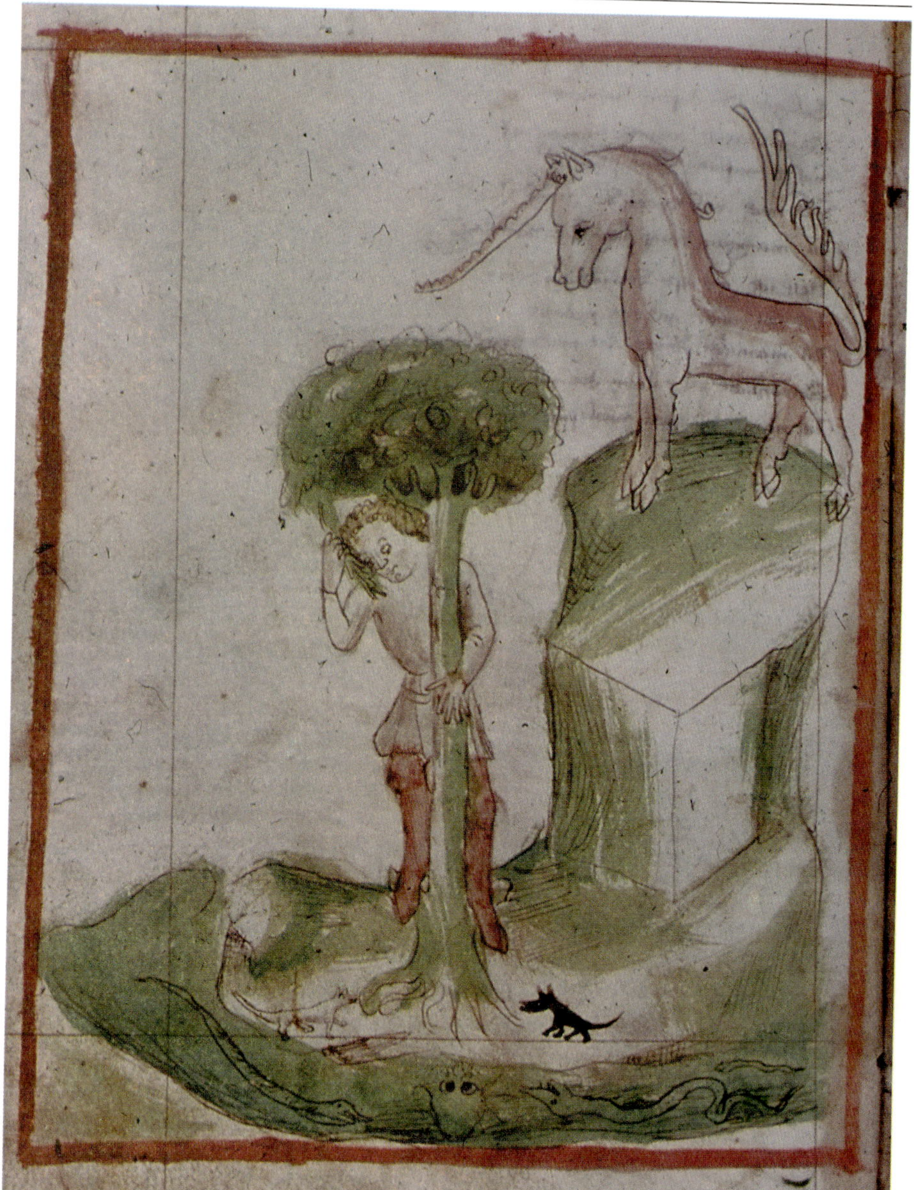

Fig. 21. Hugo von Trimberg, *Der Renner*, Munich, Bayerische Staatsbibliothek. © Bayerische Staatsbibliothek.

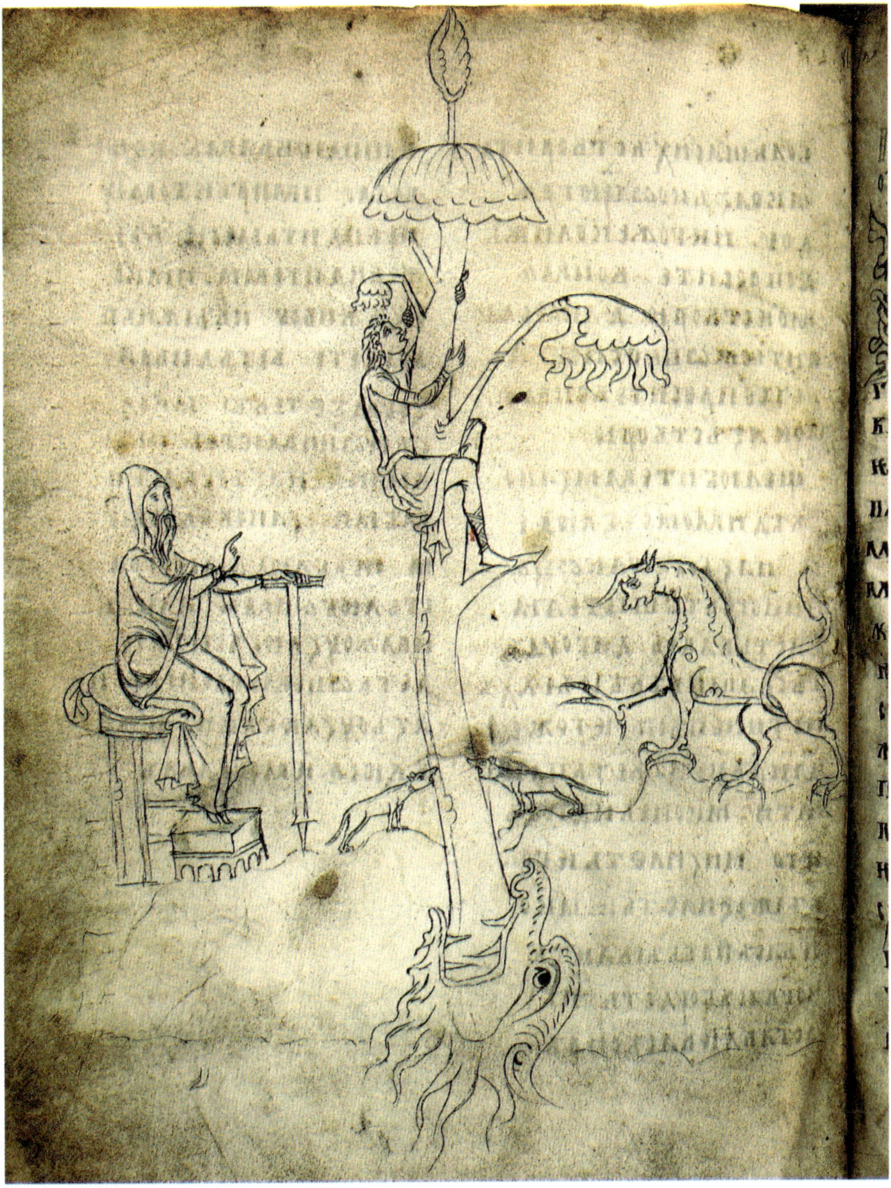

Fig. 22. Tree of Life with a man and the unicorn,
Barlaam depicted on the side. Kraków,
Czartoryskis' Library. © Fundacja Czartoryskich

Silke K. Yasmin Fischer: The Spread of Buddhism from India to Sri Lanka: Its Visual Representation, pp. 153–164:

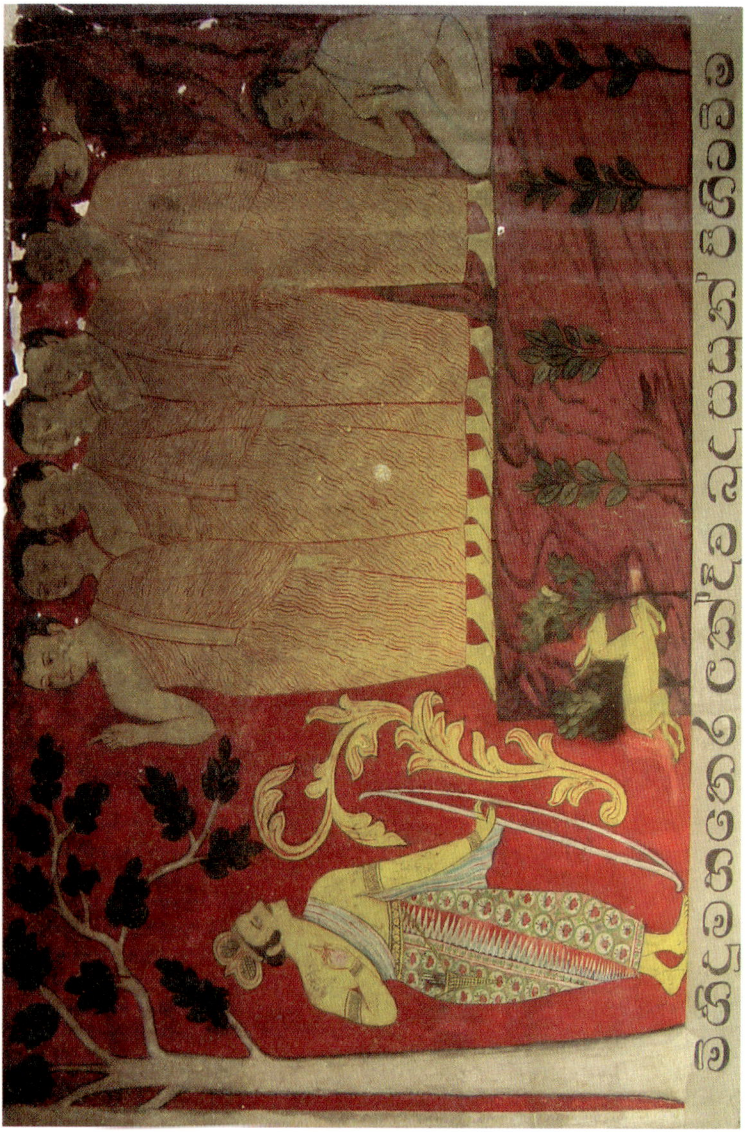

Fig. 2. Kapumulagoda Ghanāndarāmavihāra,
private collection of Dr. Rolf Heinrich Koch, Munich

Anna Œl¹czka: Temple Consecration Rituals in the Hindu Tradition of South and South-East Asia: A Study of the Textual and Archaeological Evidence, pp. 167–181:

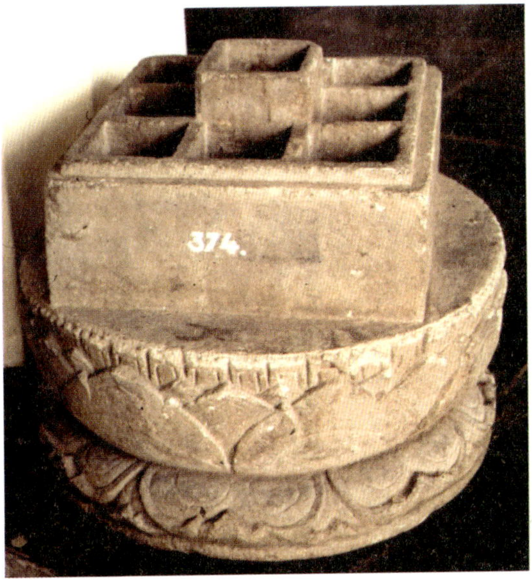

Fig. 1. Stone box found in Jolotundo (East Java).
Museum Nasional, Jakarta

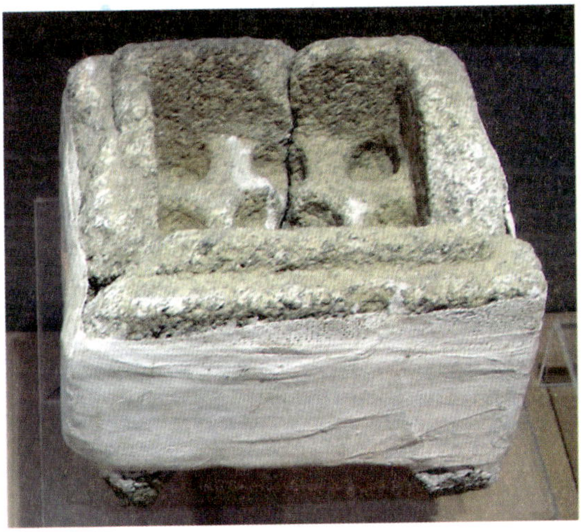

Fig. 2. Stone box found in Candi Bukit Batu Pahat.
Bujang Valley Archaeological Museum, Malaysia

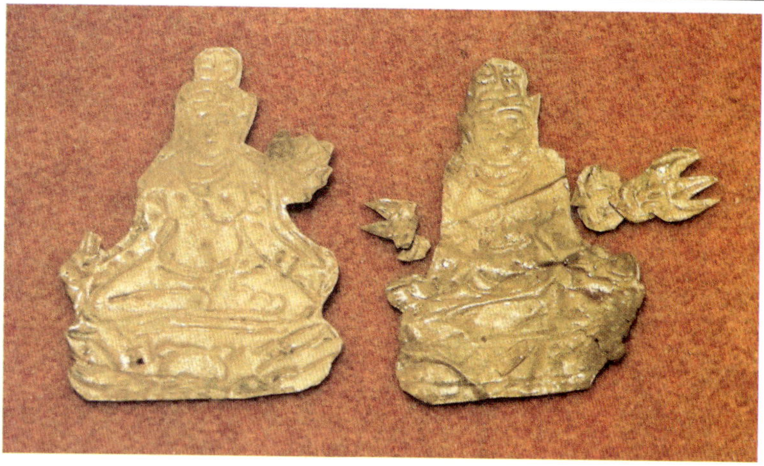

Fig. 3. Images of goddesses found in Candi Bukit Batu Pahat.
Bujang Valley Archaeological Museum, Malaysia

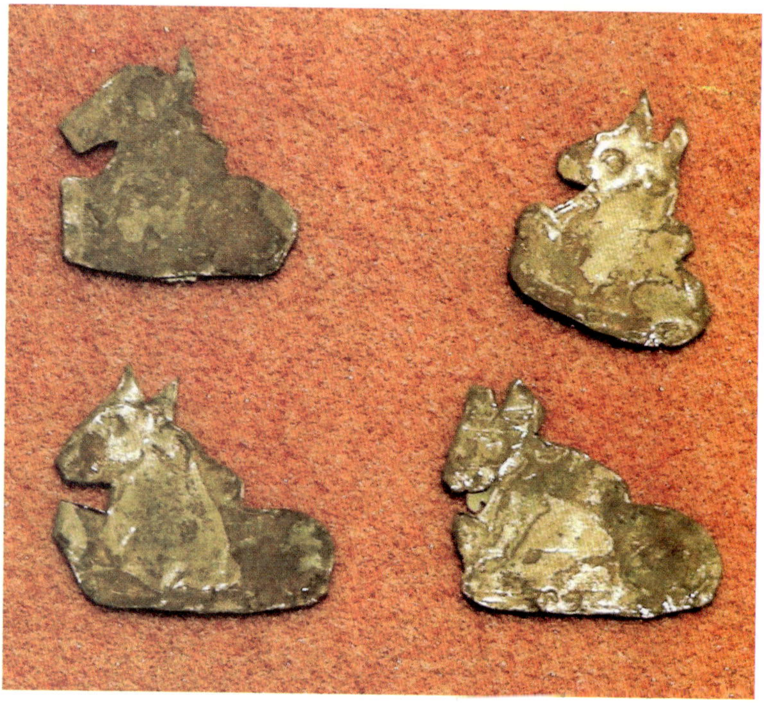

Fig. 4. Images of bulls found in Candi Bukit Batu Pahat.
Bujang Valley Archaeological Museum, Malaysia

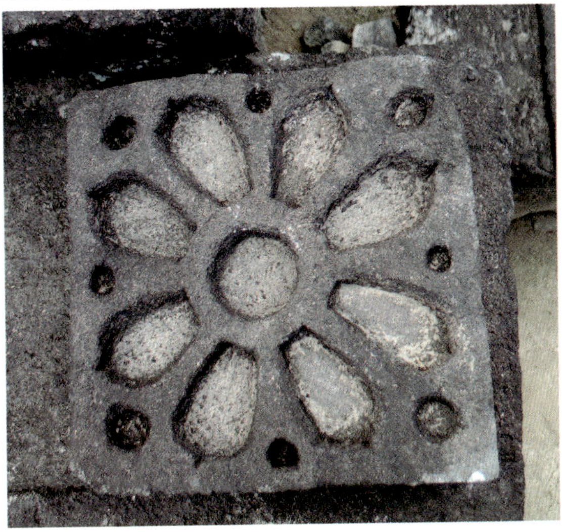

Fig. 5. Stone box in Candi Merak (Central Java)

M. Singh, R.S. Trambake, D.A. Gupta: Chemical Conservation of Hīnayāna Paintings of the 2nd BCE, Cave No. 10, Ajanta, pp. 251–259:

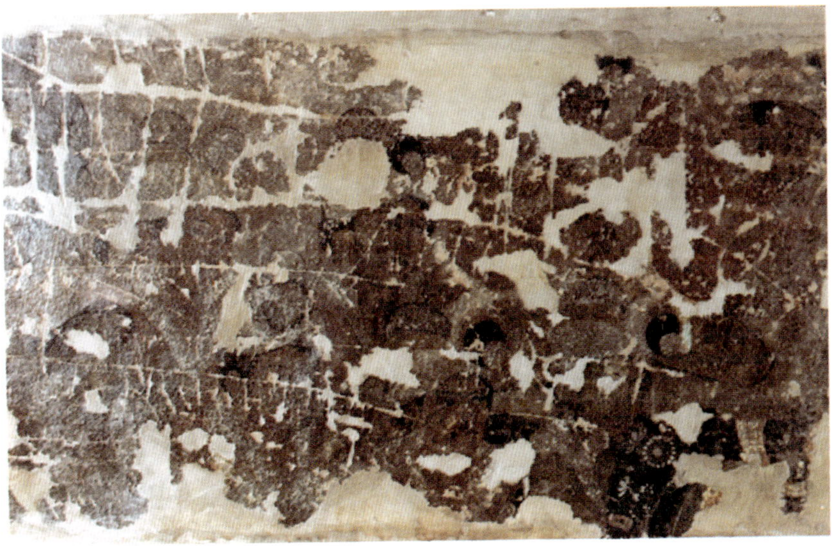

Photo 1. Visitors graffiti on painted plaster of cave no. 10, Ajanta

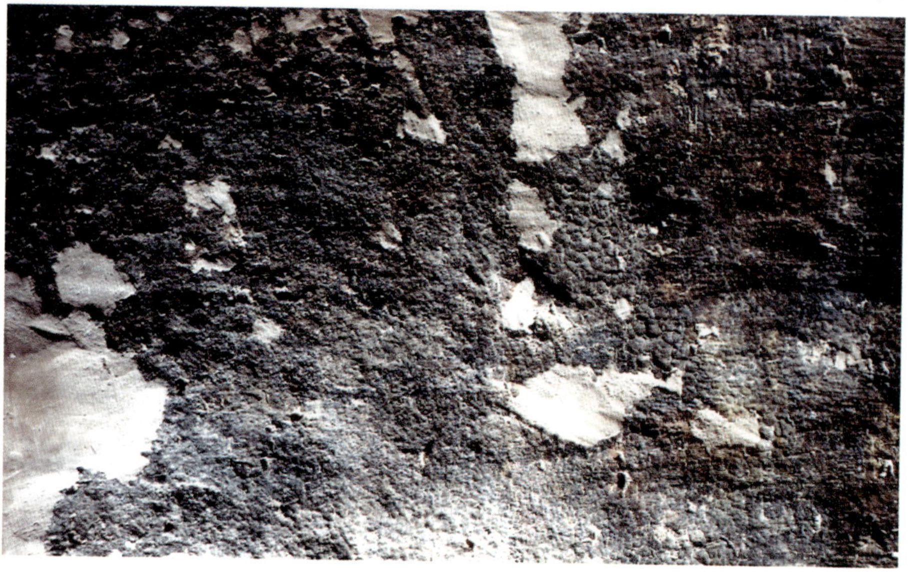

Photo 2a. Before chemical treatment, Ajantā

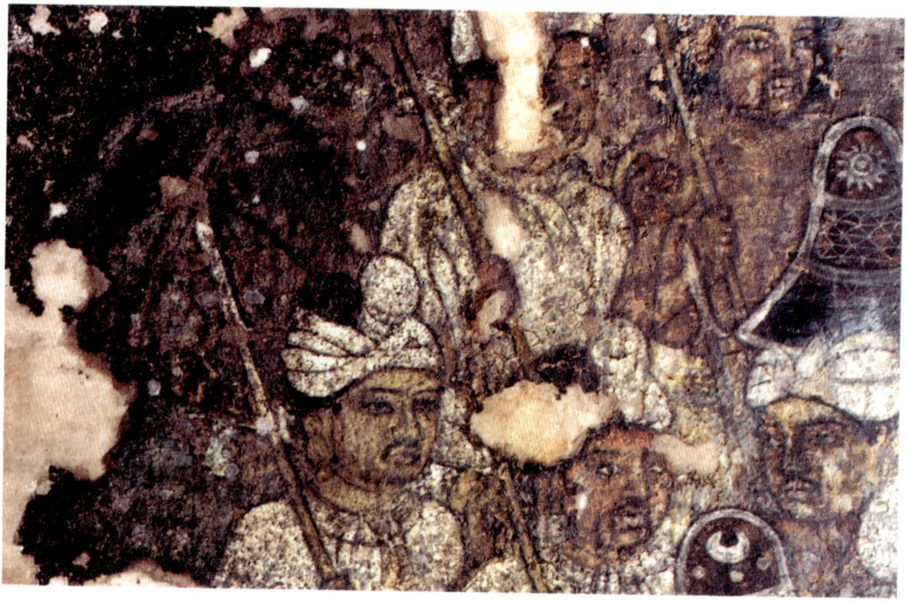

Photo 2b. After chemical conservation, Ajantā

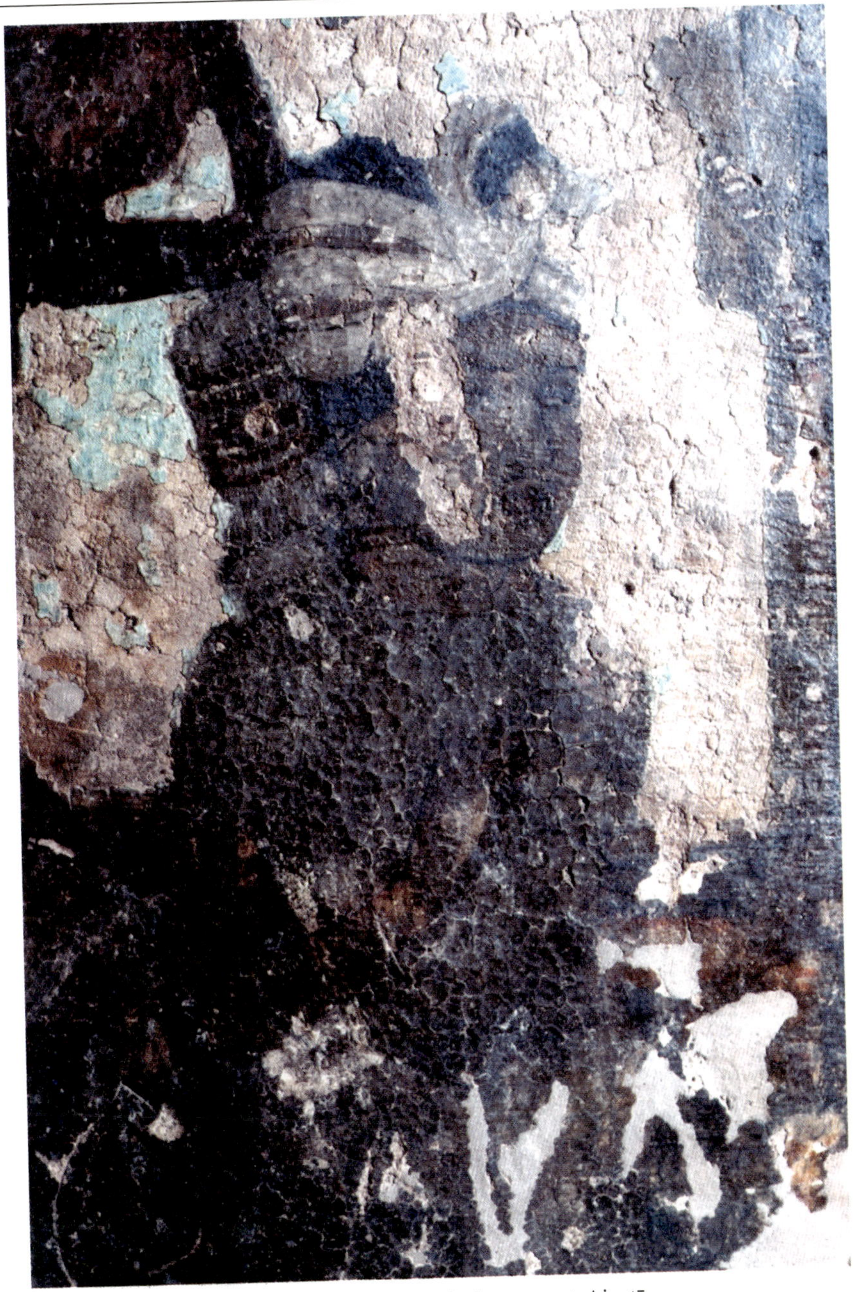

Photo 3a. Before chemical treatment, Ajantā

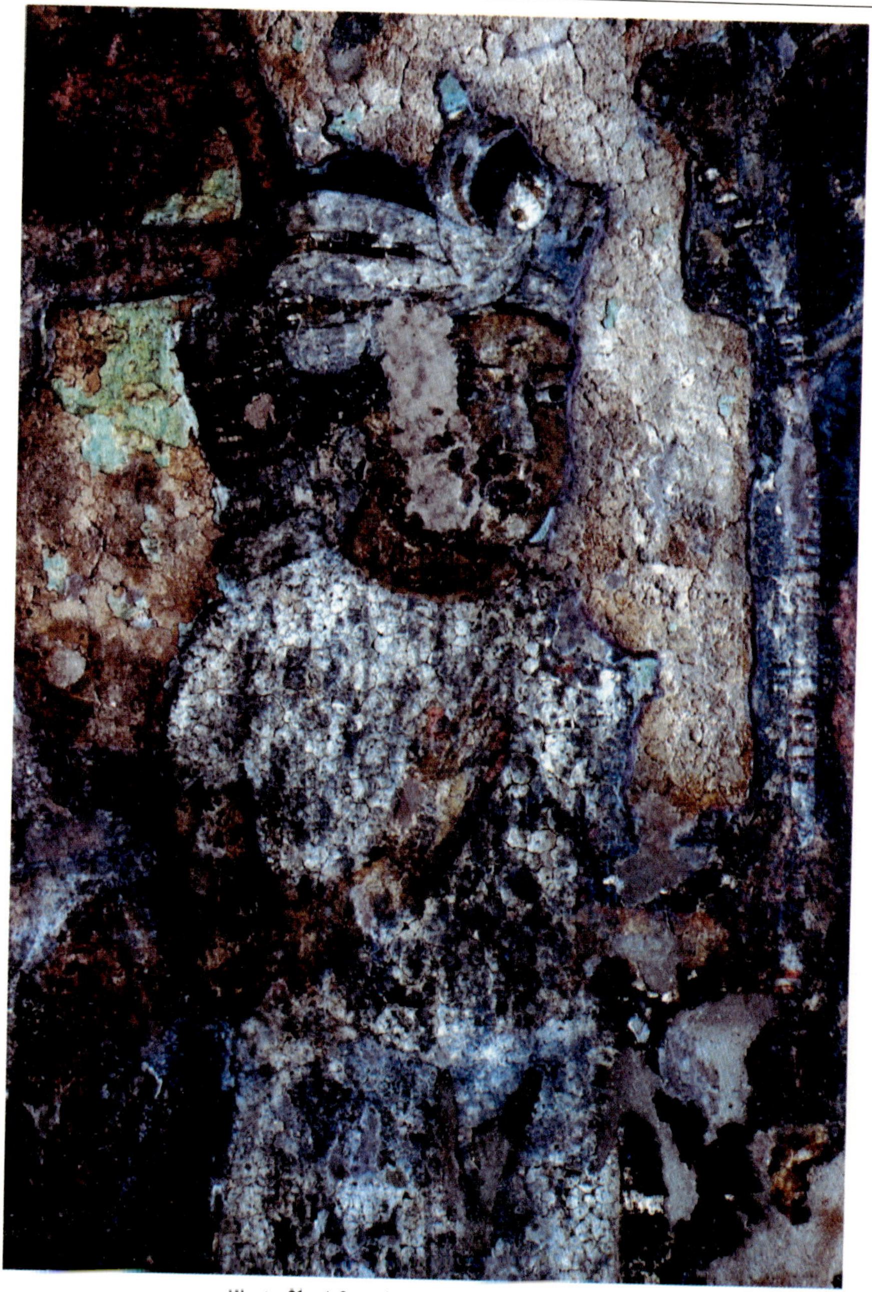

Photo 3b. After chemical treatment, Ajantā

Asoka de Zoysa: Reading Images and Interpreting the Context: Differentiating Between Iconography and Iconology According to Erwin Panofsky's Three Phase Analysis, pp. 260–291:

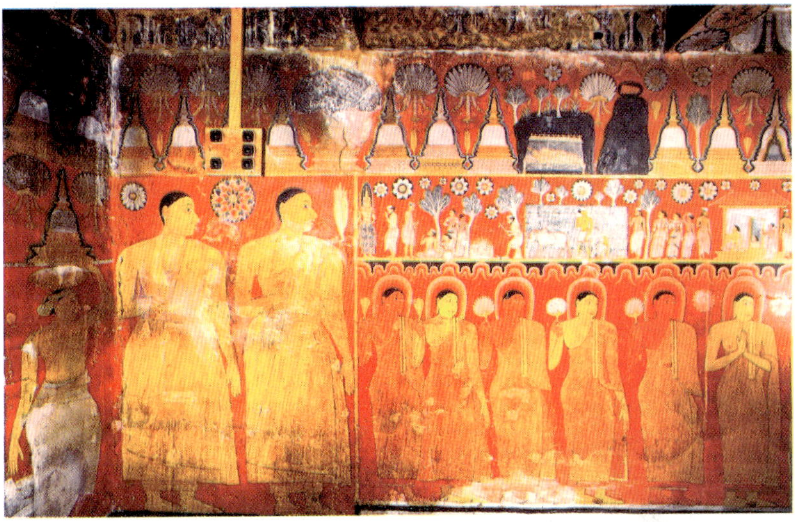

Fig. 2. Mädawala Vihāraya Sanctum. Northern (left) wall

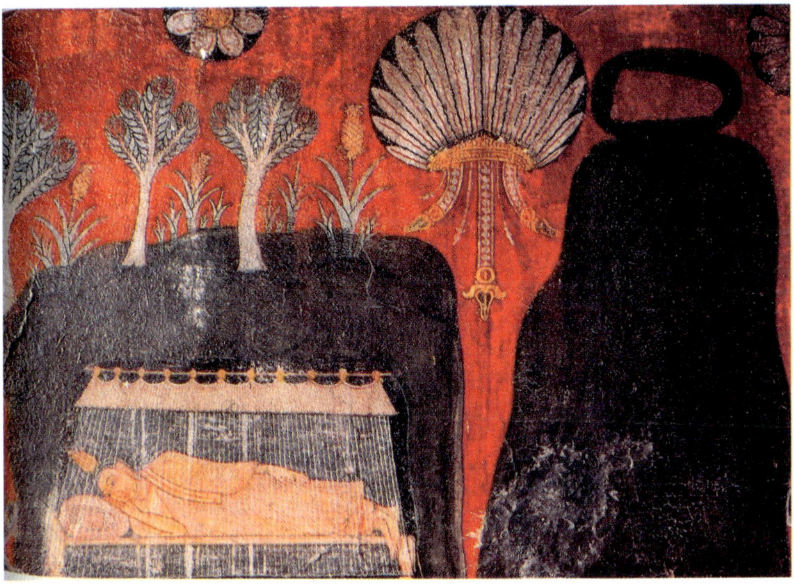

Fig. 6. Mädawala Vihāraya mountain and cave. Upper register, northern wall

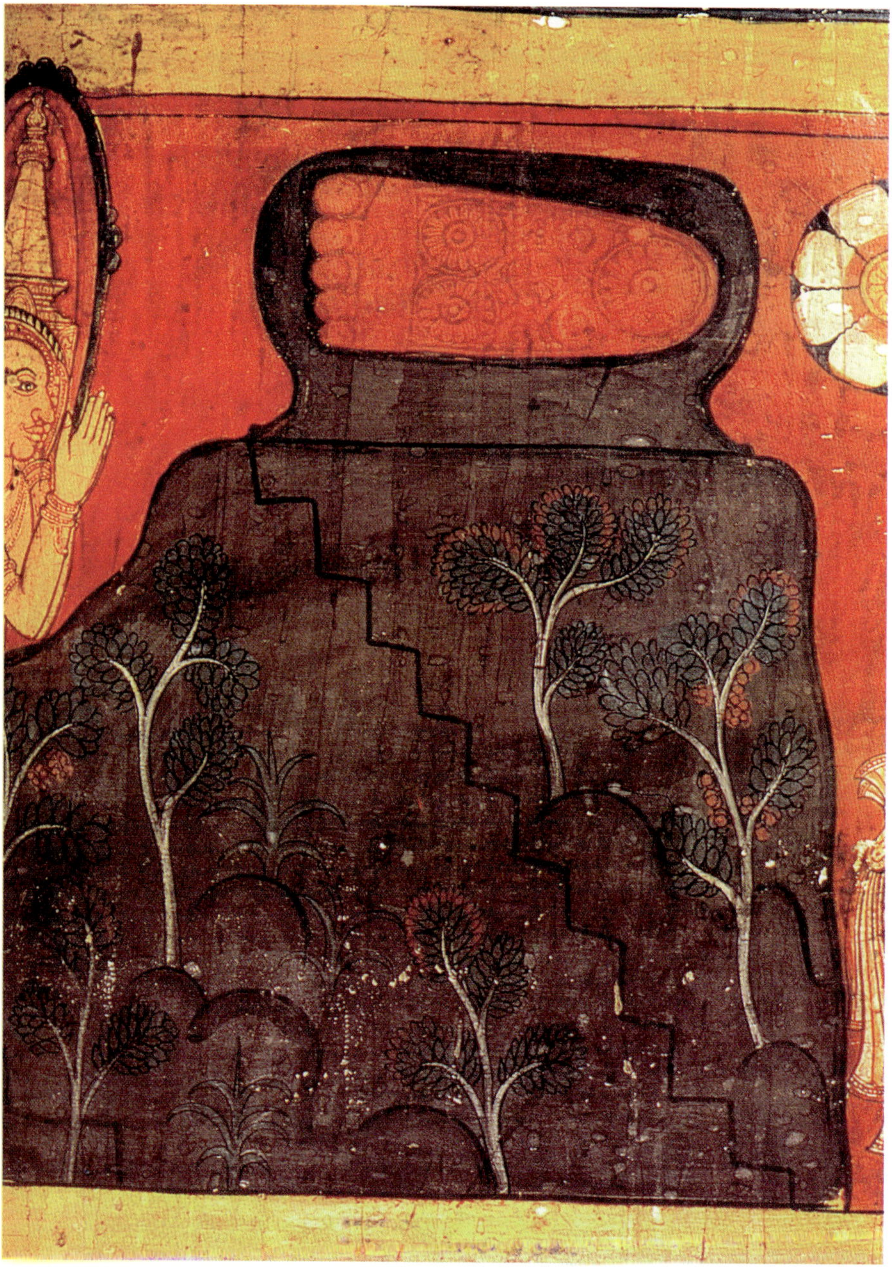

Fig. 7. Ridī Vihāraya—deity worshiping Foot Print